1932 CENSUS OF THE STANDING ROCK SIOUX RESERVATION

WITH

BIRTHS AND DEATHS 1924-1932

TRANSCRIBED BY

JEFF BOWEN

NATIVE STUDY
Gallipolis, Ohio
USA

Originally published:
Santa Maria, California
2019

Reprinted by:

Native Study LLC
Gallipolis, Ohio
www.nativestudy.com

Library of Congress Control Number: 2022906137

ISBN: 978-1-64968-161-4

Cover and Title Page Image:
Chief Rain-in-the-Face (Lakota: Ité Omáǧažu in Standard Lakota Orthography)
(c. 1835 - September 15, 1905) was a war chief of the Lakota tribe.

Made in the United States of America.

Other Books and Series by Jeff Bowen

Compilation of History of the Cherokee Indians and Early History of the Cherokees by Emmet Starr with Combined Full Name Index
(Hardbound & Softbound)

1901-1907 Native American Census Seneca, Eastern Shawnee, Miami, Modoc, Ottawa, Peoria, Quapaw, and Wyandotte Indians (Under Seneca School, Indian Territory)

1932 Census of The Standing Rock Sioux Reservation with Births And Deaths 1924-1932

Census of The Blackfeet, Montana, 1897- 1901 Expanded Edition

Eastern Cherokee by Blood, 1906-1910, Volumes I thru XIII

Choctaw of Mississippi Indian Census 1929-1932 with Births and Deaths 1924-1931   Volume I
Choctaw of Mississippi Indian Census 1933, 1934 & 1937, Supplemental Rolls to 1934 & 1935 with Births and Deaths 1932-1938, and Marriages 1936-1938 Volume II

Eastern Cherokee Census Cherokee, North Carolina 1930-1939
Census 1930-1931 with Births And Deaths 1924-1931 Taken By Agent L. W. Page Volume I
Eastern Cherokee Census Cherokee, North Carolina 1930-1939
Census 1932-1933 with Births And Deaths 1930-1932 Taken By Agent R. L. Spalsbury   Volume II
Eastern Cherokee Census Cherokee, North Carolina 1930-1939
Census 1934-1937 with Births and Deaths 1925-1938 and Marriages 1936 & 1938 Taken by Agents R. L. Spalsbury And Harold W. Foght Volume III

Seminole of Florida Indian Census, 1930-1940 with Birth and Death Records, 1930-1938

Texas Cherokees 1820-1839 A Document For Litigation 1921

Starr Roll 1894 (Cherokee Payment Rolls) Districts: Canadian, Cooweescoowee, and Delaware Volume One
Starr Roll 1894 (Cherokee Payment Rolls) Districts: Flint, Going Snake, and Illinois   Volume Two
Starr Roll 1894 (Cherokee Payment Rolls) Districts: Saline, Sequoyah, and Tahlequah; Including Orphan Roll Volume Three

Cherokee Intruder Cases Dockets of Hearings 1901-1909 Volumes I & II

Indian Wills, 1911-1921 Records of the Bureau of Indian Affairs
Books One thru Seven

Other Books and Series by Jeff Bowen

Native American Wills & Probate Records 1911-1921

Turtle Mountain Reservation Chippewa Indians 1932 Census with Births & Deaths, 1924-1932

Chickasaw By Blood Enrollment Cards 1898-1914 Volume I thru *V*

Cherokee Descendants East An Index to the Guion Miller Applications Volume I
Cherokee Descendants West An Index to the Guion Miller Applications Volume II (A-M)
Cherokee Descendants West An Index to the Guion Miller Applications Volume III (N-Z)

Applications for Enrollment of Seminole Newborn Freedmen, Act of 1905

Eastern Cherokee Census, Cherokee, North Carolina, 1915-1922, Taken by Agent James E. Henderson   *Volume I (1915-1916)*
                                        Volume II (1917-1918)
                                        Volume III (1919-1920)
                                        Volume IV (1921-1922)

Complete Delaware Roll of 1898

Eastern Cherokee Census, Cherokee, North Carolina, 1923-1929, Taken by Agent James E. Henderson   *Volume I (1923-1924)*
                                        Volume II (1925-1926)
                                        Volume III (1927-1929)

Applications for Enrollment of Seminole Newborn Act of 1905 Volumes I & II

North Carolina Eastern Cherokee Indian Census 1898-1899, 1904, 1906, 1909-1912, 1914   Revised and Expanded Edition

1932 Hopi and Navajo Native American Census with Birth & Death Rolls (1925-1931) Volume 1 - Hopi
1932 Hopi and Navajo Native American Census with Birth & Death Rolls (1930-1932) Volume 2 - Navajo

Western Navajo Reservation Navajo, Hopi and Paiute 1933 Census with Birth & Death Rolls 1925-1933

Cherokee Citizenship Commission Dockets 1880-1884 and 1887-1889
Volumes I thru *V*

Applications for Enrollment of Chickasaw Newborn Act of 1905
Volumes I thru *VII*

Other Books and Series by Jeff Bowen

Cherokee Intermarried White 1906 Volume I thru X

Applications for Enrollment of Creek Newborn Act of 1905
Volumes I thru XIV

Applications for Enrollment of Choctaw Newborn Act of 1905 Volumes I thru XX

Choctaw By Blood Enrollment Cards 1898-1914 Volumes I thru XX

Oglala Sioux Indians Pine Ridge Reservation 1932 Census Book I
Oglala Sioux Indians Pine Ridge Reservation Birth and Death Rolls 1924-1932
Book II

Census of the Sioux and Cheyenne Indians of Pine Ridge Agency
1896 - 1897 Book I
Census of the Sioux and Cheyenne Indians of Pine Ridge Agency
1898 - 1899 Book II

Northern Cheyenne Tongue River, Montana 1904 - 1932 Census
1904-1916 Volume I
Northern Cheyenne Tongue River, Montana 1904 - 1932 Census
1917-1926 Volume II

Identified Mississippi Choctaw Enrollment Cards 1902-1909   Volumes I, II & III

Sac & Fox - Shawnee Estates 1885-1910 (Under Sac & Fox Agency)
Volumes I-VIII
Sac & Fox - Shawnee Estates 1920-1924 (Under The Sac & Fox Agency,
Oklahoma) & Wills 1889-1924 Volume IX
Sac & Fox - Shawnee Deaths, Cemetery, Births, & Marriage Cards (Under The Sac
& Fox Agency, Oklahoma) 1853-1933 Volume X
Sac & Fox - Shawnee Marriages, Divorces, Estates Log Books Volumes 1 & 2, Log
Book Births & Deaths (Under Sac & Fox Agency, Oklahoma)1846-1924 Volume XI
Sac & Fox - Shawnee Guardianships Part 1 (Under Sac & Fox Agency, Oklahoma)
1892-1909 Volume XII
Sac & Fox - Shawnee Guardianships, Part 2 (Under The Sac & Fox Agency,
Oklahoma) 1902-1910 Volume XIII
Sac & Fox - Shawnee Guardianships, Part 3 (Under The Sac & Fox Agency,
Oklahoma) 1906-1914 Volume XIV

Visit our website at **www.nativestudy.com** to learn more about these
and other books and series by Jeff Bowen

Little Crow, Sioux Chief from the village of
Kaposia, 1824, Minnesota

One of the first signers of the
Treaty of Fort Laramie, 1851

This book is dedicated to
Kent Anderson
not only a friend of the Sioux but
also a kind contributor to my studies.

"One elderly Lakota chief who had witnessed the march of events from the Treaty of Fort Laramie in 1851 to the tragedy at Wounded Knee four decades later saw nothing remarkable in what had transpired. 'The [government] made us many promises,' he told a white friend, 'more than I can remember, but they never kept but one; they promised to take our land, and they took it.'

From *The Earth is Weeping*, by Peter Cozzens, pg. 466

Table of Contents

Table of Contents

INTRODUCTION

There are two separate books within this one volume that were published 23 years ago. The *1932 Census North and South Dakota Sioux on Standing Rock Reservation, North Dakota* and the *Standing Rock Sioux Reservation Births and Deaths 1924-1932* now combined. It's interesting when scanning through each page of the old books the inexperience that can be seen in the work. Over the years the quality and care has much improved through not only the records but also the knowledge gained while studying different cultures and respecting the Native Peoples and their struggles from all tribes. Never claiming to feel what they feel but respecting them for their strength and honor. The materials in this volume were transcribed from National Archive microfilm, Indian Census Rolls, 1885 - 1940; Series M-595, Roll #558. The transcriber will try to combine a brief history and study for the folks looking for their ancestors of the past and the present while at the same time hopefully giving them a taste of where they came from. Creating these genealogical books over the years has only been about helping people find their people, nothing else.

Not many people now-a-days think about the Sioux coming from Minnesota. Most think of them living as Plains Indians from the Dakota's. But, "One day in the spring of 1854, a painter of western scenes named John Mix Stanley received a visit at his studio in Washington, D.C., from a man uniquely qualified to judge the authenticity of his work. Stanley had recently returned from the Minnesota Territory, where he had sketched life among the Dakota, or Eastern Sioux--impressions he was now committing to canvas. His visitor on this occasion was none other than the Dakota spokesman Little Crow, whose native village of Kaposia was the subject of two of Stanley's paintings. Little Crow had come to Washington to confer with government officials about a treaty that would move his people westward from the woodlands near the Mississippi River, where Stanley had encountered them, to a reservation along the Minnesota River. In return, the Indians would receive annuities: regular allotments of cash from the government. A pragmatist who believed that the Dakota had more to gain by accommodating the land-hungry whites than by defying them, Little Crow supported the deal. But he wanted assurances that the government would respect the boundaries of the reservation and meet its financial obligations. And he knew that even with such promises the move would be trying for his people because they would have to abandon Kaposia and other villages. When Little Crow arrived at Stanley's studio, the artist was finishing up a study of daily life in Kaposia, showing women cleaning hides as men carried canoes down to the river. Little Crow gestured to familiar details in the scene with evident delight. But a second picture drew from him a far different response. That painting portrayed the remains of dead Indians being arrayed on a scaffold outside Kaposia in keeping with Sioux custom, which called for the deceased to be placed close to the sky and its spirits. Little Crow brooded silently over the funeral scene for a while. Then he clasped his hands above his head and walked abruptly from the room.

Those with Little Crow at the time could only guess at his somber thoughts. Perhaps the painting reminded him that moving to the reservation meant forsaking the last resting place of many of his kin. Or perhaps he saw the depiction of this solemn

ix

ceremony as an ill omen--a sign that intruders might one day capture the heritage of the Dakota along with their land and deprive them of all they held sacred."[1]

In trying to give a little of the past so the researcher can understand what their ancestors went though it always appears to be the same story only with different tribes, and different locations, while at the same time the same motives. Even with time the characters taking the land change but the tactics are always the same. Little Crow while in Minnesota was trying to save his people from the odds knowing they would lose. While trying to preserve a people he loved he saw the inevitable while making enemies of those that were his friends and family.

"Among the Indian leaders who ultimately joined in hostilities against whites in the West, few made greater concessions before taking that fateful step than the Dakota leader Little Crow. In backing the treaty that moved his people from their homeland near the Mississippi River to a reservation along the Minnesota River, he boldly defied threats by angry Dakota warriors to strike down the first chief who put pen to the treaty."[2]

Little Crow would eventually be driven to fight with the rest of his people because promises were never kept and more (land) was always wanted of them. "Until World War I, the Lakota managed to resist allotment, but in 1889--the year of the great Oklahoma land rush inspired by the Dawes Act--General Crook was dispatched to his old foes with the proposal that 9 million acres of their remaining land should be turned over to white settlement. The aging Red Cloud refused to sign such an agreement, and so did Sitting Bull, who had returned from political asylum in Canada in 1881 (for a time he appeared in 'Wild West' shows with the old railroad hunter Buffalo Bill Cody) and was living at Standing Rock on the Grand River, not far from the place where he was born:

Friends and Relatives: Our minds are again disturbed by the Great Fathers representatives, the Indian Agent, the squaw-men, the mixed-bloods, the interpreters, and the favorite-ration-chiefs. What is it they want of us at this time? They want us to give up another chunk of our tribal land. This is not the first time nor the last time. They will try to gain possession of the last piece of ground we possess. They are again telling us what they intend to do if we agree to their wishes. Have we ever set a price on our land and received such a value? No, we never did. What we got under the former treaties were promises of all sorts. They promised how we are going to live peaceably on the land we still own and how they are going to show us the new ways of living, even told us how we can go to heaven when we die....

When the white people invaded our Black Hills country our treaty agreements were still in force but the Great Father ignored it.... Therefore I do not wish to consider any proposition to cede any portion of our tribal holdings to the Great Father.... My friends and relatives, let us stand as one family as we did before the white people led us astray.

---

[1] War For The Plains, Time-Life Books; Pgs. 17-18, Para's. 1-4
[2] War For The Plains, Time-Life Books; Pg. 29, Para. 3

Due mostly to the stubborn resistance of Sitting Bull and Red Cloud, the signatures required for the cession of Indian land were not obtained, and as in the seizure of the Black Hills, it was recommended to the government that it simply ignore the 1868 Treaty, which it did. A few months later, President Benjamin Harrison proclaimed an act that dismantled the Great Sioux Reservation established at Fort Laramie and created the seven reservations that exist today; the Oglala band, which had been the most hostile, was given the dry rolling hill country between the Dakota Badlands and the Sand Hills of Nebraska, now known as the Pine Ridge Reservation."[3]

The Harrison blood line would prove disastrous to the Native American. William Henry Harrison, who Tecumseh called a liar decades earlier would eventually gain his fame and popularity through those very actions and eventually become President of the United States only to die 31 days after having entered office from typhoid, pneumonia or paratyphoid fever. Harrison's legacy would finally follow through in a grandson who also would become President of the United States and follow in his grandfather's footsteps by treating the Sioux with the same disdain by failing to keep any promises made to a Native people and totally disregarding a treaty signed at Fort Laramie in 1851. It can only be imagined how the elder Harrison would have treated the American Indian had he lived to fulfill a term or more, his grandson was bad enough openly defying the law.

There was another important man that was a friend of many native tribes like that Arapahoe, Sioux, Crow, Cheyenne and others. His name was, Thomas Fitzpatrick. He was a famous trapper and scout during the 1840's. He spoke many different native languages and the tribes trusted him greatly. Fitzpatrick married an Arapahoe woman. He later became an Indian agent and, "In 1851, Fitzpatrick assembled ten thousand Northern Plains Indians at Fort Laramie for a council of unsurpassed magnitude. The chiefs signed an agreement called the Fort Laramie Treaty--which, was nearly always the case, the Indians understood only dimly, if at all--and then joyously accepted gifts for their people from the Great Father."[4]

During the winter months of 1853 and into 1854 Thomas Fitzpatrick traveled to Washington, D.C., to make sure the treaties he had completed were accepted, but in early 1854 he died from pneumonia. Not getting to complete his task likely hurt the signers chances of having anyone to stand for their rights, at least someone with any real influence or concern for their well-being.

"The Standing Rock Indian Reservation (Lakota: *Íŋyaŋ Woslál Háŋ*/inyan bosdata) is located in North Dakota and South Dakota in the United States, and is inhabited by ethnic "Hunkpapa and Sihasapa bands of Lakota Oyate and the Ihunktuwona and Pabaksa bands of the Dakota Oyate," as well as the Hunkpatina Dakota (Lower Yanktonai). The Ihanktonwana Dakota are the Upper Yanktonai, part of the collective of Wiciyena. The sixth-largest Native American reservation in land area in the US, Standing Rock includes all of Sioux County, North Dakota, and all of

---

[3] In The Spirit of Crazy Horse; Pgs. 18-19, Para's. 3-6
[4] The Earth is Weeping; Pg. 20, Para. 2

Corson County, South Dakota, plus slivers of northern Dewey and Ziebach counties in South Dakota, along their northern county lines at Highway 20.

The reservation has a land area of 9,251.2 square kilometers (3,571.9 sq mi) and a population of 8,217 as of the 2010 census. There are 15,568 enrolled members of the tribe. The largest communities on the reservation are Fort Yates, Cannon Ball and McLaughlin.

Together with the Hunkpapa and Sihasapa bands, the Standing Rock Sioux Tribe is part of what was known as the Great Sioux Nation. The peoples were highly decentralized. In 1868 the lands of the Great Sioux Nation were reduced in the Fort Laramie Treaty to the east side of the Missouri River and the state line of South Dakota in the west. The Black Hills, considered by the Sioux to be sacred land, are located in the center of territory awarded to the tribe.

In direct violation of the treaty, in 1874 General George A. Custer and his 7th Cavalry entered the Black Hills and discovered gold, starting a gold rush. The United States government wanted to buy or rent the Black Hills from the Lakota people, but led by their spiritual leader Sitting Bull, they refused to sell or rent their lands. The Great Sioux War of 1876 was a series of battles and negotiations that occurred between 1876 and 1877, with the Lakota Sioux and Northern Cheyenne warring against the United States. Among the many battles and skirmishes of the war was the Battle of the Little Bighorn, often known as Custer's Last Stand, the most storied of the many encounters between the U.S. army and mounted Plains Native Americans. It was an overwhelming Native American victory. The U.S. with its superior resources was soon able to force the Native Americans to surrender, primarily by attacking and destroying their encampments and property. The Agreement of 1877 (19 Stat. 254, enacted February 28, 1877) officially annexed Sioux land and permanently established Native American reservations. Under the Agreement of 1877 the U.S. government took the Black Hills from the Sioux Nation.

In February 1890, the United States government broke a Lakota treaty by breaking up the Great Sioux Reservation, an area that formerly encompassed the majority of the state. It reduced it and divided it into five smaller reservations. The government was accommodating white homesteaders from the eastern United States; in addition, it intended to "break up tribal relationships" and "conform Indians to the white man's ways, peaceably if they will, or forcibly if they must". On the reduced reservations, the government allocated family units on 320-acre (1.3 km^2) plots for individual households.

Although the Lakota were historically a nomadic people living in tipis, and their Plains Native American culture was based strongly upon buffalo and horse culture, they were expected to farm and raise livestock. With the goal of assimilation, in the late 19th and early 20th centuries, they were forced to send their children to boarding schools; the schools taught English and Christianity, as well as American cultural practices. Generally, they forbade inclusion of Native American traditional culture and language. The children were beaten if they tried to do anything related to their native culture.

The farming plan failed to take into account the difficulty that Lakota farmers would have in trying to cultivate crops in the semi-arid region of South Dakota. By the end of the 1890 growing season, a time of intense heat and low rainfall, it was clear that the land was unable to produce substantial agricultural yields. As the bison had been virtually eradicated a few years earlier, the Lakota were at risk of starvation. The people turned to the Ghost Dance ritual, which frightened the supervising agents of the Bureau of Indian Affairs. Agent James McLaughlin asked for more troops. He claimed that spiritual leader Sitting Bull was the real leader of the movement. A former agent, Valentine McGillycuddy, saw nothing extraordinary in the dances and ridiculed the panic that seemed to have overcome the agencies, saying: "The coming of the troops has frightened the Indians. If the Seventh-Day Adventists prepare the ascension robes for the Second Coming of the Savior, the United States Army is not put in motion to prevent them. Why should not the Indians have the same privilege? If the troops remain, trouble is sure to come."

Thousands of additional U.S. Army troops were deployed to the reservation. On December 15, 1890, Sitting Bull was arrested for failing to stop his people from practicing the Ghost Dance. During his arrest, one of Sitting Bull's men, Catch the Bear, fired at Lieutenant "Bull Head", striking his right side. He instantly wheeled and shot Sitting Bull, hitting him in the left side, and both men subsequently died.

The Hunkpapa who lived in Sitting Bull's camp and relatives fled to the south. They joined the Big Foot Band in Cherry Creek, South Dakota, before traveling to the Pine Ridge Reservation to meet with Chief Red Cloud. The 7th Cavalry caught them at a place called Wounded Knee on December 29, 1890. The 7th Cavalry, claiming they were trying to disarm the Lakota people, killed 300 people, including women and children at Wounded Knee.

According to its constitution, Standing Rock's governing body is the elected 17-member Tribal Council, including the Tribal Chairman, Vice Chairman, Secretary, and 14 representatives. They serve terms of four years, with elections providing for staggered replacement of members. Six members are elected at-large and eight from the regional single-member districts: Fort Yates (Long Soldier), Porcupine, KenelWakpala, Running Antelope (Little Eagle), Bear Soldier (McLaughlin), Rock Creek (Bullhead)Cannonball"[5]

In hope of giving as much updated information as possible for the researcher a great deal of material has been found on Wikipedia as shown above. If there is any repeat of materials it is only because in quoting a resource it needs to be exact. The copy of the Treaty of Fort Laramie 1851 (shown on the following page) was found on the National Archives' website as a downloadable PDF. If anyone wants to see it where it is readable or would like it as their own file the link is on the next page following the image.

---

[5] Wikipedia, Standing Rock Indian Reservation

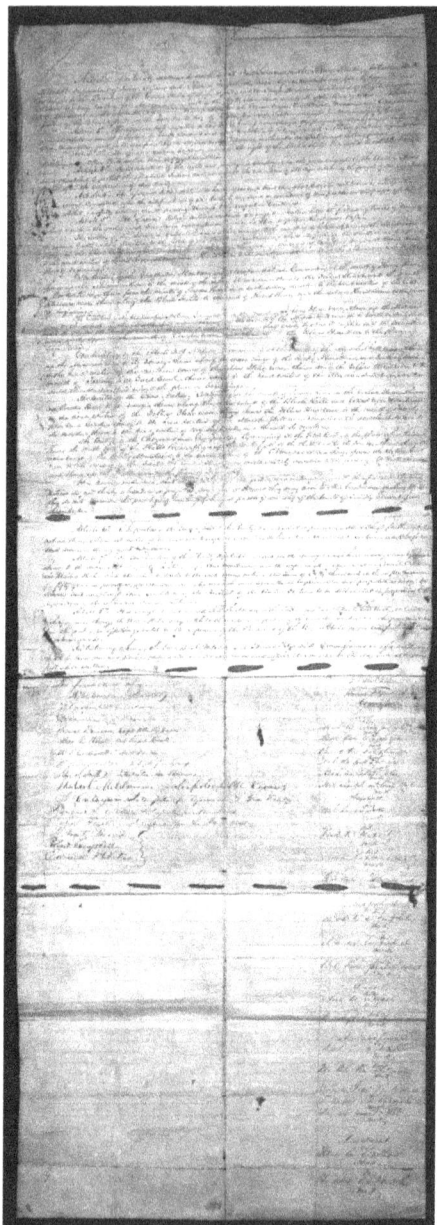

Actual Copy of the Treaty of Fort Laramie 1851
Thomas Fitzpatrick's name is among the top lines.

Link to the 1851 Treaty of Fort Laramie:
https://catalog.archives.gov/OpaAPI/media/12013686/content/arcmedia/dc-metro/rg-075/300293/26238_2012.pdf

     The study of the Sioux people was fascinating while at the same time heart wrenching. None of us can likely imagine the Tears that filled the hearts of the old ones let alone the Sioux of today. The Standing Rock Sioux Tribe has a wonderful and very informative website, if you're interested. It would never be claimed by this transcriber to ever interpret their history or culture better than the Sioux themselves. It's only wished that this work will add to a wonderful peoples' heritage and study for others.

Jeff Bowen
Gallipolis, Ohio
NativeStudy.com

1932 Census

of

NORTH DAKOTA SIOUX

on

STANDING ROCK RESERVATION,

NORTH DAKOTA

Taken by E. D. Mossman, Supt.

Ending March 31, 1932

Census of the __Standing Rock__ Reservation of the __Standing Rock__ jurisdiction, as of __April 1__, 1932, taken by __E. D. Mossman__, Superintendent. North Dakota

KEY: Number; Surname, Given; Sex; Age at Last Birthday; Tribe (Standing Rock Sioux unless otherwise noted); Degree of Blood; Marital Status; Relationship to Head of Family; At Jurisdiction where enrolled (Yes or No); (If "No", where, if given); Ward (Yes or No); Allotment, Annuity and Identification Numbers.

N. E. **ADAMS**, Frank; m; Head
1;   (Gayton), Mamie; f; 27 (3-16-05); 1/2; M; Wife; yes 1; yes; Al. 1706
2;   "   Nora F; f; 6 (6-21-26); 1/4; S; Dau; yes 2; yes; An. 2

3; **AFRAID OF HAWK**, Edward; m; 68 (1874); F; M; Head; yes 3; no;
                                                          Al. 2393
4;   (Blueboy), Louise; f; 42 (1890); F; M; Wife; yes 4; yes; Al. 1857

5; **AFRAID OF HAWK**, Louise; f; 18 (3-26-14); F; S; Head; yes 5; yes;
                                                          Al. 4572
6;   "   "   "   Unnamed; f; 1/12 (3--32); F; S; Dau; yes none; yes;
                                                          An. None.

7; **AFRAID OF HAWK**, George; m; 25 (8-15-07); F; M; Head; yes 6; yes;
                                                          Al. 2397
8;   (Red Horse), Maggie; f; 26 (12-17-05); F; M; Wife; yes 7; yes; Al. 1631
9;   "   "   "   Verne; m; 2 (7-14-29); F; S; Son; yes 8; yes; An. 10

10; **AGARD**, Cyril; m; 32 (2-14-1900); 1/2; M; Head; No 10; Whereabouts
                                          unknown; yes; Al. 1426
11;   (Pleets), Catherine; f; 33 (2-6-1899); 1/2; m; Wife; yes 11; yes; Al. 1554
12;   "   Alvina M; f; 11 (8-24-21); 1/2; s; Dau; yes 12; yes; An. 13
13;   "   Joseph; m; 8 (10-20-1923); 1/2; S; Son; yes 13; yes; An. 14
14;   "   Evelyn; f; 6 (5-25-25); 1/2; S; Dau; yes 3681; yes; An. 15
15;   "   Bernadine; f; 5 (1-14-27); 1/2; S; Dau; yes 3682; yes; An. 16

16; **AGARD**, Henry; m; 79 (1853); 1/2; M; Head; yes 14; yes; Al. 1573
17;   "   (Deroyne), Margaret; f; 79 (1853); 1/2; M; Wife; yes 15; yes;
                                                          Al. 4682

18; **ALKIRE**, James; m; 50 (1882); F; M; Head; yes 16; yes; Al. 541
19;   "   (Hona), Louise; f; 31 (2-28-1901); F; M; Wife; yes 17; yes; Al. 863
20;   "   Samuel; m; 18 (10-3-13); F; S; Son; yes 18; yes; Al. 4499
21;   "   William; m; 15 (5-20-16); F; S; Son; yes 19; yes; An. 43
22;   "   Marcella; f; 12 (10-15-19); F; S; Dau; yes 20; yes; An. 44
23;   "   Alvina; f; 9 (5-4-22); F; S; Dau; yes 21; yes; An. 45
24;   "   Ruth; f; 5 (3-24-27); F; S; Dau; yes 22; yes; An. 46
25;   "   Maude; f; 2 (7-11-29); F; S; Dau; yes 23; yes; An. 47
26;   "   Ione; f; 4/12 (11-31-31; F; S; Dau; yes none; yes; An. 48
27; Keogh, James; m; 9; 4-2-22; F; S; Son; yes 24; yes; An. 49

28; **ALL YELLOW**, James m; 67 (1865); F; Wd; Head; yes 25; yes; Al. 2020

3

Census of the __Standing Rock__ Reservation of the __Standing Rock__ jurisdiction, as of __April 1__, 1932, taken by __E. D. Mossman__, Superintendent. North Dakota

KEY: Number; Surname, Given; Sex; Age at Last Birthday; Tribe (Standing Rock Sioux unless otherwise noted); Degree of Blood; Marital Status; Relationship to Head of Family; At Jurisdiction where enrolled (Yes or No); (If "No", where, if given); Ward (Yes or No); Allotment, Annuity and Identification Numbers.

29; **ANTELOPE**, Ignatius; m; 56 (1876); F; M; Head; yes 26; yes; Al. 1667
30;   (Throws Away), Mrs; f; 65 (1867); F; M; Wife; yes 227; yes; Al. 1664
31; Whitebird, Dobson; m; 17 (2-8-14); F; S; Adpt. Son; yes 28; yes; Al. 4553

32; **ARCHAMBAULT**, Charles; m; 57 (1875); 1/2; M; Head; yes 29; No; Al. 1386
33;   (Gayton), Alice; f; 56 (1876); 1/2; M; Wife; yes 30; no; Al. 3465
34;   "   James; m; 19 (6-22-12); 1/2; S; Son; yes 31; yes; Al. 4317
35;   "   George; m; 17 (6-4-14); 1/2; S; Son; yes 32; yes; Al. 4596
36;   "   Walter; m; 14 (3-5-18); 1/2; S; Son; yes 33; yes; Al. 77
37;   "   Andrew H; m; 18 (7-25-13); 1/2; S; Nephew; yes 34; yes; Al. 4448
38;   "   Albert; m; 16 (4-30-15); 1/2; S; Nephew; yes 35; yes; Al. 4055-A
39;   "   Sophie; f; 12 (6-7-19); 1/2; S; Niece; yes 36; yes; An. 79

40; **ASHES**, Henry; m; 50 (1882); F; M; Head; yes 37; yes; Al. 676
41;   (Keeps Eagle), Ellen B; f; 38 (1893); F; M; Wife; yes 38; yes; Al. 2066
42; Elknation, Evangeline; f; 4 (7-13-27); F; S; St. Dau; yes 39; yes; An. 119

43; **ASHLEY**, Thomas P; m; 58 (1863); F; Wd; Head; yes 40; yes; Al. 2162

44; **AZURE**, Agnes L; f; 23 (4-30-08); 1/2; S; Head; yes 41; yes; Al. 2965

45; **AZURE**, Henry; m; 72 (1860); 1/2; M; Head; yes 42; yes; Al. 2958
46;   (Longee), Mary; f; 76 (1866); 1/2; M; Wife; yes 43; yes; Al. 2559

47; **AZURE**, George; m; 25 (9-5-06); 1/2; M; Head; yes 44; yes; Al. 2963
48;   "   Henry; m; 2 (3-27-30); 1/2; S; Son; yes 46; yes; An. 124

N. E. **BAILEY**, Charles; m; Head
49;   "   Henry; m; 21 (8-31-10); 1/4; S; Son; yes 47; yes; Al. 4047
50;   "   Katherine; f; 17 (1-1-15); 1/4; S; Dau; yes 48; yes; Al. 4680
51;   "   Ellen; f; 11 (6-18-20); 1/4; S; Dau; yes 49; yes; An. 136
52;   "   Ernest; m; 5 (9-27-22); 1/4; S; Son; yes 50; yes; An. 137
53;   "   William; m; 5 (1-6-25); 1/4; S; Son; yes 51; yes; An. 138

N. E. **BAUMAN**, Oscar; m; Head
54;   (Witzleben), Jean; f; 41 (11-16-91); 1/8; M; Wife; no 52; Linton, Emmons Co, ND; no; Al. 2874
55; Bauman, Martin E; 15 (1-28-17); 1/16; S; Son; no 53; Linton, Emmons Co, ND; yes; An. 152
56;   "   Bernedette; 12 (2-2-20); 1/16; S; Dau; no 54; Linton, Emmons Co, ND; yes; An. 153
57;   "   Letitia; f; 8 (1924); 1/16; S; Dau; no 55; Linton, Emmons Co, ND; yes; An. 154

Census of the __Standing Rock__ Reservation of the __Standing Rock__ jurisdiction, as of __April 1__, 1932, taken by __E. D. Mossman__, Superintendent. North Dakota

N. E. **BARDSLEY**, Floyd; m; Head
58;   (Demery), Catherine; f; 23 (6-4-09); 1/2; M; Wife; yes 56; yes; Al. 3908
59;   "   Floyd, Jr; m; 1 (5-31-30); 1/4; S; Son; yes 57; yes; An. 149
60;   "   Margaret; f; 5/12 (10-20-31); 1/4; S; Dau; yes --; yes; An. 150

61; **BEARBOY**, Peter; m; 58 (1874); F; M; Head; yes 58; yes; Al. 2560
62;   (Matoinapewin), Mrs; f; 67 (1865); F; M; Wife; yes 59; yes; Al. 2138

63; **BEARPAW**, Paul; m; 65 (1867); F; M; Head; yea 60; yes; Al. 2152
64;   (Winyanskawin), Mrs. F; 69 (1863); F; M; Wife; yes 61; yes; Al. 3178

65; **BEARSHIELD**, Julius; m; 37 (1895); F; M; Head; yes 72; yes; Al. 1819
66;   (Grindstone), Pearl; f; 27 (9-10-04); F; M; Wife; yes 845; yes; Al. 521
67;   "   Joseph; m; 8 (1924); F; S; Son; yes 74; yes; An. 203
68;   "   Cecelia; f; 6 (12-3-25); F; S; Dau; yes 75; yes; An. 204
69; Grindstone, May B; f; 6 (7-7-25); F; S; s-Dau; yes 846; yes; An. 1349
70; Grindstone, Amy B; f; 2 (5-26-29); F; S; s-Dau; yes 847; yes; An. 1354

71; **BEARSHIELD** (Brave), Susan; f; 25 (9-1-06); F; Div; Head; yes 77; yes; Al. 2687
72;   "   Mary Ann; f; 1 (8-15-30); F; S; Dau; yes 78; yes; An. 202

N. E. **BELASQUE**, John; m; Head
73;   (No Heart), Elizabeth; f; 26 (4-7-05); F; M; Wife; yes 79; yes; Al. 338
74;   "   Bernice D; f; 2 (5-6-29); F; S; Dau; yes 80; yes; An. 213

N. E. **BENDICKSON**, John; m; Head
75;   (Azure), Louise; f; 30 (9-3-01); 1/2; M; Wife; yes 81; yes; Al. 2959
76;   "   Evelyn; f; 10 (11-23-21); 1/4; S; Dau; yes 82; yes; An. 216
77;   "   Josephine; f; 8 (11-30-23); 1/4; S; Dau; yes 83; yes; An. 217
78;   "   Lucille; f; 6 (2-3-26); 1/4; S; Dau; yes 84; yes; An. 218
79;   "   John; m; 3 (11-8-28); 1/4; S; Son; yes 85; yes; An. 219

N. E. **BERGEN**, Richard; m; Head
80;   (Schoenhut), Evelyn; f; 24 (12-13-07); 1/2; M; Wife; no 86; Sisseton, Roberts Co, SD; yes; Al. 2902

81; **BIGHEAD** (Tanyanmani), Mrs. Chase; f; 74 (1858); F; Wd; Head; yes 87; yes; Al. 3198

82; **BIGHEAD** (Marpiya), Mrs. Jas; f; 78 (1854); F; Wd; Head; yes 88; yes; Al. 3136

5

Census of the __Standing Rock__ Reservation of the __Standing Rock__ jurisdiction, as of __April 1__, 1932, taken by __E. D. Mossman__, Superintendent. North Dakota

KEY: Number; Surname, Given; Sex; Age at Last Birthday; Tribe (Standing Rock Sioux unless otherwise noted); Degree of Blood; Marital Status; Relationship to Head of Family; At Jurisdiction where enrolled (Yes or No); (If "No", where, if given); Ward (Yes or No); Allotment, Annuity and Identification Numbers.

83; **BIGHORNELK**, Louis; m; 40 (1892); F; M; Head; yes 89; yes; Al. 2980
84;   (BlackPlume), Bessie; f; 35 (9-15-97); F; M; Wife; yes 90; yes; Al. 2730
85; "   Francis; m; 10 (7-24-21); F; S; Son; yes 91; yes; An. 227
86; "   William; m; 4 (4-24-28); F; S; Son; yes 92; yes; An. 228
87; "   Mary; f; 6/12 (9-25-31); F; S; Son; yes --; yes; An. 229

88; **BIGMOCCASIN** (Moccasin), Mary; f; 78 (1854); F; Wd; Head; yes 93; yes;
Al. 3153

89; **BIGSHIELD**, Marcella; f; 23 (9-2-09); F; S; Head; yes 94; yes; Al 3909

90; **BIGSHIELD**, Pius; m; 56 (1876); F; M; Head; yes 95; yes; Al. 2415
91;   (No Two Horns), Isabelle; f; 44 (1888); F; M; Wife; yes 96; yes; Al. 2104
92; "   Charlotte; f; 10 (10-16-21); F; S; Dau; yes 97; yes; An. 236
93; "   Sylvester; m; 8 (3-19-24); F; S; Son; yes 98; yes; An. 237
94; "   Ned; m; 6 (2-26-26); F; S; Son; yes 99; yes; An. 238
95; "   Angela; f; 1 (6-1-30); F; S; Dau; yes 100; yes; An. 239

96; **BLACKBEAR**, Charles; m; 54 (1878); F; M; Head; No 101; Fort Berthold
Reservation, ND; yes; Al. 2221

97; **BLACKCLOUD**, Felix; m; 49 (1883); F; M; Head; yes 105; no; Al. 620
98;   (Thompson), Sarah; f; 24 (9-12-07); F; M; Wife; yes 106; yes; Al. 2544
99; "   Sophie; f; 14 (8-8-17); F; S; Dau; yes 107; yes; An. 260
100; "   Patrick; m; 12 (3-21-21); F; S; Son; yes 108; yes; An. 261
101; "   Peter; m; 8 (8-14-23); F; S; Son; yes 109; yes; An. 262
102; "   Anastatia; f; 4 (5-1-27); F; S; Dau; yes 110; yes; An. 264
103; "   Louis; m; 3 (9-27-28); F; S; Son; yes 111; yes; An. 265
104; "   Pauline; f; 1 (7-15-30); F; S; Dau; yes 112; yes; An. 266

105; **BLACKHOOP**, Barney; m; 28 (3-1-03); F; S; Head; yes 113; yes; Al. 2766

106; **BLACKHOOP**, David; m; 35 (1-27-97); F; M; Head; no 114; Venice, CA;
no; Al. 1999
107;   (Zahn), Irene; f; 28 (7-15-03); 1/2; M; Wife; no 115; Venice. CA; yes;
Al. 2726

108; **BLACKHOOP**, William; m; 25 (12-6-06); F; S; Head; yes 116; yes; Al. 2787

109; **BLACKPLUME**, James; m; 18 (12-10-13); F; S; Head; yes 117; yes; Al 4549

110; **BLACKPRAIRIEDOG**; 87 (1845); F; Wd; Head; yes 118; yes; Al. 2125

Census of the **Standing Rock** Reservation of the **Standing Rock** jurisdiction, as of **April 1**, 1932, taken by **E. D. Mossman**, Superintendent. North Dakota

111; **BLACKPRAIRIEDOG**, James; m; 39 (1893); F; Wd; Head; yes 119; no; Al. 2576

112; " " Bede; m; 13 (1-16-19); F; S; Son; yes 121; yes; An. 288

113; " " Virginia; f; 5 (6-22-26); F; S; Dau; yes 122; yes; An. 289

114 " " Martin; m; 2 (11-7-29); F; S; Son; yes 123; yes; An. 290

115; **BLACKTOMAHAWK**, Barney; m; 24 (11-3-07); F; M; Head; yes 124; yes; Al. 2987

116; (Goodwood), Grace; f; 19 (9-12-12); F; M; Wife; yes 521; yes; Al. 4342

117; " James; m; 6/12 (9-19-31); F; S; Son; yes ---; yes; An. 294

118; **BLACKTOMAHAWK**, Jasper; m; 26 (3-26-05); F; M; Head; yes 125; yes; Al. 2480

119; (Goodwood), Agnes; f; 33 (10-27-99); F; M; Wife; yes 126; yes; Al. 2381

120; **BLACKTOMAHAWK**, Thomas; m; 53 (1879); F; M; Head; yes 129; yes; Al. 2478

121; (DifferentCloud), Lillian; f; 49 (1882); F; M; Wife; yes 130; yes; Al. 2729

122; " Mable; f; 18 (3-14-14); F; S; Dau; yes 131; yes; Al. 4567

123; " Molisa; f; 11 (6-16-20); F; S; Dau; yes 132; yes; An. 299

124; Redstone, Nellie; f; 11 (12-12-19); F; S; St-Dau; yes 133; yes; An. 301

125; **BLACKTONGUE**, Frank; m; 75 (1857); F; M; Head; yes 134; yes; Al. 1760

126; (Irontomahawk), Victoria; f; 59 (1873); F; M; Wife; yes 135; yes; Al. 3116

127; " Emma; f; 18 (2-18-14); F; S; Dau; yes 136; yes; Al. 4550

128; **BLACKTONGUE**, Mary; f; 32 (2-11-1900); F; S; Head; yes 137; yes; Al. 1761

129; **BLUEBOY** (Wiciga), Clara; f; 59 (1873); F; Wd; Head; no 138; Fort Peck Reservation, MT; yes; Al. 3155

130; **BOBTAILBEAR**, Joseph; m; 77 (1855); F; Wd; Head; yes 139; yes; Al. 2601

131; **BRAVE** (Chasing Bear), Francis; f; 59; (1873); F; M; Head; yes 140; yes; Al. 3463

132; " Joseph; m; 21 (8-20-11); F; S; Son; yes 141; yes; Al. 4195

133; " Wilson; m; 18 (12-15-13); F; S; Son; yes 142; yes; Al. 4529

134; " Bessie; f; 15 (1916); F; S; Dau; yes 143; yes; An. 329

135; **BRAVE**, Moses; m; 23 (5-1-09); F; M; Head; yes 144; yes; Al. 3815

136; **BRAVEBULL**, Claude; m; 58 (1874); F; M; Head; yes 145; yes; Al. 2189;

137; (Hat), Mollie; f; 68 (1864); F; M; Wife; yes 146; yes; Al. 1987

Census of the **Standing Rock** Reservation of the **Standing Rock** jurisdiction, as of **April 1**, 19**32**, taken by **E. D. Mossman**, Superintendent. North Dakota

KEY: Number; Surname, Given; Sex; Age at Last Birthday; Tribe (Standing Rock Sioux unless otherwise noted); Degree of Blood; Marital Status; Relationship to Head of Family; At Jurisdiction where enrolled (Yes or No); (If "No", where, if given); Ward (Yes or No); Allotment, Annuity and Identification Numbers.

138; **BRAVEBULL**, John; m; 35 (5-7-97); F; M; Head; yes 147; yes; Al. 2708
139; " Alice; f; 11 (5-30-21); 1/2; S; Dau; yes 148; yes; An. 334
140; " Josephine; f; 8 (3-6-24); 1/2; S; Dau; yes 149; yes; An. 335
141; " John, Jr; m; 5 (5-4-26); 1/2; S; Son; yes; 150; yes; An. 336
142; " Frank; m; 3 (8-8-28); 1/2; S; Son; yes 151; yes; An. 337
143; " Florence; f; 5/12; 1/2; S; Dau; yes ---; yes; An. ---.

N. E. **BREINER**, J.E; m; Head
144; (Goodreau), Josephine; f; 35 (1-31-97); 1/4; M; Wife; yes 152; no;
Al. 2437
145; " Theodore; m; 8 (12-29-23); 1/8; S; yes 153; yes; An. 356
146; " Marie C; f; 6 (8-11-25); 1/8; S; Dau; yes 154; yes; An. 357
147; " Joseph P; m; 5 (9-15-26); 1/8; S; Son; yes 155; yes; An. 358
148; " Alfred W; m; 2 (10-17-28); 1/8; S; Son; yes 156; yes; An. 359

149; **BRINGS THEM**, Mary; f; 28; (11-1-03); F; S; Head; yes 157; yes; Al. 2650

150; **BRINGS WATER**, Emma; f; 98 (1834); F; Wd; Head; yes 158; yes; Al. 3541

151; **BRISTLING**, (Wankankoyakewin), Mrs. Lucas; f; 82 (1850); F; Wd; Head;
yes 159; yes; Al. 3057

152; **BROUGHT PLENTY**, John; m; 37 (5-95); F; M; Head; yes 160; no;
Al. 1794
153; (LaFrombois), Lucy; f; 49 (1883); F; M; Wife; yes 161; yes; Al. 1981
154; Brought Plenty, Kenneth; m; 1 (5-31-30); F; S; Son; yes 162; yes; An. 372
155; LaFrombois, Cecelia; f; 15 (11-6-16); F; S; St-Dau; yes 163; yes; An. 371

156; **BROWNFOREHEAD**, (Kipanpiwin), Mrs. Wm; f; 67 (1865); F; Wd; Head;
yes 164; yes; Al. 3144
157; " James; m; 18 (12-22-13); F; S; Son; yes 165; yes; Al. 4546

158; **BUCKLEY**, Charles; m; 34 (7-10-98); 1/2; M; Head; yes 166; yes; Al. 2972
159; (Wells), Hazel; f; 28 (2-11-04); 1/4; M; Wife; no 167; Tacoma,
Pierce Co, WA; yes; Al. 2199
160; " Beverley; m; 11 (12-8-21); 3/8; S; Son; no 168; Tacoma, Pierce Co,
WA; yes; An. 412
161; " Edwin; m; 9 (2-2-23); 3/8; S; Son; no 169; Tacoma, Pierce Co,
WA; yes; An. 413
162; " Rebecca; f; 8 (11-16-24); 3/8; S; Dau; no 170; Tacoma, Pierce Co,
WA; yes; An. 414

163; **BUCKLEY**, John; m; 52 (1880); 1/2; M; Head; yes 171; no. Al. 2102
164; (Blackhoop), Maggie; f; 35 (8-4-97; F; M; Wife; yes 172; yes; Al 2704

Census of the **Standing Rock** Reservation of the **Standing Rock** jurisdiction, as of **April 1**, 1932, taken by **E. D. Mossman**, Superintendent. North Dakota

KEY: Number; Surname, Given; Sex; Age at Last Birthday; Tribe (Standing Rock Sioux unless otherwise noted); Degree of Blood; Marital Status; Relationship to Head of Family; At Jurisdiction where enrolled (Yes or No); (If "No", where, if given); Ward (Yes or No); Allotment, Annuity and Identification Numbers.

165;   "   Henry; m; 19 (4-24-12); 3/4; S; Son; yes 173; yes; Al. 4294
166; Jackson, Helen; f; 5 (11-7-26); 3/4; S; St-Dau; yes 174; yes; An. 402;

167; **BUCKLEY**, Joseph; m; 46 (1886); 1/2; M; Head; yes 175; no; Al. 2013
168;   "   Ernest J; m; 14 (2-24-17); 1/4; S; Son; yes 176; yes; An. 405
169;   "   James F; m; 12 (2-7-19); 1/4; S; Son; yes 177; yes; An. 406
170;   "   Evelyn; f; 10 (6-7-21); 1/4; S; Dau; yes 178; yes; An. 407
171;   "   Lorraine; f; 6 (3-26-26); 1/4; S; Dau; yes 179; yes; An. 408

172; **BUCKLEY**, Stephen; m; 50 (1882); 1/2; S; Head; yes 180; no; Al. 2971

173; **BUFFALOBOY** (Mazaskawin), Mrs; f; 69 (1853); F; Wd; Head; yes 181;
                                                                            yes; Al. 3209

174; **BUFFALOBOY** (Whitecloud), Josie; f; 53 (1879); F; Wd; Head; yes 183;
                                                                            yes; Al. 3208
175;   "   Alice; f; 20 (4-1-12); F; S; Dau; yes 184; yes; Al. 4166
176;   "   Rosaline; f; 17 (1-19-15); F; S; Dau; yes 185; yes; An. 417
177;   "   Elizabeth; f; 14 (12-28-17); F; S; Dau; yes 186; yes; An. 418
178;   "   Herbert, Jr; m; 10 (11-3-20); F; S; Son; yes 187; yes; An. 419

179; **BULLBEAR**, Eugene; m; 6- (1872); F; M; Head; yes 188; yes; Al. 2140
180;   (Bullbear), Julia; f; 55 (1877); F; M; Wife; yes 189; yes; Al. 3149
181;   "   Ruby; f; 20 (11-21-11); F; S; Dau; yes 190; yes; An. 423
182;   "   Louis; m; 13 (5-22-18); F; S; Son; yes 191; yes; An. 423

183; **BULLBEAR**, Frank; m; 57 (1873); F; Wd; Head; yes 192; yes; Al. 2791

184; **BULLBEAR**, Leo; m; 28 (2-21-04); F; S; Head; yes 193; yes; Al. 2142

185; **BULLHEAD**, Philip; m; 76 (1856); F; M; Head; yes 194; yes; Al. 1638
186;   (Bullhead), Henrietta; f; 72 (1860); F; M; Wife; yes 195; yes; Al. 3133

N. E. **BYINGTON**, George; m; Head
187;   (Buckley), Hattie; f; 45 (1888); 1/2; M; Wife; yes 196; yes; Al. 2974
188;   "   Charles; m; 19 (8-22-11); 1/4; S; Son; yes 197; yes; Al. 4190
189;   "   Arthur; m; 16 (5-18-15); 1/4; S; Son; yes 198; yes; An. 436
190;   "   Melvin L; m; 14 (6-26-17); 1/4; Son; yes 199; yes; An. 437
191;   "   Thomas; m; 11 (3-2-21); 1/4; S; Son; yes 200; yes; An. 438
192;   "   Dorothy; f; 6 (3-21-26); 1/4; S; Dau; yes 201; yes; An. 439
193;   "   Lawrence; m; 2 (7-15-28); 1/4; S; Son; yes 202; yes; An. 440

194; **BYINGTON**, James; m; 22 (2-21-10); 1/4; S; Head; yes 203; yes; Al. 4057

9

Census of the **Standing Rock** Reservation of the **Standing Rock** jurisdiction, as of **April 1**, 1932, taken by **E. D. Mossman**, Superintendent. North Dakota

195; **CALLOUSLEG**, Amos; m; 74 (1858); F; M; Head; yes 204; yes; Al. 1679
196;   (Flyinghorse), Louisa; f; 60 (1852); F; M; Wife; yes 205; yes; Al. 3184

197; **CALLOUSLEG**, David; m; 24 (6-9-08); F; S; Head; yes 206; yes; Al. 3820

198; **CALLOUSLEG**, Edward; m; 48 (1884); F; M; Head; yes 207; no; Al. 1684
199;   (Longbull), Mary; f; 47 (1885); F; M; Wife; yes 208; yes; Al. 566
200;   "   Paul; m; 20 (6-6-13); F; S; Son; yes 209; yes; Al. 4442
201;   "   Eleanor; f; 12 (9-22-19); F; S; Dau; yes 210; yes; An. 473
202;   "   Edmund; m; 8 (2-15-23); F; S; Son; yes 212; yes; An. 474

203; **CALLOUSLEG**, Francis; m; 25 (8-20-06); F; S; Head; yes 213; yes; Al. 1685

204; **CALLOUSLEG**, Joshua; m; 38 (1894); F; M; Head; yes 214; no; Al. 1681
205;   (Crowman), Maude; f; 48 (1884); F; M; Wife; yes 215; yes; Al. 3230
206;   "   Vincent; m; 10 (7-12-21); F; S; Son; yes 216; yes; An. 478
207;   "   Lucille; f; 8 (9-9-23); F; S; Dau; yes 217; yes; An. 479
208;   "   Francis; m; 6 (10-4-25); F; S; Son; yes 218; yes; An. 480
209; White, Margaret; f; 12 (7-6-20); F; S; St-Dau; yes 219; yes; An. 482

210; **CALLOUSLEG**, Lucy; f; 20 (12-28-10); F; S; Head; yes 223; yes; Al. 4082

211; **CALLOUSLEG**, Leo; L; m; 40 (1891); F; M; Head; yes 220; yes; Al. 1683
212;   (Strikes Ree), Mable; f; 40 (1891); F; M; Wife; yes 221; yes; Al. 1748
213;   "   Beatrice; f; 5 (1-24-27); F; S; Dau; yes 222; yes; An. 485

214; **CALLOUSLEG**, Theodore; m; 24 (8-9-07); F; S; Head; yes 224; yes;
                                                                Al. 3611
N. E. **CARIGNAN**, Jack; m; Head
215;   (Witzleben), Hermine; f; 38 (4-10-94); 1/8; M; Wife; yes 225; no;
                                                                Al. 2875
216;   "   Virginia; f; 14 (5-23-17); 1/16; S; Dau; yes 226; yes; An. 493
217;   "   John E; m; 13 (1-14-19); 1/16; S; Son; yes 227; yes; An. 494
218;   "   Lawrence M; 11 (8-20-20); 1/16; S; Son; yes 228; yes; An. 495
219;   "   Mary J; f; 8 (12-21-23); 1/16; S; Dau; yes 229; yes; An. 496
220;   "   Alfred J; m; 3 (9-28-28); 1/16; S; Son; yes 230; yes; An. 497

221; **CARRYTHEMOCCASIN**, James; m; 27 (1-26-04); F; S; Head; yes 231; yes;
                                                                Al. 2587

222; **CARRYTHEMOCCASIN**, Thomas; m; 30 (7-4-01); F; M; Head; yes 232;
                                                                yes; Al. 2455
223;   (One Hawk), Josephine; f; 19 (1-1-13); F; M; Wife; yes 233; yes;

Census of the **Standing Rock** Reservation of the **Standing Rock** jurisdiction, as of **April 1**, 1932, taken by **E. D. Mossman**, Superintendent. North Dakota

Al. 4391

224; " Jesse; m; 2 (4-14-30); F; S; Son; yes 234; yes; An. 503

225; **CASKE**, David; m; 32 (4-5-1900); F; M; Head; yes 235; yes; Al. 1823
226; (Shoots The Enemy), Agnes; f; 29 (8-6-02); F; M; Wife; yes 236; yes;
Al. 2267
227; " Annie; f; 9 (7-6-22); F; S; Dau; yes 237; yes; An. 508
228; " Josephine; f; 4 (6-23-27); F; S; Dau; yes 238; yes; An. 509

229; **CASKE**, David, Sr; m; 63 (1869); F; Wd; Head; yes 239; yes; Al. 1821

N. E. **CASKE**, Fred; m; Head
230; " Isabelle; f; 10 (12-11-21); F; S; Dau; yes 244; yes; An. 512

231; **CASKE**, Joseph; m; 24 (12-18-07); F; M; Head; yes 240; yes; Al. 2575
232; (Has Tricks), Alice; f; 21 (2-24-11); F; M; Wife; yes 241; yes; Al. 4121
233; Caske, Leo; m; 1 (9-1-30); F; S; Son; yes 242; yes; An. 511

N. E. **CHAPMAN**, Ernest; m; Head
234; (Jordan), Mary L; f; 27 (2-7-05); 1/2; M; Wife; yes 243; yes; Al. 1844
235; " Lythia; f; 8 (12-4-23); 3/4; S; Dau; yes 246; yes; An. 530
236; " Wilmer; m; 4 (12-4-26); 3/4; S; Son; yes 247; yes; An. 531
237; " Grace; f; 3 (1928); 3/4; S; Dau; yes 248; yes; An. 532
238; " Delphine; f; 1 (3-30-31); 3/4; S; Dau; yes 249; yes; An. 533

239; **CHARGING EAGLE**, John; m; 38 (1894); F; M; Head; yes 250; yes;
Al. 1739
240; (RedHawk), Ida; f; 31 (5-14-01); F; M; Wife; yes 251; yes; Al. 2610
241; " Josephine; f; 8 (4-25-23); F; S; Dau; yes 252; yes; An. 538
242; " Jennie; f; 2 (1929); F; S; Dau; yes 253; yes; An. 537

N. E. **CHASE**, Frank; m; Head
666; (Standing Soldier), Louise; f; 51 (1881); F; M; Wife; no 254; Fort
Berthold Reservation, McLean, ND; no; Al. 1864

243; **CHASING BEAR** (Wicite), Mrs; f; 87 (1845); F; Wd; Head; yes 255; yes;
Al. 3464

244; **CHASE THE BEAR**, John; m; 45 (1887); F; M; Head; yes 256; yes;
Al. 1870
245; (Two Shield), Nellie; f; 40 (1893); F; M; Wife; yes 257; yes;
Al. 1832
246; " " Rose; f; 17 (8-9-14); F; S; Dau; yes 258; yes; Al. 4625
247; " " Philip; m; 15 (1916); F; S; Son; yes 259; yes; An. 547

Census of the **Standing Rock** Reservation of the **Standing Rock** jurisdiction, as of **April 1**, 1932, taken by **E. D. Mossman**, Superintendent. North Dakota

KEY: Number; Surname, Given; Sex; Age at Last Birthday; Tribe (Standing Rock Sioux unless otherwise noted); Degree of Blood; Marital Status; Relationship to Head of Family; At Jurisdiction where enrolled (Yes or No); (If "No", where, if given); Ward (Yes or No); Allotment, Annuity and Identification Numbers.

248; " " Joseph; m; 12 (9-1-19); F; S; Son; yes 260; yes. Al. 1832-A
249; " " Maggie; f; 10 (2-5-22); F; S; Dau; yes 261; yes; Al. 1832-B
250; " " Catherine; f; 5 (9-9-26); F; S; Dau; yes 262; yes; Al. 1832-C
251; " " Florence; f; 2 (1929); F; S; Dau; yes 263; yes; Al. 1832-D

252; **CHASE IN THE WOODS**; m; 69 (1863); F; Wd; Head; yes 264; yes;
Al. 2253

253; **CHOOSES**, John; m; 51 (1881); F; M; Head; yes; 265; yes; Al. 1900
254; (Loon), Alma; f; 40 (1892); F; M; Wife; yes 266; yes; Al. 1782

255; **CHOPPER**, Frank; m; 19 (3-23-13); F; S; Alone; yes 267; yes; Al. 4425
256; " Lena; f; 12 (4-23-16); F; S; Alone; yes 268; yes; An. 574
257; Chopper, Abraham; m; 10 (1-4-20); F; S; Alone; yes 269; yes; An. 575

258; **COLDHAND**, Clement; m; 65 (1867); F; M; Head; yes 270; no; Al. 2450
259; (Yellowbird), Mrs; f; 64 (1868); F; M; Wife; yes 271; yes; Al. 3523
260; " Charles A; m; 10 (1-22-22); F; S; Adpt. Son; yes 272; yes; An. 602

261; **COLDHAND**, Daniel; m; 63 (1869); F; M; Head; yes 273; no; Al. 2312
262; (Treetop), Annie; f; 51 (1881); F; M; Wife; yes 274; yes; Al. 3213

263; **CONICA**, Andrew; m; 34 (1898); F; M; Head; yes 275; yes; Al. 2323
264; (Ireland), Helen; f; 24 (6-4-07); F; M; Wife; yes 276; yes; Al. 2261
265; " Lydia; f; 10 (9-13-21); F; S; Dau; yes 277; yes; An. 619
266; " Jacob; m; 8 (12-3-23); F; S; Son; yes 278; yes; An. 620
267; " Magdalene; f; 2 (9-1-29); F; S; Dau; yes 279; yes; An. 621
268; Paints Brown, Clifford; m; 9 (11-24-22); F; S; St-Son; yes 280; yes; An. 623
269; " " Mary M; f; 7 (2-15-25); F; S; St-Dau; yes 281; yes; An. 624

270; **CONICA**, George; m; 26 (7-30-05); F; M; Head; yes 282; yes; Al. 2688
271; (Eagleboy), Mary A; 17 (10-17-14); F; M; Wife; yes 283; yes; Al. 4656
272; " Marvin; m; 2 (1-13-30); F; S; Son; yes 284; yes; An. 627

273; **CONICA**, Henry; m; 28 (12-22-03); F; M; Head; yes 285; yes; Al. 2324
274; (Redhawk), Annie; f; 28 (5-5-03); F; M; Wife; yes 286; yes; Al. 2509
275; " Sylvester; m; 8 (5-25-24); F; S; Son; yes 287; yes; An. 630
276; " Marcelian; f; 6 (7-1-26); F; S; Dau; yes 288; yes; An. 631
277; " Stella; f; 3 (8-10-28); F; S; Dau; yes 289; yes; An. 632
278; " Henry, Jr; m; 1 (7-1-30); F; S; Son; yes 290; yes; An. 633

279; **COTTONWOOD**, Asa; m; 29 (4-30-02); 1/2; M; Head; yes 291; yes;
Al. 2663

Census of the **Standing Rock** Reservation of the **Standing Rock** jurisdiction, as of **April 1**, 1932, taken by **E. D. Mossman**, Superintendent. North Dakota

KEY: Number; Surname, Given; Sex; Age at Last Birthday; Tribe (Standing Rock Sioux unless otherwise noted); Degree of Blood; Marital Status; Relationship to Head of Family; At Jurisdiction where enrolled (Yes or No); (If "No", where, if given); Ward (Yes or No); Allotment, Annuity and Identification Numbers.

280;   (Walker) Gertrude; f; 33 (3-6-99); F; M; Wife; yes 292; yes; Al. 2595
281;   "   Asa, Jr; m; 8 (2-18-24); 3/4; S; Son; yes 293; yes; An. 640
282;   "   Beatrice; f; 4 (5-27-27); 3/4; S; Dau; yes 294; yes; An. 636
283;   "   Christina; f; 3 (5-8-28); 3/4; S; Dau; yes 295; yes; An. 639
284;   "   Agnes F; f; 11/12 (4-26-31); 3/4; S; Dau; yes ---; yes; An. 637

285; **COTTONWOOD**, Austin; m; 53 (1879); F; M; Head; yes 296; no; Al. 2671
286;   (Douglas), Esther; f; 21 (8-13-10); F; M; Wife; yes 22297; yes;
                                           Al. 4030
287;   "   Abel; m; 2 (1-25-30); F; S; Son; yes 298; yes; An. 643

288; **COTTONWOOD**, Jerome; m; 28 (1-5-04); F; M; Head; yes 299; yes;
                                           Al. 2664
289;   (Goodiron). Benedicta; f; 24 (11-16-07); F; M; Wife; yes 300; yes;
                                           Al. 2585
290;   "   Ramona; f; 1 (6-4-30); F; S; Dau; yes 301; yes; An. 651

291; **COTTONWOOD**, Jerome, Sr; m; 64 (1868); F; M; Head; yes 302; yes;
                                           Al. 2361
292;   (Swifthawk), Laura; f; 50 (1882); F; M; Wife; yes 303; yes;
                                           Al. 3237
293; Cottonwood, George; m; 12 (5-26-19); F; S; Son; yes 304; yes; An. 647
294;   "   Joseph; m; 10 (11-26-21); F; S; Son; yes 305; yes; An. 646
295;   "   Eunice; f; 3 (3-30-29); F; S; Dau; yes 307; yes; An. 648

296; **COTTONWOOD**, John S; m; 22 (8-19-09); F; M; Head; yes 308; yes;
                                           Al. 3938
297;   (Returns Last), Mildred E; f; 16 (8-2-15); F; M; Wife; yes 1120; yes;
                                           An. 653
298;   "   Walter; m; 1/12 (2-23-32); F; S; Son; yes ---; yes; An. ---.

299; **COTTONWOOD**, Thomas; m; 43 (1889); F; M; Head; yes 309; yes;
                                           Al. 2673
300;   (Onjinca), Emily; f; 34 (1898); F; M; Wife; yes 310; yes; Al. 1383
301;   "   Bruno; m; 15 (6-26-16); F; S; Son; yes 311; yes; An. 660
302;   "   Oscar; m; 13 (11-11-18); F; S; Son; yes 312; yes; An. 659
303;   "   Thomas, Jr; m; 9 (10-28-22); F; S; Son; yes 313; yes; An. 656
304;   "   Louise; f; 8 (2-20-24); F; S; Dau; yes 314; yes; An. 657
305;   "   Mary; f; 4 (1927); F; S; Dau; yes 315; yes; An. 658
306;   "   Isabelle; f; 3/12 (12-22-31); F; S; Dau; yes ---; yes; An. 661

307; **CRAZYWALKING**, Miles; m; 88 (1844); F; Wd; Head; yes 317; yes;
                                           Al. 2061

Census of the **Standing Rock** Reservation of the **Standing Rock** jurisdiction, as of **April 1**, 1932, taken by **E. D. Mossman**, Superintendent. North Dakota

KEY: Number; Surname, Given; Sex; Age at Last Birthday; Tribe (Standing Rock Sioux unless otherwise noted); Degree of Blood; Marital Status; Relationship to Head of Family; At Jurisdiction where enrolled (Yes or No); (If "No", where, if given); Ward (Yes or No); Allotment, Annuity and Identification Numbers.

308; **CRAZYWALKING**, Paul; m; 50 (1882); F; M; Head; yes 318; no; Al. 2062
309; (Graybear), Emma; f; 38 (1894); F; M; Wife; yes 319; yes; Al. 2553
310; " Margaret; f; 18 (8-21-13); F; S; Dau; yes 320; yes; Al. 4485
311; " Clara; f; 11 (10-31-20); F; S; Dau; yes 321; yes; An. 682
312; " Charles; m; 6 (12-30-25); F; S; Son; yes 322; yes; An. 683
313; " Henry; m; 4 (2-1-28); F; S; Son; yes 323; yes; An. 684
314; " Joseph; m; 2 (3-12-30); F; S; Son; yes 324; yes; An. 685

315; **CROSS**, William; m; 67 (1875); F; M; Head; yes 326; yes; Al. 2342
316; (Miniopta), Mrs. Wm; f; 61 (1871); F; M; Wife; yes 327; yes; Al. 3132

317; **CROW**, George P; m; 35 (2-5-97); F; M; Head; yes 328; yes; Al. 2574
318; (Bullhead), Kate; f; 30 (11-27-01); F; M; Wife; yes 329; yes; Al. 1640
319; " George, Jr; m; 8 (11-17-23); F; S; Son; yes 330; yes; An. 696
320; " Theron; m; 5 (10-11-26); F; S; Son; yes 331; yes; An. 697
321; " Lavern B; m; 2 (5-17-29); F; S; Son; yes 332; yes; An. 698
322; " Duane L; m; 4/12 (12-8-31); F; S; Son; yes ---; yes; An. 698

323; **CROWMAN**, John; m; 65 (1867); F; M; Head; yes 1947; yes; Al. 3232
324; (Wankanluta), Mrs; f; 63 (1869); F; M; Wife; yes 1948; yes; Al. 3095

325; **CROWNECKLACE**, Barney; m; 29 (2-12-03); F; S; Head; no 333; Vancouver, WA; yes; Al. 2513

326; **CROWNECKLACE**, Charles; m; 56 (1876); F; M; Head; yes 334; no; Al. 1892
327; " Felix; m; 16 (6-18-15); F; S; Son; yes 335; yes; An. 717
328; " Lorene; f; 11 (5-29-20); F; S; Dau; yes 336; yes; An. 718

N. E. **DeCOTEAU**, Fred; m; Head
329; (Azure), Adelia; f; 33 (4-9-99); F; M; Wife; no 337; Fort Peck Res, Poplar, Mt; yes; Al. 2961
330; " Jerry; m; 14 (8-11-17); F; S; Son; yes 338; yes; An. 738

331; **DEFENDER**, George; m; 41 (1891); 1/2; M; Head; yes 339; no; Al. 739
332; (See The Bear), Helen; f; 30 (11-1-01); F; M; Wife; yes 340; yes; Al. 2205
333; " Earl; m; 10 (8-8-21); 3/4; S; Son; yes 341; yes; An. 741
334; " Max J; m; 8 (12-3-23); 3/4; S; Son; yes 342; yes; An. 742
335; " Daniel; m; 6 (12-3-23); 3/4; S; Son; yes 343; yes; An. 743
336; " Olivia; f; 1 (10-14-30); 3/4; S; Dau; yes 344; yes; An. 744

N. E. **DEMERY**, Joe; m; Head

Census of the **Standing Rock** Reservation of the **Standing Rock** jurisdiction, as of **April 1**, 1932, taken by **E. D. Mossman**, Superintendent. North Dakota

KEY: Number; Surname, Given; Sex; Age at Last Birthday; Tribe (Standing Rock Sioux unless otherwise noted); Degree of Blood; Marital Status; Relationship to Head of Family; At Jurisdiction where enrolled (Yes or No); (If "No", where, if given); Ward (Yes or No); Allotment, Annuity and Identification Numbers.

337;   (Halsey), Martha; f; 50 (1882); 1/2; M; Wife; yes 345; no; Al. 406
338;   "   Joseph W; 11 (8-23-20); 1/2; S; Son; yes 346; yes; An. 771

N. E. **DEUCHANEAU**, Albert; m; Head
339;   (Demery), Louisa; f; 24 (12-20-07); 1/2; M; Wife; no 347; Chey. River
Res, Promise, SD; yes; Al. 3014

340; **DIFFERENT OWL**, James; m; 79 (1853); F; M; Head; yes 348; yes;
Al. 1742
341;   (Bigeagle), Mary; f; 47 (1885); F; M; Wife; yes 349; yes; Al. 3763
342;   " Samuel; m; 13 (6-19-18); F; S; Son; yes 350; yes; An. 815
343;   " Cecelia; f; 11 (8-1-20); F; S; Dau; yes 351; yes; An. 816

344; **DIFFERENT TRACK BULL** (Wankangliskawin), Mrs; f; 77 (1855); F; Wd;
Head; yes 352; yes; Al. 3501

345; **DOGSKIN**, Edward; m; 21 (3-22-11); F; S; Head; yes 1051; yes; Al. 4232

346; **DOGSKIN**, Louis; m; 32 (4-9-99); F; M; Head; yes 353; yes; Al. 2572
347;   (Bigboy), Rose; f; 29 (8-13-02); F; M; Wife; yes 354; yes; Al. 1978
348;   " Lawrence; m 7 (10-28-24); F; S; Son; yes 355; yes; An. 855
349;   " Allen; m; 5 (2-29-27); F; S; Son; yes 356; yes; An. 856
350;   " Thomas; m; 3 (2-12-29); F; S; Son; yes 357; yes; An. 857
351;   " Tony; m; 10/12 (5-9-31); F; S; Son; yes ---; yes; An. 858

352; **DOUBLERIDER**, Richard; m; 54 (1878); F; M; Head; yes 358; no;
Al. 2325
353;   (Bringsthem), Julia; f; 53 (1879); F; M; Wife; yes 359; yes; Al. 3726
354; Bringsthem, Cyril; m; 16 (10-9-15); F; S; St-Son; yes 360; yes; An. 861
355; Bringsthem, Josephine; f; 13 (7-25-18); F; S; St-Dau; yes 361; yes; An. 862
356; Bringsthem, Sampson; m; 11 (11-3-20); F; S; St-Son; yes 361; yes; An. 863

357; **DOUGLAS**, Joseph; m; 16 (11-27-18); F; S; Alone; yes; 363; yes; An. 869
358;   " Cordelia; f; 9 (9-8-22); F; S; Alone; yes 364; yes; An. 870

N. E. **DOUGLAS**, Jacob; m; Head
359;   (Manyhorses), Louise; f; 25 (5-3-06); F; M; Wife; yes 365; yes; Al. 2257
360;   " Cecelia; f; 13 (11-27-15); F; S; Dau; yes 366; yes; An. 865
361;   " Jacob; m; 9 (9-8-22); F; S; Son; yes 367; yes; An. 866
362;   " Cynthia; f; 1 (10-31-30); F; S; Dau; yes 368; yes; An. 867
363;   " Florence; f; 5/12 (10-30-31); F; S; Dau; yes ---; yes; An. 868

364; **DUNN**, Charles; m; 48 (1885); F; M; Head; yes 369; no; Al. 1982
365;   (Standing Soldier), Rachael; f; 57 (1875); F; M; Wife; yes 370; yes;

15

KEY: Number; Surname, Given; Sex; Age at Last Birthday; Tribe (Standing Rock Sioux unless otherwise noted); Degree of Blood; Marital Status; Relationship to Head of Family; At Jurisdiction where enrolled (Yes or No); (If "No", where, if given); Ward (Yes or No); Allotment, Annuity and Identification Numbers.

Al. 1866

366; " Charles, Jr; m; 18 (4-11-13); F; S; Son; yes 371; yes; Al. 4434
367; " Herbert; m; 15 (9-17-16); F; S; Son; yes 372; yes; An. 887
368; " Louis G; m; 10 (4-22-21); F; S; Son; yes 373; yes; An. 888

369; **DWARF**, Claude; m; 54 (1878); F; M; Head; yes 374; yes; Al. 1929
370; (Windy), Annie; f; 49 (1883); F; M; Wife; yes 375; yes; Al. 3044

371; **DWARF**, Joseph; m; 31 (8-1-1900); F; S; Head; yes 379; yes; Al. 930

372; **EAGLEBOY**, Ambrose; m; 33 (2-15-99); F; M; Head; yes 380; yes; Al. 2718
373; (Blackcloud), Edith; f; 35 (1-13-97); F; M; Wife; yes 102; yes; Al. 680
374; Blackcloud, Narcisse; m; 12 (6-13-19); F; S; St-Son; yes 103; yes; An. 913
375; Blackcloud, Melvin; m; 2 (10-18-29); F; S; St-Son; yes 104; yes; An. 914
376; Eagleboy, Serena; f; 9/12 (7-18-31); F; S; Dau; yes ---; yes; An. 915

3777[sic]; **EAGLEBOY**, Matthew; m; 23 (6-16-09); F; M; Head; yes 381; yes;
Al. 3829

378; **EAGLEBOY**, Nelson; m; 67 (1865); F; M; Head; yes 382; yes; Al. 2286
379; (Redstone), Lizzie; f; 32 (1890); F; M; Wife; yes 383; yes; Al. 2351
380; " Martha; f; 16 (10-9-15); F; S; Dau; yes 384; yes; An. 921
381; " Jennie; f; 14 (3-18-17); F; S; Dau; yes 385; yes; An. 922

382; **EAGLEBOY**, Samuel; m; 56 (1876); F; Wd; Head; yes 387; yes; Al. 2360

383; **EAGLEMAN**, William; m; 26 (9-23-05); F; S; Head; yes 388; yes; Al. 2648

384; **EAGLESTAFF**; m; 66 (1866); F; M; Head; yes 389; yes; Al. 2274
385; (Chief Woman), Mrs. F; 66 (1866); F; M; Wife; yes 390; yes; Al. 3199
386; Thunder, Raymond; m; 14 (2-7-18); F; S; Gr-Son; yes 391; yes; An. 962

387; **EHAKEKU**; m; 62 (1870); F; M; Head; no 392; Ft. Peck Agcy, MT; yes;
Al. 2159

388; **ELK**, John; m; 36 (1896); F; M; Head; yes 393; yes; Al. 3108
389; (Streakedeye), Catherine; f; 34 (1895); F; M; Wife; yes 394; yes;
Al. 2758
390; " John, Jr; m; 5 (3-15-27); F; S; Son; yes 395; yes; An. 975
391; Thunder, Belina; f; 9 (8-25-22); F; S; St-Dau; yes 396; yes; An. 976
392; Thunder, Josephine; f; 7 (5-24-24); F; S; St-Dau; yes 397; yes; An. 977

N. E. **ENDRES**, Louis; m; Head
393; (Washington), Ada; f; 56 (1876); 1/2; M; Wife; yes 398; no; Al. 1771

Census of the **Standing Rock** Reservation of the **Standing Rock** jurisdiction, as of **April 1**, 1932, taken by **E. D. Mossman**, Superintendent. North Dakota

KEY: Number; Surname, Given; Sex; Age at Last Birthday; Tribe (Standing Rock Sioux unless otherwise noted); Degree of Blood; Marital Status; Relationship to Head of Family; At Jurisdiction where enrolled (Yes or No); (If "No", where, if given); Ward (Yes or No); Allotment, Annuity and Identification Numbers.

N. E. **EVANS**, Frank; (m); Head
394;   (Goodiron), Cecelia; f; 32 (2-10-1900; 3/4; M; Wife; no 399; Mandan,
                                                  Morton Co, ND; yes; Al. 2489
395;   "   Willard; m; 10 (5-16-21); 3/8; S; Son; no 400; Mandan, Morton Co,
                                                  ND; yes; An. 1003
396;   "   Percy Lee; m; 9 (7-5-22); 3/8; S; Son; no 401; Mandan, Morton Co,
                                                  ND; yes; An. 1004
397;   "   Charlotte; f; 7 (8-26-24); 3/8; S; Dau; no 402; Mandan, Morton Co,
                                                  ND; yes; An. 1005

398; **EVANS**, Robert; m; 23 (4-28-09); 1/2; S; Head; no 403; Bismarck, Burleigh
                                                  Co, ND; yes; Al. 3802

399; **EVANS**, Iola; f; 17 (9-26-14); 1/2; S; Alone; yes 404; yes; An. 1006
400;   "   May; f; 14 (11-24-17); 1/2; S; Alone; yes 405; yes; An. 1007
401;   "   Francis; m; 5 (3-12-27); 1/2; S; Alone; yes 406; yes; An. 1008

402; **FASTHORSE**, Henry; m; 32 (5-31-1900); F; M; Head; yes 408; yes;
                                                  Al. 2242
403;   (Welsh), Lillian; f; 32 (5-20-1900); F; M; Wife; yes 409; yes; Al. 160
404;   "   Edward; m; 4 (10-8-27); F; S; Son; yes 410; yes; An. 1012
405;   "   Herbert K; m; 11/12 (4-6-31); F; S; Son; yes ---; yes; An. 1013

N. E. **FAULKNER**, Charles E; m; Head
406;   (Murphy), Dora C; f; 27 (3-13-05); 1/2; M; Wife; yes 415; yes; Al. 3707

407; **FASTHORSE**, Paul; m; 62 (1870); F; M; Head; yes 414; yes; Al. 2241
408;   (Bigmoccasin), Jane; f; 57 (1875); F; M; Wife; yes 415; yes; Al. 3707

409; **FASTHORSE**, Samuel; m; 28 (4-1-05); F; M; Head; yes 417; yes; Al. 2243
410;   "   Frederick; m; 4/12 (11-7-31); F; S; Son; yes ---; yes; An. 1024

N. E. **FERO**, Chas. W; m; Head
411;   (Gilland), Bessie; f; 36 (1896); 1/2; M; Wife; yes 418; yes; Al. 2845
412;   "   Lucille E; f; 14 (1-20-18); 1/4; S; Dau; yes 419; yes; an. 1033
413;   Fero, Caroline; f; 8 (10-4-23); 1/4; S; Dau; yes 420; yes; An. 1034
414;   "   Mary Lee; f; 5 (12-4-26); 1/4; S; Dau; yes 421; yes; An. 1035

N. E. **FIRECLOUD**, Robert; m; Head
415;   (Redhorse), Gertrude; f; 20 (4-4-11); F; M; Wife; yes 422; yes; Al. 4122

N. E. **FIRECLOUD**, Ludia; f; Head
416;   Zahn, John E; m; 1 (5-30-30); 1/2; S; Son; yes 423; yes; An. 1051

> **KEY:** Number; Surname, Given; Sex; Age at Last Birthday; Tribe (Standing Rock Sioux unless otherwise noted); Degree of Blood; Marital Status; Relationship to Head of Family; At Jurisdiction where enrolled (Yes or No); (If "No", where, if given); Ward (Yes or No); Allotment, Annuity and Identification Numbers.

N. E. **FISHER**, Jacob; m; Head
417;   (Harrison), Lavina; f; 20 (7-28-11); 1/4; M; Wife; yes 424; yes; Al. 4183

N. E. **FISCHER**, George; m; Head
418;   (Gayton), Trivian; f; 30 (2-1-02); 1/2; M; Wife; no 425; Bismarck,
                                                              Burleigh Co, ND; yes; Al. 1710
419;   "   Norodny, m; 4 (1-24-28); 1/4; S; Son; no 426; Bismarck, Burleigh Co,
                                                              ND; yes; An. 1054

420;   **FLY**, Louise; f; 63 (1869); F; S; Head; yes 427; yes; Al. 1767

421;   **FOLLOWS THE ROAD**; m; 75 (1857); F; M; Head; yes 428; yes;
                                                              Al. 2277
422;   (White), Mrs; f; 78 (1854); F; M; Wife; yes 429; yes; Al. 3561

423;   **FOLLOWS THE ROAD**, Noel; m; 27 (2-2-05); F; M; Head; yes 430; yes;
                                                              Al. 2696
424;   "   "   John; m; 2 (1-31-30); F; S; Son; yes 431; yes; An. 1084
425;   "   "   Nellie; f; 2d (3-29-32); F; S; day; yes ---; yes; An. ---.

426;   **FOLLOWS THE ROAD**, Thomas; m; 32 (1900); F; M; Head; yes 432; yes;
                                                              Al. 2695
427;   (Choose), Matilda; f; 24 (9-17-07); F; M; Wife; yes 433; yes; Al. 2750
428;   "   Leo; m; 3 (1-30-29); F; S; Son; yes 434; yes; An. 1087
1274;   "   Eli; m; 11/12 (4-5-31); F; S; Son; yes ---; yes; An. 1088

429;   **FOOLBEAR**, Annie; f; 44 (1888); F; S; Head; yes 435; yes; Al. 2116

430;   **FOOLBEAR**, Charles; m; 46 (1886); F; M; Head; yes 436; no; Al. 2115
431;   (Graytrack), Rose; f; 33 (1899); F; M; Wife; yes 437; yes; Al. 3808
432;   "   Chas, Jr; m; 15 (11-9-16); F; S; Son; yes 438; yes; An. 1092
433;   "   Myrtle; f; 7 (8-12-24); F; S; Dau; yes 439; yes; An. 1093
434;   Foolbear, Grace; f; 4 (9-25-27); F; S; Dau; yes 440; yes; An. 1094
435;   "   Flossie; f; 1 (3-22-31); F; S; Dau; yes 441; yes; An. 1095

436;   **FOUR**, Edward; m; 34 (1899); F; M; Head; yes 442; yes; Al. 3766
437;   "   Eugene; m; 4 (2-28-28); F; S; Son; yes 443; yes; An. 1119
438;   "   Alvera; f; 6/12 (9-5-31); F; S; Dau; yes --- yes; An. 1120

439;   **FOX**, Rose; f; 16 (1915); F; S; Alone; yes 444; yes; An. 1122

440;   **FREDETTE**, Agnes; f; 62 (1860); F; S; Head; yes[sic] 445; Faribault, MN;
                                                              no; Al. 2493

Census of the **Standing Rock** Reservation of the **Standing Rock** jurisdiction, as of **April 1**, 1932, taken by **E. D. Mossman**, Superintendent. North Dakota

KEY: Number; Surname, Given; Sex; Age at Last Birthday; Tribe (Standing Rock Sioux unless otherwise noted); Degree of Blood; Marital Status; Relationship to Head of Family; At Jurisdiction where enrolled (Yes or No); (If "No", where, if given); Ward (Yes or No); Allotment, Annuity and Identification Numbers.

441; **FROSTED**, Thomas; m; 75 (1857); F; M; Head; yes 446; no; Al. 1698
4422[sic]; (Frosted), Susan; f; 68 (1864); F; M; Wife; yes 447; yes; Al. 3228

443; **GATES**, John; m; 42 (1891); 1/2; m; Head; yes 448; no; Al. 1938

444; **GATES** (Twobears), Nellie; f; 78 (1886); F; Wd; Head; yes 449; yes; Al. 3345

445; **GAYTON**, Alfred; m; 24 (11-22-07); 1/2; Head; yes 450; yes; Al. 3002

446; **GAYTON**, Arthur; m; 26 (1-4-06); 1/2; S; Head; yes 451; yes; Al. 1719

447; **GAYTON**, Effie; f; 31 (3-3-01); 1/2; S; Head; no 452; Pierre, Hughes Co, SD; yes; Al. 1704

448; **GAYTON**, Henry; m; 30 (4-15-02); 1/2; M; Head; yes 453; yes; Al. 1717
449; " Henry J; m; 1 (11-26-30); 1/4; S; Son; yes 454; yes; An. 1178

450; **GAYTON**, James; m; 20 (12-17-11); 1/2; S; Alone; yes 455; yes; Al. 4258
451; " Geo. M; m; 18 (1-3-14); 1/2; S; Alone; yes 456; yes; Al. 4543
452; " Winston; m; 14 (1-19-18); 1/2; S; Alone; yes 457; yes; Al. 1174
453; " Lindie; f; 13 (4-2-19); 1/2; S; Alone; yes 458; yes; An. 1175
454; " Warren; m; 11 (3-26-21); 1/2; S; Alone; yes 459; yes; an. 1176

455; **GAYTON**, James; m; 45 (1887); 1/2; M; Head; yes 460; yes; Al. 1728
456; " Dora; f; 18 (2-18-24); 3/4; S; Dau; yes 461; yes; Al. 4554
457; " Mary L; f; 13 (4-27-18); 1/4; S; Dau; yes 462; yes; An. 1182
458; " Joseph; m; 10 (1-15-22); 1/4; S; Son; yes 463; yes; An. 1183
459; " Gladys; f; 11 (5-28-20); 1/4; S; Dau; yes 464; yes; An. 1184
460; Gayton, Irene; f; 4 (3-25-28); 1/4; S; Dau; yes 465; yes; An. 1185

461; **GAYTON**, John; m; 62 (1870); 1/2; M; Head; yes 466; no; Al. 1708
462; (White Eagle), Sophie; f; 52 (1880); 1/2 M; Wife; yes 467; yes; Al. 3087

463; **GAYTON**, John; m; 27 (12-23-04); 1/2; M; Head; yes 468; yes; Al. 1718
464; " Lorraine; f; 6 (4-6-26); 1/4; S; Dau; no 469; St. Paul, MN; yes; An. 1191
465; " Dorothy; f; 2 (4-5-29); 1/4; S; Dau; no 470; St. Paul, MN; yes; An. 1192

466; **GAYTON** (Mulhern), Maggie; f; 60 (1872); 1/2; Wd; Head; yes 474; no; Al. 3467
467; " Minnie; f; 19 (7-21-12); 1/2; S; Dau; yes 475; yes; Al. 4322

KEY: Number; Surname, Given; Sex; Age at Last Birthday; Tribe (Standing Rock Sioux unless otherwise noted); Degree of Blood; Marital Status; Relationship to Head of Family; At Jurisdiction where enrolled (Yes or No); (If "No", where, if given); Ward (Yes or No); Allotment, Annuity and Identification Numbers.

468;   "   Evelyn; f; 17 (1-30-15); 1/2; S; Dau; yes 476; yes; Al. 4685

469; **GAYTON**, Robert; m; 25 (2-6-07); 1/2; S; Head; yes 471; yes; Al. 1707

470; **GAYTON**, Ruby; f; 22 (8-18-09); 1/2; S; Head; yes 477; yes; Al. 3904

471; **GAYTON**, William J; m; 33 (1899); 1/2; S; Head; yes 478; yes; Al. 1716

472; **GAYTON**, William; m; 52 (1870); 1/2; M; Head; yes 479; yes; Al. 1703
473;   (Bullhead), Esther; f; 54 (1878); F; M; Wife; yes 480; no; Al. 3466
474;   "   Mable; f; 20 (2-28-12); 3/4; S; Dau; yes 481; yes; Al. 4268
475;   "   Leslie W; m; 13 (2-15-19); 3/4; S; Son; yes 482; yes; An. 1201
476;   "   Elsie; f; 8 (3-6-24); 3;4; S; Dau; yes 483; yes; An. 1202

477; **GILLAND**, James; m; 31 (9-15-1900); 1/2; M; Head; yes 485; yes; Al. 2847
478;   "   Viola J; f; 3 (6-24-28); 1/4; S; Dau; yes ---; yes; An. ----.

479; **GILLAND**, Robert; m; 45 (1887); 1/2; M; Head; yes 486; no; Al. 2844
480;   "   Robert, Jr; m; 5/12 (10-27-30); 1/4; S; Son; yes ---; yes; An. ---.

481; **GILLAND** (Kempton), Viola; f; 39 (4-1-01); 1/2; Wd; Head; yes 487; yes;
                                                                            Al. 2809

482; **GIPP**, Louis W; m; 20 (5-20-13); 1/2; M; Head; yes 488; yes; Al. 4174
483;   (Partain), Maggie; f; 18 (10-22-13); 1/2; M; Wife; yes 489; yes; Al. 4321
484;   "   Albert; m; 1 (12-4-30); 1/2; S; Son; yes 490; yes; An. 1210
485;   "   Frank B; m; 5/12 (11-26-31); 1/2; S; Son; yes ---; yes; An. 1211

486; **GODFREY**, John F; m; 15 (1-7-17); 1/2; S; Alone; yes 491; yes; An. 1216

487; **GOODBOY**, Oscar; m; 68 (1864); F; M: Head; yes 492; yes; Al. 2051
488;   (Goodboy), Bessie; f; 65 (1867); F; M; Wife; yes 493; yes; Al. 3180

489; **GOODCLOUD**, Frank; m; 58 (1874); F; M: Head; yes 494; yes; Al. 1811
490;   (Hinskawin), Matilda; f; 64 (1868); F; M; Wife; yes 495; yes; Al. 3058

491; **GOODCLOUD**, Mrs; f; 68 (1864); F; S; Head; yes 496; yes; Al. 2494

492; **GOODCROW**; m; 67 (1865); F; M; Head; yes 497; yes; Al. 2094
493;   (Tipi or Redbull); Mrs; f; 67 (1865); F; M; Wife; yes 498; yes; Al. 3684

494; **GOODIRON**, Louis; m; 51 (1881); F; M: Head; yes 499; yes; Al. 2679
495;   (Hairychin), Kate; f; 54 (1878); F; M; Wife; yes 500; yes; Al. 2350
496;   "   Francis; m; 13 (7-26-18); F; S; Son; yes 501; yes; Al. 4519-A.
497; Hairychin, Catherine; f; 13 (6-18-18); F; S; St-Dau; yes 502; yes; An. 1249

Census of the **Standing Rock** Reservation of the **Standing Rock** jurisdiction, as of **April 1**, 1932, taken by **E. D. Mossman**, Superintendent. North Dakota

KEY: Number; Surname, Given; Sex; Age at Last Birthday; Tribe (Standing Rock Sioux unless otherwise noted); Degree of Blood; Marital Status; Relationship to Head of Family; At Jurisdiction where enrolled (Yes or No); (If "No", where, if given); Ward (Yes or No); Allotment, Annuity and Identification Numbers.

498; Hairychin, Francis; m; 16 (2-16-16); F; S; St-Son; yes 503; yes; An. 1248

499; **GOODIRON** (Walker), Mary; f; 37 (1895); F; M; Head; yes 504; yes; Al. 2594

500; " Hermine; f; 14 (10-16-17); F; S; Dau; yes 505; yes; An. 1251

501; " Joseph; m; 10 (3-10-22); F; S; Son; yes 506; yes; An. 1252

502; " Gilbert; m; 8 (3-8-24); F; S; Son; yes 507; yes; An. 1253

503; " Theresa; f; 4 ; F; S; Dau; yes 508; yes; An. 1254

504; **GOODIRON**, Samuel; m; 31 (9-4-02); F; M; Head; yes 509; yes; Al. 2490

505; " Magdaline; f; 4 (5-14-27); F; S; Dau; yes 510; yes; An. 1256

506; " Carl; m; 3 (1-23-29); F; S; Son; yes 511; yes; An. 1257

507; " Percy; m; 6/12 (9-13-31); F; S; Son; yes ~~512~~; yes; An. ---.

508; **GOODIRON**, William; m; 26 (6-13-05); F; M; Head; yes 512; yes; Al. 2136

509; (Carry Moccasin), Elizabeth; f; 26 (6-30-05); F; M; Wife; yes 513; yes; Al. 2598

510; " Lucille; f; 4 (1-19-28); F; S; Dau; yes 514; yes; An. 1261

511; **GOODLEFTHAND**; m; 64 (1867); F; M; Head; yes 516; yes; Al. 1917

512; (Wakawin), Mrs; f; 63 (1869); F; M; Wife; yes 517; yes; Al. 3681

513; **GOODLEFTHAND**, Lake; m; 20 (10-15-10); F; M; Head; yes 518; yes; Al. 4043

514; (Tail), Rose M; f; 20 5-14-11; F; M; Wife; yes 519; yes; Al. 4300

515; " Wilmer; m; 5/12 (10-10-31); F; S; Son; yes ---; yes; An. 1266

516; **GOODWOOD** (Keepseagle), Ellen; f; 52 (1880); F; M; Head; yes 520; yes; Al. 3538

517; " Grace; f; 19 (9-12-12); F; S; Dau; yes 521; yes; Al. 4342

518; " Beatrice; f; 15 (6-30-16); F; S; Dau; yes 522; yes; Al. 2383-A.

519; " Florence; f; 13 (11-26-18); F; S; Dau; yes 523; yes; Al. 2382-A.

520; " George; m; 8 (1-31-24); F; S; Son; yes 524; yes; An. 1272

521; **GOODREAU**, Charles; m; 25 (2-8-07); 1/2; M; Head; yes 525; yes; Al. 2792

522; **GOODREAU**, Joseph; m; 23 (1-11-09); 1/2; S; Head; yes 526; yes; Al. 3780

523; **GOODREAU**, Mamie; f; 24 (5-26-07); 1/4; S; Head; yes 527; yes; Al. 2442

524; **GOODREAU**, Robert; m; 64 (1868); 1/2; M; Head; yes 528; yes; Al. 2511

525; (Lanigan), Annie; f; 50 (1862); 1/2; M; Wife; yes 529; yes; Al. 2477

526; " Louise; f; 19 (2-26-13); 1/2; S; Dau; yes 530; yes; Al. 4411

527; " Mollie; f; 15 (8-23-16); 1/2; S; Dau; yes 531; yes; An. 1278

528; Goodreau, Alvin; m; 11 (10-21-20); 1/2; S; Son; yes 532; yes; An. 1279

Census of the **Standing Rock** Reservation of the **Standing Rock** jurisdiction, as of **April 1**, 1932, taken by **E. D. Mossman**, Superintendent. North Dakota

KEY: Number; Surname, Given; Sex; Age at Last Birthday; Tribe (Standing Rock Sioux unless otherwise noted); Degree of Blood; Marital Status; Relationship to Head of Family; At Jurisdiction where enrolled (Yes or No); (If "No", where, if given); Ward (Yes or No); Allotment, Annuity and Identification Numbers.

529;   "   Alvina; f; 11 (10-21-20); 1/2; S; Dau; yes 533; yes; An. 2288
530;   "   Barney; m; 10 (8-8-22); 1/2; S; Son; yes 534; yes; An. 1280
531;   "   Mila F; m; 7 (4-30-24); 1/2; S; Son; yes; 535; yes; An. 1281

532; **GOODREAU**, Samuel; m; 62 (1870); 1/2; M; Head; yes 536; no; Al. 2873

533; **GOODREAU**, Samuel S; m; 21 (10-31-10); 1/4; S; Head; yes 537; yes;
                          Al. 4058

534; **GOODREAU**, Theodore; m; 28 (10-6-03); 1/4; m; Head; yes 538; yes;
                          Al. 2440
535;   "   Patricia; f; 3 (3-10-28); 1/8; S; Dau; yes ---; yes; An. ---

536; **GRAYBEAR**, Harry; m; 42 (1890); F; M; Head; yes 539; yes; Al. 2552
537;   (Standing Soldier), Maggie; f; 42 (1860); F; M; Wife; yes 540; yes;
                          Al. 1861
538;   "   Henry; m; 14 (5-8-17); F; S; Son; yes 541; yes; An. 1288
539;   "   William; m; 11 (12-20-20); F; S; Son; yes 542; yes; An. 1289
540;   "   Leo L; m; 8 (12-8-23); F; S; Son; yes 543; yes; An. 1290
541;   "   Joseph; m; 3 (2-15-29); F; S; Son; yes 544; yes; An. 1291
542;   "   Eva M; f; 23d (3-8-32); F; S; Dau; yes ---; yes; An. ---.

543; **GRAYBEAR**, Jesse; m; 44 (1888); F; M; Head; yes 545; yes; Al. 2551
544;   (Hodgkinson), Ella; f; 35 (1897); 1/4; M; Wife; yes 546; no; Al. 2857
545;   "   Lucille; f; 11 (2-1-21); 5/8; S; Dau; yes 547; yes; An. 1295
546;   "   Mae; f; 7 (7-25-24); 5/8; S; Dau; yes 548; yes; An. 1296
547;   "   Raymond; m; 2 (4-5-29); 5/8; S; Son; yes 549; yes; An. 1296

548; **GRAYBULL**; m; 79 (1853); F; M; Head; yes 560; yes; Al. 2203
549;   (Sisakewin), Mrs; f; 75 (1857); F; M; Wife; yes; 561; yes; Al. 3543

550; **GRAYBULL**, Arthur; m; 38 (4-18-94); F; M; Head; yes; 562; no; Al. 2583
551;   (Mulhern), Emma; f; 38 (1-22-94); 1/2; M; Wife; yes 563; no; Al. 2556
552;   "   William; m; 16 (6-29-15); 3/4; S; Son; yes 564; yes; An. 1301
553;   "   Ethel; f; 10 (7-12-21); 3/4; S; Dau; yes 565; yes; An. 1302
554;   "   Gladys; f; 8 (1-8-24); 3/4; S; Dau; yes 566; yes; An. 1303

555; **GRAYBULL** (Youngbear), Josephine; f; 38 (1894); F; Wd; Head; yes 568;
                          yes; Al. 2156

556; **GRAYBULL**, Thomas; m; 35 (1897); F; M; Head; yes; 567; yes; Al. 2582
557;   (Mentz), Melda; f; 29 (0-13-03); 3/4; M; Wife; yes 924; yes; Al. 2216
558;   "   Thomas, Jr; m; 13 (8-2-18); F; S; Son; yes 569; yes; An. 1306
559;   "   Edgar; m; 11 (5-12-20); F; S; Son; yes 570; yes; An. 1307

Census of the **Standing Rock** Reservation of the **Standing Rock** jurisdiction, as of **April 1**, 1932, taken by **E. D. Mossman**, Superintendent. North Dakota

KEY: Number; Surname, Given; Sex; Age at Last Birthday; Tribe (Standing Rock Sioux unless otherwise noted); Degree of Blood; Marital Status; Relationship to Head of Family; At Jurisdiction where enrolled (Yes or No); (If "No", where, if given); Ward (Yes or No); Allotment, Annuity and Identification Numbers.

560; " Elmer; m; 6 (11-8-25); F; S; Son; yes 572; yes; An. 1308
561; " Matt; m; 2 (2-6-30); F; S; Son; yes 573; yes; An. 1309
562; Mulhern, Aurelia; f; 9 (8-17-22); 5/8; S; St-Dau; yes 925; yes; An. 1311
563; Mulhern, Hildegard; m; 4 (12-22-27); 5/8; S; St-Son; yes 926; yes; An. 1312

564; **GRAYDAY**, Joseph; m; 35 (1897); F; M; Head; yes 573; yes; Al. 2407
565; " Gladys; f; 4 (8-11-27); 1/2; S; Dau; yes 574; yes; An. 1314
566; " Joseph D; m; 2 (1929); 1/2; S; Son; yes 575; yes; An. 1315

567; **GRAYDOG**, Rose; f; 75 (1857); F; S; Head; yes 576; yes; Al. 3733

N. E. **GRAYHAWK**, Benjamin; m; Head
568; (Kidder), Josephine; f; 35 (1897); F; M: Wife; no 577; Fort Peck Res, Poplar, Roosevelt Co, MT; yes; Al. 1953

569; **GRAYSTONE**, Roger; m; 49 (1883); F; M; Head; yes 578; no; Al. 2370
570; (Kidder), Jennie; f; 58 (1874); F; M; Wife; yes 579; yes; Al. 3229
571; " Placida; f; 9 (9-12-22); F; S; Dau; yes 580; yes; An. 1334
572; " Matthew; m; 13 (9-2-17); F; S; Son; yes 581; yes; An. 1335
573; Kidder, John; m; 19 (12-9-12); F; S; St-Son; yes 582; yes; Al. 4387
574; Kidder, James; m; 17 (9-19-14); F; S; St-Son; yes 583; yes; An. 1337
575; " Bessie A; f; 12 (8-22-19); F; S; St-Dau; yes 584; yes; An. 1338

N. E. **GROVER**, O.W; m; Head
576; (Archambault), Clara; f; 40 (1892); 1/2; M; Wife; yes 586; no; Al. 1410
577; " Louis; m; 13 (3-16-19); 1/4; S; Son; yes 587; yes; An. 1356
578; " Erwin C; m; 11 (10-19-20); 1/4; S; Son; yes 588; yes; An. 1357
579; " Hermine; f; 9 (1-30-23); 1/4; S; Dau; yes 589; yes; An. 1358
580; " Milton A; m; 7 (1-20-26); 1/4; S; Son; yes 590; yes; An. 1359
581; " Memoree; f; 5 (11-11-26); 1/4; S; Dau; yes 591; yes; An. 1360
582; " John C; m; 2 (7-25-29); F; S; Son; yes 592; yes; An. 1361
583; " Marie; f; 11/12 (4-27-31); 1/4; S; Dau; yes 593; yes; An. 1362

584; **HAIRYCHIN**, Elizabeth; f; 21 (3-1-12); F; S; Head; yes 593; yes; Al. 4272

593; **HALSEY**, Jacob; m; 59 (1873); 1/2; M; Head; yes 602; no; Al. 786
594; (Endres), Bessie; f; 39 (1893); 1/2; M; Wife; yes 603; yes; Al. 1772
595; " Ada M; f; 18 (11-28-13); 1/2; S; Dau; yes 604; yes; Al. 4524
596; Halsey, Rhabana; f; 15 (9-24-16); 1/2; S; Dau; yes 605; yes; An. 1388
597; " John D; m; 13 (6-18-18); 1/2; S; Son; yes 606; yes; An. 1389
598; " William; m; 11 (5-9-20); 1/2; S; Son; yes 607; yes; An. 1390
599; " Rose J; f; 6 (2-20-26); 1/2; S; Dau; yes 608; yes; An. 1391
600; " George J; m; 3 (4-26-28); 1/2; S; Son; yes 609; yes; An. 1392

KEY: Number; Surname, Given; Sex; Age at Last Birthday; Tribe (Standing Rock Sioux unless otherwise noted); Degree of Blood; Marital Status; Relationship to Head of Family; At Jurisdiction where enrolled (Yes or No); (If "No", where, if given); Ward (Yes or No); Allotment, Annuity and Identification Numbers.

601; **HALSEY**, Jerome; m; 23 (6-19-09); 1/2; S; Head; yes 610; yes; An. 1392
602; **HALSEY**, Lillian; f; 20 (11-15-10); 1/2; S; Alone; yes 612; yes; Al. 4059

603; **HALSEY**, Louis; m; 47 (1885); 1/2; M; Head; yes 613; no; Al. 2474
604;   (Ironeyes), Christine; f; 52 (1880); F; M; Wife; yes 614; yes; Al. 192
605;   "   Marcella; f; 20 (11-26-11); 3/4; S; Dau; yes 615; yes; Al. 4237
606;   "   Alice; f; 17 (10-16-14); 3/4; S; Dau; yes 616; yes; Al. 4652
607;   "   Margaret; f; 13 (2-28-19); 3/4; S; Dau; yes 617; yes; An. 1401
608;   "   Henry; m; 10 (7-2-21); 3/4; S; Son; yes 618; yes; An. 1402

609; **HALSEY**, Michael; m; 36 (1896); 1/2; M; Head; yes 620; no; Al. 1627;
610;   "   Gladys M; f; 5 (7-18-26); 5/8; S; Dau; yes 621; yes; An. 1405
611;   "   Michael, Jr; m; 3 (10-17-28); 5/8; S; Son; yes 622; yes; An. 1406
612;   "   Wesley B; m; 1 (12-7-30); 5/8; S; Son; yes 623; yes; An. 1407

613; **HALSEY**, Peter; m; 34 (1898); 1/2; M; Head; no 624; Kansas City,
                                Jackson Co, MO; no; Al. 794

N. E. **HARRIS**, Larry; m; Head
620;   (Pleets), Annie; f; 38 (1894); 3/4; m; Wife; no 632; Hopeville, Fulton
                               Co, GA; no; Al. 1617
621;   "   Lawrence; m; 12 (8-31-19); 3/8; S; Son; no 633; Hopeville, Fulton,
                               Co, GA; yes; An. 1433
622;   "   George E; m; 10 (7-16-21); 3/8; S; Son; no 634; Hopeville, Fulton
                               Co, GA; yes; An. 1434

N. E. **HARRIS**, Joseph; m; Head
623;   (Loan Him Arrows), Kate; f; 32 (11-6-1900); F; M; Wife; no 637; Fort
                        Peck Res, Poplar, Roosevelt Co, MT; yes; Al. 1909
624   "   Chauncey; m; 8 (12-77[sic]-23); F; S; Son; no 638; Fort Peck Res,
                        Poplar, Roosevelt Co, MT; yes; An. 1440

625; **HARRIS**, Henry; m; 25 (5-6-06); 1/4; M; Head; yes 639; yes; Al. 3991
626;   "   James E; m; 4 (10-11-27); 1/8; S; Son; yes 640; yes; An. 1436
627; Harris, Mary A; f; 3 (12-?-28); 1/8; S; day; yes 641; yes; An. 1437
628;   "   Charles H; m; 1 (7-24-30); 1/8; S; Son; yes 642; yes; An. 1438
629;   "   David D; m; 1 da (3-30-31); 1/8; S; Son; yes ---; yes; An. ---.

630; **HAS KNIFE**, Mrs. F; 80 (1852); F; S; Head; yes 643; yes; Al. 3721

631; **HAS TRICKS**, Jerome; m; 65 (1867); F; M; Head; yes 644; yes; Al. 1943
632;   (Marpiya), Jane; f; 65 (1867); F; M; yes 645; yes; Al. 3052

633; **HAS TRICKS**, Mary; f; 33 (12-29-99); F; S; Head; yes 646; yes; Al. 1944

Census of the **Standing Rock** Reservation of the **Standing Rock** jurisdiction, as of **April 1**, 1932, taken by **E. D. Mossman**, Superintendent. North Dakota

KEY: Number; Surname, Given; Sex; Age at Last Birthday; Tribe (Standing Rock Sioux unless otherwise noted); Degree of Blood; Marital Status; Relationship to Head of Family; At Jurisdiction where enrolled (Yes or No); (If "No", where, if given); Ward (Yes or No); Allotment, Annuity and Identification Numbers.

634; **HAWKSHIELD**, Herbert; m; 67 (1865); F; M; Head; yes 647; no; Al. 158
635; (Cross), Mary A; f; 58 (1874); F; M; Wife; yes 648; yes; Al. 3130
636; Tail, Jerry; m; 17 (5-1-14); F; S; St-Son; yes 649; yes; Al. 4593

637; **HAWKSHIELD**, Herbert, Jr; m; 29 (7-25-02); F; S; Head; no 651; Fort
Totten Res, ND; yes; Al. 159

638; **HIS HORSE APPEARS**, Isaac; m; 42 (1890); F; M; Head; yes 652; yes;
Al. 2528
639; (Blacktomahawk), Mary Lucy; f; 29 (3-24-04); F; M; Wife; yes 653;
yes; Al. 2479
640; " Bertha; f; 9 (5-21-22); F; S; Dau; yes 654; yes; An. 1513
641; " Joe Mark; m; 6 (4-23-25); F; S; Son; yes 655; yes; An. 1514

642; **HIS CHASE**, Pius; m; 28 (7-20-03); F; M; Head; yes 656; yes; Al. 1768
643; (Black Tongue), Rose; f; 29 (5-11-02); F; M; Wife; yes 657; yes;
Al. 1762
644; " Pius, Jr; m; 5 (10-2-26); F; S; Son; yes 658; yes; An. 1508
645; " Joan R; f; 2 (8-13-29); F; S; Dau; yes 659; yes; An. 1509
646; " Elizabeth; f; 1 (3-22-31); F; S; Dau; yes 660; yes; An. 1510

647; **HODGKINSON**, Agnes; f; 19 (9-1-12); 1/4; S; Head; no 661; Blackwell, OK;
yes; Al. 4331

N. E. **HODGKINSON**, Edward; m; Head
648; (Mentz), Annie; f; 56 (1876); 1/2; M; Wife; yes 660; yes; Al. 2855
649; " Lucille; f; 17 (10-20-14); 1/4; S; Dau; yes 662; yes; Al. 4677
650; " Orlando; m; 13 (11-20-18); 1/4; S; Son; yes 663; yes; An. 1522
651; " Caroline; f; 10 (1-17-22); 1/4; S; Dau; yes 664; yes; An. 1523

652; **HODGKINSON**, Charles; m; 24 (2-24-08); 1/4; S; Head; yes 665; yes;
Al. 2829

653; **HODGKINSON**, Frederick; m; 33 (1-24-99); 1/4; M; Head; no 666; San
Francisco, CA; no; Al. 2825

N. E. **HOISINGTON**, C.L; m; Head
654; (Kempton), Evelyn; f; 23 (9-6-08); 1/4; M; Wife; yes 667; no;
Al. 3837
655; " Clarence; m; 3 (6-17-28); 1/8; S; Son; yes 668; yes; An. 1543
656; " Calvin C; m; 2 (6-25-29); 1/8; S; Son; yes 669; yes; An. 1544
657; " Richard K; m; 1 (10-8-30); 1/8; S; Son; yes 670; yes; An. 1545

KEY: Number; Surname, Given; Sex; Age at Last Birthday; Tribe (Standing Rock Sioux unless otherwise noted); Degree of Blood; Marital Status; Relationship to Head of Family; At Jurisdiction where enrolled (Yes or No); (If "No", where, if given); Ward (Yes or No); Allotment, Annuity and Identification Numbers.

658; **HOLY ELK FACE**, John W; m; 19 (9-14-12); F; M; Head; yes 673; yes; Al. 4343

659;   (Tail), Eva; f; 16 (2-6-16); F; M; Wife; yes 650; yes; An. 1485

660; **HOLY ELK FACE** (Ironshield), Nellie; f; 42 (1890); F; Wd; Head; yes 672; yes; Al. 2590

661;   "   Carlisle; m; 12 (12-11-19); F; S; Son; yes 674; yes; A. 1550

662;   "   Peter, m; 9 (6-15-22); F; S; Son; yes 675; yes; An. 1551

663;   "   Agatha; f; 2 (1-2-30); F; S; Dau; yes 676; yes; An. 1552

664; **HONA**, Hona; m; 81 (1851); F; Wd; Head; yes 676; yes; Al. 1580

665; **HONA**, George; m; 49 (1893); F; S; Head; yes 677; yes; Al. 1581

667; **HOOTING OWL** (Tipiwastewin), Mrs; f; 80 (1852); F; Wd; Head; yes 679; yes; Al. 1942

N. E. **HOPKINS**, William; m; Head

668;   (Take The Shield), Emma; f; 32 (1900); F; M; Wife; yes 680; yes; Al. 2463

669;   "   Daniel; m; 2 (12-8-29); F; S; Son; yes 681; yes; An. 1558

670; **HOWARD**, Antoine; m; 20 (8-6-11); 1/2; S; Head; no 682; Lawrence, Douglas Co, KS; yes; Al. 4184

671; **HOWARD**, James; m; 50 (1882); 1/2; M; Head; yes 683; no; Al. 1104

672;   "   Carter E; m; 12 (5-28-18); 1/2; S; Son; yes 684; yes; An. 1587

673; Ironnecklace, Theresa; f; 20 (5-22-11); 1/2; S; St-Dau; yes 685; yes; Al. 4157

674;   "   Florence; f; 18 (2-12-14); 1/2; S; St-Dau; yes 686; yes; Al. 4565

675;   "   Thomas; m; 16 (10-7-15); 1/2; S; St-Son; yes 687; yes; An. 1589

676;   "   Clayton; m; 15 (1-1-17); 1/2; S; St-Son; yes 688; yes; An. 1590

677;   "   Lang; m; 13 (10-13-18); 1/2; S; St-Son; yes 689; yes; An. 1591

678; **HOWARD**, John, Jr; m; 22 (6-3-10); 1/2; S; Head; no 690; Lawrence, Douglas Co, KS; yes; Al. 3988

679; **HUFF**, Joseph; m; 50 (1882); 1/2; M; Head; yes 691; no; Al. 2335

680;   (Mulhern), Nellie; f; 51 (1881); 1/2; M; Wife; yes 692; no; Al. 2591

681;   "   Norman; m; 19 (6-5-12); 1/2; S; Son; yes 692; yes; Al. 4305

682;   "   Mildred; f; 16 (7-4-15); 1/2; S; Dau; yes 694; yes; An. 1514

683;   "   Lucille; f; 14 (6-4-17); 1/2; S; Dau; yes 695; yes; An. 1615

684; **HUFF**, Luella; f; 11 (8-12-20); 1/2; S; Dau; yes 696; yes; An. 1616

Census of the **Standing Rock** Reservation of the **Standing Rock** jurisdiction, as of **April 1**, 1932, taken by **E. D. Mossman**, Superintendent. North Dakota

KEY: Number; Surname, Given; Sex; Age at Last Birthday; Tribe (Standing Rock Sioux unless otherwise noted); Degree of Blood; Marital Status; Relationship to Head of Family; At Jurisdiction where enrolled (Yes or No); (If "No", where, if given); Ward (Yes or No); Allotment, Annuity and Identification Numbers.

685; **HUFF**, Peter; m; 24 (5-4-08); 1/2; M; Head; yes 698; yes; Al. 2593

686; **IRELAND**, Andrew; m; 59 (1873); F; M; Head; yes 699; no; Al. 2260
687;   (Wakannajin), Mrs; f; 60 (1872); F; M; Wife; yes 700; yes; Al. 3689
688;   "   Elizabeth; f; 19 (11-18-12); F; S; Dau; yes 701; yes; Al. 4377

689; **IRELAND**, Francis; m; 48 (1884); F; M; Head; yes 702; no; Al. 2348
690;   (Ashley), Martha; f; 38 (1894); F; M; Wife; yes 703; yes; Al. 2163
691;   "   Samuel; m; 21 (11-2-10); F; S; Son; yes 704; yes; Al. 4052
692;   "   Rufus; m; 18 (8-13-13); F; S; Son; yes 705; yes; Al. 4484
693;   "   Agatha; f; 16 (2-15-25); F; S; yes 706; yes; An. 1634
694;   "   Christine; f; 5 (3-28-27); F; S; Dau; yes 707; yes; An. 1635
695;   "   Irene; f; 2 (10-6-29); F; S; Dau; yes 708; yes; An. 1636
696;   "   Alvin A; m; 6 da (3-24-32); F; S; Son; yes ---; yes; An. 1637

697; **IRONBOULDER**, John; m; 52 (1880); F; M; Head; yes 709; no; Al. 2616
698;   (Redfox), Emma; f; 61 (1881); F; M; Wife; yes 710; yes; Al. 3617
699;   "   Leo; m; 14 (11—19-17); F; S; Son; yes 711; yes; An. 1644
700; Redfox, Melda; f; 15 (1-8-17); F; S; Adpt-Dau; yes 712; yes; An. 1645

701; **IRONBULL**, Martin; m; 58 (1874); F; M; Head; yes 713; yes; Al. 2368
702;   (NoTwoHorn), Harriet; f; 55 (1877); F; M; Wife; yes 714; yes; Al. 3672
703;   "   Lillian; f; 16 (7-26-15); F; S; Dau; yes 715; yes; Al. 2368-A.

704; **IRONEYES**, Edward; m; 31 (10-6-1900); F; M: Head; yes 716; yes; Al. 193
705;   (ChasingBear), Agnes; f; 20 (8-31-11); F; M; Wife; yes 717; yes;
                          Al. 4194
706;   "   Jerome; m; 1 (2-25-31); F; S; Son; yes 718; yes; An. 1654

N. E. **IRONNNEST**, Philip; m; Head
707;   (Leandog), Christine; f; 23 (6-29-09); F; M: Wife; no 719; Cheyenne
                          Agency, SD; yes; Al. 3906

708; **IRONROAD**, Andrew; m; 59 (1873); F; M; Head; yes 720; no; al. 2330
709;   (Winyanehake), Mary; f; 63 (1869); F; M; Wife; yes 721; yes; Al. 3090
710;   "   Josephine; f; 20 (2-16-11); F; S; Dau; yes 722; yes; Al. 4103

711; **IRONROAD**, Daniel; m; 78 (1854); F; M; Head; yes 723; yes; Al. 2298
712;   (Ironroad), Helen; f; 57 (1875); F; M; Wife; yes 724; yes; Al. 3111

713; **IRONROAD**, Ignatius; m; 51 (1881); F; M; Head; yes 725; no; Al. 2301
714;   (DifferentTrackBull), Mary; f; 45 (1887); F; M; Wife; yes 726; yes;
                          Al. 2133

Census of the **Standing Rock** Reservation of the **Standing Rock** jurisdiction, as of **April 1**, 1932, taken by **E. D. Mossman**, Superintendent. North Dakota

KEY: Number; Surname, Given; Sex; Age at Last Birthday; Tribe (Standing Rock Sioux unless otherwise noted); Degree of Blood; Marital Status; Relationship to Head of Family; At Jurisdiction where enrolled (Yes or No); (If "No", where, if given); Ward (Yes or No); Allotment, Annuity and Identification Numbers.

715; " Mila; m; 12 (1-23-20); F; S; Son; yes 727; yes; Al. 2133-A.
716; **IRONROAD**, John; m; 25 (2-22-07); F; M; Head; yes 728; yes; Al. 2333
717; (Fourswords), Julia; f; 20 (6-2-11); F; M; Wife; yes 729; yes; Al. 4145
718; " Albert J; m; 9/12 (6-27-31); F; S; Son; yes ---; yes; An. 1683

719; **IRONROAD**, Nellie; f; 25 (7--06); F; S; Head; yes 730; yes; Al. 2299
720; " Grace; f; 2 (6-2-29); F; S; Dau; yes 731; yes; An. 1685

721; **IRONROAD**, Ruth; f; 23 (3-5-09); F; S; Head; yes 732; yes; Al. 3825

722; **IRONROAD**, Samuel; m; 33 (1899); F; M; Head; yes 733; yes; Al. 2300
723; (Many Horses), Estella; f; 28 (11-28-03); F; M; Wife; yes 734; yes; Al. 2258
724; " Gertrude; f; 9 (7-25-22); F; S; Dau; yes 735; yes; An. 1689
725; " Charlotte; f; 5 (1-20-26); F; S; Dau; yes 736; yes; An. 1690
726; " Leon; m; 4 (1-26-28); F; S; Son; yes 737; yes; An. 1691
727; " Lyman; m; 2 (3-11-29); F; S; Son; yes 739; yes; An. 1692
728; " Shirley; f; 1/12 (2-3-32); F; S; Dau; yes –; yes; An. ---.

729; **IRONSHIELD**, Bernard; m; 50 (1882); M; Head; yes 739; no; Al. 2250
730; (Yellowhawk), Mary; f; 58 (1874); F; M; Wife; yes 740; yes; Al. 3537

731; **IRONSHIELD**, John; m; 32 (1900); F; M; Head; yes 741; yes; Al. 2436
732; (Tail), Daisy; f; 25 (11-15-05); F; M; Wife; yes 742; yes; Al. 2355
733; " Sylvan; f (8-23-25); F; S; Dau; yes 743; yes; An. 1700
734; " Evelyn; f; 3 (10-19-28); F; S; Dau; yes 744; yes; An. 1701
735; " Elenor M; f; 9/12 (6-22-31); F; S; Dau; yes none; yes; An. 1702

736; **IRONSHIELD** (Ironbull), Josephine; f; 25 (8-2-08); F; Wd; Head; yes 745; yes; Al. 3582
737; " Jane V; f; 3 (5-13-28); F; S; Dau; yes 746; yes; An. 1704
738; " Aaron; m; 1 (9--30); F; S; Son; yes 747; yes; An. 1705

739; **IRONTOMAHAWK**, Paul; m; 24 (5-11-07); F; S; Head; yes 748; yes; Al. 2618

N. E. **JAMERSON**, James; m; Head
740; " Charles; m; 20 (10-28-11); 1/2; S; Son; yes 749; yes; Al. 4229
741; " Adeline; f; 17 (2-27-15); 1/2; S; Dau; yes 750; yes; Al. 4704
742; " Theron; m; 15 (9-5-16); 1/2; S; Son; yes 751; yes; An. 1720
743; " Theodore; m; 13 (6-18-18); 1/2; S; Son; yes 752; yes; An. 1721
744; " Agnes C; f; 11 (8-20-20); 1/2; S; Dau; yes 753; yes; An. 1722
745; " Bertha L; f; 9 (9-14-22); 1/2; S; Dau; yes 754; yes; An. 1723
746; " Thomas P; m; 8 (10-17-24); 1/2; S; Son; yes 755; yes; An. 1724

KEY: Number; Surname, Given; Sex; Age at Last Birthday; Tribe (Standing Rock Sioux unless otherwise noted); Degree of Blood; Marital Status; Relationship to Head of Family; At Jurisdiction where enrolled (Yes or No); (If "No", where, if given); Ward (Yes or No); Allotment, Annuity and Identification Numbers.

747;   "   William; m; 4 (5-6-27); 1/2; S; Son; yes 756; yes; An. 1725

N. E.   **JONES**, Rolla; m; Head

748;   (Gayton), Rosalind; f; 28 (8-22-03); 1/2; M; Wife; yes 472; yes; Al. 1705

749;   "   Marlene; f; 4/12 (11-15-31); 3/4; S; Dau; yes ---; yes; An. 1195

750;   **JORDAN**, Jacob; m; 46 (1886); 1/2; M; Head; yes 757; no; Al. 1612

751;   (Azure), Nancy; f; 47 (1884); 1/2; M; Wife; yes 758; no; Al. 2964

752;   "   Leo; m; 18 (10-20-12); 1/2; S; Son; yes 759; yes; Al. 4365

753;   "   Henry; m; 17 (4-27-14); 1/2; S; Son; yes 760; yes; Al. 4579

754;   "   Mary C; f; 14 (6-22-17); 1/2; S; Dau; yes 761; yes; An. 1733

755;   "   Louise; f; 12 (5-22-19); 1/2; S; Dau; yes 762; yes; An. 1734;

756;   "   Bessie; f; 11 (3-21-25); 1/2; S; Dau; yes 763; yes; An. 1735

757;   "   Margaret; f; 8 (6-15-23); 1/2; S; Dau; yes 764; yes; An. 1746

758;   **JORDAN**, William; m; 57 (1875); 1/2; Wd; Head; yes 765; no; Al. 1843

759;   "   Wallace; m; 20 (1-23-12); 3/4; S; Son; yes 766; yes; Al. 4257

760;   "   Rose; f; 16 (1-3-16); 3/4; S; Dau; yes 767; yes; An. 1749

761;   "   Caroline; f; 14 (9-2-17); 3/4; S; Dau; yes 768; yes; An. 1750

762;   Jordan, Michael; m; 12 (8-4-19); 3/4; S; Son; yes 769; yes; An. 1751

763;   "   Lena; f; 10 (5-25-21); 3/4; S; Dau; yes 770; yes; An. 1752

764;   "   Julia; f; 7 (1-15-22); 3/4; S; Dau; yes 771; yes; An. 1753

765;   **KARNIGA**, Bessie; f; 32 (1-4-1900); F; S; Head; yes 772; yes; Al. 2229

766;   **KARNIGA**, Giles; m; 55 (1877); F; M; Head; yes 773; yes; Al. 2537

767;   (Littleshield), Annie; f; 66 (1866); F; M; Wife; yes 774; yes; Al. 3723

768;   **KARNIGA**, Julia; f; 20 (3-14-11); F; S; Head; yes 775; yes; Al. 4114

769;   **KEEPS EAGLE**, James; m; 46 (1886); F; S; Head; yes 776; yes; Al. 2958

770;   **KEEPS EAGLE**, John; m; 51 (1851); F; S; Head; yes 777; yes; Al. 2065

771;   **KEEPS EAGLE**, Joseph P; m; 38 (10-22-94); F; S; Head; yes 778; yes; Al. 2067

772;   **KELLEY**, Charles C; m; 39 (1893); 1/2; M; Head; no 779; Whereabouts unknown; yes; Al. 1464

773;   (Gates), Josephine; f; 44 (1888); 1/2; M; Wife; yes 780; no; Al. 1937

774;   "   Helen; f; 9 (5-21-22); 1/2; S; Dau; yes 781; yes; An. 1767

775;   "   Elsie M; f; 8 (12-2-23); 1/2; S; Dau; yes 782; yes; An. 1768

776;   "   Susan L; f; 7 (1-22-25); 1/2; S; Dau; yes 783; yes; An. 1769

777;   "   Theodora; f; 5 (3-6-27); 1/2; S; Dau; yes 784; yes; An. 1770

Census of the __Standing Rock__ Reservation of the __Standing Rock__ jurisdiction, as of __April 1__, 1932, taken by __E. D. Mossman__, Superintendent. North Dakota

KEY: Number; Surname, Given; Sex; Age at Last Birthday; Tribe (Standing Rock Sioux unless otherwise noted); Degree of Blood; Marital Status; Relationship to Head of Family; At Jurisdiction where enrolled (Yes or No); (If "No", where, if given); Ward (Yes or No); Allotment, Annuity and Identification Numbers.

778;   "   Calvin F; m; 3 (7-8-28); 1/2; S; Son; yes 785; yes; An. 1771

779;   "   Patrick; m; 2 (11-14-29); 1/2; S; Son; yes 786 Yes; An. 1772

780; **KEMPTON**, Amy C; f; 27 (8-31-04); 1/4; S; Head; yes 787; yes; Al. 2808

781; **KEMPTON**, Asa F; m; 55 (11-15-1877); 1/4; M; Head; yes 788; yes;
                            Al. 2811
782;   "   Orphie C; f; 19 (12-16-12); 1/8; S; Dau; yes 789; yes; Al. 4392

N. E. **KEOGH**, Leo P; m; Head
783;   (Harrison), Leona; f; 28 (2-4-04); 1/4; M; Wife; yes 790; no; Al. 3990
784;   "   Edith A; f; 11 (9-25-23); 1/8; S; Dau; yes 791; yes; An. 1810
785;   "   Elmer E; m; 5 (7-14-26); 1/8; S; Son; yes 792; yes; An. 1811
786;   "   Margaret; f; 4 (2-17-28); 1/8; S; Dau; yes 793; yes; An. 1812
787;   "   Aubrey P; f; 10/12 (5-23-31); 1/8; S; Dau; yes ---; yes; An. 1813

788; **KIDDER**, Bertha; f; 23 (5-19-09); F; S; Head; yes 794; yes; Al. 3842

789; **KIDDER**, Daniel; m; 29 (5-19-09); F; M; Head; yes 795; yes; Al. 1954
790;   (Crowman), Jennie I; f; 35 (1897); F; M; Wife; yes 796; yes; Al. 1677
791;   "   Magdalene; f; 3 (8-27-28); F; S; Dau; yes 797; yes; An. 1817
792;   "   Daniel, Jr; m; 1 (5-21-30); F; S; Son; yes 798; yes; An. 1820
793;   "   Bertha; f; 9/12 (6-12-31); F; S; Dau; yes ---; yes; An. 1821
794; See The Elk, John; m; 8 (9-7-23); F; S; St-Son; yes 799; yes; An. 1819

795; **KIDDER**, Patrick; m; 26 (4-27-06); F; S; Head; yes 800; yes; Al. 1955

N. E. **KING**, James; m; Head
796;   (Gayton), Inez A; f; 26 (8-3-05); 1/2; M; Wife; yes 2610; yes; Al. 1711
797;   "   Amos; m; 7 (2-18-25); 1/4; S; Son; yes 2611; yes; An. 1864
798;   "   Melvin; m; 4 (4-11-27); 1/4; S; Son; yes 2612; yes; An. 1865
799;   "   Leona M; f; 2 (4-25-29); 1/2; S; Dau; yes; 2613; yes; An. 1866
800;   "   Renee D; f; 10/12 (5-13-31); 1/4; S; Dau; yes ---; yes; An. 1867

801; **KIDDER**, Thomas, Jr; m; 33 (8-12-99); F; M; Head; yes 801; yes; Al. 1952
802;   (Dwarf), Martha; f; 20 (10-17-11); F; M; Wife; yes; 378; yes; Al. 4217

803; **KILLS SPOTTED**, Claude; m; 58 (1874); F; M; Head; yes 805; yes;
                            Al. 2086
804;   (Shelltrack), Mary; f; 40 (11-23-92); F; M; Wife; yes 806; yes; Al. 2308
805;   "   Rose; f; 19 (10-30-12; F; S; Dau; yes 807; yes; Al. 4512
806;   "   Lawrence; m; 15 (7-12-15); F; S; yes 808; yes; An. 1856
807;   "   Victor; m; 13 (2-21-19); F; S; Son; yes 809; yes; An. 1857
808;   "   James; m; 10 (9-1-21); F; S; Son; yes; 3684; yes; An. 1858

Census of the **Standing Rock** Reservation of the **Standing Rock** jurisdiction, as of **April 1**, 1932, taken by **E. D. Mossman**, Superintendent. North Dakota

KEY: Number; Surname, Given; Sex; Age at Last Birthday; Tribe (Standing Rock Sioux unless otherwise noted); Degree of Blood; Marital Status; Relationship to Head of Family; At Jurisdiction where enrolled (Yes or No); (If "No", where, if given); Ward (Yes or No); Allotment, Annuity and Identification Numbers.

809; " Tony; m; 8 (12-17-23); F; S; Son; yes; 3685; yes; An. 1859
810; " Winifred; f; 4 (4-28-27); F; S; Dau; yes 3686; yes; An. 1860
811; " Lucille; f; 1 (3-31-31); F; S; Dau; yes 3687; yes; An. 1861

812; **KING**, Jerome; m; 23 (3-23-09); F; M; Head; yes 810; yes; Al. 3798

813; **KING**, Samuel; m; 51 (1881); F; M; Head; yes 811; yes; Al. 2083

N. E. **KITTELSTVEDT**, Raymond; m; Head
814; (Whiteeagle), Melda A; f; 22 (2-1-10); 3/4; M; Wife; yes 812; yes; Al. 4119
815; " Ronald; m; 1 (6-6-30); 3/8; S; Son; yes 813; yes; An. 3498

N. E. **KROUSER**, Jack; m; Head
816; (McLaughlin), Melda; f; 29 (7-14-02); 1/2; M; Wife; yes 814; yes; Al. 2467
817; Krouser, John C; m; 7 (1-24-25); 1/4; S; Son; yes 815; yes; An. 1874
818; " Helen L; f; 5 (5-5-26); 1/4; S; Dau; yes 816; yes; An. 1875
819; " Deloris; f; 3 (4-12-28); 1/4; S; Dau; yes 817; yes; An. 1876

N. E. **LaFROMBOIS**, Moses; m; Head
820; (Blue Earth), Mable; f; 44 (1888); F; M; Wife; yes 818; yes; Al. 1814
821; Blue Earth, Richard; m; 11 (8-29-30); F; S; St-Son; yes 819; yes; An. 1886
822; Blue Earth, Alice; f; 13 (6-1-18); F; S; St-Dau; yes 820; yes; An. 1885
823; " Jane; f; 8 (10-3-23); F; S; St-Dau; yes 821; yes; An. 1887

N. E. **LAMBIE**, John E; m;; Head
824; (Melvin), Laura; f; 46 (1886); 1/2; M; Wife; no 822; Swastika, ND; yes; Al. 3553
825; " Thomas; m; 19 (3-27-12); 1/4; S; Son; no 823; Swastika, ND; yes; Al. 4306
826; " Emma M; f; 16 (7-14-15); 1/4; S; Dau; no 824; Swastika; ND; yes; An. 1892
827; " Theodore; m; 15 (10-22-16); 1/4; S; Son; no 825; Swastika; ND; yes; An. 1893
828; " Robert; m; 11 (1-23-20); 1/4; S; Son; no 826; Swastika, ND; yes; An. 1894
829; " Patrick; m; 7 (3-17-25); 1/4; S; Son; no 827; Swastika, ND; yes; An. 1895

830; **LAMBIE**, Mary L; f; 24 (5-21-07); 1/4; S; Head; yes 828; yes; Al. 3554

831; **LAMBIE**, William; m; 23 (12-16-09); 1/4; S; Head; yes 829; yes; Al. 4022

Census of the **Standing Rock** Reservation of the **Standing Rock** jurisdiction, as of **April 1**, 1932, taken by **E. D. Mossman**, Superintendent. North Dakota

KEY: Number; Surname, Given; Sex; Age at Last Birthday; Tribe (Standing Rock Sioux unless otherwise noted); Degree of Blood; Marital Status; Relationship to Head of Family; At Jurisdiction where enrolled (Yes or No); (If "No", where, if given); Ward (Yes or No); Allotment, Annuity and Identification Numbers.

832; **LANGER**, David; m; 62 (1860); 1/4; M; Head; yes 830; yes; Al. 4021

833; **LITTLE BEAR**, Bert; m; 29 (7-7-02); F; M; Head; yes 2691; yes; Al. 2059

834; **LITTLE BEAR** (Archambault), Irene; f; 22 (2-4-10); 1/2; M; Head; yes 2692; yes; Al. 4276

835; " Bernice; f; 1 (10-6-30); 3/4; S; Dau; yes 2693; yes; An. 1967

836; " Aleck C; m; 16 da (3-14-32); 3/4; S; Son; yes ---; yes; An. ---.

837; **LITTLECHIEF** (Whitehawk), Mrs; f; 74 (1858); F; M; Head; yes 831; yes; Al. 2319

838; **LITTLECHIEF** (Capa), Agnes; f; 67 (1866); F; Wd; Head; yes 833; no; Al. 2063

839; **LITTLECHIEF**, Charles; m; 37 (1895); F; M; Head; yes 2707; no; Al. 2320

840; (Redfish), Eva; f; 40 (4-22-92); F; M; Wife; yes 2708; yes; Al. 2423

841; " Germaine; f; 5 (2-12-27); F; S; Dau; yes 2709; yes; An. 1985

842; **LITTLECROW**, John; m; 47 (1885); F; M; Head; yes 833; no; Al. 2063

843; (Thunderhawk), Susan; f; 48 (1884); F; M; Wife; yes 834; no; Al. 3197

844; **LITTLE WARRIOR**, Annie; f; 36 (12-17-95); F; S; Head; yes 835; yes; Al. 2033

845; " " William; m; 17 (1-12-15); F; S; Son; yes 836; yes; An. 2020

846; " " Joseph; m; 7 (6-30-24); F; S; Son; yes 837; yes; An. 2021

847; **LOAN HIM ARROWS**; m; 92 (1850); F; M; Head; yes 838; yes; Al. 478

848; (KillsCrowIndian), Mrs; f; 70 (1862); F; M; Wife; yes 839; yes; Al. 3283

849; **LONEMAN**, Annie; f; 32 (7-19-1900); F; S; Head; yes 840; yes; Al. 141

850; **LOOKING HORSE**, Peter; m; 20 (7-29-12); F; M; Head; yes 1402; yes; Al. 4324

851; (Fasthorse), Camille; f; 26 (2-20-06); F; M: Wife; yes 407; yes; Al. 2244

852; " Peter; m; 9/12 (6-30-31); F; S; Son; yes –; yes; An. 2085

853; **LOON**, Edward H; m; 33 (1899); F; M; Head; yes 2796; yes; Al. 1784

854; " Rita Ella; f; 2 (11-22-29); F; S; Dau; yes 2797; yes; An. 2088

855; **LOON**, Theodore; m; 61 (1871); F; M; Head; yes 841; yes; Al. 1781

856; (Gray Horns), Mrs; f; 61 (1877); F; M; Wife; yes 842; yes; Al. 3231

857; " Edward; m; 20 (11-8-11); F; S; Son; yes 843; yes; Al. 4239

858; **LOVEJOY**, Eugene; m; 36 (1896); F; M; Head; yes 844; no; Al. 1997

Census of the **Standing Rock** Reservation of the **Standing Rock** jurisdiction, as of **April 1**, 1932, taken by **E. D. Mossman**, Superintendent. North Dakota

KEY: Number; Surname, Given; Sex; Age at Last Birthday; Tribe (Standing Rock Sioux unless otherwise noted); Degree of Blood; Marital Status; Relationship to Head of Family; At Jurisdiction where enrolled (Yes or No); (If "No", where, if given); Ward (Yes or No); Allotment, Annuity and Identification Numbers.

859; **LOWELL** (Pleets), Mary; f; 40 (1892); 1/2; Wd; Head; yes 848; no; Al. 721

860; **LYONS**, Raphael; m; 36 (10-24-96); 1/4; M; Head; yes 849; no; Al. 1557

861; " Betty J; f; 10 (4-30-1); 1/8; S; Dau; yes 850; yes; An. 2108

862; " Ramona; f; 2 (10-21-29); 1/8; S; Dau; yes 851; yes; An. 2109

N. E. **MADDOCKS**, ?; m; Head

863; (McLaughlin), Melda; f; 33 (7-17-99); 1/4; M; Wife; no 852; Bismarck, Burleigh Co, ND; no; Al. 283

864; Fischer, Joan; f; 11 (12-17-20); 1/8; S; St-Dau; no 853; Bismarck, Burleigh Co, ND; yes; An. 2114

865; **MAGPIE EAGLE**, Lawrence; m; 50 (1882); F; M; Head; yes 854; no; Al. 774

866; (Zintkalaziwin), Ella; f; 60 (1873); F; M; Wife; yes 855; yes; Al. 3240

867; " Martina; f; 20 (8-6-10); F; S; Dau; yes 856; yes Al. 4060

868; **MANY HORSES**; m; 73 (1859); F; M; Head; yes 857; yes; Al. 2254

869; (Black Eyes); Mrs; f; 57 (1875); F; M; Wife; yes 858; yes; Al. 3125

870; **MANY HORSES**, Felix; m; 41 (1891); F; M; Head; yes 859; yes; Al. 2255

871; " " Michael; m; 15 (10-4-16); F; S; Son; yes 860; yes; Al. 1673

872; " " Louis; m; 12 (4-14-19); F; S; Son; yes 861; yes; An. 1674

873; " " Carl; m; 6 (5-29-25); F; S; Son; yes 862; yes; An. 2156

874; **MANY WOUNDS**, George; m; 47 (1885); F; M; Head; yes 863; no; Al. 1632

875; (Halsey), Mary; f; 42 (1889); 1/2; M; Wife; yes 864; no; Al. 795

876; " Leona; f; 11 (6-18-20); 3/4; S; Dau; yes 865; yes; An. 2175

877; " Phyllis; f; 9 (9-22-22); 3/4; S; Dau; yes 866; yes; An. 2169

878; " Geo, Jr; m; 5 (8-26-26); 3/4; S; Son; yes 867; yes; An. 2170

879; " Peter; m; 2 (5-30-29); 3/4; S; Son; yes 868; yes; An. 2171

880; Howard, Joseph; m; 14 (5-29-17); 3/4; S; St-Son; yes 869; yes; An. 2174

881; " Marion E; f; 16 (9-12-15); 3/4; S; St-Dau; yes 870; yes; An. 2173

882; **MARSHALL**, Charles; m; 40 (9-17-92); F; M; Head; yes 871; no; Al. 1459

883; (TwoBear), Bessie; f; 30 (2-27-02); F; M; Wife; yes 872; yes; Al. 2364

884; " Christina; f; 12 (12-26-19); F; S; Dau; yes 873; yes; An. 2186

885; " Gertrude; f; 10 (3-2-22); F; S; Dau; yes 874; yes; An. 2187

886; " Mary R; f; 8 (11-2-24); F; S; Dau; yes 875; yes; An. 2188

887; **McLAUGHLIN** (Lanigan), Nellie; f; 57 (1875); 1/2; M; Head; yes 876; no; Al. 3083

888; " John; m; 20 (8-5-11); 1/2; S; Son; yes 877; yes; Al. 4185

889; " Charles; m; 11 (8-26-20); 1/2; S; Son; yes 878; yes; An. 2255

890; **McLAUGHLIN**, Robert S; m; 23 (7-13-08); 1/2; S; Head; yes 897; yes;

Census of the **Standing Rock** Reservation of the **Standing Rock** jurisdiction, as of **April 1**, 1932, taken by **E. D. Mossman**, Superintendent. North Dakota

KEY: Number; Surname, Given; Sex; Age at Last Birthday; Tribe (Standing Rock Sioux unless otherwise noted); Degree of Blood; Marital Status; Relationship to Head of Family; At Jurisdiction where enrolled (Yes or No); (If "No", where, if given); Ward (Yes or No); Allotment, Annuity and Identification Numbers.

Al. 3547

N. E. **MEANS**, Wesley; m; Head
891; (Short); Alma; f; 32 (9-8-1900); 1/2; M; Wife; yes 880; yes; Al. 2564
892; " Lavina; f; 8 (9-11-23); 1/2; S; Dau; yes 881; yes; An. 2275
893; " Wesley W; m; 7 (3-13-25); 1/2; S; Son; yes 882; yes; An. 2276
894; " Mary J; f; 5 (2-13-27); 1/2; S; Dau; yes 883; yes; An. 2277

895; **MELVIN**, John; m; 55 (1877); 1/2; M; Head; yes 884; no; Al. 2832
896; (Lanigan), Mamie; f; 50 (1882); 1/2; M; Wife; yes 885; no; Al. 2555

897; **MENTZ**, Geo. F; m; 24 (11-5-07); 1/2; M; Head; yes 886; yes; Al. 3494
898; (White), Mildred; f; 27 (4-14-04); 1/2; M; Wife; yes 887; yes; Al. 1736
899; LaPlant, Kenneth D; m; 3 (6-18-28); 1/2; S; St-Son; yes 1439; yes; An. 2298

900; **MENTZ**, Henry; m; 45 (1887); 1/2; M; Head; no 888; Jamestown, ND; no;
Al. 3018
901; " Margaret; f; 13 (5-3-18); 1/4; S; Dau; yes 889; yes; An. 2300
902; " Agnes; f; 12 (8-2-19); 1/4; S; Dau; yes 890; yes; An. 2301
903; " Henry G; m; 11 (12-19-20); 1/4; S; Son; yes 891; yes; An. 2302
904; " William; m; 9 (2-25-22); 1/4; S; Son; yes 892; yes; An. 2303
905; " Rose; f; 8 (11-8-18); 1/4; S; Dau; yes 893; yes; An. 2304
906; " Marcella; f; 7 (3-5-25); 1/4; S; Dau; yes 894; yes; An. 2305
907; " Antoine; m; 5 (2-12-27); 1/4; S; Son; yes 895; yes; An. 2306
908; " Walter J; m; 3 (9-26-28); 1/4; S; Son; yes 896; yes; An. 2307
909; " Marie R; f; 1 (2-1-31); 1/4; S; Dau; yes 897; yes; An. 2308

910; **MENTZ**, Joseph; m; 47 (1885); 1/2; M; Head; yes 898; no; Al. 2888
911; " Marie S; f; 15 (9-6-16); 1/2; S; Dau; yes 899; yes; Al. 4178
912; " Ruth E; f; 12 (6-22-19); 1/2; S; Dau; yes 900; yes; An. 2311
913; " John E; m; 9 (8-21-22); 1/2; S; Son; yes 901; yes; An. 2312
914; " Bernadine; f; 8 (2-26-24); 1/2; S; Dau; yes 902; yes; An. 2313

915; **MENTZ** (Zahn), Josephine; f; 39 (3-20-93); 1/2; Div; Head; yes 905; no;
Al. 2724
916; Gipp, James F; m; 18 (12-24-13); 1/4; S; Son; yes 909; yes; Al. 4717
917; " Christine; f; 6 (3-14-26); 1/4; S; Dau; yes 910; yes; An. 2320

918; **MENTZ**, Thomas; m; 62 (1880); 1/2; M; Head; yes 904; yes; Al. 2214
919; " Hermine; f; 11 (6-28-21); 3/4; S; Dau; yes 906; yes; An. 2316
920; " Melda; f; 8 (11-11-24); 3/4; S; Dau; yes 907; yes; An. 2317
921; " Thomas, Jr; m; 3 (3-4-29); 3/4; S; Son; yes 908; yes; An. 2381

N. E. **MERRILL**, George; m; Head

34

Census of the **Standing Rock** Reservation of the **Standing Rock** jurisdiction, as of **April 1**, 1932, taken by **E. D. Mossman**, Superintendent. North Dakota

KEY: Number; Surname, Given; Sex; Age at Last Birthday; Tribe (Standing Rock Sioux unless otherwise noted); Degree of Blood; Marital Status; Relationship to Head of Family; At Jurisdiction where enrolled (Yes or No); (If "No", where, if given); Ward (Yes or No); Allotment, Annuity and Identification Numbers.

922;   (Gayton), Jane S; f; 39 (1893); 1/2; M; Wife; no 911; Detroit, MI; no; Al. 1713

923;   " Francis; m; 11 (4-12-20); 1/2; S; Son; no 912; Detroit, MI; yes; An. 2322

924;   " Violet; f; 9 (9-29-22); 1/2; S; Dau; no 913; Detroit, MI; yes; An. 2323

N. E. **MOLASH**, William; m; Head

925;   (Buckley), Mandy; f; 55 (1877); 1/2; M; Wife; yes 914; no; Al. 2563

926;   " Annie L; f; 18 (5-24-14); 1/4; S; Dau; yes 915; yes; Al. 4574

927;   " Rosie; f; 16 (3-30-16); 1/4; S; Dau; yes 917; yes; An. 2337

928;   " Marie G; f; 12 (1-16-20); 1/4; S; Dau; yes 918; yes; An. 2338

929;   " Nellie L; 11 (5-10-21); 1/4; S; Dau; yes 919; yes; An. 2339

930;   " Charles; m; 9 (10-23-23); 1/4; S; Son; yes 920; yes; An. 2340

N. E. **MOOREHEAD**, Theodore; m; Head

931;   (Skye), Josephine; f; 20 (7-11-10); 1/2; M; Wife; yes 921; yes; Al. 3959

932;   " Beatrice; f; 1 (3-9-31); 1/4; S; Dau; yes 922; yes; An. 2344

933; **MULHERN**, Maggie; f; 82 (1850); 1/2; Wd; Head; no 927; Fort Rice, Morton Co, ND; no; Al. 2181

934; **MURPHY**, Bernard; m; 24 (9-2-07); 1/2; M; Head; yes 928; yes; Al. 3006

935;   " Doris May; f; 1 (11-16-30); 1/4; S; Dau; yes 929; yes; An. 2357

936;   " Woodrow; m; 23d (3-7-32); 1/4; S; Son; yes ---; yes; An. ---.

937; **MURPHY**, Henry; m; 43 (1889) 1/2; M; Head; yes 930; no; Al. 2994

938;   (Walking Cloud), Jennie; f; 36 (7-4-96); F; M; Wife; yes 931; yes; Al. 2588

939;   " Mary Ann; f; 15 (4-27-16); F; S; Dau; yes 932; yes; An. 2361

940;   " Lenore; f; 14 (7-15-17); F; S; Dau; yes 933; yes; An. 2362

941;   " Joshua; m; 12 (1-21-19); F; S; Son; yes 934; yes; An. 2363

942;   " Harry C; m; 11 (2-28-21); F; S; Son; yes 935; yes; An. 2364

942[sic]; " Ruth A; f; 1 (10-15-30); F; S; Dau; yes 936; yes; An. 2365

943; **MURPHY**, James; m; 36 (4-22-95); 1/2; S; Head; yes 937; no; Al. 2996

944; **MURPHY**, Joseph; m; 39 (6-6-93); 1/2; M; Head; yes 938; no; Al. 2995

945;   (Ramsey), Elizabeth; f; 34 (7-31-98); 1/2; M; Wife; yes 939; yes; Al. 2390

946;   " Joseph T; m; 14 (9-2-17); 1/2; S; Son; yes 940; yes; An. 2369

947;   " Iola May; f; 11 (1-13-21); 1/2; S; Dau; yes 941; yes; An. 2370

948;   " Harold M; m; 2 (5-23-29); 1/2; S; Son; yes 942; yes; An. 2371

949; **MURPHY**, Robert; m; 29 (3-1-03); 1/2; M; Head; yes 943; yes; Al. 2997

Census of the **Standing Rock** Reservation of the **Standing Rock** jurisdiction, as of **April 1**, 1932, taken by **E. D. Mossman**, Superintendent. North Dakota

KEY: Number; Surname, Given; Sex; Age at Last Birthday; Tribe (Standing Rock Sioux unless otherwise noted); Degree of Blood; Marital Status; Relationship to Head of Family; At Jurisdiction where enrolled (Yes or No); (If "No", where, if given); Ward (Yes or No); Allotment, Annuity and Identification Numbers.

950;   "   Robert, Jr; m; 4 (6-16-27); 1/4; S; Son; yes 944; yes; An. 2373
951;   "   Sylvia M; f; 2 (3-3-29); 1/4; S; Dau; yes 945; yes; An. 2374
952;   "   Elenor J; f; 11/12 (4-13-31); 1/4; S; Dau; yes ---; yes; An. 2375

N. E.   **MUTH**, F. C; m; Head; yes
953;   (Kempton), Viola E; f; 26 (1-16-06); 1/8; M; Wife; yes 946; yes; Al. 2813

N. E.   **NOEL**, Leon; m; Head
954;   (Short), Lodina; f; 33 (1-29-99); 1/2; M; Wife; yes 947; no; Al. 2563
955;   "   Leola C; f; 9 (9-22-22); 1/4; S; Dau; yes 948; yes; An. 2394
956;   "   Louis C; m; 8 (4-15-24); 1/4; S; Son; yes 949; yes; An. 2395
957;   "   Leon W; m; 6 (8-1-25); 1/4; S; Son; yes 950; yes; An. 2396
958;   "   Eloise R; f; 5 (10-16-26); 1/4; S; Dau; yes 951; yes; An. 2397
959;   "   Donald F; m; 3 (911-28); 1/4; S; Son; yes 952; yes; An. 2398
960;   "   Paul R; m; 1 (8010-30); 1/4; S; Son; yes 953; yes; An. 2399

961;   **NOHEART**, Albert; m; 59 (1873); F; M; Head; yes 954; yes; Al. 1746
962;   (Lean Elk), Lucille; f; 47 (1885); F; M; Wife; yes 955; yes; Al. 3094
963;   "   Agnes; f; 15 (5-6-16); F; S; Dau; yes; 956; yes; An. 2403
964;   "   Albert, Jr; m; 13 (10-14-18); F; S; Son; yes 957; yes; An. 2404
965;   "   Harry; m; 9 (4-11-22); F; S; Son; yes 958; yes; An. 2405

966;   **NO HEART**, Joseph; m; 90 (1842); F; Wd; Head; yes 959; yes; Al. 1745

N. E.   **NORD**, A. L.; m; Head
967;   (Gayton), Vivian; f; 33 (4-7-99); 1/2; M; Wife; yes 960; yes; Al. 1709
968;   "   Edwin C; m; 6 (6-18-25); 1/4; S; Son; yes 961; yes; An. 2420
969;   "   Raymond; m; 3 (12-14-28); 1/4; S; Son; yes 962; yes; An. 2421
970;   "   Wayne R; m; 1 (9-13-30); 1/4; S; Son; yes 963; yes; An. 2422

971;   **NO TWO HORNS**; m; 80 (1852); F; M; Head; yes 964; yes; Al. 2367
972;   (See The Bear), Margaret; f; 75 (1857); F; M; Wife; yes 965; yes;
                                                                       Al. 2368

973;   **OCANKUTAWA**; m; 88 (1844); F; Wd; Head; yes 966; yes; Al. 2546

974;   **ONEFEATHER**, Henry; m; 36 (1896); F; M; Head; yes 967; yes; Al. 1082
975;   (Swiftcloud), Lucy; f; 34 (4-16-98); F; M; Wife; yes 968; yes; Al. 2450
976;   "   Clifford; m; 2 (12-15-29); F; S; Son; yes 969; yes; An. 2451

977;   **ONE HORN**, Edward; m; 45 (1887); F; M; Head; yes 970; yes; Al. 2753
978;   (Highbear), Maggie; f; 36 (1895); F; M; Wife; yes 971; yes; Al. 2538
979;   "   Lizzie L; f; 19 (9-24-12); F; S; Dau; yes 972; yes; Al. 4376
980;   "   Edith; f; 16 (10-20-15); F; S; Dau; yes 973; yes; An. 2458

Census of the __Standing Rock__ Reservation of the __Standing Rock__ jurisdiction, as of __April 1__, 1932, taken by __E. D. Mossman__, Superintendent. North Dakota

KEY: Number; Surname, Given; Sex; Age at Last Birthday; Tribe (Standing Rock Sioux unless otherwise noted); Degree of Blood; Marital Status; Relationship to Head of Family; At Jurisdiction where enrolled (Yes or No); (If "No", where, if given); Ward (Yes or No); Allotment, Annuity and Identification Numbers.

981;   "   Stephen; m; 8 (1-16-24; F; S; Son; yes 974; yes; An. 2459

982;   "   Pauline; f; 5 (2-6-27); F; S; Dau; yes 975; yes; An. 2460

983;   One Horn, Lucas Ed; m; 2 (1929); F; S; Son; yes 976; yes; An. 2461

984;   **ONIHAN** (Higheagle), Anna; f; 40 (1892); F; Wd; Head; yes 977; yes; Al. 2689

985;   "   Josephine; f; 12 (4-18-19); F; S; Dau; yes 978; yes; An. 2464

986;   "   Selina; f; 4 (1-12-28); F; S; Dau; yes 979; yes; An. 2465

987;   "   Lynas; m; 1 (3-30-31); F; S; Son; yes 980; yes; An. 2466

988;   **OWNS MEDICINE**, Henry; m; 65 (1868); F; M; Head; yes 981; yes; Al. 2419

989;   (Take The Hat), Catherine f; 73 (1859); F; M; Wife; yes 982; yes; Al. 3066

990;   **OWNS MEDICINE**, Peter; m; 39 (1893); F; M; Head; yes 983; no; Al.2421

991;   **PANHICIYA**, Daniel; m; 54 (1878); F; M; Head; yes 984; yes; Al. 3981

992;   (Tatiopalutawin), Bertha; f; 51 (1881); F; M; Wife; yes 985; yes; Al. 2670

993;   "   Mary E; f; 12 (6-23-19); F; S; Dau; yes 986; yes; An. 2483

994;   "   Henry S; m; 10 (9-10-21); F; S; Son; yes 987; yes; An. 2484

995;   "   Francis; m; 8 (1924); F; S; Son; yes 988; yes; An. 2486

996;   "   Julia; f; 5 (1-19-26); F; S; Dau; yes 989; yes; An. 2485

997;   **PARKHURST**, Alexander; m; 57 (1875); 1/2; M; Head; no 990; Lucky Lake, Sask Co, Canada; yes; Al. 2976

998;   **PARKHURST**, Charles; m; 47 (1885); 1/2; M; Head; no 991; Lucky Lake, Sask Co, Canada; no; Al. 3811

999;   "   Lyle F; m; 18 (5-5-13); 1/4; S; Son; no; 992; Lucky Lake, Sask Co, Canada; yes; Al. 4626

1000;   "   Percy A; m; 16 (6-15-15); 1/4; S; Son; no 993; Lucky Lake, Sask Co, Canada; yes; An. 2499

1001;   **PARKHURST**, Claude I; m; 22 (9-8-09); 1/4; S; Head; no 994; Lucky Lake, Sask Co, Canada; yes; Al. 3920

1002;   **PARKIN**, Lewis C; m; 49 (1883); 1/2; M; Head; no 995; Whereabouts unknown; no; Al. 2553

1003;   **PARTAIN**, Minnie; f; 21 (2-14-11); 1/4; S; Head; no 996; Lawrence, Douglas Co, KS; yes; Al. 4098

KEY: Number; Surname, Given; Sex; Age at Last Birthday; Tribe (Standing Rock Sioux unless otherwise noted); Degree of Blood; Marital Status; Relationship to Head of Family; At Jurisdiction where enrolled (Yes or No); (If "No", where, if given); Ward (Yes or No); Allotment, Annuity and Identification Numbers.

1004; **PLEETS**, George; m; 56 (1866); 1/2; M; Head; yes 997; no; Al. 1619
1005;   "   Samuel; m; 21 (3-3-11); 1/2; S; Son; no 998; Phoenix San. Phoenix,
                                       AZ; yes; Al. 4101

1006; **PLEETS**, Jesse; m; 48 (4-9-84); 1/2; Wd; Head; yes 999; no; Al. 1645
1007;   "   Robert M; m; 12 (10-15-19); 1/2; S; Son; yes 1000; yes; An. 2525
1008; Winters, Francis; m; 4 (4-27-27); 1/2; S; Nephew; yes 1001; yes; Al. 1709-A

1009; **PLEETS**, Joseph; m; 62 (1870); 1/2; M; Head; yes 1002; no; Al. 1646
1010;   (Little Eagle), Augustine; f; 59 (1873); 1/2; M; Wife; yes 1003; yes;
                                       Al. 3560

1011; **PLEETS**, Josephine; f; 26 (1-7-06); 1/2; S; Head; yes 1004; yes; Al. 1647

1012; **PLEETS**, Walter; m; 29 (11-16-02); 1/2; M; Head; yes 1005; yes; Al. 1553
1013;   (Buffaloboy), Agatha; f; 27 (7-27-04); F; M; Wife; yes 1006; yes; Al. 1881
1014;   "   Helen F; f; 8 (1-10-24); F; S; Dau; yes 1007; yes; An. 2532
1015;   "   Henrietta; f; 5 (12-30-26); 3/4; S; Dau; yes 1007; yes; An. 2533
1016;   "   Laverne; m; 5 (1928); 3/4; S; Son; yes 1008; yes; An. 2534
1017;   "   Jean; f; 9/12 (6-20-31); 3/4; S; Dau; yes ---; yes; An. 2535

N. E. **PLENTYCHIEF**, Walter; m; Head
1018;   (Coldhand), Mary; f; 35 (7-6-97); F; M; Wife; yes 1009; yes; Al. 2313
1019; Chapman, Joseph; m; 11 (5-12-20); F; S; St-Son; yes 1010; yes; An. 2537

N. E. **PLOOG**, Hugo; m; Head
1020;   (Kempton), Esther; f; 36 (6-11-96); 1/8; M; Wife; yes 1011; yes;
                                       Al. 2804
1021;   "   Hugo L; m; 6 (4-25-25); 1/8; S; Son; yes 1012; yes; An. 2539
1022;   "   Sylvan L; f; 5 (2-4-27); 1/8; S; Dau; yes 1013; yes; An. 2540

N. E. **POOR DOG**, Harry; m; Head
1023;   (Highcat), Rose; f; 41 (1-12-91); F; M; Wife; yes 1014; yes; Al. 2532

1024; **PORCUPINE TAIL**; m; 55 (1877); F; S; Head; yes 1015; yes; Al. 702

1025; **POWERS**, Albert; m; 35 (10-30-97); 1/4; M; Head; yes 1016; no; Al. 2852
1026;   "   Nell Rose; f; 8 (12-16-24); 1/8; S; Dau; yes 1017; yes; An. 2544
1027;   "   Doris Ann; f; 4 (10-24-28); 1/8; S; Dau; yes 1018; yes; An. 2545

Census of the **Standing Rock** Reservation of the **Standing Rock** jurisdiction, as of **April 1**, 1932, taken by **E. D. Mossman**, Superintendent. North Dakota

KEY: Number; Surname, Given; Sex; Age at Last Birthday; Tribe (Standing Rock Sioux unless otherwise noted); Degree of Blood; Marital Status; Relationship to Head of Family; At Jurisdiction where enrolled (Yes or No); (If "No", where, if given); Ward (Yes or No); Allotment, Annuity and Identification Numbers.

1028; **PRETENDS EAGLE**, Joseph; m; 40 (7-30-92); F; M; Head; yes 1019; no; Al. 823

1029; (Buffaloboy), Benedicta; f; 38 (12-29-94); F; M; Wife; yes 1020; yes; Al. 1879

1030; " Alice J; f; 14 (9-27-17); F; S; Dau; yes 1021; yes; An. 2552

1031; " Joseph M; m; 12 (1-17-20); F; S; Son; yes 1022; yes; An. 2553

1032; " Josephine; f; 10 (12-11-21); F; S; Dau; yes 1023; yes; An. 2554

1033; " Bernard; m; 5 (4-4-27); F; S; Son; yes 1024; yes; An. 2555

1034; " James M; m; 3 (12-11-28); F; S; Son; yes 1025; yes; An. 2556

1035; " Leo Dan; m; 1 (9-25-30); F; S; Son; yes 1026; yes; An. 2557

1036; **PRETTY BEAR**; m; 85 (1847); F; M; Head; yes 1027; yes; Al. 2682

1037; (Hinyanjicawin), Mrs; f; 79 (1853); F; M; Wife; yes 1028; yes; Al. 2470

1038; **PRETTY BEAR**, John; m; 62 (1880); F; M; Head; yes 1029; yes; Al. 2111

1039; " " Nancy; f; 17 (1-10-10); F; S; Dau; yes 1030; yes; Al. 4711

1040; **PRETTY BIRD**; m; 70 (1862); F; m; Head; yes 1031; yes; Al. 3843

N. E. **RAINBOW**; m; Head

1041; (Kill Spotted), Carrie; f; 31 (1900); F; M; Wife; no 1033; Fort Totten Res, Fort Totten, ND; yes; Al. 2606

1042; " Mary G; f; 10 (5-30-21); F; S; Dau; no 1034; Fort Totten Res, Fort Totten, ND; yes; An. 2587

1043; " Cecelia; f; 9 (4-19-23); F; S; Dau; no 1035; Fort Totten Res, Fort Totten, ND; yes; An. 2589

1044; " Lucille; f; 4 (9-29-27); F; S; Dau; no 1036; Fort Totten Res, Fort Totten, ND; yes; An. 2590

1045; " Amelia; f; 3 (1-27-29); F; S; Dau; no ---; Fort Totten Res, Fort Totten, ND; yes; An. 2588

N. E. **RAMEY**, J.T; m; Head

1046; (Zahn), Clara; f; 36 (1895); 1/2; M; Wife; yes 1037; no; Al. 2725

1047; " Albert; m; 8 (10-22-23); 1/4; S; Son; yes 1038; yes; An. 2595

1048; " Josephine; f; 8 (10-22-23); 1/4; S; Dau; yes 1039; yes; An. 2596

1049; " James; m; 6 (8-19-27); 1/4; S; Son; yes 1040; yes; An. 2597

1050; " Aaron; m; 2 (4-7-29); 1/4; S; Son; yes 1041; yes; An. 2598

1051; Jordan, Clara; f; 15 (9-29-16); 1/2; S; St-Dau; yes 1042; yes; An. 2592

1052; " William; m; 13 (1918); 1/2; S; St-Son; yes 1043; yes; An. 2593

1053; " Helen; f; 11 (1921); 1/4; S; St-Dau; yes 1044; yes; An. 2594

1054; **RAMSEY**, Charles; m; 63 (1869); 1/2; M; Head; yes 1045; no; Al. 2389

1055; (Bighead), Laura C; f; 40 (4-21-1891); F; M; Wife; yes 1046; yes; Al. 2024

Census of the **Standing Rock** Reservation of the **Standing Rock** jurisdiction, as of **April 1**, 1932, taken by **E. D. Mossman**, Superintendent. North Dakota

1056;   "   Joseph; m; 19 (2017013); 3/4; S; Son; yes 1047; yes; Al. 4475

1057;   "   Patrick; m; 8 (3-17-24); 3/4; S; Son; yes 1048; yes; An. 2601

1058;   "   Regina; f; 5 (6-1-26); 3/4; S; Dau; yes 1049; yes; An. 2602

1059;   "   Sidney J; m; 3 (5-22-28); 3/4; S; Son; yes 1050; yes; An. 2605

1060;   "   Julia A; f; 9/12 (6-4-31); 3/4; S; Dau; yes ---; yes; An. 2606

1061; Dogskin, Benedict; m; 13 (8-27-18); 3/4; S; St-Son; yes 1052; yes; An. 2603

1062;   "   James; m; 11 (10-9-20); 3/4; S; St-Son; yes 1053; yes; An. 2604

1063; **RATTLINGHAIL**, George; m; 45 (1887); F; M; Head; yes 1054; no; Al. 1586

1064;   "   Irvin; m; 4 (7-28-27); F; S; Son; yes 1055; yes; An. 2611

1065; Brownotter, Clayton; m; 13 (11-28-18); F; S; St-Son; yes 1056; yes; An. 2609

1066; Brownotter, Sophie; F; 9 (6-8-22); F; S; St-Dau; yes 1057; yes; An. 2610

1067; **RATTLINGHAIL**, John; m; 65 (1867); F; M; Head; yes 1058; yes; Al. 1590

1068;   (Longchase), Emma; f; 53 (1879); F; M; Wife; yes 1059; yes; Al. 1590

1069; Rattlinghail, Patrick; m; 8 (10-15-23); F; S; Son; yes 1060; yes; An. 2614

1070; **RATTLING LODGE**, Tipi; f; 81 (1851); F; S; Head; yes 1061; yes; Al. 2272

1071; **RATTLINGHAIL**, George; m; 50 (1882); F; M; Head; yes 1062; yes; Al. 2172

1072;   (Conica), Mary; f; 60 (1872); F; M; Wife; yes 1063; yes; Al. 3217

1073; **RATTLINGTAIL** (White Woman), Mrs; f; 77 (1855); F; Wd; Head; yes 1064; yes; Al. 3712

1074; **RATTLINGTAIL**, Mary; f; 20 (9-9-12); F; S; Alone; yes 1065; yes; Al. 4366

1075; **REDBEAR**, George; m; 48 (1884); F; M; Head; yes 1066; yes; Al. 3827

1076;   (Pretty Eagle), Mrs; f; 56 (1876); F; M; Wife; yes 1067; yes; Al. 3619

1077;   "   Charles; m; 18 (1-16-14); F; S; Son; yes 1068; yes; An. 2626

1078;   "   Nancy E; f; 13 (7-6-18); F; S; Dau; yes 1069; yes; An. 2627

1079; **REDBOW** (Brow Eyes), Mrs; f; 83 (1849); F; Wd; Head; yes 1070; yes; Al. 3182

1080; **REDBOW**, Robert; m; 28 (4-22-03); F; M; Head; yes 1071; yes; Al. 2030

1081;   (Twin), Mary C; f; 33 (1899); F; M; Wife; yes 1072; yes; Al. 2326

1082; **REDBULL**, Thomas; m; 29 (12-18-02); F; S; Head; yes 1073; yes; Al. 2039

1083; **REDDOG**, Peter; m; 23 (9-13-08); F; M; Head; yes 1074; yes; Al. 3812

Census of the **Standing Rock** Reservation of the **Standing Rock** jurisdiction, as of **April 1**, 1932, taken by **E. D. Mossman**, Superintendent. North Dakota

KEY: Number; Surname, Given; Sex; Age at Last Birthday; Tribe (Standing Rock Sioux unless otherwise noted); Degree of Blood; Marital Status; Relationship to Head of Family; At Jurisdiction where enrolled (Yes or No); (If "No", where, if given); Ward (Yes or No); Allotment, Annuity and Identification Numbers.

1084; (Rabbithead), Fannie; f; 20 (7-5-12); F; M; Wife; yes 3120; yes; Al. 4210

1085; **REDDOG**, Paul; m; 19 (8-6-12); F; S; Alone; yes 1075; yes; Al. 4378

1086; **REDEARS**, Adolph; m; 62 (1870); F; Wd; Head; yes 1076; yes; Al. 2147

1087; **REDEARS**, Philip; m; 39 (1893); F; M; Head; yes 1077; yes; Al. 2150
1088;   (Longchase), Sadie; f; 26 (10-19-06); F; M: Wife; yes 1078; yes;
Al. 1591
1089; " Irene M; f; 7/12 (8-27-31); F; S; Dau; yes ---; yes; An. 2658
1090; Rattlinghail, Cyril; m; 6 (3-5-27); F; S; St-Son; yes 1079; yes; An. 2656
1091; " Joseph; m; 3 (1928); F; S; St-Son; yes 1080; yes; An. 2657

1092; **REDEARS**, Robert; m; 44 (6-18-88); F; S; Head; yes 1081; yes; Al. 3154

1093; **REDFOX**, Charles; m; 57 (1876); F; M; Head; yes 1082; yes; Al. 2647
1094;   (Croweagle), Maude; f; 47 (1885); F; M; Wife; yes 1083; yes; Al. 3675
1095; " Sadie; f; 16 (2-22-16); F; S; Dau; yes 1084; yes; Al. 3675-A.
1096; " Patrick; m; 8 (12-22-24); F; S; Son; yes 1085; yes; Al. 3675-B.

1097; **REDFOX**, Joseph; m; 47 (1885); F; M; Head; yes 1086; yes; Al. 2626
1098;   (Yellowhawk), Jennie; f; 47 (1885); F; M; Wife; yes 1087; no; Al. 2676
1099; " Philomene; f; 18 (1-27-14); F; S; Dau; yes 1088; yes; An. 2673

1100; **REDFOX**, Paul; m; 39 (6-19-93); F; M; Head; yes 1089; no; Al. 2629
1101;   (KillsTheEnemy), Mary; f; 40 (9-1-91); F; M; Wife; yes 1090; yes;
Al. 106
1102; " Leo B; m; 15 (1-20-17); F; S; Son; yes 1091; yes; An. 2676
1103; " Victor B; m; 13 (11-15-18); F; S; Son; yes 1092; yes; An. 2677
1104; " Alvina; f; 3 (8-12-27); F; S; Dau; yes 1093; yes; An. 2678

1105; **REDFOX**, William; m; 29 (6-2-02); F; S; Head; no 1094; Fort Peck Res, MT;
yes; Al. 2639

1106; **REDHORSE**, Alfred; m; 34 (1-23-98); F; M; Head; yes 1095; yes; Al. 1630
1107;   (Winter), Susan; f; 19 (6-12-12); F; M; Wife; yes 1096; yes; Al. 4316

1108; **REDHORSE**, Chase; m; 58 (1874); F; M; Head; yes 1097; yes; Al. 1629
1109;   (Stripedcloud), Caroline; f; 48 (1884); F; M; Wife; yes 1098; yes;
Al. 3046
1110; " Lee; m; 17 (11-30-14); F; S; Son; yes 1099; yes; Al. 4672

1111; **REDSTONE**, Agnes; f; 29 (2-16-03); F; S; Head; yes 1100; yes; Al. 2448

Census of the **Standing Rock** Reservation of the **Standing Rock** jurisdiction, as of **April 1**, 1932, taken by **E. D. Mossman**. Superintendent. North Dakota

KEY: Number; Surname, Given; Sex; Age at Last Birthday; Tribe (Standing Rock Sioux unless otherwise noted); Degree of Blood; Marital Status; Relationship to Head of Family; At Jurisdiction where enrolled (Yes or No); (If "No", where, if given); Ward (Yes or No); Allotment, Annuity and Identification Numbers.

1112; **REDSTONE**, Asa; m; 37 (11-28-94); F; M; Head; yes 1101; no; Al. 2170
1113;   (Onehorn), Susan; f; 31 (1900); F; M; Wife; yes 1102; yes; Al. 2471
1114;   "   Seraphine; f; 7 (4-20-24); F; S; Dau; yes 1103; yes; An. 2718
1115;   "   Virginia; f; 9 (4-13-22); F; S; Dau; yes 1104; yes; An. 2716
1116;   "   Melvin; m; 4 (6-26-27); F; S; Son; yes 1105; yes; An. 2719
1117;   "   Cecelia; f; 1 (8-2-30); F; S; Dau; yes 1106; yes; An. 2720

1118; **REDTOMAHAWK**, Barnabus; m; 38 (7-22-93); F; M; Head; yes 1107; no;
                                                                            Al. 2003
1119;   (Mentz), Louisa; f; 31 (5-23-1900); F; M; Wife; yes 1108; yes; Al. 2215
1120; Redtomahawk, Mary; f; 11 (9-8-20); F; S; Dau; yes 1109; yes; An. 2723
1121;   "   Joseph; m; 10 (12-20-21); F; S; Son; yes 1110; yes; An. 2724
1122;   "   Leonard; m; 7 (5-25-24); F; S; Son; yes 1111; yes; An. 2725
1123;   "   Peter; m; 5 (11-16-26); F; S; Son; yes 1112; yes; An. 2726
1124;   "   Courtney; m; 2 (5-22-29); F; S; Son; yes 1113; yes; An. 2727
1125;   "   Bernard; m; 3/12 (122-16-31); F; S; Son; yes ---; yes; An. 2728

1126; **REDTOMAHAWK**, Henry; m; 32 (11-20-1890); F; S; Head; yes 1114; yes;
                                                                            Al. 2004

N. E. **REEDY**, T. J.; m; Head
1127;   (Reedy), Agnes B; f; 76 (1856); 1/8; M; Wife; no 1116; Seattle, King Co,
                                                                       WA; no; Al. 1925

1128; **REEDY**, Philip; m; 50 (1882); 1/8; M; Head; no 1117; Casselton, Cass Co,
                                                                       ND; no; Al. 1926

N. E. **REGER**, Ben; m; Head
1129;   (Watson), Mary; f; 32 (9-1-99); 1/4; M; Wife; no 1118; Fargo, Cass Co,
                                                                       ND; no; Al. 2936

1130; **RETURNS LAST**, Thomas; m; 57 (1875); F; M; Head; yes 1119; no;
                                                                            Al. 2694
1131;   (Ireland), Lucy; f; 34 (1898); F; Wife; yes 1120; yes; Al. 2736
1132;   "   Christine; f; 2 (7-24-29); F; S; Dau; yes 1122; yes; An. 2744

1133; **RUNS THE MIDDLE**, (Tawokanzewakanwin), Mrs; f; 63 (1849); F; Wd;
                                                           Head; yes 1124; yes; Al. 2160

1134; **RUNS THE HOOP** (Laughling), Mrs; f; 83 (1849); F; Wd; Head; yes 123;
                                                                       yes; Al. 2549

N. E. **RUSSELL**, Howard; m; Head
1135;   (Greystone), Margaret; f; 44 (1888); F; M; Wife; yes 1125; yes; Al. 4410

Census of the **Standing Rock** Reservation of the **Standing Rock** jurisdiction, as of **April 1**, 1932, taken by **E. D. Mossman**, Superintendent. North Dakota

KEY: Number; Surname, Given; Sex; Age at Last Birthday; Tribe (Standing Rock Sioux unless otherwise noted); Degree of Blood; Marital Status; Relationship to Head of Family; At Jurisdiction where enrolled (Yes or No); (If "No", where, if given); Ward (Yes or No); Allotment, Annuity and Identification Numbers.

1136; **SANTEE**, Eugene; m; 26 (2-18-06); F; S; Head; yes 1126; yes; Al. 2579

1137; **SANTEE**, George; m; 42 (1890); F; M; Head; yes 1127; no; Al. 2623
1138; (Onehawk), Melda; f; 32 (7-2-1900); F; M; Wife; yes 1128; yes;
Al. 2399
1139; " Etta V; f; 12 (2-14-20); F; S; Dau; yes 1129; yes; An. 2790

1140; **SANTEE** (Tanyanglinajin), Mrs. Haskell; f; 74 (1858); F; Wd; Head; yes
1130; yes; Al. 3222

1141; **SANTEE**, Louis; m; 45 (10-26-86); F; M; Head; yes 1131; yes; Al. 2636
1142; (Redfox), Cecelia; f; 42 (1890); F; M; Wife; yes 1132; yes; Al. 2628
1143; " James; m; 14 (2-17-18); F; S; Son; yes 1133; yes; An. 2795

N. E. **SCHOCK**, Emil; m; Head
1144; (Jordan), Mary L; f; 24 (1-28-07); 1/2; M; Wife; no 1134; Yakima,
WA; yes; Al. 2966
1145; " Jacqueline; f; 6 (1-18-26); 1/4; S; Dau; no 1135; Yakima, WA; yes;
An. 2805
1146; " Evangeline; f; 4 (10-8-27); 1/4; S; Dau; no 1136; Yakima, WA; yes;
An. 2806
1147; " Agnes M; f; 2 (4-15-29); 1/4; S; Dau; no 1137; Yakima. WA; yes;
An. 2807

1148; **SCHOENHUT**, Courtney; m; 27 (5-27-05); 1/4; M; Head; no 1138; Emmett,
Gem Co, ID; no; Al. 2901

1149; **SCHOENHUT** (Murphy), Nellie; f; 52 (1880); 1/2; Wd; Head; yes 1139; no;
Al. 2900

1150; **SCHOENHUT**, Robert; m; 22 (7-3-09); 1/2; S; Head; yes 1140; yes; Al. 3934

N. E. **SEARS**, Joseph; m; Head
1151; (Hodgkinson), Mary; f; 28 (1-1-04); 1/4; M; Wife; no 1141; Blackwell,
OK; yes; Al. 2859
1152; " Raymond; m; 5 (7-22-26); 1/4; S; Son; no 1142; Blackwell, OK; yes;
An. 2812

1153; **SEE THE BEAR**; m; 83 (1849); F; Wd; Head; yes 1143; yes; Al. 2204

1154; **SEE THE BEAR**, Rebecca; f; 71 (1861); F; S; Head; yes 1144; yes; Al. 3084

Census of the __Standing Rock__ Reservation of the __Standing Rock__ jurisdiction, as of __April 1__, 1932, taken by __E. D. Mossman__, Superintendent. North Dakota

KEY: Number; Surname, Given; Sex; Age at Last Birthday; Tribe (Standing Rock Sioux unless otherwise noted); Degree of Blood; Marital Status; Relationship to Head of Family; At Jurisdiction where enrolled (Yes or No); (If "No", where, if given); Ward (Yes or No); Allotment, Annuity and Identification Numbers.

1155; **SHELLTRACK** (Yellow Elk), Annie; f; 32 (1900); F; Wd; Head; yes 1146; yes; Al. 2569

1156; " Mary V; f; 11 (7-26-20); F; S; Dau; yes 1147; yes; An. 2822
1157; " Stanley; m; 8 (7-26-24); F; S; Son; yes 1148; yes; An. 2823
1158; " Wesley; m; 6 (3-20-26); F; S; Son; yes 1149; yes; An. 2824
1159; **SHELL TRACK**, Charles; m; 31 (12-26-1900); F; M; Head; yes 1150; yes; Al. 2310
1160; (Bullbear), Helen; f; 31 (1901); F; M; Wife; yes 1151; yes; Al. 2141
1161; " Victoria; f; 7 (7-25-25); F; S; Dau; yes 1152; yes; An. 2827
1162; " Viola; f; 4 (7-27-27); F; S; Dau; yes 1153; yes; An. 2828
1163; " Elmer; m; 3 (10-7-28); F; S; Son; yes 1154; yes; An. 2829
1164; " Alvin; m; 5/12; (10-11-31); F; S; Son; yes ---; yes; An. 2830

1165; **SHELL TRACK** (Good Woman), Mrs; f; 62 (1870); F; Wd; Head; yes 1155; yes; Al. 3562

1166; **SHELL TRACK**, Samuel F; m; 23 (7-13-09); F; S; Head; yes 1156; yes; Al. 3970

1167; **SHIELDNECKLACE**, Leo; m; 48 (1884); F; M; Head; no 1157; Fort Berthold Res, ND; no; Al. 2402

1168; **SHOOTER** (Many Horse), Mrs. Philip; f; 73 (1859); F; WD; Head; yes 1158; yes; Al. 3093

1169; **SHOOT HOLY**; m; 87 (1845); F; Wd; Head; yes 1159; yes; Al. 2734

1170; **SHOOTS BUFFALO**; m; 68 (1864); F; M; Head; yes 1160; yes; Al. 2247
1171; (Matokenapewin); f; 65 (1867); F; M; Wife; yes 1161; yes; Al. 3499

1172; **SHOOT THE ENEMY** (Wincincala), Mrs; f; 79 (1853); F; Wd; Head; yes 1162; yes; Al. 2239

1173; **SHORT**, George; m; 26 (6-27-05); 1/4; S; Head; yes 1163; yes; Al. 3566

1174; **SHORT**, Margaret; f; 24 (12-23-07); 1/4; S; Head; no 1164; Bismarck, Burleigh Co, ND; yes; Al. 2567

1175; **SHORT**, Thomas; m; 29 (7-31-02); 1/4; M; Head; yes 1165; yes; Al. 2565
1176; (Pleets), Julia; f; 26 (5-1-05); 1/2; M; Wife; yes 1166; yes; Al. 1675
1177; " Thomasine; f; 5 (5-31-26); 3/8; S; Dau; yes 1167; yes; An. 2880
1178; " Bernice; f; 3 (8-13-28); 3/8; S; Dau; yes 1168; yes; An. 2881
1179; " Colleen M; f; 1 (11-25-30); 3/8; S; Dau; yes 1169; yes; An. 2882

Census of the **Standing Rock** Reservation of the **Standing Rock** jurisdiction, as of **April 1**, **1932**, taken by **E. D. Mossman**, Superintendent. North Dakota

KEY: Number; Surname, Given; Sex; Age at Last Birthday; Tribe (Standing Rock Sioux unless otherwise noted); Degree of Blood; Marital Status; Relationship to Head of Family; At Jurisdiction where enrolled (Yes or No); (If "No", where, if given); Ward (Yes or No); Allotment, Annuity and Identification Numbers.

1180; **SIAKA**, Clarence; m; 49 (1883); F; M; Head; yes 1170; no; Al. 1896
1181;   "   Felix; m; 8 (12-3-24); F; S; Son; yes 1171; yes; An. 2827
1182; Siaka, Virginia; f; 2 (9-27-29); F; S; Dau; yes 1172; yes; An. 2888

1183; **SIAKA** (Hesapaspewin), Francis; f; 62 (1870); F; M; Head; yes 3276; yes;
Al. 1642

1184; **SIAKA**, Thomas; m; 32 (1900); F; M; Head; no 1173; Fort Totten, ND; yes;
Al. 1830
1185;   "   Clarence; m; 10 (12-8-21); F; S; Son; no 1174; Fort Totten, ND; yes;
Al. 4723
1186;   "   Veronica; f; 3 (3-4-29); F; S; Dau; no ---; Fort Totten, ND; yes;
An. 2891
1187;   "   Sylvia; f; 1 (12-5-30); F; S; Dau; no ---; Fort Totten, ND; yes;
An. 2892

1188; **SILK**, Arthur; m; 20 (10-18-10); 1/2; M; Head; yes 1184; yes; Al. 4118
1189;   (Yellowhammer), Marcella; f; 19 (3-1-13); F; M; Wife; yes 1534; yes;
Al. 4413

1190; **SILK**, Charles; m; 27 (7-28-04); 1/2; S; Head; yes 1175; yes; Al. 868

1191; **SILK**, Harry; m; 43 (1889); 1/2; M; Head; yes 1176; no; Al. 2952
1192;   (Halsey), Josephine; f; 44 (1888); 1/2; M; Wife; yes 1177; yes; Al. 788
1193;   "   Stephen; m; 19 (5-13-12); 1/2; S; Son; yes 1178; yes; Al. 4275
1194;   "   Harry, Jr; m; 17 (3-27-15); 1/2; S; Son; yes 1179; yes; An. 19,
1195;   "   Helen F; f; 15 (10-15-16); 1/2; S; Dau; yes 1180; yes; An. 20

1196; **SILK**, Elizabeth; f; 19 (10-25-12); 1/2; S; Alone; yes 1181; yes; Al. 4402

1197; **SILK**, John; m; 62 (1870); 1/2; M; Head; yes 1182; no; Al. 866
1198;   "   (Halsey), Bridget; f; 53 (1879); 1/2; M; Wife; yes; 1183; yes; Al. 3569
1199;   "   Jennie; f; 16 (3-23-16); 1/2; S; Dau; yes 1185; yes; An. 2902
1200;   "   Emma; f; 15 (3-29-17); 1/2; S; Dau; yes 1186; yes; An. 2903
1201;   "   Allen D; m; 9 (9-29-22); 1/2; S; Son; yes 1188; yes; An. 2905
1202;   "   Thomas; m; 11 (4-11-20); 1/2; S; Son; yes 1187; yes; An. 2904

1203; **SILK**, John, Jr; m; 25 (6-23-06); 1/2; m; Head; yes 1189; yes; Al. 1223
1204;   (Treetop), Agnes; f; 32 (4-13-99); F; M; Wife; yes 1190; yes; Al. 1947
1205;   "   Charles; m; 5 (2-10-27); 3/4; S; Son; yes 1191; yes; An. 2909
1206;   "   Edith; f; 3 (3-11-29); 3/4; S; Dau; yes 1192; yes; An. 2910
1207;   "   Elizabeth; f; 9/12 (6-26-31); 3/4; S; Dau; yes ---; yes; An. 2911

Census of the **Standing Rock** Reservation of the **Standing Rock** jurisdiction, as of **April 1**, 1932, taken by **E. D. Mossman**, Superintendent. North Dakota

KEY: Number; Surname, Given; Sex; Age at Last Birthday; Tribe (Standing Rock Sioux unless otherwise noted); Degree of Blood; Marital Status; Relationship to Head of Family; At Jurisdiction where enrolled (Yes or No); (If "No", where, if given); Ward (Yes or No); Allotment, Annuity and Identification Numbers.

1208; **SILK**, Lawrence; m; 23 (8-2-08); 1/2; M; Head; no 1193; White Earth, Becker Co, MN; yes; Al. 3849

1209; **SKYE**, Amelia; f; 24 (10-23-07); 1/2; S; Head; no 1194; c/o Indian Ofc, Washington, DC; yes; Al. 2782

1210; **SKYE**, Douglas; m; 26 (10-19-05); 1/2; M; Head; no 1195; Rosebud Res, Rosebud, SD; yes; Al. 2781

1211; (Mentz), Margaret; f; 20 (6-10-11); 1/2; M; Wife; no 1196; Rosebud Res, Rosebud, SD; yes; An. 4178

1212; " Harriet I; f; 3/12 (12-6-31); 1/2; S; Dau; no ---; Rosebud Res, Rosebud, SD; yes; An. 2934

N. E. **SKYE**, Thomas; m; Head
1213; (Murphy), Annie; f; 48 (1884); 1/2; M; Wife; yes 1196; no; Al. 2780

1214; **SLEEPSFROMHOME**, George; m; 39 (1893); F; M; Head; yes 1201; no; Al. 709

1215; (Yellowfat), Julia; f; 29 (1902); F; M; Wife; yes 1202; yes; Al. 771
1216; " Daniel; m; 9 (2-16-23); F; S; Son; yes 1203; yes; An. 2940
1217; " William; m; 7 (9-5-24); F; S; Son; yes 1204; yes; An. 2941
1218; " Mary L; f; 6 (1-25-26); F; S; Dau; yes 1205; yes; An. 2942
1219; " Margaret; f; 2 (9-5-29); F; S; Dau; yes 1206; yes; An. 2943
1220; " Wallace; m; 1 (3-31-32); F; S; Son; yes---; yes; An. ----

1221; **SLEEPSFROMHOME** (Ptesanlutatewin), Mrs. Oliver; f; 72 (1860); yes 1207; yes; Al. 3584

N. E. **SMITH**, William; m; Head
1222; (Zahn), Alice; f; 35 (1897); 1/2; M; Wife; no 1208; Fort Totten, ND; yes; Al. 2723

1223; " Mary L; f; 10 (2-29-22); 1/2; S; Dau; no 1209; Fort Totten, ND; yes; An. 2953

1224; " Alice E; f; 8 (3-15-24); 1/2; S; Dau; no 1210; Fort Totten, ND; yes; An. 2954

1225; **SMITE**, William; m; 58 (1874); F; M; Head; yes 1211; no; Al. 2410
1226; (Onehorn), Jessie; f; 39 (1892); F; M; Wife; yes 1212; yes; Al. 2472
1227; " Raymond; m; 19 (6-1-12); F; S; Son; yes 1213; yes; Al. 4307

1228; **SNOW**, Charles; m; 21 (3-9-10); F; S; Alone; yes 1214; yes; Al. 4004

1229; **SPEAKSWALKING**, Joseph; m; 27 (7-11-04); F; M; Head; no 1215; Fort Berthold Res, Halliday, Dunn Co, ND; yes; Al. 1746

Census of the **Standing Rock** Reservation of the **Standing Rock** jurisdiction, as of **April 1**, 1932, taken by **E. D. Mossman**, Superintendent. North Dakota

1230; **SPEAKSWALKING**, Omar; m; 23 (2-9-09); F; M; Head; yes 1216; yes; Al. 3797

1231; (Twiggs), Nellie H; f; 18 (7-29-13); F; M; Wife; yes 1229; yes; Al. 4462

1232; **SPOTTEDBIRD**, John; m; 38 (1866); F; S; Head; no 1217; Fort Peck Res, MT; no; Al. 2387

1233; **SPOTTED ELK**, Agnes; f; 15 (1-30-17); F; S; Alone; yes 3320; yes; An. 2980

1234; **SPOTTED ELK**, Hugh; m; 34 (1898); F; M; Head; yes 1218; yes; Al. 2715
1235; (Wisespirit), Sarah; f; 25 (7-1-06); F; M; Wife; yes 1219; yes; Al. 2268
1236; " Merriel; f; 3 (3-1-29); F; S; Dau; yes 1220; yes; An. 2983
1237; " Hermine; f; 1 (2-11-31); F; S; Dau; yes 1221; yes; An. 2984

1238; **SPOTTED ELK** (Sasawin), Mrs. Luke; f; 76 (1856); F; Wd; Head; yes 1222; yes; Al. 2281

1239; **SPOTTED HORSE**, David; m; 22 (2-?-1910); F; S; Head; yes 3688; yes; Al. 3949

1240; **SPOTTED HORSE**, Francis; m; 36 (5-23-96; F; M; Head; yes 1223; yes; Al. 1597
1241; (Bullhead), Mary; f; 50 (1882); F; M; Wife; yes 1224; yes; Al. 3042
1242; " David; m; 16 (5-29-16); F; S; Son; yes 1225; yes; An. 2989
1243; " Joseph; m; 11 (3-11-21); F; S; Son; yes 1226; yes; An. 2991
1244; " Henry E; m; 7 (7-2-25); F; S; Son; yes 1227; yes; An. 2990
1245; Twiggs, Victoria; f; 12 (11-11-19); F; S; St-Dau; yes 1228; yes; An. 2993

1246; **STANDING SOLDIER**, Bernard; m; 45 (1887); F; M; Head; yes 1230; yes; Al. 1862
1247; " Mary; f; 9 (6-25-22); F; S; Dau; yes 1231; yes; An. 2999
1248; " Bernard; m; 3 (7-29-28); F; S; Son; yes 1232; yes; An. 3010

1249; **STANDING SOLDIER**, Jerome; m; 54 (1878); F; M; Head; yes 1233; yes; Al. 1865
1250; (Elk), Nellie; f; 61 (1871); F; M; Wife; yes 1234; yes; Al. 3734

1251; **STONEMAN**, Thomas; m; 78 (1854); F; Wd; Head; yes 1235; yes; Al. 1809

N. E. **STRAMPHER**, Carl; m; Head
1252; (Duncan), Imelda; f; 31 (6-8-1900); 1/4; M; Wife; yes 1237; yes; Al. 2838
1253; " Babe; f; 12 (12-6-19); 1/8; S; Dau; yes 1238; yes; An. 3018

KEY: Number; Surname, Given; Sex; Age at Last Birthday; Tribe (Standing Rock Sioux unless otherwise noted); Degree of Blood; Marital Status; Relationship to Head of Family; At Jurisdiction where enrolled (Yes or No); (If "No", where, if given); Ward (Yes or No); Allotment, Annuity and Identification Numbers.

1254; " Alberta; f; 10 (11-23-21); 1/8; S; Dau; yes 1239; yes; An. 3019
1255; " Phyllis; f; 8 (10-16-24); 1/8; S; Dau; yes 1240; yes; An. 3020
1256; " George; m; 5 (2-1-27); 1/8; S; Son; yes 1241; yes; An. 3021
1257; " Doris E; f; 1 (12-27-30); 1/8; S; Dau; yes 1242; yes; An. 3022

1258; **STREAKED EYE**, Caske; m; 36 (1895); F; S; Head; yes 1243; yes; Al. 2856

N. E. **STREAKED EYE**, Robert; m; Head
1259; (Runs The Hoop), Mary; f; 46 (1886); F; M; Wife; yes 1244; yes; Al. 2292
1260; " Saul; m; 17 (1-6-15); F; S; Son; yes 1245; yes; Al. 4678
1261; " Regina; f; 15 (1916); F; S; Dau; yes 1246; yes; An. 3026
1262; " Louisa; f; 12 (12-29-20); F; S; Dau; yes 1247; yes; An. 3027

1263; **STREAKED EYE**, Norbert; m; 56 (1876); F; M; Head; yes 1248; no;
Al. 2304
1264; (Topala), Emma; f; 31 (1901); F; M; Wife; yes 1249; yes; Al. 2079
1265; " Edna; f; 6 (3-27-26); F; S; Dau; yes 1250; yes; An. 3030

1266; **STRETCHES HIMSELF**, Chas; m; 33 (12-4-99); F; M; Head; yes 1251;
yes; Al. 2698

1267; **STRETCHES HIMSELF**, Clementine; f; 20 (9-15-11); F; S; Alone; no
1252; Fort Peck Res, MT; yes; Al. 4199

1268; **STRETCHES HIMSELF**, Laura; f; 37 (1892); F; S; Head; yes 1254; yes;
Al. 2148
1269; " Levi; m; 18 (5-7-13); F; S; Son; yes 1255; yes; Al. 4431
1270; " Johnathan; m; 16 (8-3-15); F; S; Son; yes 1256; yes; An. 3035
1271; " Phoebe; f; 14 (9-1-27); F; S; Dau; yes 1257; yes; An. 3036
1272; " Laura; f; 1 (2-24-31); F; S; Dau; yes 1258; yes; An. 3037

1273; **STRIPED CLOUD** (Tiyopasnawin), Mrs; f; 73 (1859); F; Wd; Head; yes
1259; yes; Al. 3048

1275; **SWIFTBIRD**, George; m; 32 (10-4-99); F; M; Head; yes 1260; yes; Al. 2686
1276; (Owens), Georgia; f; 30 (12-17-03); F; M; Wife; yes 1261; yes; Al. 2483

1277; **SWIFTBIRD**, Hugh; m; 56 (1876); F; Wd; Head; yes 1262; yes; Al. 2134

1278; **SWIFTBIRD**, John; f[sic]; 43 (1889); F; S; Head; no 1263; Manitoba, Canada;
no; Al. 2684

1279; **SWIFTEAGLE**, Eli; m; 64 (1868); F; M; Head; yes 1264; yes; Al. 2098
1280; (Graybear), Mary; f; 56 (1876); F; M; Wife; yes 1265; yes; Al. 3080

Census of the **Standing Rock** Reservation of the **Standing Rock** jurisdiction, as of **April 1**, 1932, taken by **E. D. Mossman**, Superintendent. North Dakota

KEY: Number; Surname, Given; Sex; Age at Last Birthday; Tribe (Standing Rock Sioux unless otherwise noted); Degree of Blood; Marital Status; Relationship to Head of Family; At Jurisdiction where enrolled (Yes or No); (If "No", where, if given); Ward (Yes or No); Allotment, Annuity and Identification Numbers.

1281; **SWIFTHAWK,** Hugh; m; 71 (1861); F; M; Head; yes 1266; yes; Al. 2251
1282; (Swifthawk), Annie R; f; 68 (1864); F; M; Wife; yes 1267; yes; Al. 3236

1283; **TAOKATEWIN**; f; 74 (1858); F; S; Head; no 1268; Fort Berthold Res, ND; yes; Al. 2009

1284; **TAIL,** George; m; 30 (1901); F; M; Head; yes 1269; yes; Al. 2353
1285; (Belland), Rose; f; 21 (6-15-10); F; M; Wife; yes 1270; yes; Al. 4032
1286; " Margaret; f; 4 (6-12-28); F; S; Dau; yes 1271; yes; An. 3070
1287; " Milton; m; 2 (8-31-29); F; S; Son; yes 1272; yes; An. 3071
1288; " Dorothy E; f; 11/12 (5-15-31); F; S; Dau; yes ---; yes; An. 3072

1289; **TAKE THE SHIELD,** Edwin; m; 50 (1882); F; M; Head; yes 1273; yes; Al. 2462
1290; (Feather), Flora; f; 49 (1883); F; m; Wife; yes 1274; yes; Al. 2233
1291; One Hawk, Carl; m; 20 (7-17-01); F; S; St-Son; yes 1275; yes; Al. 4031

1292; **TAKE THE SHIELD** (Name), Mrs; f; 79 (1853); F; Wd; Head; no 1276; Fort Peck Res, MT; yes; Al. 726

1293; **TATTOOED,** Eugene; m; 30 (1901); F; S; Head; yes 1277; yes; Al. 1659

1294; **TATTOOED,** James; m; 37 (1895); F; M; Head; yes 1278; no; Al. 1661
1295; (McLean), Melda; f; 35 (1897); F; M; Wife; yes 1279; yes; Al. 186
1296; " William B; m; 12 (1-11-20); F; S; Son; yes 1280; yes; An. 3113
1297; " Marie; f; 9 (9-9-22); F; S; Dau; yes 1281; yes; An. 3114
1298; " Morris; m; 7 (2-22-25); F; S; Son; yes 1282; yes; An. 3115
1299; " Margaret; f; 4 (5-11-27); 3/4; S; Dau; yes 1283; yes; An. 3116
1300; " Torrence; m; 1 (10-14-30); 3/4; S; Son; yes 1284; yes; An. 3117

1301; **THOMPSON,** Obed; m; 30 (1901); F; M; Head; yes 1285; yes; Al. 2445
1302; " Ambrose; m; 5 (7-20-26; F; S; Son; yes 1286; yes; An. 3149
1303; " Veronica; f; 3 (5-13-28); F; S; Dau; yes 1287; yes; An. 3150
1304; " Olivia M; f; 2 (3-30-30); F; S; Dau; yes 1288; yes; An. 3151

1305; **THUNDER,** Charles; m; 42 (12-15-90); F; S; Head; yes 1289; no; Al. 2427

1306; **THUNDER,** Merrill; m; 42 (12-15-90; F; M; Head; yes 1290; no; Al. 2426
1307; (Ironroad), Agnes; f; 32 (9-1-99); F; M; Wife; yes 1291; yes; Al. 2332
1308; " Casper; m; 14 (3-6-18); F; S; Son; yes 1292; yes; An. 52
1309; " Wallace; m; 10 (1-7-22); F; S; Son; yes 1293; yes; An. 3156
1310; " Jacob; m; 5 (8-10-26); F; S; Son; yes 1294; yes; An. 3157

Census of the **Standing Rock** Reservation of the **Standing Rock** jurisdiction, as of **April 1**, 1932, taken by **E. D. Mossman**, Superintendent. North Dakota

KEY: Number; Surname, Given; Sex; Age at Last Birthday; Tribe (Standing Rock Sioux unless otherwise noted); Degree of Blood; Marital Status; Relationship to Head of Family; At Jurisdiction where enrolled (Yes or No); (If "No", where, if given); Ward (Yes or No); Allotment, Annuity and Identification Numbers.

1311; " Alma; f; 1 (3-12-31); F; S; Dau; yes 1295; yes; An. 3158

1312; **TIBBETTS**, Arthur; m; 63 (1869); F; M; Head; yes 1296; yes; Al. 2041

1313; **TIBBETTS**, Percy; m; 28 (7-3-03); F; M; Head; yes 1297; yes; Al. 2042
1314; " Wayne A; m; 7/12 (8-18-31); F; S; Son; yes ---; yes; An. 3170

1315; **TIOKASIN**, David; m; 26 (6-12-05); F; S; Head; no 1298; U.S. Army, Fort
        Snelling, Hennepin, MN; yes; Al. 2775

1316; **TIOKASIN**, Moses; m; 39 (5-14-92); F; M; Head; yes 1299; no; Al. 2774
1317;   (Bravebull), Marie; f; 34 (1898); F; M; Wife; yes 1300; yes; Al. 2707
1318; " Albert; m; 17 (2-18-15); F; S; Son; yes; 1301; yes; Al. 4687
1319; " Sophie; f; 14 (6-29-17); F; S; Dau; yes 1302; yes; An. 3181
1320; " John; m; 9 (6-9-30); F; S; Son; yes 1303; yes; An. 3182
1321; " George; m; 5 (1926); F; S; Son; yes 1304; yes; An. 3183
1322; Tiokasin, Clifford; m; 1 (6-26-30); F; S; Son; yes 1305; yes; An. 3184

1323; **TIOKASIN**, Richard; m; 47 (1884); F; Wd; Head; yes 1305; yes; Al. 1694

1324; **TIOKASIN** (Pleets), Rose; f; 59 (1863); F; Wd; Head; yes 1307; yes;
        Al. 3438

1325; **TIOKASIN**, Samuel J; m; 35 (1897); F; M; Head; yes 1308; yes; Al. 2772
1326; " Joseph; m; 4 (6-15-27; F; S; Son; yes 1309; yes; An. 3188
1328; " Antoine; m; 1 (8-21-30); F; S; Son; yes 1310; yes; An. 3189

1329; **TIBONA**, Henry; m; 59 (1863); F; M; Head; yes 1313; yes; Al. 2359
1330; Fourswords, Jean; f; 18 (9-14-13); F; S; Gr.Dau; yes 1314; yes; Al. 4476
1331; Fourswords, Luella; f; 15 (3-15-17); F; S; Gr.Dau; yes 1315; yes; An. 3195

1332; **TOPALA**, Henry; m; 24 (12-24-07); F; S; Head; yes 1316; yes; Al. 2706

1333; **TRAVERSIE**, Alexander; m; 38 (11-15-94); 1/2; M; Head; no 1317;
        Mandan, Morton Co, ND; yes; Al. 2014

1334; **TREETOP** (Keeps Eagle), Mrs. Louisa; f; 52 (1880); F; Wd; Head; yes 1318;
        yes; Al. 2069

1335; **TREETOP**, John; m; 52 (1880); F; M; Head; yes 1319; no; Al. 1574
1336;   (Lovejoy), Mary; f; 54 (1878); F; M; Wife; yes 1320; no; Al. 1996
1337; " Percy; m; 12 (3-18-20); F; S; Son; yes 1321; yes; An. 3200
1338; Firecloud, Susan; f; 21 (8-10-10); F; S; St-Dau; yes 1322; yes; Al. 4159
1339; Lovejoy, James; m; 18 (12-27-14); F; S; St-Son; yes 1323; yes; Al. 4614

Census of the **Standing Rock** Reservation of the **Standing Rock** jurisdiction, as of **April 1**, 1932, taken by **E. D. Mossman**, Superintendent. North Dakota

KEY: Number; Surname, Given; Sex; Age at Last Birthday; Tribe (Standing Rock Sioux unless otherwise noted); Degree of Blood; Marital Status; Relationship to Head of Family; At Jurisdiction where enrolled (Yes or No); (If "No", where, if given); Ward (Yes or No); Allotment, Annuity and Identification Numbers.

1340; **TUSK** Charles; m; 32 (2-6-1900) F; M; Head; yes 1324; yes; Al. 1868
1341; (Medicine Stone), Rebecca; f; 29 (7-8-02); F; M; Wife; yes 1325; yes; Al. 1751
1342; " Charles; m; 5 (1-9-27); F; S; Son; yes; 1326; yes; An. 3211
1343; " Leonard; m; 3 (6-11-28); F; S; Son; yes 1327; yes; An. 3212
1344; " Laura; f; 11 (3-4-20); F; S; Dau; yes 1328; yes; An. 3213

1345; **TUSK**, Mrs. Reuben; f; 73 (1859); F; Wd; Head; yes 1329; yes; Al. 2770

1346; **TWIGGS**, Annie; f; 64 (10-22-04); F; S; Head; yes 1330; yes; Al. 2633

1347; **TWIGGS**, Mary; f; 64 (1868); F; S; Head; yes 1331; yes; Al. 2604

1348; **TWIGGS**, Serena; f; 22 (3-26-10); F; S; Head; no; 1332; Chemawa, Marion Co, OR; yes; Al. 3985

1349; **TWIN**, Joseph; m; 25 (9-20-06); F; M; Head; yes 1333; yes; Al. 1657
1350; (Redstone), Lucy; f; 17 (10-13-14); F; M; Wife; yes 1334; yes; Al. 4659
1351; " Joseph, Jr; m; 1 (10-18-30); F; S; Son; yes 1335; yes; An. 3225

1352; **TWIN**, Joseph; m; 70 (1862); F; M; Head; yes 1336; yes; Al. 1635
1353; (Wahapawin), Emma; f; 74 (1858); F; M; Wife; yes 1337; yes; Al. 3544

1354; **TWOBEARS**, Basil; m; 48 (1884); F; M; Head; yes 1338; yes; Al. 2608
1355; (Alkire), Annie; f; 57 (1875); F; M; Wife; yes 1339; yes; Al. 3688
1356; " Alma L; f (11-12-16); F; S; Dau; yes 1340; yes; An. 3230
1357; " Albert; m; 12 (5-30-19); F; S; Son; yes 1341; yes; An. 3231

1358; **TWOBEARS**, Edward; m; 34 (1898); F; S; Head; yes 1342; yes; Al. 2613

1359; **TWOBEARS**, George; m; 23 (5-28-99); F; M; Head; yes 1343; yes; Al. 2363
1360; (Twiggs), Esther; f; 24 (10-5-07); F; M; Wife; yes 1344; yes; Al. 2635
1361; " June; f; 9/12 (6-26-31); F; S; Dau; yes ---; yes; An. 3235

1362; **TWOBEARS**, Joseph; m; 66 (1866); F; M; Head; yes 1346; yes; Al. 2362
1363; (Twobears), Mary; f; 62 (1870); F; M; Wife; yes 1347; yes; Al. 3727

1364; **TWOBEARS**, Joseph; m; 38 (4-8-94); F; M; Head; yes 1348; yes; Al. 2612
1365; (Tail), Dora; f; 28 (10-8-03); F; M; Wife; yes 1349; yes; Al. 2354
1366; " Gilbert; m; 10 (3-26-22); F; S; Son; yes 1350; yes; An. 3240
1367; " Verna; f; 5 (4-30-25); F; S; Dau; yes 1351; yes; An. 3241
1368; " Patrick; m; 4 (5-17-27); F; S; Son; yes 1352; yes; An. 3242

51

Census of the **Standing Rock** Reservation of the **Standing Rock** jurisdiction, as of **April 1**, 1932, taken by **E. D. Mossman**, Superintendent. North Dakota

KEY: Number; Surname, Given; Sex; Age at Last Birthday; Tribe (Standing Rock Sioux unless otherwise noted); Degree of Blood; Marital Status; Relationship to Head of Family; At Jurisdiction where enrolled (Yes or No); (If "No", where, if given); Ward (Yes or No); Allotment, Annuity and Identification Numbers.

1369; " Neal W; f; 2 (12-9-29); F; S; Son; yes 1353; yes; An. 3243
1370; " Selma; f; 4/12 (11-2-31); F; S; Dau; yes 13--; yes; An. 3244

1371; **TWOBEARS**, Josephine; f; 22 (10-3-09); F; S; Head; yes 1354; yes; Al. 3932

1372; **TWOBEARS**, Louis; m; 26 (1-22-06); F; S; Head; yes 1355; yes; Al. 2615
1373; **TWOBEARS**, Mandan; m; 29 (9-24-02); F; S; Head; yes 1356; yes; Al. 2614

1374; **TWOBEARS**, Stephen; m; 68 (1864); F; M; Head; yes 1357; yes; Al. 2293
1375; (Cross), Henrietta; f; 62 (1870; F; M; Wife; yes 1358; yes; Al. 3205

1376; **TWOBULLS**, Walter; m; 78 (1854); F; M; Head; yes 1359; yes; Al. 2337
1377; (Tawasusnawin), Annie; f; 69 (1863); F; M; Wife; yes 1360; yes; Al. 3203

1378; **TWOHORSES**, Frank; m; 36 (8-17-96); F; M; Head; yes 1361; no; Al. 2047
1379; (Bighead), Alice; f; 33 (1899); F; M; Wife; yes 1362; yes; Al. 2744
1380; " Harding; m; 11 (10-26-21); F; S; Son; yes 1363; yes; An. 3270
1381; " Melda; f; 8 (10-8-23); F; S; Dau; yes 1364; yes; An. 3271
1382; " Grady; m; 4 (10-8-27); F; S; Son; yes 1365; yes; An. 3272
1383; " Ray; m; 2 (3-4-30); F; S; Son; yes 1366; yes; An. 3273

1384; **TWOHORSES**, Harry; m; 34 (12-18-98); F; S; Head; yes 1367; yes; Al. 2044

1385; **TWOHORSES**, Leo; m; 80 (1852); F; S; Head; yes 1368; yes; Al. 2043

1386; **TWOHORSES**, Pius; m; 46 (1886); F; S; Head; yes 1369; no; Al. 2043

1387; **TWOPARENTS** (Capawin), Mrs; f; 88 (1844); F; Wd; Head; yes 1370; yes; Al. 3716

1388; **TWOSHIELDS**, Antoine; m; 59 (1873); F; M; Head; yes 1372; no; Al. 2227
1389; (Bigboy), Jennie; f; 43 (1889); F; M; Wife; yes 1373; yes; Al. 1976
1390; " Agnes; f; 18 (7-5-13); F; S; Dau; yes; 1374; yes; Al. 4480
1391; " Sampson; m; 14 (1-16-18); F; S; Son; yes 1375; yes; An. 3282
1392; " Cecelia; f; 12 (12(22(19); F; S; Dau; yes 1376; yes; An. 3283
1393; " Ellis; m; 9 (7-6-22); F; S; Son; yes 1377; yes; An. 3284
1394; " Elsie; f; 17 (12-22-14); F; F; S; Dau; yes 1378; yes; Al. 4688
1395; " Nora; f; 7/12 (8-5-31); F; S; Dau; yes ---; yes; An. 3285

1396; **TWOSHIELDS**, Anthony; m; 51 (1881); F; M; head; no 1379; Sisseton
Res, SD; yes; Al. 2225

1397; **TWOSHIELDS**, John; m; 70 (1862); F; M; Head; yes 1380; yes; Al. 1829
1398; (Fasthorse), Martha; f; 44 (1886); F; M; Wife; yes 1198; yes; Al. 3809

Census of the __Standing Rock__ Reservation of the __Standing Rock__ jurisdiction, as of __April 1__, 1932, taken by __E. D. Mossman__, Superintendent. North Dakota

KEY: Number; Surname, Given; Sex; Age at Last Birthday; Tribe (Standing Rock Sioux unless otherwise noted); Degree of Blood; Marital Status; Relationship to Head of Family; At Jurisdiction where enrolled (Yes or No); (If "No", where, if given); Ward (Yes or No); Allotment, Annuity and Identification Numbers.

1399; Slater, Isabelle; f; 13 (1-15-22); F; S; St-Dau; yes 1199; yes; Al. 3809-A.
1400; Slater, Ruby; f; 8 (10-20-23); F; S; St-Dau; yes 1200; yes; Al. 3809-B.

1401; **VAULTER**, James; m; 35 (1897); F; M; Head; yes 1382; yes; Al. 1800
1402; (Wears Horn), Alice; f; 26 (1905); F; M; Wife; yes 1383; yes; Al. 4591
1403; Vaulter, Alice; f; 3 (8-8-28); F; S; Dau; yes 1384; yes; An. 3290
1404; " Evelyn; f; 1 (11-5-30); F; S; Dau; yes 1385; yes; An. 3291

N. E. **VENNERI**, Cecil; Head
1405; (Zahn), Helen; f; 31 (6-18-1900); 1/2; M; Wife; no 1386; Denver,
Colo; yes; Al. 2722

1406; **WALKER**, Albert; m; 56 (1876); F; M; Head; yes 1387; no; Al. 2443
1407; (Bringswater), Lucy; f; 57 (1875); F; M; Wife; yes 1388; yes; Al. 3540
1408; " Susan V; f; 18 (8-26-13); F; S; Dau; yes 1389; yes; Al. 4477
1409; " Scholastica; f; 16 (2-18-16); F; S; Dau; yes 1390; yes; An. 3330

1410; **WALKINGCLOUD**, Charles; m; 64 (1868); F; M; Head; yes 1391; yes;
Al. 2403
1411; (Wincincala), Mrs; f; 61 (1871); F; M; Wife; yes 1392; yes; Al. 3579

1412; **WALKINGCLOUD**, Nancy; f; 26 (11-1-05); F; S; Head; yes 1393; yes;
Al. 2584

1413; **WALKING THUNDER**; m; 64 (1868); F; M; Head; yes; 1394; no;
Al. 2249
1414; (Wiciqa[sic]), Mrs; f; 62 (1870); F; m; Wife; yes 1395; yes; Al. 3720

1415; **WANKICUN**, Bede; m; 65 (1867); F; m; Head; yes 1396; yes; Al. 2119
1416; (Grindstone), Louise; f; 65 (1887); F; M; Wife; yes 1397; yes; Al. 497
1417; " Christina; f; 12 (12-7-19); F; S; Dau; yes 1398; yes; An. 3358
1418; " Evan; m; 9 (7-9-22); F; S; Son; yes 1399; yes; An. 3359
1419; " Noah; m; 7 (8-14-25); F; S; Son; yes 1400; yes; An. 3360
1420; " Calvin; m; 3 (4-3-29); F; S; Son; yes 1401; yes; An. 3361
1421; Lookinghorse, Mamie; f; 15 (11-1-16); F; S; St-Dau; yes 1402; yes; An. 3362

1422; **WANOQUIPI**, Bebe; m; 27 (10-17-04); F; M; Head; yes 1404; yes; Al. 1911
1423; (White Eagle), Mary L; f; 18 (5-24-13); F; M; Wife; yes 1459; yes;
Al. 4436
1424; Cottonwood, Margaret; f; 4 (1-14-28); F; S; St-Dau; yes 1460; yes; An. 3375

1425; **WANOQUPI**, Edward; m; 49 (1883); F; M; Head; yes 1405; yes; Al. 1908
1426; (Gray Horns), Mrs; f; 43 (1879); F; M; Wife; yes 1406; yes; Al. 3063
1427; " Thomas; m; 20 (2-28-12); F; S; Son; yes 1407; yes; Al. 4271

Census of the __Standing Rock__ Reservation of the __Standing Rock__ jurisdiction, as of __April 1__, 1932, taken by __E. D. Mossman__, Superintendent. North Dakota

KEY: Number; Surname, Given; Sex; Age at Last Birthday; Tribe (Standing Rock Sioux unless otherwise noted); Degree of Blood; Marital Status; Relationship to Head of Family; At Jurisdiction where enrolled (Yes or No); (If "No", where, if given); Ward (Yes or No); Allotment, Annuity and Identification Numbers.

1428; **WANOQUPI**, John; m; 23 (5-30-09); F; M; Head; yes 1408; yes; Al. 3948
1429;   (Has Tricks), A. Jennie; f; 26 (2-28-06); F; M; Wife; yes 1409; yes; Al. 1945
1430;   "   Lorene; f; 1 (7-23-30); F; S; Dau; yes 1410; yes; An. 3381
1431; **WAONJINIAYUHA**, William; m; 71 (1861); F; Wd; Head; no 1411; Crow Creek Agcy, SD; yes; Al. 2085

N. E.   **WAREHAM**, Alfred W; m; Head
1432;   (Goodreau), Ruth; f; 32 (12-16-99); 1/2; M; Wife; no 1412; St Paul, Ramsey Co, MN; yes; Al. 2439
1433;   "   Audrey H; f; 8 (12-1-23); 1/8; S; Dau; no ---; St Paul, Ramsey Co, MN; yes; An. ---
1434;   "   Shirley M; f; 7 (11-24-24); 1/8; S; Dau; no ---; St Paul. Ramsey Co, MN; yes; An.---
1435;   "   John R; m; 5 (8-8-26); 1/8; S; Son; no ---; St Paul, Ramsey Co, MN; yes; An. ---

1436; **WARNER**, Edgar; m; 23 (12-22-08); 1/2; S; Head; no 1413; Rosebud Res, SD; yes; Al. 3610

1437; **WARRIOR**, Martin; m; 73 (1859); F; Wd; Head; yes 1414; yes; Al. 1400

N. E.   **WAYMAN**, W. C; m; Head
1438;   (Mulhern), Catherine; f; 41 (1891); 1/2; M; Wife; yes 1415; no; Al. 2655
1439;   "   Warren M; m; 7 (1-1-25); 1/4; S; Son; yes 1416; yes; An. 3412
1440; Partain, Hazel; f; 17 (5-14-14); 1/2; S; St-Dau; yes 1417; yes; Al. 4583
1441;   "   Francis; m; 16 (3-14-16); 1/2; S; St-Son; yes 1418; yes; An. 3409
1442;   "   Nadine; f; 15 (1-16-18); 1/2; S; St-Dau; yes 1419; yes; An. 3410
1443;   "   Florence; f; 10 (9-9-21); 1/2; S; St-Dau; yes 1420; yes; An. 3411

1444; **WELLS**, Aaron; m; 77 (1855); 1/4; M; Head; yes 1421; no; Al. 2195

1445; **WELLS**, Agnes; f; 24 (3-5-08); 1/4; S; Head; no 1422; Tacoma, Pierce Co, Wash; yes; Al. 2969

1446; **WELLS**, Francis; m; 27 (8-13-04); 1/4; M; Head; no 1423; Chicago, Cook Co, Ill; no; Al. 2967

1447; **WELLS**, Frank G; m; 54 (1878); 1/4; M; Head; yes 1424; no; Al. 2201

1448; **WELLS**, James; m; 55 (1877); 1/4; M; Head; yes 1425; no; Al. 2198

Census of the **Standing Rock** Reservation of the **Standing Rock** jurisdiction, as of **April 1**, 1932, taken by **E. D. Mossman**, Superintendent. North Dakota

KEY: Number; Surname, Given; Sex; Age at Last Birthday; Tribe (Standing Rock Sioux unless otherwise noted); Degree of Blood; Marital Status; Relationship to Head of Family; At Jurisdiction where enrolled (Yes or No); (If "No", where, if given); Ward (Yes or No); Allotment, Annuity and Identification Numbers.

1449; **WELLS**, Joseph; m; 52 (1888); 1/4; M; Head; yes 1426; no; Al. 2197

1450; **WELLS**, Laura; f; 25 (5-10-06); 1/4; S; Head; no 1427; Tacoma, Pierce Co, Wash; yes; Al. 2200

1451; **WELLS**, Victor L; m; 25 (11-15-06); 1/4; S; Head; no 1429; Chicago, Cook Co, IL; yes; Al. 2068

N. E. **WHEELER**, D.V; m; Head
1452; (Wells), Clara; f; 46 (1886); 1/4; M; Wife; yes 1430; no; Al. 2196

N. E. **HELGESON**, Theodore; m; Head
1453; (White), Angeline; f; 25 (2-14-07); 1/2; M; Wife; no 1431; Aberdeen, Brown Co, S.D.; yes; Al. 3706

1454; **WHITE**, Bede; m; 42 (2-18-90); F; M; Head; yes 1432; no; Al. 574
1455; " Louis; m; 10 (7-4-21); F; S; Son; yes; 1434; yes; An. 3439
1456; " Leonard; m; 9 (3-29-23); F; S; Son; yes 1435; yes; An. 3440

1457; **WHITE**, Benjamin; m; 59 (5-15-73); 1/2; M; Head; yes 1436; no; Al. 1732
1458; (Gayton), Abbie; f' 64 (11-15-68); 1/2; M; Wife; yes 1437; no; Al. 3673
1459; Vidovich, Geraldine; f; 5 (6-6-26); 1/2; S; Gr-Dau; yes 1438; yes; An. 344

1460; **WHITE**, Benjamin; m; 29 (3-18-03); 1/2; S; Head; yes 1440; yes; Al. 1735

1461; **WHITE**, Francis; m; 36 (7-24-95); F; M; Head; yes 1441; no; Al. 572

1462; **WHITE**, Josephine; f; 22 (3-7-10); 1/2; S; Head; no 1442; Minneapolis, MN; yes; Al. 3986

1463; **WHITE**, William; m; 26 (7-22-05); 1/2; S; Head; yes 1443; yes; Al. 1737

1464; **WHITEBEARD** (Sungleska), Mrs; f; 81 (1851); F; Wd; Head; yes 1444; yes; Al. 3568

1465; **WHITEBIRD**, Henry P; m; 29 (1895); F; M; Head; yes 1445; yes; Al. 1731
1466; (Hawk), Mary P; f; 26 (4-26-02); F; M; Wife; yes 1446; yes; Al. 1273
1467; " Gloria M; f; 5/12 (10-26-31); F; S; Dau; yes 1447; yes; An. 3469

1468; **WHITEBIRD**, Phillip; m; 68 (1864); F; Wd; Head; yes 1447; yes; Al. 1730

1469; **WHITECLOUD**, William; m; 46 (1886); F; M; head; yes 1448; no; Al. 1924

Census of the __Standing Rock__ Reservation of the __Standing Rock__ jurisdiction, as of __April 1__, 1932, taken by __E. D. Mossman__, Superintendent. North Dakota

KEY: Number; Surname, Given; Sex; Age at Last Birthday; Tribe (Standing Rock Sioux unless otherwise noted); Degree of Blood; Marital Status; Relationship to Head of Family; At Jurisdiction where enrolled (Yes or No); (If "No", where, if given); Ward (Yes or No); Allotment, Annuity and Identification Numbers.

1470; (LoanHimArrows), Emma; f; 30 (5-15-01); F; M; Wife; yes 1449; yes; Al. 1910

1471; " William; m; 10 (3-20-22); F; M; Son; yes 1450; yes; Al. 1910A

1472; " Gordon; m; 5 (7-26-26); F; S; Son; yes 1451; yes; Al. 1910B

1473; **WHITE EAGLE**, Jacob; m; 42 (1890); F; M; Head; yes 1453; no; Al. 2016

1474; (No Two Horns), Helen; f; 35 (3-9-97); F; M; Wife; yes 1454; yes; Al. 2384

1475; " " Edward; m; 10 (9-4-21); F; S; Son; yes 1455; yes; An. 3503

1476; " " Jacob, Jr; m; 15 da (3-16-31); F; S; Son; yes ---; yes; An. 3504

1477; **WHITE EAGLE**, Jerome; m; 62 (1870); F; m; Head; yes 1456; yes; Al. 2177

1478; (Wablezela); f; 54 (1878); F; M; Wife; yes 1457; yes; Al. 2444

1479; " Jerome, Jr; m; 12 (4-22-19); F; S; Son; yes 1458; yes; An. 3507

1480; **WHITE EAGLE**, Milan; m; 32 (5-6-99); F; m; Head; yes 1461; yes; Al. 2188

1481; (Graybull), Annie; f; 31 (1-21-09); F; M; Wife; yes 1462; yes; Al. 2206

1482; " Melvin; m; 5 (9-27-26); F; S; Son; yes 1463; yes; An. 3510

1483; " Wesley; m; 3 (10-7-28); F; S; Son; yes 1464; yes; An. 3511

1484; " Earl; m; 1 (11-1-30); F; S; Son; yes 1465; yes; An. 3512

1485; **WHITE EAGLE**, Richard; m; 40 (8-16-91); F; m; Head; yes 1466; no; Al. 1775

1486; (Jordan), Margaret; f; 45 (8-15-91); F; M; Wife; yes 1467; no; Al. 1614

1487; " " Sarah; f; 15 (4-15-18); F; S; Dau; yes 1468; yes; An. 3515

1488; " " Edna; f; 11 (3-15-21); F; S; Dau; yes 1469; yes; An. 3516

1489; " " Joseph; m; 8 (4-4-23); F; S; Son; yes 1470; yes; An. 3517

1490; " " Irene M; f; 5 (7-19-26); F; S; Dau; yes 1471; yes; An. 3518

1491; " " Leonard; m; 1 (7-1-30); F; S; Son; yes 1472; yes; An. 3519

1492; **WHITEFACE BEAR**; m; 76 (1853); F; Wd; Head; yes 1473; yes; Al. 1779

1493; **WHITELIGHTNING** (Tarcaokawin), Mrs; f; 76 (1856); F; Wd; Head; yes 1475; yes; Al. 3160

1494; **WHITELIGHTNING**, Harry; m; 39 (1893); F; M; Head; yes 1476; yes; Al. 2193

1495; (Streaked Eye), Elizabeth; f; 36 (1895); F; M; Wife; yes 1477; yes; Al. 2757

1496; " Josephine; f; 14 (5-30-17); F; S; Dau; yes 1478; yes; An. 3533

1497; " Mamie; f; 8 (11-18-23); F; S; Dau; yes 1479; yes; An. 3534

1498; " Peter; m; 3 (10-18-28); F; S; Son; yes 1480; yes; An. 3535

Census of the__Standing Rock__Reservation of the__Standing Rock__jurisdiction, as of__April 1__, 1932, taken by__E. D. Mossman__, Superintendent. North Dakota

KEY: Number; Surname, Given; Sex; Age at Last Birthday; Tribe (Standing Rock Sioux unless otherwise noted); Degree of Blood; Marital Status; Relationship to Head of Family; At Jurisdiction where enrolled (Yes or No); (If "No", where, if given); Ward (Yes or No); Allotment, Annuity and Identification Numbers.

1499; " Jerome; m; 2/12 (1-19-32); F; S; Son; yes ---; yes; An. ---.

1500; **WHITELIGHTNING**, Joseph; m; 58 (1874); F; M; Head; yes 1481; yes; Al. 2190

1501; **WHITELIGHTNING**, Paul; m; 42 (1890); F; M; Head; yes 1482; yes; Al. 2192

1502;   (Redears), Margaret; f; 34 (1898); F; M; Wife; yes 1483; yes; Al. 2149
1503; " John; m; 6 (10-20-25); F; S; Son; yes 1484; yes; An. 3540
1504; " Luke; m; 4 (9-20-27); F; S; Son; yes 1485; yes; An. 3541
1505; " Edward; m; 1 (7-24-30); F; S; Son; yes 1486; yes; An. 3542

1506; **WHITETWIN**; m; 58 (1874); F; M; Head; yes 1487; yes; Al. 2755
1507;   (Tasinatawin), Mary; f; 52 (1880); F; M; Wife; yes 1488; yes; Al. 3225
1508; " George; m; 15 (10-20-16); F; S; Son; yes 1489; yes; An. 3581
1509; " Robert; m; 14 (1-14-18); F; S; Son; yes 1490; yes; An. 3582
1510; " Paul; m; 10 (7-17-21; F; S; Son; yes 1491; yes; An. 3583

1511; **WHITETWIN**, Charles; m; 30 (8-5-01); F; M; Head; yes 1492; yes; Al. 2328
1512;   (Cottonwood), Mable; f; 35 (1897); F; M; Wife; yes 1493; yes; Al. 2672
1513; " Margaret; f; 2 (3-15-29); F; S; Dau; yes 1494; yes; An. 3575
1514; " Agnes; f; 1 (3-19-31); F; S; Head[sic]; yes 1495; yes; Al. 3578
1514; Zahn, Lorene R; f; 10 (12-27-21); F; S; St-Dau; yes 1496; yes; An. 2795A
1515; Zahn, Geraldine; f; 6 (3-29-26); F; S; St-Dau; yes 1497; yes; An. 2795B

N. E. **WICKS**, Joseph; m; Head
1517;   (Mentz), Marcella; f; 30 (2-4-02); 1/2; M; Wife; yes; 1498; no; Al. 2218
1518; " Chaske F; m; 6 (5-10-25); 1/4; S; Son; yes 1499; yes; An. 3585
1519; " Joseph J; m; 5 (2-26-27) 1/4; S; Son; yes 1500; yes; An. 3586

N. E. **WILKIE**, Michael; m; Head
1520;   (Goodreau), Lulu; f; 34 (7-17-98); 1/4; M; Wife; no 1501; St Paul; MN; no; Al. 3438

N. E. **WILLIAMS**, George; m; Head
1521;   (Goodlefthand), Maggie; f; 32 (6-7-99); F; M; Wife; yes 73; yes; Al. 1922

1522; **WINDY**, Albert; m; 80 (1852); F; M; Head; yes 1502; yes; Al. 2375
1523;   (Lean Elk), Bessie; f; 71 (1861); F; M; Wife; yes 1503; yes; Al. 2586

1524; **WINDY**, James; m; 42 (3-21-90; F; M; Head; yes 1504; yes; Al. 2377
1525;   (Thigh), Jennie; f; 38 (7-?-1894); F; M; Wife; yes 1505; yes; Al. 2263
1526; " Dorothy; f; 11 (1-18-21); F; S; Dau; yes 1506; yes; An. 3596
1527; " Eugene; m; 9 (1-5-25); F; S; Son; yes 1507; yes; An. 3597

KEY: Number; Surname, Given; Sex; Age at Last Birthday; Tribe (Standing Rock Sioux unless otherwise noted); Degree of Blood; Marital Status; Relationship to Head of Family; At Jurisdiction where enrolled (Yes or No); (If "No", where, if given); Ward (Yes or No); Allotment, Annuity and Identification Numbers.

1528;   "   Francis; m; 6 (8-23-25); F; S; Son; yes 1508; yes; An. 3598

1529;   "   Edna P; f; 4 (2-28-28); F; S; Dau; yes 1509; yes; An. 3599

1530;   "   Chester; m; 1 (7-23-30); F; S; Son; yes 1510; yes; An. 3600

1531;   **WINTERS**, Asa; m; 25 (3-23-07); F; S; Head; yes 1511; yes; Al. 1792

1532;   **WINTERS**, Francis; m; 31 (4-18-01); F; S; Head; yes 1512; yes; Al. 1790

1533;   **WISESPIRIT**, Adolph; m; 60 (1871); F; M; Head; yes 1513; yes; Al. 2211

1534;   (ShootsTheEnemy), Josephine; f; 50 (1882); F; M; Wife; yes 1514; yes; Al. 2265

1535;   "   Grace; f; 12 (6-26-19); F; S; Dau; yes 1515; yes; Al. 2266-A.

1536;   **WISESPIRIT**, Charles; m; 23 (9-12-08); F; M; Head; yes 1516; yes; Al. 3776

1537;   (Siaka), Mary; f; 22 (11-14-09); F; M; Wife; yes 1517; yes; Al. 3916

1538;   "   Quinton; m; 2 (9-20-29); F; S; Son; yes 1518; yes; An. 3608

1539;   "   Unnamed; m; 16 da (3-15-32); F; S; Son; yes ---; yes; An. ---

1540;   **WISESPIRIT**, George; m; 21 (2-14-11); F; m; Head; yes 1519; yes; Al. 4094

1541;   (Cottonwood), Kate; f; 17 (9-26-14); F; M; Wife; yes 1520; yes; Al. 4646

1542;   "   Veronica; f; 2 (3-11-30); F; S; Dau; yes 1521; yes; An. 3611

1543;   **WITZLEBEN**, Agnes; f; 27 (9-23-04); 1/8; S; Head; no 1522; Bismarck, Burleigh Co, ND; yes; Al. 2877

1544;   **WITZLEBEN**, Leo; m; 29 (9-5-02); 1/8; M; Head; no 1523; Gladstone, Stark Co, ND; yes; Al. 2876

1545;   **WOODPECKER** (Redbird), Mrs. Tail; f; 69 (1863); F; Wd; Head; yes 1525; yes; Al. 3536

1546;   **YELLOW**, Cecelia; f; 69 (1862); F; S; Head; yes 1526; yes; Al. 3531

1547;   **YELLOW**, James; m; 37 (2-10-95); F; M; Head; yes 1527; no; Al. 1655

1548;   (Striped Cloud), Cecelia; f; 48 (1884); F; M; Wife; yes 1528; yes; Al. 801

1549;   "   Louis J; m; 14 (6-19-17); F; S; Son; yes 1529; yes; An. 3622

1550;   **YELLOW**, John; m; 29 (4-21-02); F; S; Head; yes 1530; yes; Al. 1646

1551;   **YELLOWBIRD**, Charles; m; 28 (8-4-03); F; S; Head; yes 1531; yes; Al. 1875

1552;   **YELLOWHAMMER**, Edward; m; 54 (1878); F; M; Head; yes 1532; yes; Al. 1964

1553;   (Hairychin), Flavia; f; 55 (1877); F; M; Wife; yes 1553; yes; Al. 3226

Census of the __Standing Rock__ Reservation of the __Standing Rock__ jurisdiction, as of __April 1__, 1932, taken by __E. D. Mossman__, Superintendent. North Dakota

KEY: Number; Surname, Given; Sex; Age at Last Birthday; Tribe (Standing Rock Sioux unless otherwise noted); Degree of Blood; Marital Status; Relationship to Head of Family; At Jurisdiction where enrolled (Yes or No); (If "No", where, if given); Ward (Yes or No); Allotment, Annuity and Identification Numbers.

1554; " Richard; m; 17 (1-24-15); F; S; Son; yes 1535; yes; An. 3655

1555; " William; m; 10 (11-13-21); F; S; Son; yes 1536; yes; An. 3656

1556; **YELLOWHAMMER**, Ed. Jr; m; 29 (9-19-04); F; M; Head; yes 1537; yes; Al. 1966

1557; (Twoshields), Nancy; f; 23 (12-2-08); F; M; Wife; yes 1538; yes; Al. 3778

1558; " Angeline; f; 1 (6-20-30); F; S; Dau; yes 1539; yes; An. 3659

1559; **YELLOWHAMMER**, Martin; m; 29 (8-20-02); F; S; Head; yes 1540; yes; Al. 1965

1560; **YELLOWLODGE**, Francis; m; 25 (7-3-03); F; M; Head; yes 1541; yes; Al. 1852

1561; (HolyElkFace), Clementine; f; 21 (9-18-10); F; M; Wife; yes 1542; yes; Al. 4161

1562; " Agatha; f; 6/12 (9-20-31); F; S; Dau; yes ---; yes; An. ---

1563; **YELLOWLODGE** (Four), Theresa; f; 54 (1878); F; M; Head; yes 1543; yes; Al. 3765

1564; " Mary; f; 15 (4-11-16); F; S; Dau; yes 1544; yes; An. 3666

1565; **YOUNGBEAR**, Frank; m; 29 (12-24-02); F; M; Head; yes 1545; no; Al. 2155

1566; (Rattlingcloud), Margaret; f; 29 (4-12-02); F; M; Wife; yes 1546; yes; Al. 2662

1567; " Frank, Jr; m; 9 (8-20-21); F; S; Son; yes 1547; yes; Al. 2662A

1568; " Kingman; m; 8 (10-28-23); F; S; Son; yes 1548; yes; An. 3672

1569; " Calvin; m; 6 (2-6-26) F; S; Son; yes 1549; yes; An. 3673

1570; " Estelle; f; 4 (8-18-28); F; S; Dau; yes 1550; yes; An. 3674

1571; **YOUNGBEAR** (Tasinawaste), Mrs; f; 73 (1859); F; Wd; Head; yes 1551; yes; Al. 3092

1572; **ZAHN**, Aaron; m; 25 (2-8-07); 1/2; S; Head; yes 1552; yes; Al. 2727

1573; **ZAHN**, Emma; f; 21 (7-8-10); 1/2; S; Head; yes 1553; yes; Al. 4104

1574; " Helen C; f; 4 (1-6-28); 1/2; S; Dau; yes 1554; yes; An. 3686

1575; **ZAHN**, Francis; m; 40 (5-4-91); 1/2; S; Head; yes 1555; no; Al. 2721

1576; **ZAHN**, John; m; 52 (1880); 1/2; M; Head; yes 1556; no; Al. 2316

1577; (Gates), Mary; f; 49 (1883); 1/2; M; Wife; yes 1557; yes; Al. 1940

1578; " Bennett; m; 14 (1-31-18); 1/2; S; Son; yes 1558; yes; An. 3690

1579; Gates, James; m; 20 (2-3-12); 1/2; S; St-Son; yes 1559; yes; Al. 4128

Census of the **Standing Rock** Reservation of the **Standing Rock** jurisdiction, as of **April 1**, 19**32**, taken by **E. D. Mossman**, Superintendent. North Dakota

KEY: Number; Surname, Given; Sex; Age at Last Birthday; Tribe (Standing Rock Sioux unless otherwise noted); Degree of Blood; Marital Status; Relationship to Head of Family; At Jurisdiction where enrolled (Yes or No); (If "No", where, if given); Ward (Yes or No); Allotment, Annuity and Identification Numbers.

N. E. **ZAHN**, William; m; Head
1580;   (Flying Cloud), Josephine; f; 63 (1869); F; M; Wife; yes 1560; yes; Al. 2315

1581;   **ZAHN**, Robert; m; 32 (2-3-1900); 1/2; M; Head; yes 1561; yes; Al. 2795
1582;   (Halsey), Christina; f; 30 (7-4-1901); 1/2; M; Wife; yes 1562; yes; Al. 1609
1583;   "   Lavon; f; 3 (7-2-28); 3/4; S; Dau; yes 1563; yes; An. 3696
1584;   "   Carmen L; f; 2 (10-1-29); 3/4; S; Dau; yes 1564; yes; An. 3697
1585;   "   Keith; m; 1/12 (2-6-31); 3/4; S; Son; yes ---; yes; An. 3698
1586;   Mentz, Fay Marie; f; 8 (6-6-23); 3/4; S; St-Dau; yes 1565; yes; An. 3694
1587;   Mentz; William; m; 6 (8-7-25); 3/4; S; St-Son; yes 1566; yes; An. 3695

1588;   **ZAHN**, William; m; 47 (1885); 1/4; M; Head; yes 1567; no; Al. 2318
1589;   "   John V; m; 18 (12-13-13); 1/8; S; Son; yes 1569; yes; Al. 4526
1590;   "   Wilma; f; 13 (6-10-18); 1/8; S; Dau; yes 1570; yes; An. 3701
1591;   "   George; m; 6 (7-28-25); 1/8; S; Son; yes 1571; yes; An. 3702

1592;   **ZAHN**, William V; m; 21 (10-21-10); 1/8; m; Head; yes 1568; yes; Al. 4196

Supplemental Sheet:

3713;   **HALSEY**, Leo; m; 23 (12-25-09); 1/2; S; Head; yes 611; yes; Al. 3983

3714;   **WHITE COW WALKING**; m; 78 (1854); F; Wd; Head; yes 1452; yes;
                                                              Al. 2219

1932 Census

of

SOUTH DAKOTA SIOUX

on

STANDING ROCK RESERVATION,

NORTH DAKOTA

Taken by E. D. Mossman, Supt.

Ending March 31, 1932

Census of the **Standing Rock** Reservation of the **Standing Rock** jurisdiction, as of **April 1**, 1932, taken by **E. D. Mossman**, Superintendent. South Dakota

KEY: Number; Surname, Given; Sex; Age at Last Birthday; Tribe (Standing Rock Sioux unless otherwise noted); Degree of Blood; Marital Status; Relationship to Head of Family; At Jurisdiction where enrolled (Yes or No); (If "No", where, if given); Ward (Yes or No); Allotment, Annuity and Identification Numbers.

1593; **AGARD**, James; m; 40 (1892); 1/2; M; Head; yes 1572; no; Al. 1422
1594;   (Shoestring), Isabelle; f; 38 (1894) F; M; Wife; yes 1573; yes; Al. 1486
1595;   "   Jennie; f; 15 (11-9-16); 3/4; S; Dau; yes 1574; yes; An. 22
1596;   "   William; m; 12 (5-29-19); 3/4; S; Son; yes 1575; yes; An. 23
1597;   "   Louis H; m; 11 (6-9-21); 3/4; S; Son; yes 1576; yes; An. 24
1598;   "   Dixie B; f; 8 (9-18-23); 3/4; S; Dau; yes 1577; yes; An. 25
1599;   "   Al Joseph; m; 4 (6-14-28); 3/4; S; Son; yes ---; yes; An. 28
1600;   "   Seraphine; f; 2 (12-1-29); 3/4; S; Dau; yes 1579; yes; An. 27

1601; **AGARD**, Jerry; m; 29 (2-24-03); 1/2; S; Head; yes 1580; yes; Al. 1427

1602; **AGARD**, Louis; m; 68 (1864); 1/2; M; Head; yes 1581; no; Al. 1420
1603;   "   Harry; m; 18 (10-8-13); 1/2; S; Son; yes 1582; yes; Al. 4510
1604;   "   Louisa; f; 16 (7-17-15); 1/2; S; Dau; yes 1583; yes; An. 31

1605; **AGARD**, Louis, Jr; m; 33 (12-3-99); 1/2; M; Head; yes 1584; no; Al. 1424
1606;   (Archambault), Blanche; f; 32 (12-31-99); 1/4; M; Wife; yes 1585; yes;
                                                                          Al. 1387
1607;   "   Louis J; m; 12 (12-1-19); 3/8; S; Son; yes 1586; yes; An. 34
1608;   "   Joseph; m; 10 (11-20-21); 3/8; S; Son; yes 1587; yes; An. 35
1609;   "   Wallace; m; 8 (5-18-23); 3/8; S; Son; yes 1588; yes; An. 36
1610;   "   Quentin; m; 6 (6-20-25); 3/8; S; Son; yes 1589; yes; An. 37
1611;   "   Wyln[sic] M; f; 4 (9-11-27); 3/8; S; Dau; yes 1590; yes; An. 38
1612;   "   Theresa M; f; 1 (7-14-30); 3/8; S; Dau; yes 1591; yes; An. 39

1613; **AGARD**, William; m; 25 (11-21-06); 1/2; S; Head; yes 1592; yes; Al. 1425

N. E. **AMERICAN HORSE**, Charles; m; Head
1614; (Kills Crow), Louise; f; 28 (5-1-03); F; M; Wife; No 1593; Pine Ridge Res,
                                                                 SD; yes; Al. 443

1615; **AMIDST**, James; m; 69 (1863); F; M; Head; yes 1594; yes; Al. 624
1616;   (Oyankela); f; 63 (1869); F; M; Wife; yes 1595; yes; Al. 3641

1617; **AMIDST**, James, Jr; m; 26 (9-17-05); F; S; Head; yes 1596; yes; Al. 627

1618; **ANKLE**, Henry A; m; 39 (1893); F; M; Head; yes 1597; no; Al. 3928
1619; (Many Deeds), Ethel; f; 30 (11-17-1901); F; M; Wife; yes 1598; yes; Al. 1141
1620;   "   Jesse; m; 10 (11-20-21); F; S; Son; yes 1599; yes; An. 60
1621;   "   Henry W; m; 8 (2-12-24); F; S; Son; yes 1600; yes; An. 61
1622; Ankle, Lorraine; f; 2 (2-8-30); F; S; Dau; yes 1601; yes; An. 62

1623; **ANKLE**, Matthew; m; 58 (1874); F; M; Head; yes 1602; yes; Al. 2831

Census of the __Standing Rock__ Reservation of the __Standing Rock__ jurisdiction, as of __April 1__, 1932, taken by __E. D. Mossman__, Superintendent. South Dakota

1624; **ANTELOPE**, Albert; m; 50 (1882); F; M; Head; yes 1603; no; Al. 1510
1625;   (Bullghost), Bessie; f; 51 (1880); F; M; Wife; yes; 1604; yes; Al. 3405
1626;   "   Mamie; f; 16 (6-23-15); F; S; Dau; yes 1605; yes; Al. 1511
1627;   "   Noble; m; 6 (9-11-25); F; S; Son; yes 1605; yes; An. 66

1628; **ANTELOPE**, Edwin; m; 57 (1875); F; M; Head; yes 1607; no; Al. 1509
1629;   (Shoestring), Annie; f; 57 (1875); F; M; Wife; yes 1608; yes; Al. 3426
1630;   "   Levi; m; 10 (2-5-22); F; S; Son; yes 1609; yes; An. 68
1631; Shoestring, Jerome; m; 19 (2-16-13); F; S; St-Son; yes 1610; yes; Al. 4414
1632; Shoestring, Ambrose; m; 16 (4-1-16); F; S; St-Son; yes 1611; yes; An. 70

1633; **ARCHAMBAULT**, Charles; m; 28 (11-10-03); 1/2; S; Head; yes 1612; yes;
Al. 1413

1634; **ARCHAMBAULT**, Harry; m; 55 (1887); 1/4; M; Head; yes 1614; no;
Al. 1392
1635;   "   John G; m; 19 (8-5-12); 1/8; S; Son; yes 1615; yes; Al. 4327

1636; **ARCHAMBAULT**, John; m; 40 (1892); 1/2; M; Head; yes 1616; no;
Al. 1391
1637;   (Little Eagle), Margaret; f; 40 (1892); F; M; Wife; yes 1617; yes; Al. 1368
1638;   "   Cyril; m; 18 (1-11-14); F; S; Son; yes 1618; yes; Al. 4539
1639;   "   Oscar; m; 16 (3-29-16); F; S; Son; yes 1619; yes; An. 89
1640;   "   Leola; f; 13 (10-4-18); F; S; Dau; yes 1620; yes; An. 90
1641;   "   Edgar; m; 11 (7-25-20); F; S; Son; yes 1621; yes; An. 91
1642;   "   Clayton; m; 8 (3-16-24); F; S; Son; yes 1622; yes; An. 92
1643;   "   Germaine; f[sic]; 4 (7-1-27); F; S; Son; yes 1623; yes; An. 93
1644;   "   Ray; m; 9/12 (8-29-31); F; S; Son; yes ---; yes; An. 94

1645; **ARCHAMBAULT**, Joseph; m; 63 (1869); 1/2; M; Head; no 1624; Sioux
Falls, Minnehaha Co, SD; no; Al. 1409
1646;   (Gates), Mary; f; 48 (1884); 1/2; M; Wife; yes 1625; no; Al. 878
1647;   "   Ruby; f; 21 (3-15-11); 1/2; S; Dau; yes 1626; yes; Al. 4108
1648;   "   Frank; m; 19 (1-4-13); 1/2; S; Son; yes 1627; yes; Al. 4389
1649;   "   Sibley; m; 19 (1-4-13); 1/2; S; Son; yes 1628; yes; Al. 4390
1650;   "   Patrick; m; 11 (7-16-20); 1/2; S; Son; yes 1629; yes; An. 97

1651; **ARCHAMBAULT**, Leo; m; 38 (5-1-94); 1/2; M; Head; no 1630; Beulah,
Crook Co, WY; no; Al. 1411
1652;   "   Lola; f; 9 (5-10-22); 1/2; S; Dau; no 1631; Beulah, Crook Co; WY; yes;
An. 99

Census of the **Standing Rock** Reservation of the **Standing Rock** jurisdiction, as of **April 1**, 1932, taken by **E. D. Mossman**, Superintendent. South Dakota

KEY: Number; Surname, Given; Sex; Age at Last Birthday; Tribe (Standing Rock Sioux unless otherwise noted); Degree of Blood; Marital Status; Relationship to Head of Family; At Jurisdiction where enrolled (Yes or No); (If "No", where, if given); Ward (Yes or No); Allotment, Annuity and Identification Numbers.

1653; **ARCHAMBAULT**, Louis; m; 51 (1881); 1/2; m; Head; yes 1632; no;
Al. 1388
1654;   "   Phoebe; f; 19 (11-7-12); 1/2; S; Dau; yes 1633; yes; Al. 4374
1655;   "   Louis; m; 16 (6-15-15); 1/2; S; Son; yes 1634; yes; An. 101
1656;   "   Lenora; f; 14 (5-4-17); 1/2; S; Dau; yes 1636; yes; An. 102

1657; **ARCHAMBAULT**, Paul J; m; 24 (3-22-08); 1/2; S; Head; no 1638;
Baltimore (Ind State), MD; yes; Al. 3344

1658; **ARCHAMBAULT**, Richard, C; m; 5 (2-24-27); 1/4; S; Alone; yes 1637; yes;
An. 105

1659; **ARCHAMBAULT**, Robert; m; 25 (9-11-06); 1/2; M; Head; yes 1638; yes;
Al. 2759
1660;   (Spottedhorse), Josephine; f; 22 (6-1-09); F; M; Wife; yes 1639; yes;
Al. 3885
1661;   "   Marie V; f; 3 (3-22-29); 3/4; S; Dau; yes 1640; yes; An. 108
1662;   "   Maurice; m; 1 (1930); 3/4; S; Son; yes 1641; yes; An. 109

1663; **ARCHAMBAULT**, Samuel; m; 56 (1876); 1/2; M; Head; no 1642; Harlem,
Mont; no; Al. 3346

1664; **ARCHAMBAULT**, Sophie; f; 27 (7-16-04); 1/2; S; Head; yes 1643; yes;
Al. 2768

1665; **ARCHAMBAULT**, William; m; 29 (10-19-02); 1/2; M; Head; yes 1644; yes;
Al. 2767
1666;   (Shields), Amelia; f; 24 (9-28-07); 1/2; M; Wife; yes 1645; yes; Al. 3314

1667; **ARMSTRONG**, Edward; m; 15 (1881); F; M; Head; yes 1646; yes; Al. 349

1668; **ASHES**, Jacob; m; 54 (1878); F; M; Head; yes 1647; yes; Al. 675

N. E.   **BABBITT**, Dave; m; Head
1669;   (Tiokasin), Bridget; f; 36 (1895); F; Wife; yes 1648; no; Al. 2773
1670;   "   Rose; f; 13 (8-23-18); 1/2; S; Dau; yes 1649; yes; An. 128
1671;   "   David, Jr; m; 11 (11-3-20); 1/2; S; Son; yes 1650; yes; An. 129

1672; **BADGER**, Jovita; m; 77 (1865); F; m: Head; yes 1651; no; Al. 827
1673;   (NoEyeBrows), Maggie; f; 62 (1870); F; M; Wife; yes 1652; yes; Al. 3138
1674;   "   Katherine; f; 18 (4-26-13); F; S; Dau; yes 1653; yes; Al. 4428

Census of the **Standing Rock** Reservation of the **Standing Rock** jurisdiction, as of **April 1**, 1932, taken by **E. D. Mossman**, Superintendent. South Dakota

KEY: Number; Surname, Given; Sex; Age at Last Birthday; Tribe (Standing Rock Sioux unless otherwise noted); Degree of Blood; Marital Status; Relationship to Head of Family; At Jurisdiction where enrolled (Yes or No); (If "No", where, if given); Ward (Yes or No); Allotment, Annuity and Identification Numbers.

1675; **BAINE**, Clarence; m; 57 (6-30-07); 1/4; S; Head; no 1656; Redrock, Noble Co, OK; yes; Al. 2514

1676; **BAINE**, George; m; 57 (1875); 1/2; M; Head; no 1657; Tulalip Agency, Tulalip, Wash; no Al. 629
1677;   "   Edmund; m; 21 (5-4-10); 1/4; S; Son; no 1658; Tulalip Agency, Tulalip, Wash; yes; Al. 3892
1678;   "   Anna J; f; 17 (2-18-15); 1/4; S; Dau; no 1659; Tulalip Agency, Tulalip, Wash; yes; An. 142
1679;   "   Margaret; f; 15 (2-17-17); 1/4; S; Dau; no 1660; Tulalip Agency, Tulalip, Wash; yes; An. 143
1680;   "   Patricia; f; 10 (1921); 1/4; S; Dau; no 1661; Tulalip Agency, Tulalip, Wash; yes; An. 144

1681; **BAINE**, John; m; 57 (1875); 1/2; M; Head; yes 1662; no; Al. 655

N. E.   **BARADA**, WE; m; Head
1682;   (Hourigan), Mary; f; 38 (4-28-95); 1/4; M; Wife; no 2459; San Francisco, Cal; no; Al. 2867

1683; **BEARCATCHES**, Alexander; m; 45 (1886); F; S; Head; yes 1663; yes; Al. 490

1684; **BEARFACE**, Vital; m; 58 (1874); F; M; Head; yes 1664; yes; Al. 752
1685; (Rough Surface), Jean; f; 38 (10-25-94); F; M; Wife; yes 1665; yes; Al. 714
1686;   "   William; m; 5 (4-11-26); F; S; Son; yes 1666; yes; An. 161
1687;   "   Doraphine   f; 4 (10-17-27); F; S; Dau; yes 1667; yes; An. 162

1688; **BEARKING**, Eugene m; 57 (1875); 1/2; M; Head; yes 1668; no; Al. 696
1689; (FeatherEarring), Rose; f; 61 (1871); 1/2; M; Wife; yes 1669; yes; Al. 3576
1690; "   Lawrence; m; 17 (6-6-14); 1/2; S; Son; yes 1671; yes; Al. 4603

1691; **BEARKING**, John; m; 20 (8-8-11); 1/2; M; Head; yes 1670; yes; Al. 4193
1692; (Halsey), Mable; f; 20 (5-4-10); 1/2; M; Wife; yes 619; yes; Al. 4003

1693; **BEARKING**, George; m; 28 (6-119-03); 1/2; M; Head; yes 1672; yes; Al. 700
1694;   (White), Laura; f; 28 (10-1-03); F; M; Wife; yes 1673; yes; Al. 545
1695; "   Bernice; f; 6 (11-1-25); F; S; Dau; yes 1674; yes; An. 168
1696; "   Lucille; f; 4 (4-16-28); F; S; Dau; yes 1675; yes; An. 169
1697; "   Leonard; m; 2 (2-15-29); F; S; Son; yes 1676; yes; An. 170
1698; "   Loretta C; f; 5/12 (10-3-31); F; S; Dau; yes ---; yes; An. 171

Census of the **Standing Rock** Reservation of the **Standing Rock** jurisdiction, as of **April 1**, 1932, taken by **E. D. Mossman**, Superintendent. South Dakota

KEY: Number; Surname, Given; Sex; Age at Last Birthday; Tribe (Standing Rock Sioux unless otherwise noted); Degree of Blood; Marital Status; Relationship to Head of Family; At Jurisdiction where enrolled (Yes or No); (If "No", where, if given); Ward (Yes or No); Allotment, Annuity and Identification Numbers.

1699; **BEARNECKLACE**; m; 72 (1860); F; M; Head; yes 1677; yes; Al. 1047
1700;   (Cetanskawin), Mrs; f; 72 (1860); F; M; Wife; yes 1678; yes; Al. 3319

1701; **BEARSCARESAWAY**, George; m; 42 (3-5-90); F; S; Head; yes 1679; yes; Al. 691

1702; **BEARRIBS**, Andrew; m; 24 (1-15-08); F; S; Head; yes 1680; yes; Al. 3387

1703; **BEARRIBS**, James; m; 66 (1876; F; M; Head; yes 1681; yes; Al. 1289
1704;   (Onefeather), Lucy; f; 50 (1882); F; M; Wife; yes 1681; yes; Al. 3142
1705;   "   Walter J; m; 21 (1-15-11); F; S; Son; yes 1682; yes; Al. 4139
1706;   "   Eugene; m; 11 (5-1-20); F; S; Son; yes 1684; yes; An. 182

1707; **BEARSHEART**, Sidney; m; 42 (1890); F; M; Head; yes 1685; no; Al. 2386
1708;   (Pehinsakiya), Gertrude; f; 39 (1893); F; M; Wife; yes 1686; yes; Al. 272
1709;   "   Lawrence; m; 10 (11-28-21); F; S; Son; yes 1687; yes; An. 195
1710;   "   Wilbert; m; 4 (3-25-28); F; S; Son; yes 1688; yes; An. 196

1711; **BEARSHIELD**, James; m; 78 (1854); F; M; Head; yes 1689; yes; Al. 775
1712;   (Bearface), Otilia; f; 55 (1877); F; M; Wife; yes 1690; yes; Al. 3505
1713; Bearface, Annie; f; 23 (8-31-09); F; S; St-Dau; yes 1691; yes; Al. 4130

1714; **BEARWEASEL**, James; m; 42 (1890); F; M; Head; yes 1693; no; Al. 1436
1715;   (BullHead), Josephine; f; 33 (6-4-99); F; M; Wife; yes 1694; yes; Al. 1639
1716;   "   Eva; f; 12 (12-30-19); F; S; Dau; yes 1695; yes; An. 208
1717;   "   Maxine; f; 9 (8-14-22); F; S; Dau; yes 1696; yes; An. 209

1718; **BEARSOLDIER**, George; m; 78 (1844); F; Wd; Head; yes 1692; yes; Al. 542

1718[sic]; **BEARWEASEL**, Leo; m; 64 (1848); F; M; Head; yes 1697; yes; Al. 1435

N. E. **BENSON**, Eugene; m; Head
1719;   (Kempton), Fern; f; 25 (4-20-06); 1/4; M; Wife; yes 1698; yes; Al. 2810
1720;   "   Louis E; m; 2 (5-18-29); 1/8; S; Son; yes 1699; yes; An. 221

1721; **BIGMANE**, David; m; 36 (1895); F; M; Head; no 1700; Fort Peck Res, Mont; no; Al. 1458

1722; **BIGMANE**, Thomas; m; 31 (5-3-01); F; M; Head; no 1701; Fort Peck Res, Mont; no; Al. 1461

Census of the __Standing Rock__ Reservation of the __Standing Rock__ jurisdiction, as of __April 1__, 1932, taken by __E. D. Mossman__, Superintendent. South Dakota

KEY: Number; Surname, Given; Sex; Age at Last Birthday; Tribe (Standing Rock Sioux unless otherwise noted); Degree of Blood; Marital Status; Relationship to Head of Family; At Jurisdiction where enrolled (Yes or No); (If "No", where, if given); Ward (Yes or No); Allotment, Annuity and Identification Numbers.

N. E.   **BIRDEAGLE**, George; m; Head
1723;   (Kills Crow), Julia; f; 57 (1876); F; M; Wife; no 1702; Pine Ridge Res, SD; yes; Al. 3122
1724;   Kills Crow, Theodore; m; 19 (6-23-12); F; S; St-Son; no 1703; Pine Ridge Res, SD; yes; Al. 4313

1725;   **BIRDHORSE**, Leon; m; 25 (6-8-06); F; M: Head; yes 1704; yes; Al. 3761

1726;   **BIRDHORSE**, Robert; m; 28; F; M; Head; yes 1707; yes; Al. 256
1727;   "   Wilmer R; m; 5 (9-28-26); F; S; Son; yes 1708; yes; An. 243
1728;   "   Dallas R; m; 4 (10-26-28); F; S; Son; yes 1709; yes; An. 244

1729;   **BIRDHORSE**, William; m; 16 (5-16-15); F; S; Alone; yes 1710; yes; An. 245

N. E.   **BIRDNECKLACE**, Moses; m; Head
1730;   (Iron), Louise; f; 25 (9-3-06); F; M; Wife; no 1711; Chey River Res, yes; Al. 1241

1731;   **BLACKBEAR**, (Snow), Harriet; f; 32 (1890); F; Wd; Head; yes 1712; yes; Al. 177
1732;   "   George; m; 15 (8-22-12); F; S; Son; yes 1713; yes; An. 250
1733;   "   William; m; 10 (1-24-16); F; S; Son; yes 1714; yes; An. 248
1734;   "   Chauncey; m; 1 (12-20-21); F; S; Son; yes 1715; yes; An. 249

1735;   **BLACKBEAR**, Walter W; m; 81 (1851); F; Wd; Head; yes 1716; yes; Al. 583

1736;   **BLACKCLOUD**, Aloysius; m; 57 (1875); F; M; Head; yes 1717; yes; Al. 603
1737;   (Blackcloud), Matilda; f; 51 (1881); F; M; Wife; yes 1718; yes; Al. 3419

1738;   **BLACKCLOUD**, David; m; 11-28-03); F; M; Head; yes 1719; yes; Al. 604
1739;   (Bearking), Josephine; f; 25 (8-4-06); 1/2; M; Wife; yes 1720; yes; Al. 2505
1740;   "   Loretta L; f; 5 (11-11-26); 3/4; S; Dau; yes 1721; yes; An. 256
1741;   "   Aloysius; m; 3 (10-5-28); 3/4; S; Son; yes 1722; yes; An. 257
1742;   "   Vendeline J; m; 1 (3-26-31); 3/4; S; Son; yes ---; yes; An. 258

1743;   **BLACKCLOUD**, Joseph; m; 34 (1898); F; S; Head; yes 1723; yes; Al. 679

N. E.   **BLACKEAGLE**, Luke; m; Head
1744;   (Loves War), Elizabeth; f; 27 (1903); F; M; Wife; yes 1724; yes; Al. 3784

Census of the __Standing Rock__ Reservation of the __Standing Rock__ jurisdiction, as of __April 1__, 1932, taken by __E. D. Mossman__, Superintendent.   South Dakota

KEY: Number; Surname, Given; Sex; Age at Last Birthday; Tribe (Standing Rock Sioux unless otherwise noted); Degree of Blood; Marital Status; Relationship to Head of Family; At Jurisdiction where enrolled (Yes or No); (If "No", where, if given); Ward (Yes or No); Allotment, Annuity and Identification Numbers.

1745; **BLACKFOX** (Pankeska), Mrs Herman; f; 75 (1854); F; Wd; Head; yes 1725;
yes; Al. 3385

1746; " Hermine; f; 16 (3-12-16); F; S; Gr-Dau; yes 1726; yes; An. 268

1747; **BLACKHOOP**, Benedict; m; 64 (1868); F; Wd; Head; yes 1727; no;
Al. 1998

1748; **BLACKHOOP**, Joseph; m; 32 (3-16-1900); F; M; Head; yes 1728; yes;
Al. 2785

1749; (Redtomahawk), Louise; f; 27 (12-16-04); F; M; Wife; yes 1729; yes;
Al. 2002

1750; " Pearl; f; 7 (3-18-25); F; S; Dau; yes 1730; yes; An. 275
1751; " Robert; m; 4 (12-20-27); F; S; Son; yes 1731; yes; An. 276

1752; **BLACKHOOP**, Martin; m; 58 (1874); F; M; Head; yes 1732; yes; Al. 2270
1753; " Bessie; f; 16 (9-5-15); F; S; Dau; yes 1733; yes; An. 278
1754; " Mabel; f; 13 (8-18-18); F; S; Dau; yes 1734; yes; An. 279

1755; **BLACKHOOP**, Thomas; m; 24 (9-25-08); F; M; yes 1735; yes; Al. 3800
1756; (Cottonwood), Nellie; f; 24 (1907); F; M; Wife; yes 1736; yes; Al. 2666
1757; " Arnold; m; 4 (3-14-28); F; S; Son; yes 1737; yes; An. 282

1758; **BLACKHOOP**, William J; m; 25 (10-?-06); F; S; Head; yes 1738; yes;
Al. 3847

1759; **BLACKTHUNDER** (Wasu), Mrs; f; 79 (1843); F; Wd; Head; yes 1739; yes;
Al. 3311

1760; **BLANKET**, Nicholas; m; 63 (1869); F; M; Head; yes 1740; yes; Al. 2916
1761; (Onjinca), Nellie E; f; 39 (1898); F; M; Wife; yes 1741; yes; Al. 1381,

N. E. **BLENDER**, L. E.; m; Head
1762; (Duncan), Bertha; f; 35 (1897); 1/4; M; Wife; no 1742; Bison, Perkins Co,
SD; no; Al. 2837

1763; **BOBTAILBEAR**, William; m; 20 (12-25-11); F; S; Head; yes 2407; yes;
Al. 4282

1764; **BLUE EARTH**, Paul; m; 34 (1898); F; M; Head; no 1743; Chey River Res,
SD; yes; Al. 1691

1765; **BOBTAILTIGER**, Edward; m; 77 (1855); F; M; Head; yes 1744; yes;
Al. 200
1766; (Sitomni), Mrs; f; 71 (1861); F; M; Wife; yes 1745; yes; Al. 3455

KEY: Number; Surname, Given; Sex; Age at Last Birthday; Tribe (Standing Rock Sioux unless otherwise noted); Degree of Blood; Marital Status; Relationship to Head of Family; At Jurisdiction where enrolled (Yes or No); (If "No", where, if given); Ward (Yes or No); Allotment, Annuity and Identification Numbers.

1767; **BOBTAIL TIGER**, John; m; 35 (1897); F; M; Head; yes 1746; yes; Al. 202
1768;　　　　(Gabe), Rose; f; 30 (6-29-02); F; M; Wife; yes 1747; yes; Al. 126
1769;　　" 　L. Malenia; f; 1 (10-29-30); F; S; Dau; yes 1748; yes; An. 317
1770;　　" 　Genevieve; f; 5/12 (10-23-31); F; S; Dau; yes ---; yes; An. 318
1771; Gabe, Rufus; m; 10 (2-7-22); F; S; St-Son; yes 1749; yes; An. 1140
1772; Gabe, Berneta; f; 6 (8-5-25); F; S; St-Dau; yes 1750; yes; An. 1149

1773; **BONECLUB**, Harry; m; 28 (4-13-03); F; M; Head; yes 1751; yes; Al. 234
1774;　　　(Noheart), Annie; f; 30 (4-26-01); F; M; Wife; yes 1752; yes; Al. 336
1775;　　" 　Agnes J; f; 2 (5-12-29); F; S; Dau; yes 1753; yes; An. 322
1776;　　" 　Minerva; f; 4/12 (11-16-31); F; S; Dau; yes ---; yes; An. 323

1777; **BRAVECROW**, Samuel; m; 41 (1891); F; M; Head; yes 1754; yes; Al. 1130
1778;　　　(Hawk), Julia; f; 36 (12-8-96); F; M; Wife; yes 1755; yes; Al. 2945
1779;　　" 　Mildred; f; 11 (7-15-28); F; S; Dau; yes 1756; yes; An. 340

1780; **BRAVECROW**, Walter; m; 36 (1896); F; M; Head; yes 1757; yes; Al. 1131
1781;　　　(Cedar), Mary; f; 32 (3-11-1900); F; M; Wife; yes 1758; yes; Al. 1481
1782;　　" 　Amelia; f; 10 (1-28-22); F; S; Dau; yes 1759; yes; An. 343
1783;　　" 　Paul; m; 1 (7-25-31); F; S; Son; yes 1760; yes; An. 345

1784; **BRAVETHUNDER**, Barney; m; 29 (1893); F; S; Head; yes 1761; yes;
Al. 1209

1785; **BRAVETHUNDER**, John; m; 48 (1882); F; M; Head; yes 1762; no;
Al. 820

1786; **BRAVETHUNDER**, Joseph; m; 55 (1877); F; M; Head; yes 1763; yes;
Al. 1210
1787;　　　(Bravethunder), Ida; f; 48 (1882); F; M; Wife; yes 1764; yes; Al. 3082
1788;　　" 　Rose; f; 16 (3-6-16); F; S; Dau; yes 1675; yes; An. 351
1789;　　" 　Mary E; f; 10 (11-25-21); F; S; Dau; yes 1766; yes; An. 352
1790;　　" 　Joseph, Jr; m; 4 (2-22-28); F; S; Son; yes 1767; yes; An. 353

1791; **BRAVETHUNDER**, Julia; f; 73 (1859); F; S; Head; yes 1768; yes; Al. 3105

1792; **BREAST**, Charles; m; 47 (1885); F; S; Head; yes 1769; yes; Al. 3353

1793; **BROUGHT**, Pius; m; 69 (1863); F; S; Head; yes 1770; yes; Al. 2923

1794; **BROUGHT PLENTY**, August; m; 32 (5-9-1900); F; M; Head; yes 1771; yes;
Al. 1796
1795;　　　(End of Horn), Lulu; f; 32 (8-7-1900); F; M; Wife; yes 1772; yes; Al. 596
1796;　　" 　" 　Genevieve; f; 4 (5-18-27); F; S; Dau; yes 1773; yes; An. 367

70

Census of the __Standing Rock__ Reservation of the __Standing Rock__ jurisdiction, as of __April 1__, 1932, taken by __E. D. Mossman__, Superintendent. South Dakota

KEY: Number; Surname, Given; Sex; Age at Last Birthday; Tribe (Standing Rock Sioux unless otherwise noted); Degree of Blood; Marital Status; Relationship to Head of Family; At Jurisdiction where enrolled (Yes or No); (If "No", where, if given); Ward (Yes or No); Allotment, Annuity and Identification Numbers.

1797; Brought Plenty, Cyril E; m; 7/12 (8-12-31); F; S; Son; yes ~~1~~---; yes; An. 368

1798; **BROWN**, (Onebull), Cecelia; f; 39 (1893); F; M; Head; no 1774; Chey River
Res, SD; yes; Al. 992

1799; **BROWN**, Elsie; f; 36 (1895); 1/2; M; Head; yes 1775; yes; An. 376
1800;   "   Sophie; f; 8 (1923); 1/2; S; Dau; yes 1776; yes; An. 377
1801;   "   Nora; f; 1 (12-4-30); 1/2; S; Dau; yes 1777; yes; An. 378

1802; **BROWN**, James; m; 56 (1876); F; M; Head; no 1778; Columbia Falls,
Flathead Co, Mont; no; Al. 2841

1803; **BROWNMAN** (Isnawin), Mrs Elias; f; 67 (1865); F; Wd; Head; yes 1779;
yes; Al. 3337

1804; **BROWNOTTER**, Jacob; m; 24 (7-26-07); F; M; Head; yes 1780; yes;
Al. 3350
1805;   (Dogeagle), Maude; f; 23 (12-18-08); F; M; Wife; yes 1781; yes; Al. 3840

1806; **BROWNOTTER**, Leo; m; 28 (12-18-04); F; M: Head; yes 1782; yes;
Al. 1517
1807;   "   Henry H; m; 3 (8-26-28); F; S; Son; yes 1784; yes; An. 385

1808; **BRUCE**, Lillian; f; 26 (8-28-05); 1/2; S; Head; no 1785; Sioux City,
Woodbury Co, IA; yes; Al. 1726

1809; **BRUGUIER**, Leo C; m; 51 (1881); 1/2; M; Head; no 1786; Fort Peck Res,
Mont; no; Al. 1094
1810;   (Forte), Emma; f; 71 (1861); 1/2; M; Wife; yes 1787; no; Al. 1095

1811; **BRUSHHORNS** (Hintunkasan), Mrs. Emma; f; 72 (1860); F; Wd; Head; yes
1788; yes; Al. 3664

1812; **BRUSHHORNS**, Emma; f; 19 (3-9-13); F; S; Alone; yes 1789; yes; Al. 4463

1813; **BRUSHHORNS**, Joseph; m; 33 (3-20-99); F; S; Head; no 1790; Fort Peck,
Mont; yes; Al. 113

N. E. **BUCK**, Dennis; m; Head
1814;   (Little Eagle), Angela; f; 44 (1888); F; M; Wife; no 1791; Cheyenne River
Res, SD; no; Al. 3278

1815; **BUCKLEY**, Abraham; m; 50 (1881); 1/2; M; Head; yes 1792; yes; Al. 1115
1816;   (Blackfox), Maude; f; 48 (1884); F; M; Wife; yes 1793; yes; Al. 3263

Census of the **Standing Rock** Reservation of the **Standing Rock** jurisdiction, as of **April 1**, **1932**, taken by **E. D. Mossman**, Superintendent. South Dakota

KEY: Number; Surname, Given; Sex; Age at Last Birthday; Tribe (Standing Rock Sioux unless otherwise noted); Degree of Blood; Marital Status; Relationship to Head of Family; At Jurisdiction where enrolled (Yes or No); (If "No", where, if given); Ward (Yes or No); Allotment, Annuity and Identification Numbers.

1817;   "   Raymond; m; 14 (5-22-16) 3/4; S; Son; yes 1794; yes; An. 395
1818;   "   Wilson; m; 9 (4-8-22); 3/4; S; Son; yes 1795; yes; An. 396
1819;   "   Philomene; f; 7 (12-28-24); 3/4; S; Dau; yes 1796; yes; An. 397
1820;   "   Ruth; f; 1 (6-30-30); 3/4; S; yes 1797; yes; An. 398

1821;   **BULLGHOST** (Hunkpatewin), Mrs; f; 84 (1848); F; Wd; Head; yes 1798;
                                                                        yes; Al. 2930

1822;   **BULLHEAD**, Francis; m; 45 (1887); F; M; Head; yes 1799; yes; Al. 1179
1823;   "   Evelyn; f; 19 (2-21-13); F; S; Dau; yes 1800; yes; Al. 4420
1824;   "   Xavior; m; 17 (11-25-14); F; S; Son; yes 1801; yes; An. 428
1825;   "   Christine; f; 13 (4-18-18); F; S; Dau; yes 1802; yes; An. 429

1826;   **BURSHIA**, William; m; 49 (1884); F; M; Head; yes 1803; yes; Al. 223

1827;   **CADOTTE**, Benjamin; m; 55 (1877); 1/2; M; Head; yes 1804; no; Al. 72
1828;   "   Vivian; f; 20 (4-8-12); 1/2; S; Dau; yes 1805; yes; Al. 4319
1829;   "   Benjamin, Jr; m; 19 (2-25-23); 1/2; S; Son; yes 1806; yes; An. 444
1830;   "   Clarence; m; 16 (7-8-25); 1/2; S; Son; yes 1807; yes; An. 445
1831;   "   Lillian; f; 13 (2-4-28); 1/2; S; Dau; yes 1808; yes; An. 446

1832;   **CADOTTE**, Gilbert; m; 33 (1-8-99); 1/2; M; Head; no; 1809; US Navy,
                              New York City, New York Co, NY; no; Al. 90

1833;   **CADOTTE**, Ignatius; m; 29 (6-29-02); 1/2; S; Head; yes 1810; yes; Al. 175

1834;   **CADOTTE**, Jerome; m; 40 (1891); 1/2; M; Head; yes 1811; yes; Al. 86
1835;   (Madbear), Scholastica; f; 40 (1891); 1/2; M; Wife; yes 1812; yes; Al. 671
1836;   "   Verna; f; 16 (10-9-15); 1/2; S; Dau; yes 1813; yes; An. 451
1837;   "   Ethel; f; 14 (2-7-18); 1/2; S; Dau; yes 1814; yes; An. 452
1838;   "   Wilfred; m; 11 (9-13-20); 1/2; S; Son; yes 1815; yes; An. 452[sic]
1839;   "   Roger; m; 9 (3-24-23); 1/2; S; Son; yes 1816; yes; An. 453
1840;   "   Mary J; 6 (4-5-25); 1/2; S; Dau; yes 1817; yes; An. 454
1841;   "   Dorothy I; f; 1 (11-7-30); 1/2; S; Dau; yes 1818; yes; An. 456

1842;   **CADOTTE**, John; m; 57 (1875); 1/2; M; Head; yes 1819; yes; Al. 173
1843;   (McLean), Hattie; f; 52 (1880); 1/2; M; Wife; yes 1820; yes; Al. 3461
1844;   "   Aaron; m; 20 (9-16-11); 1/2; S; Son; yes 1821; yes; Al. 4209
1845;   "   Theresa; f; 13 (5-10-18); 1/2; S; Dau; yes 1822; yes; An. 459

1846;   **CADOTTE**, Raymond; m; 23 (2-23-09); 1/2; S; Head; yes 1823; yes;
                                                                        Al. 3775

Census of the **Standing Rock** Reservation of the **Standing Rock** jurisdiction, as of **April 1**, 1932, taken by **E. D. Mossman**, Superintendent.   South Dakota

KEY: Number; Surname, Given; Sex; Age at Last Birthday; Tribe (Standing Rock Sioux unless otherwise noted); Degree of Blood; Marital Status; Relationship to Head of Family; At Jurisdiction where enrolled (Yes or No); (If "No", where, if given); Ward (Yes or No); Allotment, Annuity and Identification Numbers.

1847;   **CADOTTE**, Samuel; m; 51 (1881); 1/2; M; Head; yes 1824; no; Al. 345
1848;   (Swiftcloud), Nellie; f; 49 (1883); 1/2; M; Wife; yes 1825; yes; Al. 61

1849;   **CADOTTE**, Samuel, Jr; m; 27 (11-8-04); 1/2; S; Head; yes 1826; yes; Al. 346

N. E.   **CADOTTE**, Joe; M; Head
1850;   (KillsCrowIndian), Sarah; f; 23 (9-17-09); F; M; Wife; yes 1827; yes;
                                                                        Al. 3918
1851;   Joseph D; m; 8/12 (9-8-31); F; S; Son; yes ---; yes; An. 464

N. E.   **CAIRNS**, Henry; m; Head
1852;   (Traversie), Maude; f; 57 (1875); 1/2; M; Wife; yes 1825; no; Al. 316

N. E.   **CAMPBELL**, N H; m; Head
1853;   (Hodgkinson), Louisa; f; 36 (1896); 1/4; M; Wife; yes 1829; yes;
                                                                        Al. 2856
1854;   "   Mildred; f; 19 (12-22-13); 1/8; S; Dau; yes 1830; yes; Al. 4426
1855;   "   Edna L; f; 16 (8-2-15); 1/8; S; Son; yes 1831; yes; An. 489
1856;   "   Raymond; m; 14 (6-17-17); 1/8; S; Son; yes 1832; yes; An. 490

1857;   **CARRY MOCCASIN**, Chester; m; 72 (1860); F; M; Head; yes 1835; yes;
                                                                        Al. 455
1858;   (Carry Moccasin), Martha; f; 71 (1861); F; m; Wife; yes 1836; yes;
                                                                        Al. 3388

1859;   **CATCHBEAR**, Benedict; m; 72 (1869); F; Wd; Head; yes 1837; yes; Al. 128

1860;   **CATCHBEAR**, Bernard; m; 27 (10-26-04); F; M; Head; yes 1838; yes;
                                                                        Al. 132
1861;   (Looking Back), Grace; f; 19 (9-2-12); F; M; Wife; yes 1839; yes;
                                                                        Al. 4341
1862;   "   Clayton; m; 2 -3-16-30); F; S; Son; yes 1840; yes; An. 517
1863;   "   Abel; m; 5/12; (10-6-31); F; S; Son; yes ---; yes; An. 518

1864;   **CATKA**, Emma; f; 80 (1853); F; S; Head; yes 1841; yes; Al. 65

1865;   **CEDARBOY**, David; m; 24 (9-14-09); F; S; Head; yes 1842; yes; Al. 3479

1866;   **CEDARBOY**, James; m; 71 (1861); F; M; Head; yes 1843; yes; Al. 1480
1867;   (Eagleman), Susan; f; 61 (1871); F; M; Wife; yes 1844; yes; Al. 3473

1868;   **CETANWICKTE**, Robert; m; 71 (1899); F; Wd; Head; yes 1845; yes;
                                                                        Al. 1500

73

Census of the **Standing Rock** Reservation of the **Standing Rock** jurisdiction, as of **April 1**, 1932, taken by **E. D. Mossman**, Superintendent. South Dakota

N. E. **CHAPMAN**, Guy; m; Head
1869;   (Carrier), Mabel; f; 21 (5-6-10); F; M; Wife; yes 1834; yes; Al. 4006
1870;   "   James G; m; 11 (12-12-20); 1/2; S; Son; yes 1846; yes; An. 524
1871;   "   Mildred; f; 7 (5-13-24); 1/2; S; Dau; yes 1847; yes; An. 525
1872;   "   Clement C; m; 4 (4-18-28); 1/2; S; Son; yes 1848; yes; An. 526
1873   "   Guy, Jr; 5/12 (10-24-31); 1/2; S; Son; yes ---; yes; An. 528

1874; **CHASEALONE**, Luke; m; 61 (1871); F; M; Head; yes 1851; yes; Al. 692
1875;   "   George; m; 13 (1918); F; S; Son; yes 1852; yes; An. 539
1876;   "   Julia; f; 11 (7-15-20); F; S; Dau; yes 1853; yes; An. 540
1877;   "   Evelyn; f; 6 (7-6-25); F; S; Dau; yes 1854; yes; An. 541

1878; **CHASEALONE**, Peter; m; 78 (1854); F; M; Head; yes 1855; yes; Al. 45

1879; **CHASEOFTEN**, Joseph; m; 63 (1869); F; M; Head; yes 1856; yes; Al. 382
1880;   (Wiocan), Matilda; f; 57 (1875); F; M; Wife; yes 1857; yes; Al. 3619

1881; **CHASING HAWK**, Ambrose; m; 19 (10-29-12); F; M; Head; yes 1860; yes; Al. 4359
1882;   (Has Horns), Louise; f; 18 (8-7-13); F; M; Wife; yes 2365; yes; Al. 4474

1883; **CHASING HAWK**, Burt; m; 47 (1885); F; M; Head; yes 1858; no; Al. 516
1884;   (Onefeather), Annie; f; 42 (1890); F; M; Wife; yes 1859; yes; Al. 1296
1885;   "   Leo; m; 16 (7-25-15); F; S; Son; yes 1860; yes; An. 557
1886;   "   Josephine; f; 12 (3-4-19); F; S; Dau; yes 1861; yes; An. 559
1887;   "   Mary; f; 13 (4-28-17); F; S; Dau; yes 1863; yes; An. 558
1888;   "   Vincent; m; 10 (4-28-21); F; S; Son; yes 1864; yes; An. 560
1889;   "   Laura; f; 6 (6-30-25); F; S; Dau; yes 1865; yes; An. 561
1890;   "   Jennie; f; 4 (12-17-27); F; S; Dau; yes 1866; yes; An. 562
1891;   "   Nancy; f; 1 (4-18-30); F; S; Dau; yes 1867; yes; An. 563

1892; **CHASINGHAWK**, James; m; 63 (1869); F; M; Head; yes 1868; yes; Al. 514
1893;   (His Red Horse), Elizabeth; f; 64 (1868); F; M; Wife; yes 1869; yes; Al. 3367

1894; **CHEYENNE**, Albert; m; 40 (1891); F; M; Head; yes 1870; yes; Al. 3859
1895;   (Redfox), Annie; f; 32 (1900); F; M; Wife; yes 1871; yes 2630
1896;   "   Mary; f; 5 (10-2-26); F; S; Dau; yes 1872; yes; An. 570

1897; **CIRCLINGHAWK**, Edward; m; 93 (1839); F; M; Head; yes 1873; yes; Al. 899
1898; (Sunkawastewin), Mrs; f; 79 (1853); F; M; Wife; yes 1874; yes; Al. 3847

Census of the **Standing Rock** Reservation of the **Standing Rock** jurisdiction, as of **April 1**, 1932, taken by **E. D. Mossman**, Superintendent. South Dakota

KEY: Number; Surname, Given; Sex; Age at Last Birthday; Tribe (Standing Rock Sioux unless otherwise noted); Degree of Blood; Marital Status; Relationship to Head of Family; At Jurisdiction where enrolled (Yes or No); (If "No", where, if given); Ward (Yes or No); Allotment, Annuity and Identification Numbers.

N. E. **CLAYMORE**, Charles; m; Head
1899;   (Whitesell), Elizabeth; f; 35 (5-18-97); 1/2; M; Wife; yes 1876; no; Al. 552

1900; **CLAYMORE** (LaFrombois), Jennie; f; 72 (1850); F; M; Head; yes 1875; yes; Al. 3393

1901; **CLAYMORE**, Joseph, Jr; m; 46 (1886); 1/2; M; Head; yes 1877; no; Al. 427
1902;   (McLean), Mary; f; 44 (1888); 1/2; M; Wife; yes 1878; no; Al. 645

1903; **CLAYMORE**, Mary Ann; f; 9 (6-25-22); 1/4; S; Alone; yes 1879; yes; An. 582

N. E. **CLAYMORE**, Peter; m; Head
1904;   (Bearking), Mary; f; 32 (11-10-1900); 1/2; M; Wife; yes 1880; yes; Al. 699

1905; **CLAYMORE**, Paul; m; 39 (1893); 1/2; M; Head; yes 1881; no; Al. 429
1906;   (Gayton), Rose; f; 39 (1893); 1/2; M; Wife; yes 1882; yes; Al. 1714
1907;   "   Samuel A; m; 17 (2-28-15); 1/2; S; Son; yes 1883; yes; An. 4692
1908;   "   Sylvia M; f; 14 (71-17[sic]); 1/2; S; Dau; yes 1884; yes; An. 587
1909;   "   Clifford; m; 12 (8-18-19); 1/2; S; Son; yes 1885; yes; An. 588
1910;   "   Wesley; m; 10 (8-31-21); 1/2; S; Son; yes 1886; yes; An. 589
1911;   "   Helen L; f; 8 (10-10-23); 1/2; S; Dau; yes 1887; yes; An. 590
1912;   "   Mary L; f; 6 (2-4-26); 1/2; S; Dau; yes 1888; yes; An. 591
1913;   "   Evelyn; f; 4 (8-15-28); 1/2; S; Dau; yes 1889; yes; An. 592

1914; **CLAYMORE**, Philip; m; 10 (2-8-22); 1/4; S; Alone; no 1890; Mobridge, Walworth Co, SD; yes; An. 593

1915; **CLAYMORE**, William; m; 51 (1881); 1/2; M; Head; no 1891; Mobridge, Walworth Co, SD; no; Al. 22
1916;   "   William C; m; 15 (4-27-16); 1/4; S; Son; no 1892; Mobridge, Walworth Co, SD; yes; An. 595
1917;   "   Joseph; m; 12 (2-11-19); 1/4; S; Son; no 1893; Mobridge, Walworth Co, SD; yes; An. 596
1918;   "   Richard; m; 10 (3-6-21); 1/4; S; Son; no 1894; Mobridge, Walworth Co, SD; yes; An. 597
1919;   "   Billy S; m; 7 (6-30-24); 1/4; S; Son; no 1895; Mobridge; Walworth Co, SD; yes; An. 598

1920; **CLOUD** (Marpiya), Louise; f; 86 (1846); F; Wd; Head; yes 1896; yes; Al. 706

N. E. **CLOWN**, James; m; Head
1921;   (Redbear), Mary; f; 33 (1899); F; M; Wife; yes 1897; yes; Al. 1011

Census of the **Standing Rock** Reservation of the **Standing Rock** jurisdiction, as of **April 1**, 1932, taken by **E. D. Mossman**, Superintendent. South Dakota

KEY: Number; Surname, Given; Sex; Age at Last Birthday; Tribe (Standing Rock Sioux unless otherwise noted); Degree of Blood; Marital Status; Relationship to Head of Family; At Jurisdiction where enrolled (Yes or No); (If "No", where, if given); Ward (Yes or No); Allotment, Annuity and Identification Numbers.

N. E.   **COLLINS**, Lemuel; m; Head
1922;   (McLaughlin), Helen; f; 26 (11-8-05); 1/2; M; Wife; yes 1898; yes;
                                                                                  Al. 2468
1923;   "   Charles H; m; 1 (4-2-30); 1/4; S; Son; yes 1899; yes; An. 606

1924; **COMEAU**, Joseph; m; 23 (7-12-09); 1/4; S; Head; yes 1900; yes; Al. 3851

N. E.   **COMEAU**, Edward; m; Head
1925;   (Traversie), Lillie; f; 54 (1878); 1/2; M; Wife; yes 1901; no; Al. 1090
1926;   "   Edwin; m; 21 (3-18-11); 1/4; S; Son; yes 1902; yes; Al. 4313
1927;   "   Whitney; m; 19 (2-5-13); 1/4; S; Son; yes 1903; yes; Al. 4399
1928;   "   Catherine; f; 16 (11-19-15); 1/4; S; Dau; yes 1904; yes; An. 610
1929;   "   Gladys; f; 13 (4-25-18); 1/4; S; Dau; yes 1905; yes; An. 611

1930; **COMEAU**, Orville; m; 30 (2-8-02); 1/4; M; Head; yes 1906; yes; Al. 1091

1931; **COMEAU**, Vera; f; 25 (2-20-07); 1/4; S; Head; yes 1907; yes; Al. 3162

1932; **COMEAU**, Virgil; m; 26 (7-9-05); 1/4; M; Head; yes 1908; yes; Al. 1093
1933;   "   Rita J; f; 3 (5-20-28); 1/8; S; Dau; yes 1909; yes; An. 615
1934;   "   Donna J; f; 1 (8-21-30); 1/8; S; Dau; yes 1910; yes; An. 616

1935; **COTTONWARE** (Dupree), Mary; f; 59 (1873); 1/2; M; Head; no 1912;
                                                     Portland, Muttnomal[sic] Co, OR; no; Al. 437

1936; **COTTREL** (Claymore), Abbie; f; 53 (1879); 1/4; M; Head; no 1913;
                                                                        Sanator, SD; no; Al. 24
1937;   "   Philip E; m; 11 (4-16-20); 1/8; S; Son; no 1914; Sanator, SD; yes;
                                                                                  An. 663

1938; **COUNT**, Fridolin; m; 61 (1871); F; S; Head; yes 1915; yes; Al. 1079

1939; **COURNOYER**, Joseph; m; 28 (6-11-03); 1/2; S; Head; no 1917; Yankton
                                                     Res, Wagner, SD; yes; Al. 1268

1940; **CRAWLER** (Tasinamaniwin), Mary; f; 59 (1853); F; Wd; Head; yes 1918;
                                                                        yes; Al. 3362

1941; **CRAZYBEAR**; m; 59 (1853); F; Wd; Head; yes 1919; yes; Al. 2052

1942; **CRAZYBEAR**, Johnson; m; 63 (1869); F; M; Head; yes 1920; yes; Al. 1374
1943;   (Istaziwin), Annie; f; 80 (1852); F; M; Wife; yes 1921; yes; Al. 3248

Census of the **Standing Rock** Reservation of the **Standing Rock** jurisdiction, as of **April 1**, 1932, taken by **E. D. Mossman**, Superintendent. South Dakota

KEY: Number; Surname, Given; Sex; Age at Last Birthday; Tribe (Standing Rock Sioux unless otherwise noted); Degree of Blood; Marital Status; Relationship to Head of Family; At Jurisdiction where enrolled (Yes or No); (If "No", where, if given); Ward (Yes or No); Allotment, Annuity and Identification Numbers.

1944; **CRAZYBEAR**, Peter; m; 33 (1899); F; M; Head; yes 1922; yes; Al. 1376
1945; (Harris), Mary f; 22 (8-26-09); F; M; Wife; no 1922; Omaha, Neb; yes; Al. 4011
1946; " Victor G; m; 3 (3-13-29); F; S; Son; no 1923; Omaha, Neb; yes; An. 671

1947; **CRAZYHAWK**; m; 71 (1861); F; M; Head; yes 1925; yes; Al. 1144
1948; (Tiwanyankapi), Mrs; f; 73 (1859); F; M; Wife; yes 1926; yes; Al. 3257

1949; **CRAZYHAWK**, Barney; m; 35 (1897); F; M; Head; yes 1927; yes; Al. 1145
1950; (Mountain), Susan; f; 33 (1899); F; M; Wife; yes 1928; yes; Al. 1101
1951; " Mary; f; 11 (10-7-20); F; S; Dau; yes 1929; yes; An. 676
1952; " Robert; m; 10 (12-12-21); F; S; Son; yes 1930; yes; An. 677
1953; " James; m; 5 (4-28-26); F; S; Son; yes 1931; yes; An. 678

1954; **CROSS** (Grass Shield), Theresa; f; 72 (1860); F; Wd; Head; yes 1932; yes; Al. 3407

1955; **CROSSBEAR**, Jacob; m; 98 (1844); F; M; Head; yes 1933; yes; Al. 962

1956; **CROSSBEAR**, Walter; m; 36 (1896); F; M; Head; yes 1934; yes; Al. 1177
1957; " Phoebe; f; 7 (8-24-23); F; S; Dau; yes 1935; yes; An. 692

N. E. **CREEK**, James; m; Head
1958; (Hailhawk), Josephine; f; 48 (1884); F; M; Wife; yes 1936; yes; Al. 340

1959; **CROWFEATHER**, Charles; m; 24 (3-29-08); F; S; Head; yes; 1947; yes; Al. 3615

1960; **CROWFEATHER**, Francis; m; 51 (1881); F; M; Head; yes 1938; yes; Al. 806
1961; (Charging Eagle), Mamie; f; 48 (1884); F; M; Wife; yes 1939; yes; Al. 3614
1962; " Marcella; f; 17 (10-15-14); F; S; Dau; yes 1940; yes; Al. 4653
1963; " Louis; m; 12 (12-15-18); F; S; Son; yes 1941; yes; An. 704
1964; " Grace; f; 6 (11-10-25); F; S; Dau; yes 1942; yes; An. 705

1965; **CROWFEATHER**, Frowin; m; 22 (3-10-10); F; S; Head; yes 1943; yes; Al. 3956

1966; **CROWGHOST** (Zuyala), Mrs Lawrence; f; 83 (1849); F; Wd; Head; yes 1944; yes; Al. 3091

1967; **CROWGHOST**, Leo; m; 26 (8-20-05); F; S; Head; yes 1945; yes; Al. 1288

Census of the **Standing Rock** Reservation of the **Standing Rock** jurisdiction, as of **April 1**, 1932, taken by **E. D. Mossman**, Superintendent. South Dakota

KEY: Number; Surname, Given; Sex; Age at Last Birthday; Tribe (Standing Rock Sioux unless otherwise noted); Degree of Blood; Marital Status; Relationship to Head of Family; At Jurisdiction where enrolled (Yes or No); (If "No", where, if given); Ward (Yes or No); Allotment, Annuity and Identification Numbers.

1968; **CROWGHOST**, Samuel; m; 23 (11-21-09); F; M: Head; yes 1946; yes;
Al. 3937

1969; (Whitebearclaws), Winifred; f; 19 (3-26-13); F; m; Wife; yes 3568; yes;
Al. 4419

1970; **CROWNECKLACE**, Thomas; m; 40 (1892); F; M: Head; yes 1949; no;
Al. 2512

1971; (Has Horns), Alice; f; 34 (1-29-98); F; M; Wife; yes 1950; yes; Al. 1166
1972; " Thos, Jr; m; 13 (8-17-18); F; S; Son; yes 1952; yes; An. 721
1973; " Christie; f; 10 (7-17-21); F; S; Dau; yes 1953; yes; An., 722
1974; " Viola E; f; 8 (11-23-23); F; S; Dau; yes 1954; yes; An. 723
1975; " Cora; f; 6 (12-31-25); F; S; Dau; yes 1955; yes; An. 724
1976; " Serena; f; 3 (3-26-29); F; S; Dau; yes 1956; yes; An. 725

1977; **CROWSKIN**, Louis; m; 38 (6-7-94); F; S; Head; yes 1959; no; Al. 848

1978; **CULBERTSON**, Jack; m; 58 (1874); F; M: Head; yes 1960; no; Al. 2975
1979; (Porcupine Creek), Jennie; f; 57 (1875); F; M; Wife; yes 1961; yes;
Al. 509
1980; " Albert; m; 20 (2-7-12); F; S; Son; yes 1962; yes; Al. 4274
1981; " Esther; f; 15 (6-19-16); F; S; Dau; yes 1963; yes; An. 729
1982; " Mamie; f; 13 (10-26-18); F; S; Dau; yes 1964; yes; An. 730

1983; **CULBERTSON**, Moses; m; 29 (1902); F; M; Head; yes 1965; yes; Al. 3899
1894; (Mountain), Alice; f; 20 (12-26-10); F; M; Wife; yes 1966; yes; Al. 4066

N. E. **DAVIS**, George; m; Head
1985; (Redhorse), Annie; f; 47 (1885); F; M; Wife; yes 1967; yes; Al. 320
1986; " Melda; f; 10 (9-1-21); F; S; Dau; yes 1968; yes; An. 737

N. E. **DAVIES**, James E; m; Head
1987; (Reedy), Catherine; f; 52 (1880); 1/4; M; Wife; no 1970; Seattle, King Co,
Wash; no; Al. 1927
1988; Margaret; f; 19; 1/8; S; Dau; no 1971; Seattle, King Co, Wash; yes; Al. 4357

1989; **DEFENDER**, Benjamin; m; 39 (5-26-94); F; M; Head; yes 1972; no; Al. 740
1990; (Gilland), Sadie; f; 42 (1880); 1/2; M; Wife; yes 1973; no; Al. 3129
1991; " Benj, Jr; m; 15 (1-17-17); 1/2; S; Son; yes 1974; yes; An. 747
1992; " Nancy; f; 11 (11-15-21); 1/2; S; Dau; yes 1975; yes; An. 748
1993; " Marion; f; 7 (7-2-24); 1/2; S; Dau; yes 1976; yes; An. 750

1994; **DELORIA**, Susan; f; 36 (1896); 1/2; S; Head; no 1978; Columbia Univ,
New York, NY; no; Al. 3755

Census of the **Standing Rock** Reservation of the **Standing Rock** jurisdiction, as of **April 1**, 1932, taken by **E. D. Mossman**, Superintendent. South Dakota

KEY: Number; Surname, Given; Sex; Age at Last Birthday; Tribe (Standing Rock Sioux unless otherwise noted); Degree of Blood; Marital Status; Relationship to Head of Family; At Jurisdiction where enrolled (Yes or No); (If "No", where, if given); Ward (Yes or No); Allotment, Annuity and Identification Numbers.

1995; **DELORIA**, Vine V; m; 31 (1901); 1/2; S; Head; no 1979; Columbia Univ, New York, NY; no; Al. 3754

1996; **DEMARRIAS**, Earl; m; 21 (7-18-10); 1/2; S; Alone; yes 1980; yes; Al. 4074
1997; " Charles; m; 20 (1-25-13); 1/2; S; Alone; yes 1981; yes; Al. 4395
1998; " Pearl V; f; 17 (3-27-15); 1/2; S; Alone; yes 1982; yes; An. 755
1999; " Mary V; f; 14 (1-14-18); 1/2; S; Alone; yes 1983; yes; An. 756

N. E. **DEMERY**, James; m; Head
2000; (Vermillion), Alice; f; 38 (1894; 2/3; M; Wife; yes 1984; no; Al. 2905
2001; " Chester; m; 11 (6-15-20); 1/2; S; Son; yes 1985; yes; An. 758
2002; " Alice M; f; 9 (4-20-22); 1/2; S; Dau; yes 1986; yes; An. 759
2003; " Ernest; m; 6 (12-18-25); 1/2; S; Son; yes 1987; yes; An. 760
2004; " Florence; f; 4 (9-6-27); 1/2; S; Dau; yes 1988; yes; An. 761
2005; " Matilda; f; 3 (10-20-28); 1/2; S; Dau; yes 1989; yes; An. 762
2006; " James R; m; 1 (4-26-30); 1/2; S; Son; yes ---; yes; An. 763

N. E. **DEMERY**, Irvin; m; Head
2007; (Vermillion), Gladys; f; 21 (3-4-11); 1/4; M; Wife; yes 1990; yes; Al. 4117
2008; " Irvin C; m; 3 (9-18-28); 1/4; S; Son; yes 1991; yes; An. 773
2009; " Roy Bud; m; 2 (12-17-29); 1/4; S; Son; yes 1992; yes; An. 774

N. E. **DEMERY**, Robert; m; M; Head
2010; (Vermillion), Mary; f; 41 (1891); 1/2; M; Wife; yes 1993; no; Al. 2904
2011; " John V; m; 16 (4-5-15); 1/2; S; Son; yes 1994; yes; An. 776
2012; " Rose; f; 13 (12-13-18); 1/2; S; Dau; yes 1995; yes; An. 777
2013; " Edwin; m; 10 (3-16-24); 1/2; S; Son; yes 1996; yes; An. 778
2014; " Robert C; m; 6 (7-16-25); 1/2; S; Son; yes 1997; yes; An. 779
2015; " Dorothea; f; 5 (11-3-26); 1/2; S; Dau; yes 1998; yes; An. 780
2016; " Margaret; f; 2 (11-7-29); 1/2; S; Dau; yes 1999; yes; An. 781

N. E. **DEMPSY**, John; m; Head
2017; (Primeau), Margaret; f; 39 (1893); 1/2; M; Wife; yes 2000; yes; Al. 1430
2018; " James L; m; 15 (8-26-16); 1/2; S; Son; yes 2001; yes; An. 783
2019; " John R; m; 13 (5-28-18); 1/2; S; Son; yes 2002; yes; An. 784
2020; " Elenor[sic]; f; 12 (12-28-19); 1/2; S; Dau; yes 2003; yes; An. 785
2021; " Leona M; f; 10 (2-26-22); 1/2; S; Dau; yes 2004; yes; An. 786
2022; " Margaret; f; 8 (6-8-24); 1/2; S; Dau; yes 2005; yes; An. 787
2023; " Benj Leroy; m; (1931); 1/2; S; Ill Son; yes ---; yes; An. 788

2024; **DeROCKBRAINE**, Andrew; m; 30 (1902); 3/4; S; Head; yes 2006; yes; Al. 1256

Census of the __Standing Rock__ Reservation of the __Standing Rock__ jurisdiction, as of __April 1__, 1932, taken by __E. D. Mossman__, Superintendent. South Dakota

2025; **DeROCKBRAINE**, Antoine J; m; 37 (6-2-95); 3/4; S; Head; yes 2007; yes; Al. 1258

2026; **DeROCKBRAINE**, Antoine; m; 62 (1870); 1/2; M; Head; yes 2008; no; Al. 876
2027; (Eagleboy), Domitilla; f; 62 (1870); F; M; Wife; yes 2009; yes; Al. 3085
2028; " Grace; f; 18 (12-18-13); 3/4; S; Dau; yes 2010; yes; Al. 4530

2029; **DeROCKBRAINE**, Charles; m (8-8-97); 1/2; M; Head; no 2011; Rapid City, Pennington Co, SD; no; Al. 1257
2030; (Fox), Lucy R; f 30 (2-10-02); F; M; Wife; no 2012; Rapid City, Pennington Co; SD; yes; Al. 3196
2031; " Rose L; f; 11 (9-1-20); 3/4; S; Dau; no 2013; Rapid City, Pennington Co, SD; yes; An. 796
2032; " Joseph; m; 6 (12-23-25); 3/4; S; Son; no 2014; Rapid City, Pennington Co, SD; yes; An. 797
2033; " Nelson; m; 5 (2-7-27); 3/4; S; Son; no 2015; Rapid City, Pennington Co, SD; yes; An. 798
2034; " Effie M; f; 1 (1930); 3/4; S; Dau; no ---; Rapid City, Pennington Co, SD; yes; An. 799

2035; **DeROCKBRAINE**, Gabriel; m; 29 (10-29-03); 3/4; S; Head; yes; Al. 1255

2036; **DeROCKBRAINE**, James; m; 21 (1-1-10); 3/4; M; Head; yes 2017; yes; Al. 3941
2037; (Treetop), Lizzie; f; 20 (1-19-12); F; M; Wife; yes 2018; yes; A 4255

2038; **DeROCKBRAINE**, Thomas; m; 37; 3/4; M; Head; yes 2019; yes; Al. 1237
2039; (Hawk), Josephine; f; 30 (3-14-02); F; M; Wife; yes 2020; yes; Al. 2946
2040; " Madeline; f; 9 (11-6-22); 7/8; S; Dau; yes 2021; yes; An. 805
2041; " Dorothy; f; 6 (12-10-27); 7/8; S; Dau; yes 2022; yes; An. 807
2042; " Margaret; f; 4 (1925); 7/8; S; Dau; yes 2023; yes; An. 807
2043; " Bertha; f; 1 (1-1-31); 7/8; S; Dau; yes 2024; yes; An. 808

N. E. **DEUCHENEAU**, B. I.; m; Head
2044; (Hawkbear), Emma; f; 33 (1899); F; M; Wife; no 2025; Cheyenne; River Res, SD; yes; Al. 50

2045; **DID NOT BUTCHER**; m; 80 (1852); F; Wd; Head; yes 2026; Al. 353

2046; **DID NOT BUTCHER**, Louise; f; 34 (1898); F; S; Head; yes 2027; yes; Al. 354

Census of the **Standing Rock** Reservation of the **Standing Rock** jurisdiction, as of **April 1**, 1932, taken by **E. D. Mossman**, Superintendent. South Dakota

KEY: Number; Surname, Given; Sex; Age at Last Birthday; Tribe (Standing Rock Sioux unless otherwise noted); Degree of Blood; Marital Status; Relationship to Head of Family; At Jurisdiction where enrolled (Yes or No); (If "No", where, if given); Ward (Yes or No); Allotment, Annuity and Identification Numbers.

2047; **DISTRIBUTE**, James; m; 46 (1886); F; M; Head; yes 2028; no; Al. 82
2048;   "   Adeline; f; 18 (8--13); F; S; Dau; yes 2030; yes; An. 4457
2049;   "   Mary L; f; 15 (4-4-16); F; S; Dau; yes 2031; yes; An. 819
2050;   "   Lillian; f; 6 (12-17-25); F; S; Dau; yes 2032; yes; An. 820
2051;   "   Delphine; f; 3 (12-26-28); F; S; Dau; yes 2033; yes; An. 821

2052; **DISTRIBUTE**, James, Jr; m; 20 (12-19-11); F; S; Dau; yes 2032; yes; An. 820
2053;   (Loves War), Madeline; f; 20 (10-5-11); F; M; Wife; yes 2806; yes; Al. 419
2054;   "   Amelia; f; 2/12 (1-3-32); F; S; Dau; yes None; yes; An. ---
2055;   "   Glorietta; f; 2 (6-24-29); F; S; St-Dau; yes 2807; yes; An. 826

2056; **DOG**, Bede; m; 27 (9-29-04); F; M; Head; yes 2035; yes; Al. 580
2057;   (Dogeagle), Emma; f; 23 (12-18-08); F; M; Wife; yes 2036; yes; Al. 3481
2058;   "   Evelyn; f; 4 (5-28-27); F; S; Dau; yes 2037; yes; An. 829

2059; **DOG**, Joseph; m; 39 (1893); F; M; Head; yes 2038; yes; Al. 579
2060;   (Shot At), Mary; f; 38 (1894); F; M; Wife; yes 2039; yes; Al. 961
2061;   "   Genevieve; f; 12 (2-29-20); F; S; Dau; yes 2040; yes; An. 832
2062;   "   Helen; f; 5 (1-3-27); F; S; Dau; yes 2041; yes; An. 833

2063; **DOG**, Louis; m; 69 (1863); F; M; Head; no 2042; Rapid City, Pennington Co, SD; yes; Al. 575
2064;   "   Moses A; m; 10 (4-29-21); F; S; Son; no 2043; Rapid City, Pennington Co, SD; yes; An. 835
2065;   "   Bertha; f; 8 (1924); F; S; Dau; no 2044; Rapid City, Pennington Co, SD; yes; An. 836

2066; **DOG**, Louis, Jr; m; 43 (1899); F; M; Head; yes 2045; yes; Al. 578
2067;   (Buckley), Rachael; f; 37 (10-2-94); F; M; Wife; yes 2046; yes; Al. 1116
2068;   "   Davis; m; 3 (4-10-29); F; S; Son; yes 2047; yes; An. 839

2069; **DOG**, Moses; m; 24 (7-3-07); F; S; Head; yes 2048; yes; Al. 3060

2070; **DOGCLOUD**, Benedict; m; 39 (1893); 1/2; M; Head; no 2049; Minneapolis, Hennepin Co, Minn; no; Al. 2081
2071;   "   Donna I; f; 11 (10-19-20); 1/2; S; Dau; no 2050; Minneapolis, Hennepin Co, Minn; yes; An. 842

2072; **DOGEAGLE**, James; m; 56 (1876); F; M; Head; yes; 2051; no; Al. 3838
2073;   (Looking Elk), Lucy; f; 32 (1890); F; M; Wife; yes 2052; yes; Al. 982
2074;   "   Dominic; m; 20 (6-29-11); F; S; Son; yes 2053; yes; Al. 4181
2075;   "   Ambrose; m; 18 (1-14-14); F; S; Son; yes 2054; yes; Al. 4537

KEY: Number; Surname, Given; Sex; Age at Last Birthday; Tribe (Standing Rock Sioux unless otherwise noted); Degree of Blood; Marital Status; Relationship to Head of Family; At Jurisdiction where enrolled (Yes or No); (If "No", where, if given); Ward (Yes or No); Allotment, Annuity and Identification Numbers.

2076; " Catherine; f; 15 (10-20-16); F; S; Dau; yes 2055; yes; An. 348

2077; " George; m; 3 (5-10-28); F; S; Son; yes 2056; yes; An. 848

2078; " Theresa; F; 2/12 (1-11-32); F; S; Dau; yes ---; yes; An. ---

2079; **DOGEAGLE**, Sarah; f; 19 (4-20-12); F; S; Alone; yes 2057; yes; Al. 4303

2080; **DOGEAGLE**, Samuel D; m; 29 (10-12-02); F; S; Head; no 2058; Lantry, Dewey Co, SD; yes; Al. 1135

2081; **DOGMAN** (Heskawin), Mrs James; f; 78 (1854); F; Wd; Head; yes 2059; yes; Al. 3244

2082; **DOG ON THE BUTTE** (Igniwin), Mrs; f; 81 (1851); F; Wd; Head; no 2060; Fort Peck Res, Mont; yes; Al. 807

2083; **DRIVER**, Garfield; m; 63 (1869); F; M; Head; yes 2061; no; Al. 901

N. E. **DRAPPEAU**, Dewey; m; Head
2084; (Cournoyer), Hermine; f; 25 (12-17-06); 1/2; M; Wife; no; Yankton Res, Wagner, Chas. Mix, SD; yes; Al. 872

2085; **DUNCAN**, David; m; 26 (4-26-06); 1/2; S; Head; no 2066; Palermo, Butte Co, Cal; yes; Al. 3732

2086; **DUNCAN**, Edward; m; 40 (1871); 1/2; M; Head; no 2062; Alliance, Box Butte Co, Neb; no; Al. 2835

2087; " Ethel; f; 15 (4-16-16); 1/4 S; Dau; no 2063; Alliance, Box Butte Co, Neb; yes; An. 874

2088; " Everett; m; 13 (8-8-18); 1/4; S; Son; no 2064; Alliance; Box Butte Co, Neb; yes; An. 875

2089; " Charles; m; 10 (1-6-22); 1/4; S; Son; no 2065; Alliance, Box Butte Co, Neb; yes; An. 876

2090; **DUNCAN**, Ellen; f; 61 (1871); 1/2; S; Head; no 2066; Palermo, Butt Co, Cal; yes; Al. 3732

2091; **DUNCAN**, Daniel L; m; 20 (8-23-10); 1/2; M; Head; yes 2068; yes; Al. 4266

2092; " Richard J; m; 1 (9-29-30); 1/4; S; Son; yes 2069; yes; An. 880

2093; **DUNCAN**, George; m; 29 (2-25-03); 1/2; M; Head; no 2070; Selah, Wash; no; Al. 2839

2094; (Silk), Martha; f; 30 (12-21-02); 1/2; M; Wife; yes 2071; yes; Al. 857

Census of the __Standing Rock__ Reservation of the __Standing Rock__ jurisdiction, as of __April 1__, 1932, taken by __E. D. Mossman__, Superintendent. South Dakota

KEY: Number; Surname, Given; Sex; Age at Last Birthday; Tribe (Standing Rock Sioux unless otherwise noted); Degree of Blood; Marital Status; Relationship to Head of Family; At Jurisdiction where enrolled (Yes or No); (If "No", where, if given); Ward (Yes or No); Allotment, Annuity and Identification Numbers.

2095; **DUNCAN**, Jefferson; m; 36 (4-10-95); 1/2; S; Head; no 2072; Princeton, Cal; no; Al. 2836

2096; **DUNCAN**, Robert; m; 25 (4-20-26); 1/2; S; Head; yes 2073; yes; Al. 2840

2097; **DWARF**, Henry; m; 30 (9-14-01); F; M; Head; yes 376; yes; Al. 1931
2098; (Spottedhorse), Julia; f; 29 (8-11-02); F; M; Wife; yes 377; yes; Al. 409

2099; **EAGLE**, Francis; m; 52 (1880); F; M; Head; yes 2074; yes; Al. 220
2100; (Redbird), Susan; f; 37 (1895); F; M: Wife; yes 2075; yes; Al. 196
2101; " Felix; m; 21 (8-5-10); F; S; Son; yes 2076; yes; Al. 4093
2102; " Caroline; f; 2 (9-12-29); F; S; Dau; yes 2077; yes; An. 903
2103; Redbird, Eunice; f; 13 (1-18-20); F; S; St-Dau; yes 2078; yes; An. 901
2104; Redbird, Hazel; f; 12 (2-13-25); F; S; St-Dau; yes 2079; yes; An. 902
2105; Redbird, William; m; 7 (3-9-18) F; S; St-Son; yes 2080; yes; An. 900

2106; **EAGLE**, Frank; m; 22 (8-11-10); F; S; Head; yes 2081; yes; Al. 4028

N. E. **EAGLE**, George; m; Head
2107; (Nationshield), Mary; f; 50 (1882); F; M; Wife; yes 2082; yes; Al. 4632
2108; " Ellen; f; 16 (8-17-15); F; S; Dau; yes 2082; yes; An. 906
2109; " Sampson; m; 14 (1-15-18); F; S; Son; yes 2084; yes; An. 907
2110; " Rosaline; f; 9 (1-22-23); F; S; Dau; yes 2085; yes; An. 908
2111; " George; m; 6 (4-28-25); F; S; Son; yes 2086; yes; An. 909

2112; **EAGLEBOY**, Grover; m; 71 (1861); F; M; Head; yes 2087; yes; Al. 1213
2113; (Itazyowin), Mrs F; 78 (1854); F; M; Wife; yes 2088; yes; Al. 3389

2114; **EAGLEBOY** (Awetewin), Mrs; f; 75 (1857); F; Wd; Head; yes 2089; yes; Al. 3653

2115; **EAGLEDOG**, Amos; m; 52 (1880); F; M; Head; yes 2090; no; Al. 1060
2116; (Ironcloud), Margaret; f; 34 (1898); F; M; Wife; yes 2091; yes; Al. 30
2117; " Isaac; m; 19 (10-5-12); F; S; Son; yes 2092; yes; Al. 4351
2118; " James P; m; 7 (1925); F; S; Son; yes 2093; yes; An. 929
2119; " Solomon; m; 6 (2-25-26); F; S; Son; yes 2094; yes; An. 928
2120; " Lily M; f; 3 (11-11-28); F; S; Dau; yes 2095; yes; An. 930
2121; " Irene M; f; 9/12 (6-22-31); F; S; Dau; yes 2096; yes; An. 931

2122; **EAGLEDOG**, John; m; 73 (1859); F M; Head; yes 2096; yes; Al. 1057
2123; (Itaskawin), Mrs F; 61 (1861); F; M; Wife; yes 2097; yes; Al. 3282

2124; **EAGLEHORN**, Allen; m; 73 (1859); F; M; Head; yes 2099; yes; Al. 491
2125; (Ozanwastewin), Mrs; f; 83 (1849); F; M; Wife; yes 2100; yes; Al. 3661

Census of the **Standing Rock** Reservation of the **Standing Rock** jurisdiction, as of **April 1**, 1932, taken by **E. D. Mossman**, Superintendent. South Dakota

KEY: Number; Surname, Given; Sex; Age at Last Birthday; Tribe (Standing Rock Sioux unless otherwise noted); Degree of Blood; Marital Status; Relationship to Head of Family; At Jurisdiction where enrolled (Yes or No); (If "No", where, if given); Ward (Yes or No); Allotment, Annuity and Identification Numbers.

2126; **EAGLEHORN**, James; m; 28 (1894); F; M; Head; yes 2101; yes; Al. 492,
2127; (Take The Hat), Rose; f; 30 (3-3-02); F; M; Wife; yes 2102; yes; Al. 1205
2128; " Annabelle; f; 4 (1-6-28); F; S; Dau; yes 2103; yes; An. 937

2129; **EAGLEMAN**, Joseph; m; 48 (1884); F; M; Head; yes 2104; no; Al. 2647
2130; (DidNotButcher), Helen; f; 42 (1890); F; M; Wife; yes 2105; yes; Al. 357
2131; " Clara A; f; 8 (3-3-24); F; S; Dau; yes 2106; yes; An. 940

2132; **EAGLEMAN**, Luke; m; 54 (1878); F; M; Head; yes 2107; no; Al. 52
2133; (Shoots The Bear), Amy; f; 49 (1883); F; M; Wife; yes 2108; yes; Al.
3415
2134; " Noble A; m; 17 (6-8-14); F; S; Son; yes 2109; yes; Al. 4607
2135; " Vera M; f; 13 (6-7-18); F; S; day; yes 2110; yes; An. 946
2136; " Oliver; m; 11 (3-1-21); F; S; Son; yes 2111; yes; An. 947

2137; **EAGLEMAN**, Luke, Jr; m; 29 (12-9-06); F; M; Head; yes 2112; yes; Al. 916
2138; (Howard), Eliza; f; 21 (4-22-11); F; M; Wife; yes 2113; yes; Al. 4177

2139; **EAGLE ON HIGH**, Alma; f; 91 (1841); F; S; Head; yes 2114; yes; Al. 3165

2140; **EAGLESHIELD**; m; 73 (1859); F; M; Head; yes 2115; yes; Al. 896
2141; (White Buffalo), Mrs; f; 74 (1858); F; M; Wife; yes 2116; yes; Al. 3171

2142; **EAGLESHIELD**, Fritz W; m; 23 (12-8-09); F; S; Head; no 2117; Santee,
Neb; yes; Al. 3942

2143; **EAGLESHIELD**, John; m; 47 (1885); F; M; Head; yes 2118; yes; Al. 898
2144; (Take The Hat), Louise; f; 42 (1890); F; M; Wife; yes 2119; yes; Al. 1202
2145; " Sidney; m; 13 (10-31-19); F; S; Son; yes 2120; yes; An. 954
2146; " Ernest; m; 9 (1-12-23); F; S; Son; yes 2121; yes; An. 955
2147; " Collins; m; 8 (12-13-24); F; S; Son; yes 2122; yes; An. 956
2148; " Inez; f; 4 (12-25-27); F; S; Dau; yes 2123; yes; An. 957
2149; " Clarice; m; 2 (2-24-30); F; S; Son; yes 2124; yes; An. 958

2150; **EARRING** (Graytrack), Regina; f; 42 (11-18-90); F; M; Head; yes 2125; no;
Al. 3807

2151; **EARTHEATER**, Samuel m; 62 (1870); F; M; Head; yes 2126; yes; Al. 1419
2152; (Bearweasel), Emma; F; 56 (1876); F; M; Wife; yes 2127; yes; Al. 3254
2153; Bearweasel, Robert; m; 20 (5-28-11); F; S; Son; yes 2128; yes; Al. 44444147
2154; " Minnie; f; 17 (4-6-14); F; S; Dau; yes 2129; yes; An. 965

N. E. **ECKMAN**, Leo; m; Head
2155; (McLean), Elizabeth; f; 35 (1897); 1/2; M; Wife; yes 2130; yes; Al. 275

Census of the **Standing Rock** Reservation of the **Standing Rock** jurisdiction, as of **April 1**, 1932, taken by **E. D. Mossman**, Superintendent. South Dakota

KEY: Number; Surname, Given; Sex; Age at Last Birthday; Tribe (Standing Rock Sioux unless otherwise noted); Degree of Blood; Marital Status; Relationship to Head of Family; At Jurisdiction where enrolled (Yes or No); (If "No", where, if given); Ward (Yes or No); Allotment, Annuity and Identification Numbers.

2156; " Marie A; f; 11 (4-21-20); 11/4; S; Dau; yes 2131; yes; An. 967
2157; " Leo F; m; 10 (3-10-22); 1/4; S; Son; yes 2132; yes; An. 968
2158; " Paul A; m; 8 (6-5-24); 1/4; S; Son; yes 2133; yes; An. 969
2159; " Elizabeth; f; 5 (1-16-27); 1/4; S; Dau; yes 2134; yes; An. 970
2160; " Julia; f; 5 (1-16-27) 1/4; S; Dau; yes 2135; yes; An. 971

2170; **ELK**, Jerome; m; 83 (1849); F; M; Head; yes 2136; yes; Al. 2131

2171; **ELK**, John; m; 64 (1868); F; M; Head; no 2137; Crow Creek Res, Fort
Thompson, SD; yes; Al. 2988

2172; **ELK**, Johnson; m; 55 (1896); F; M; Head; yes 2138; yes; Al. 1072
2173; Johnson, Jr; m; 19 (8-25-12); F; S; Son; yes 2139; yes; Al. 4336
2174; Elaine F; 16 (11-20-15); F; S; Dau; yes 2141; yes; An. 981
2175; Lavina; f; 1222 (12-15-18); F; S; Dau; yes 2142; yes; An. 982
2176; Victor; m; 8 (11-24-23); F; S; Son; yes 2143; yes; An. 983

2177; **ELK EAGLE** (Loneman), Agnes; f; 52 (1880); F; Wd; Head; no 2145; Chey
River Res, SD; yes; Al. 139

2178; **ELK NATION**, Amos; m; 47 (1885); F; M; Head; yes 2146; yes; Al. 1536
2179;   (Hawkeagle), Jennie; f; 31 (2-21-91); F; M; Wife; yes 2150; yes; Al. 1493
2180; " Alvin; m; 18 (11-29-13); F; S; Son; yes 2147; yes; Al. 4517
2181; " Horace; m; 12 (3-13-20); F; S; Son; yes 2148; yes; An. 987
2182; " Ambrose; m; 8 (4-21-23); F; S; Son; yes 2149; yes; An. 988
2183; Rosebud, Irving; m; 11 (8-19-21); F; S; St-Son; yes 2151; yes; An. 990
2184; Yellowearrings, Leonard; m; 3 (1928); F; S; St-Son; yes 2152; yes; An. 991

2185; **ELKNATION**, James; m; 52 (1880); F; M; Head; yes 2153; yes; Al. 884

2186; **ELKNATION**, Louis; m; 76 (1856); F; M; Head; yes 2154; yes; Al. 1535
2187;   (Kagliwin), Mrs; f; 73 (1859); F; M; Wife; yes 2155; yes; Al. 3331
2188; Crowghost, James; m; 15 (12-16-16); F; S; gr-Son; yes 2156; yes; An. 707

2189; **END OF HORN**, Ignatius; m; 64 (1868); F; Wd; Head; yes 2157; yes; Al.103

2190; **END OF HORN**, Abraham; m; 26 (5-31-05); F; M; Head; yes 2158; yes;
Al. 598
2191;   (Crowfeather), Julia; f; 26 (1-3-06); F; M; Wife; yes 2159; yes; Al. 1605
2192; " Merril A; m; 1 (9-2-30); F; S; Son; yes 2160; yes; An. 997
2193; " Vincent C; f; 1/12 (2-22-32); F; S; Son; yes ---; yes; An. ---

2194; **END OF HORN**, William; m; 52 (1870); F; Wd; Head; yes 2161; yes;
Al. 595

KEY: Number; Surname, Given; Sex; Age at Last Birthday; Tribe (Standing Rock Sioux unless otherwise noted); Degree of Blood; Marital Status; Relationship to Head of Family; At Jurisdiction where enrolled (Yes or No); (If "No", where, if given); Ward (Yes or No); Allotment, Annuity and Identification Numbers.

2195; **FASTHORSE**, Imelda; f; 30 (4-1-02); F; S; Head; yes 411; yes; Al. 2939
2196; "   Mary; f; 2 (8-27-29); F; S; Dau; yes 412; yes; An. 1021

2197; **FASTHORSE**, Joseph; m; 55 (1877); F; M; Head; yes 2162; no; Al. 2937
2198; (Fasthorse), Louise; f; 54 (1878); F; M; Wife; yes 2163; yes; Al. 3260
2199; "   Thomas; m; 20 (11-22-11); F; S; Son; yes 2164; yes; Al. 4235
2200; "   Alma; f; 10 (1-31-22); F; S; Dau; yes 2165; yes; An. 1016

2201; **FASTHORSE**, Joseph J; m; 24 (6-?-08); F; S; Head; yes 2166; yes; Al. 2940

2202; **FASTHORSE**, Regina; f; 29 (12-13-02); F; S; Head; yes 416; yes; Al. 2938

2203; **FEARLESS**, Francis; m; 83 (1849); F; Wd; Head; yes 2167; yes; Al. 606

2204; **FEATHEREARRINGS**; m; 75 (1857); F; M; Head; yes 2168; yes; Al. 808
2205; (Ogunla), Mrs F; 83 (1849); F; M; Wife; yes 2169; yes; Al. 3577

N. E. **FENELON**, Vincent; m; Head
2206; (McLaughlin), Etta; f; 30 (11-18-02); 1/2; M; Wife; yes 2170; no; Al. 567
2207; "   James; m; 10 (4-8-22); 1/4; S; Son; yes 2171; yes; An. 1029
2208; "   William; m; 8 (5-31-23); 1/4; S; Son; yes 2172; yes; An. 1030
2209; "   Eugene; m; 4 (5-12-28); 1/4; S; yes 2173; yes; An. 1031

2210; **FIRECLOUD**, Alfred; m; 66 (1866); F; M; Head; yes 2174; yes; Al. 938
2211; (Wizizika), Mollie; f; 67 (1865); F; M; Wife; yes 2175; yes; Al. 3369

2212; **FIRECLOUD**, Ben; m; 63 (1869); F; M; Head; yes 2176; yes; Al. 894
2213; (Foster), Sarah; f; 32 (1-1111-1900); F; M; Wife; yes 2177; yes; Al. 946
2214; " Ben, Jr; m; 8 (8-4-23); F; S; Son; yes 2178; yes; An. 1040
2215; " Christopher; m; 2 (4-9-29); F; S; Son; yes 2179; yes; n 1041

2216; **FIRECLOUD**, Jacob; m; 24 (7-20-08); F; M; Head; yes 2180; yes; Al. 3370
2217; (Blackbear), Bessie; f; 19 (8-22-12); F; M; Wife; yes 2181; yes; Al. 4338

2218; **FIRECLOUD**, Joseph; m; 67 (1870); F; M; Head; yes 2182; yes; Al. 750
2219; (Crowskin), Elizabeth; f; 29 (1903); F; M; Wife; yes 2183; yes; Al. 849
2220; " Susan; f; 15 (11-11-16); F; S; Dau; yes 2184; yes; An. 1046

2221; **FIRECLOUD**, Leo S; m; 36 (1896); F; S; Head; yes 2185; yes; Al. 940

2222; **FIRECLOUD**, Leonard; m; 36 (1896); F; M; Head; yes 2186; yes; Al. 941

2223; **FLY**, Felix; m; 37 (1895); F; M; Head; yes 2187; yes; Al. 2894
2224; "   Felix F; m; 6 (1-12-26); 1/2; S; Son; yes 2188; yes; An. 1056

Census of the **Standing Rock** Reservation of the **Standing Rock** jurisdiction, as of **April 1** , 1932, taken by **E. D. Mossman** , Superintendent. South Dakota

KEY: Number; Surname, Given; Sex; Age at Last Birthday; Tribe (Standing Rock Sioux unless otherwise noted); Degree of Blood; Marital Status; Relationship to Head of Family; At Jurisdiction where enrolled (Yes or No); (If "No", where, if given); Ward (Yes or No); Allotment, Annuity and Identification Numbers.

2225; Fly, Regina; f; 5 (12-3-26); 1/2; S; Dau; yes 2189; yes; An. 1057

2226; **FLY**, Samuel; m; 29 (11-4-02); F; M; Head; yes 2190; yes; Al. 2896
2227; " Lawrence; m; 1 (1-31-31); F; S; Son; yes 2191; yes; An. 1060

2228; **FLYINGBY**, Nathan; m; 56 (1876); F; M; Head; yes 2192; yes; Al. 496
2229; (Grindstone), Eloise; f; 37 (1895); F; M; Wife; yes 2193; yes; Al. 481
2230; " Moses; m; 18 (1-16-14); F; S; Son; yes 2194; yes; Al. 4489
2231; " Joseph; m; 10 (6-5-21); F; S; Son; yes 2195; yes; An. 1065
2232; " Calvin; m; 8 (5-12-24); F; S; Son; yes 2196; yes; An. 1066

2233; **FLYINGBY**, Noel; m; 72 (1860); F; M; Head; yes 2198; yes; Al. 464
2234; " Joseph; m; 13 (2-8-19); F; S; Son; yes 2199; yes; An. 1067

2235; **FLYINGHORSE**, Anthony; m; 58 (1874); F; M; Head; no 2200; Cheyenne River Res, SD; no; Al. 1483
2236; " Victor; m; 11 (4-13-21); F; S; Son; no 2201; Cheyenne River Res, SD; yes; An. 1069

2237; **FLYINGHORSE**, James; m; 47 (1884); F; M; Head; yes 2202; no; Al. 1491
2238; " Verna; f; 18 (8-9-13); 1/2; S; Dau; yes 2203; yes; Al. 4450
2239; " Elsie; f; 15 (2-2-17); 1/2; S; Dau; yes 2204; yes; An. 1071
2240; " Roy M; m; 11 (12-7-20); 1/2; S; Son; yes 2205; yes; An. 1072

2241; **FLYINGHORSE**, William; m; 33 (9-18-99); F; M; Head; yes 2206; yes; Al. 1484
2242; (LittleEagle), Bertha; f; 31 (1901); F; M; Wife; yes 2207; yes; Al. 1372
2243; " May Ella; f; 9 (12-24-22); F; S; Dau; yes ---; yes; An. 1076
2244; " William; m; 10 (6-11-24); F; S; Son; yes 2208; yes; An. 1077
2245; " George; m; 12 (6-18-19); F; S; Son; yes 2209; yes; An. 1078
2246; " Irene; f; 4 (12-21-27); F; S; Dau; yes 2210; yes; An. 1079
2247; " Elmer; m; 2 (1-20-30); F; S; Son; yes 2211; yes; An. 1080

2248; **FORTE**, Bruce; m; 42 (1890); 1/2; M; Head; no 2212; Flathead Res, Pohlson, Mont; no; Al. 1099
2249; (Claymore), Louise; f; 43 (1889); 1/2; M; Wife; no 2213; Flathead Res, Pohlson, Mont; no; Al. 430
2250; " Edward B; m; 15 (2-20-17); 1/2; S; Son; no 2214; Flathead Res, Pohlson, Mont; yes; An. 1098
2251; " Leon; m; 12 (6-27-19); 1/2; S; Son; no 2215; Flathead Res, Pohlson, Mont; yes; An. 1099
2252; " June B; f; 9 (8-23-22); 1/2; S; Dau; no 2216; Flathead Res, Pohlson, Mont; yes; An. 1100

Census of the __Standing Rock__ Reservation of the __Standing Rock__ jurisdiction, as of __April 1__, 1932, taken by __E. D. Mossman__, Superintendent. South Dakota

KEY: Number; Surname, Given; Sex; Age at Last Birthday; Tribe (Standing Rock Sioux unless otherwise noted); Degree of Blood; Marital Status; Relationship to Head of Family; At Jurisdiction where enrolled (Yes or No); (If "No", where, if given); Ward (Yes or No); Allotment, Annuity and Identification Numbers.

2253; **FORTE**, Clyde; m; 23 (12-29-09); 1/2; S; Head; no 2217; Trenton, Mercer Co, NJ; yes; Al. 4259

2254; **FORTE**, Joseph; m; 43 (111889); 1/2; M; Head; no 2218; Flathead Res, Pohlson, Mont; no; Al. 1100

2255; **FORTE**, Margaret; f; 25 (7-20-06); 1/4; S; Head; no 2219; Trenton, Mercer Co, NJ; yes; Al. 2545

2256; **FORTE**, Mayo; m; 48 (1884); 1/2; M; Head; no 2220; Trenton, Mercer Co, NJ; no; Al. 1101
2257;   "   Maxine; f; 14 (9-13-17); 1/4; S; Dau; no 2221; Trenton, Mercer Co, NJ; yes; An. 1104
2258;   "   Mercedes; f; 9 (10-6-22); 1/4; S; Dau; no 2222; Trenton, Mercer Co, NJ; yes; An. 1105

2259; **FORTE**, Zelda; f; 27 (2-22-05); 1/4; S; Head; no 2223; Trenton, Mercer Co, NJ; yes; Al. 1102

2260; **FOSTER** (Iron), Amelia; f; 24 (1871); 1/2; S; Head; yes 2224; yes; Al. 3355

2261; **FOSTER**, Daniel; m; 24 (9-5-08); 1/2; S; Head; yes 2225; yes; Al. 3887

2262; **FOSTER**, Harry; m; 26 (3-25-06); 1/2; M; Head; yes 2226; yes; Al. 947

2263; **FOSTER**, Samuel; m; 38 (6-19-94); 1/2; M; Head; yes 227; no; Al. 945
2264;   (No Heart), Louisa; f; 36 (3-24-06); 1/2; M; Wife; yes 2228; yes; Al. 335
2265;   "   Edna J; f; 17 (1-19-15); 1/2; S; Dau; yes 2229; yes; An. 1114
2266;   "   Collins; m; 11 (7-4-20); 1/2; S; Son; yes 2230; yes; An. 1113
2267;   "   Minnie E; f; 9 (11-12-22; 1/2; S; Dau; yes 2231; yes; An. 1114
2268;   "   Selina; f; 7 (3-1-25); 1/2; S; Dau; yes 2232; yes; An. 1115
2269;   "   May J; f; 5 (12-14-26); 1/2; S; Dau; yes 2234; yes; An. 1116
2270;   "   Theresa; f; 2 (1930); 1/2; S; Dau; yes 2234; yes; An. 1117

2271; **FOX**, Andrew; m; 71 (1861); F; M; Head; no 2235; Rosebud Res, SD; no; Al. 1395

N. E. **FRANK**, Martin; m; Head
2272;   (Makes Trouble), Emma; f; 42 (1890); F; M; Wife; yes 2236; yes; Al. 1527
2273;   "   Myrtle; f; 16 (6-29-15); 1/2; S; Dau; yes 2237; yes; An. 1124
2274;   "   William; m; 14 (11-6-17); 1/2; S; Son; yes 2238; yes; An. 1125
2275;   "   Pearl; f; 11 (1-9-20); 1/2; S; Dau; yes 2239; yes; An. 1126
2276;   "   Catherine; f; 10 (8-4-21); 1/2; S; Dau; yes 2240; yes; An. 1127
2277;   "   Sylvia; f; 9 (2-28-23); 1/2; S; Dau; yes 2241; yes; An. 1128

Census of the **Standing Rock** Reservation of the **Standing Rock** jurisdiction, as of **April 1** , 1932, taken by **E. D. Mossman** , Superintendent. South Dakota

KEY: Number; Surname, Given; Sex; Age at Last Birthday; Tribe (Standing Rock Sioux unless otherwise noted); Degree of Blood; Marital Status; Relationship to Head of Family; At Jurisdiction where enrolled (Yes or No); (If "No", where, if given); Ward (Yes or No); Allotment, Annuity and Identification Numbers.

2278; Frank, Agnes L; f; 7 (12-22-24); 1/2; S; Dau; yes 2242; yes; An. 1129
2279;   "   Annie; f; 6 (3-12-26); 1/2; S; Dau; yes 2243; yes; An. 1130
2280;   "   Martin R; m; 3 (10-6-28); 1/2; S; Son; yes 2244; yes; An. 1131
2281;   "   Cecelia L; f; 11/12 (4-10-31); 1/2; S; Dau; yes ---; yes; An. ---

N. E.   **FRANK**, Mike; m; Head
2282;   (Makes Trouble), Lulu; f; 35 (5-28-97); F; M; Wife; yes; 2245; yes;
                                            Al. 1529
2283;   "   Elsie; f; 11 (11-7-20); 1/2; S; Dau; yes 2246; yes; An. 1133
2284;   "   Flora; f; 13 (12-31-18); 1/2; S; Dau; yes 2247; yes; An. 1134
2285;   "   Michael; m; 4 (8-3-27); 1/2; S; Son; yes 2248; yes; An. 1135

2286; **FRISKING ELK** (Tacuwignakaskawin), Agnes; f; 77 (1855); F; Wd; Head;
                                          yes 2249; yes; Al. 3601

N. E.   **FULMER**, Kenneth; m; Head
2287;   (Claymore), Rose; f; 49 (1883); 1/2; M; Wife; no 2250; Laguna Beach,
                                        Cal; no; Al. 21
2288;   "   Kenneth; m; 19 (7-16-12); 1/4; S; Son; no 2251; Laguna Beach, Cal; yes;
                                        Al. 4445
2289;   "   Fern R; f; 18 (10-22-12); 1/4; S; Dau; no 2252; Laguna Beach; Cal; yes;
                                        Al. 4521
2290;   "   Norma J; f; 16 (10-1-15); 1/4; S; Dau; no 2253; Laguna Beach, Cal; yes;
                                        An. 1141

N. E.   **GAY**, Harold; m; Head
2291;   (LeCompte), Julia; f; 24 (5-29-07); 1/2; m; Wife; yes 2674; yes; Al. 3749

2292; **GABE**, Ambrose; m; 41 (1-11-93); F; M; Head; yes 2254; yes; Al. 123
2293;   (Yellow); Eva; f; 29 (8-20-02); F; M; Wife; yes 2255; yes; Al. 189
2294;   "   Carl; m; 5 (9-9-28); F; S; Son; yes 2256; yes; An. 1147
2295;   "   Madeline; f; 1 (4-27-30); F; S; Dau; yes 2257; yes; An. 1150

2296; **GABE**, Baptiste; m; 68 (1864); F; M; Head; yes 2258; no; Al. 122
2297;   (Noheart), Josephine; f; 55 (1877); F; M; Wife; yes 2259; yes; Al. 3602
2298; Noheart, Frank; m; 21 (9-15-10); F; S; St-Son; yes 2260; yes; Al. 4129,
2299; Noheart, Albert; m; 15 (7-20-16); F; S; St-Son; yes 2261; yes; An. 1153

2300; **GABE**, Charles; m; 34 (1898); F; M; Head; yes 2262; yes; Al. 125

2301; **GABE**, George; m; 50 (1882); F; M; Head; yes 2263; yes; Al. 116
2302;   "   Helen E; f; 17 (1915); F; S; Dau; yes 2264; yes; An. 1156
2303;   "   Ella J; f; 9 (9-12-22); F; S; Dau; yes 2265; yes; An. 1157
2304;   "   Reuben; m; 14 (1-16-18); F; S; Son; yes 2266; yes; An. 1158

Census of the **Standing Rock** Reservation of the **Standing Rock** jurisdiction, as of **April 1**, 1932, taken by **E. D. Mossman**, Superintendent. South Dakota

KEY: Number; Surname, Given; Sex; Age at Last Birthday; Tribe (Standing Rock Sioux unless otherwise noted); Degree of Blood; Marital Status; Relationship to Head of Family; At Jurisdiction where enrolled (Yes or No); (If "No", where, if given); Ward (Yes or No); Allotment, Annuity and Identification Numbers.

2305; **GABE**, Joseph; m; 27 (2-15-05); F; M; Head; no 2267; Caryville[sic], NY; yes; Al. 127

2306; **GARTER**, John; m; 46 (1886); F; M; Head; yes 2268; no; Al. 1276
2307; (DeRockbraine), Mary Ann; f; 46 (1886); F; M; Wife; yes 2269; yes; Al. 1260
2308; " Florence; f; 15 (10-5-16); F; S; Dau; yes 2270; yes; Al. 4509
2309; " Solomon; m; 6 (3-8-25); F; S; Son; yes 2271; yes; An. 1162

2310; **GAYTON**, Claude R; m; 28 (10-22-04); 1/2; M; Head; no 2272; Aberdeen, Brown Co, SD; yes; Al. 1722
2311; (Hodgkinson), Emma; f; 26 (4-2-06); 1/4; M; Wife; no 2273; Aberdeen, Brown Co, SD; yes; Al. 2861
2312; " Waldo C; m; 2 (2-10-30); 3/8; S; Son; no 2274; Aberdeen, Brown Co, SD; yes; An. 1171

N. E. **GODFREY**, Frank; m; Head
2313; (Twiggs), Annie; f; 48 (1884); 1/2; M; Wife; yes 2275; no; Al. 3502
2314; " Norman; m; 19 (8-4-12); 1/4; S; Son; yes 2276; yes; Al. 4326
2315; " Rita M; f; 8 (8-9-23); 1/4; S; Dau; yes 2277; yes; An. 1213
2316; " Maxine; f; 15 (8-3-16); 1/4; S; Dau; yes 2278; yes; An. 1214
2317; " Thos E; m; 5 (3-12-27); 1/4; S; Son; yes 2279; yes; An. 1215

N. E. **GOINS**, Earl; m; Head
2318; (Whitebird), Gertrude; f; 42 (1890); F; M; Wife; yes 2280; yes; Al. 1317
2319; " Frank J; m; 1 (9-13-30); F; S; Son; yes 2281; yes; An. 1219
2320; Littlecrow, Joseph; m; 11 (7-7-20); F; St-Son; yes 2282; yes; An. 3472

2321; **GOODDOG**, William; m; 84 (1848); F; M; Head; yes 2283; yes; Al. 433
2322; (Takuyukasni), Mrs; f; 62 (1860); F; M; Wife; yes 2284; yes; Al. 3655

2323; **GOODEAGLE** (Beareagle), Annie; f; 47 (1885); F; M; Head; yes 2286; yes; Al. 3412

2324; **GOODEAGLE**, William; m; 38 (1893); F; M; Head; yes 2287; no; Al. 1329
2325; " Percy; m; 17 (8-26-14); F; S; Son; yes 2288; yes; Al. 4696
2326; " Josephine; f; 16 (1-16-16); F; S; Dau; yes 2289; yes; An. 1231
2327; " Daniel; m; 14 (11-6-17); F; S; Son; yes 2290; yes; An. 1232
2328; " Ethel; f; 7 (1-11-25); F; S; Dau; yes 2291; yes; An. 1233
2329; " Leon B; m; 4 (5-1-27); F; S; Son; yes 2292; yes; An. 1234

2330; **GOOD ELK** (Winyewinla), Mrs Martin; f; 73 (1859); F; Wd; Head; yes 2293; yes; Al. 3474

Census of the **Standing Rock** Reservation of the **Standing Rock** jurisdiction, as of **April 1**, **1932**, taken by **E. D. Mossman**, Superintendent. South Dakota

KEY: Number; Surname, Given; Sex; Age at Last Birthday; Tribe (Standing Rock Sioux unless otherwise noted); Degree of Blood; Marital Status; Relationship to Head of Family; At Jurisdiction where enrolled (Yes or No); (If "No", where, if given); Ward (Yes or No); Allotment, Annuity and Identification Numbers.

2331; **GOOD ELK**, Joseph; m; 45 (1887); F; M; Head; yes 2294; yes; Al. 435
2332; "   Joseph, Jr; m; 15 (1917); F; S; Son; yes 2295; yes; An. 1236
2333; "   Grace; f; 9 (12-17-22); F; S; Dau; yes 2296; yes; An. 1237

2334; **GOODFUR**, Felix; m; 66 (1866); F; M; Head; yes 2297; yes; Al. 35

2335; **GOODFUR**, Luke; m; 36 (1896); F; M; Head; yes 2298; no; Al. 36
2336;   (Redbird), Henrietta; f; 36 (1896); F; M; Wife; yes 2299; yes; Al. 287
2337; "   Mary; f; 10 (1-5-22); F; S; Dau; yes 2300; yes; An. 1242
2338; "   Lavina; f; 8 (6-12-23); F; S; Dau; yes 2301; yes; An. 1243
2339; "   Charlotte; f; 3/12 (12-1-31); F; S; Dau; yes; yes; An. 1244

2340; **GOODVOICEBULL**, Thomas; m; 55 (1877); F; M; Head; yes 2302; yes;
                                                                                Al. 208
2341;   (Bluecloud), Placida; f; 56 (1877); F; M; Wife; yes 2303; yes; Al. 3594

2342; **GRAHAM**, Mark W; m; 54 (1878); 1/2; S; Head; yes 2304; yes; Al. 513

2343; **GRAYEAGLE** (Bravethunder), Anna; f; 52 (1870); F; Wd; Head; yes 2305;
                                                                            yes; Al. 3326
2344;   "   Charles; m; 16 (1-29-16); F; S; Son; yes 2306; yes; An. 1318

2345; **GRAYEAGLE**, Clarence; m; 53 (1871); F; M; Head; yes 2307; no; Al. 1156
2346;   "   Maxine; f; 13 (3-1-19); F; S; Dau; yes 2308; yes; An. 1320

2347; **GRAYEAGLE**, Gabriel; m; 79 (1853); F; M: Head; yes 2309; yes; Al. 1148
2348;   (Winyanhanska), Mrs; f; 75 (1857); F; M; Wife; yes 2310; yes; Al. 1473

2349; **GRAYEAGLE**, John; m; 34 (7-13-98); F; M; Head; yes 2311; no; Al. 1153
2350;   (Thief), Cecelia; f; 31 (1901); F; M; Wife; yes 2312; yes; Al. 840
2351; "   Leonard; m; 12 (11-19-19); F; S; Son; yes 2313; yes; An. 1236
2352; "   Michael; m; 10 (4-3-21); F; S; Son; yes 2314; yes; An. 1327
2353; "   Marjorie; f; 9 (7-5-22); F; S; Dau; yes 2315; yes; An. 1328
2354; "   Elaine; f; 6 (1-2-26); F; S; Dau; yes 2316; yes; An. 1329

2355; **GRAYEAGLE**, Moses; m; 27 (10-4-04); F; M; Head; yes 2317; yes; Al. 1149

2356; **GRINDSTONE**, Dwight; m; 31 (1901); F; M; Head; yes 2318; yes; Al. 483
2357;   (Clark), Alice; f; 31 (10-10-1900); F; M; Wife; yes 2319; yes; Al. 2741
2358; "   Irene M; f; 8 (12-18-23); F; S; Dau; yes 2320; yes; An. 1341
2359; "   Adele F; f; 5 (7-19-26); F; S; Dau; yes 2321; yes; An. 1342

2360; **GRINDSTONE**, Frank; m; 38 (1894); F; S; Head; yes 2322; yes; Al.; 498

Census of the __Standing Rock__ Reservation of the __Standing Rock__ jurisdiction, as of __April 1__, 1932, taken by __E. D. Mossman__, Superintendent. South Dakota

KEY: Number; Surname, Given; Sex; Age at Last Birthday; Tribe (Standing Rock Sioux unless otherwise noted); Degree of Blood; Marital Status; Relationship to Head of Family; At Jurisdiction where enrolled (Yes or No); (If "No", where, if given); Ward (Yes or No); Allotment, Annuity and Identification Numbers.

2361; **GRINDSTONE**, George J; m; 25 (10-23-06); F; S; Head; yes 2323; yes;
Al. 928

2362; **GRINDSTONE**, John; m; 64 (1868); F; M; Head; yes 2324; yes; Al. 496
2363;   (Treetop), Mollie; f; 53 (1879); F; M; Wife; yes 2325; yes; Al. 3530
2364; Treetop, Margaret; f; 11 (1-17-21); F; S; St-Dau; yes 2327; yes; An. 1347

2365; **GRINDSTONE**, Paul; m; 58 (1874); F; M; Head; yes 2328; yes; Al. 517
2366;   (Longsteps), Bernadine; f; 53 (1879); F; M; Wife; yes 2329; yes; Al. 767

2367; **GRINDSTONE**, Stanton; m; 78 (1854); F; M; Head; yes 2330; yes; Al. 480
2368;   (Yellowhorse), Mrs; f; 61 (1871); F; M; Wife; yes 2331; yes; Al. 3174
2369;   "   John; m; 20 (6-25-11); F; S; Son; yes 2332; yes; Al. 4173

2370; **GROWLER**, Susan; f; 32 (3-18-1900); F; S; Head; yes 2333; yes; Al. 1032
2371;   "   John; m; 10 (5-9-21); F; S; Son; yes 2334; yes; An. 1365
2372;   "   Philomene; f; 7 (5-27-24); F; S; Dau; yes 2335; yes; An. 1364

N. E. **HAGER**, Fred; m; Head
2373;   (Low Dog), Louise; f; 50 (1882); F; M; Wife; yes 2336; no; Al. 722
2374;   "   Regina; f; 20 (6-6-11); 1/2; S; Dau; yes 2337; yes; Al. 4038
2375;   "   Alfred H; m; 19 (9-15-12); 1/2; S; Son; yes 2338; yes; Al. 4382

N. E. **HALIBURTON**, Roy; m; Head
2376;   (Taylor), Melda; f; 31 (3-9-01); 1/4; M; Wife; yes 2346; no; Al. 277
2377;   "   Marie; f; 3 (7-6-28); 1/8; S; Dau; yes 2347; yes; An. 1379

2378; **HAIRYCHIN**, Joachim; m; 50 (1882); F; M; Head; yes 2339; no; Al. 854
2379;   (DeRockbraine), Victoria; f; 39 (1893); F; M; Wife; yes 2340; yes; Al. 1254
2380;   "   Mary L; f; 10 (5-25-21); F; S; Dau; yes 2341; yes; An. 1373
2381;   "   Percy; m; 8 (8-8-23); F; S; Son; yes 2342; yes; An. 1374
2382;   "   Joseph; m; 6 (10-20-25); F; S; Son; yes 2343; yes; An. 1375
2383;   "   Cecelia; f; 4 (5-1-27); F; S; Dau; yes 2344; yes; An. 1376
2384;   "   Grace; f; 2 (4-26-29); F; S; Dau; yes 2345; yes; An. 1377

2385; **HAND**, George H; m; 31 (1-29-01); F; M; Head; yes 2348; yes; Al. 2503
2386;   "   Geo M; m; 11 (10-1620); F; S; Son; yes 2349; yes; An. 1413
2387;   "   Gertrude; f; 9 (4-5-22); F; S; Dau; yes 2350; yes; An. 1414
2388;   "   Marie; f; 7 (4-19-24); F; S; Dau; yes 51; yes; An. 1415
2389;   "   Elaine G; f; 2 (11-2-28); F; S; Dau; yes 2352; yes; An. 1416
2390;   "   Catherine; f; 1/12 (2-7-32); F; S; Dau; yes ---; yes; An. ---

2391; **HAND**, Philomene; f; 17 (6-18-14); F; S; Head; yes 3223; yes; Al. 4606
2392;   "   Henry L; m; 3/12 (12-19-32); F; S; Son; yes ---; yes; An. 142

Census of the **Standing Rock** Reservation of the **Standing Rock** jurisdiction, as of **April 1**, 1932, taken by **E. D. Mossman**, Superintendent. South Dakota

KEY: Number; Surname, Given; Sex; Age at Last Birthday; Tribe (Standing Rock Sioux unless otherwise noted); Degree of Blood; Marital Status; Relationship to Head of Family; At Jurisdiction where enrolled (Yes or No); (If "No", where, if given); Ward (Yes or No); Allotment, Annuity and Identification Numbers.

2393; **HAND**, Veremund; m; 61 (1871); F; M; Head; yes 2353; yes; Al. 850
2394; (Hand), Catherine; f; 54 (1878); F; M; Wife; yes 2354; yes; Al. 3189
2395; " Mary E; f; 20 (11-10-10); F; S; Dau; yes 2355; yes; Al. 4061
2396; " William; m; 16 (10-2-15); F; S; Son; yes 2356; yes; An. 1423
2397; " Russell; m; 14 (12-27-17); F; S; Son; yes 2357; yes; An. 1424

2398; **HANLEY**, George; m; 47 (1885); 1/2 F[sic]; M; Head; no 2358; Whereabouts unknown; no; Al. 2776

N. E. **HARRISON**, W J; m; Head
2399; (Kempton), Sarah; f; 58 (1874); 1/4; M; Wife; no 2361; Merced, Cal; yes; Al. 2802

2400; **HAS HORNS**, Benjamin; m; 51 (1881); F; M; Head; yes 2362; no; Al. 381
2401; (Wayankela), Mrs; f; 67 (1865); F; M; Wife; yes 2363; yes; Al. 133 9[sic]

2402; **HAS HORNS**, Frank; m; 57 (1875); F; M; Head; yes 2364; yes; Al. 383

2403; **HAS HORNS**, Henry; m; 30 (12-1-01); F; M; Head; yes 2366; yes; Al. 1167
2404; (Standing Near), Annie; f; 27 (1903); F; M; Wife; yes 2367; yes; Al. 4590

2405; **HAS HORNS**, Owen; m; 52 (1870); F; M; Head; yes 2368; yes; Al. 376
2406; (Whiteman), Lizzie; f; 44 (1888); F; M; Wife; yes 2369; yes; Al. 3753
2407; " Daniel; m; 17 (8-12-14); F; S; Son; yes 2370; yes; Al. 4628
2408; " Pearl; f; 14 (5-11-17); F; S; Dau; yes 2371; yes; An. 1452
2409; " Minnie; f; 11 (7-20-20); F; S; Dau; yes 2372; yes; An. 1453
2410; " Mary C; f; 9 (9-12-22); F; S; Dau; yes 2373; yes; An. 1453
2411; " Irvin C; m; 5 (8-28-26); F; S; Son; yes 2374; yes; An. 1454

2412; **HAWK**, Bede; m; 61 (1871); F; M; Head; yes 2375; no; Al. 2944
2413; (Tawacinawastewin), Mrs; f; 61 (1871); F; M; Wife; yes 2376; yes; Al. 3401
2414; " Stephen; m; 17 (5-24-14); F; S; Son; yes 2377; yes; Al. 4597

2415; **HAWK**, Duncan; m; 36 (1895); F; M; Head; yes 2378; yes; Al. 308

2416; **HAWK**, Edward; m; 56 (1876); F; M; Head; yes 2379; yes; Al. 304
2417; " Ione M; f; 5 (3-9-27); F; S; Dau; yes 2380; yes; An. 1466

2418; **HAWK**, Enoch; m; 22 (2-8-10); F; S; Head; yes 2381; yes; Al. 4008

2419; **HAWK**, George; m; 20 (4-23-10); F; S; Alone; yes 2382; yes; Al. 3980

2420; **HAWK**, Victoria; f; 27 (6-13-04); F; S; Head; yes 2383; yes; Al. 163

KEY: Number; Surname, Given; Sex; Age at Last Birthday; Tribe (Standing Rock Sioux unless otherwise noted); Degree of Blood; Marital Status; Relationship to Head of Family; At Jurisdiction where enrolled (Yes or No); (If "No", where, if given); Ward (Yes or No); Allotment, Annuity and Identification Numbers.

2421; **HAWK**, William; m; 54 (1878); F; M; Head; yes 2384; yes; Al. 161
2422;　(Swiftcloud), Annie; f; 52 (1880); F; M; Wife; yes 2385; yes; Al. 3433
2423;　" Andrew; m; 18 (6-1313); F; S; Son; yes 2386; yes; An. 1471
2424;　" Lizzie; f; 15 (12-27-16); F; S; Dau; yes 2387; yes; An. 1472
2425;　" Edith; f; 12 (2-12-20); F; S; Dau; yes 2388; yes; An. 1473

2426; **HAWKBEAR**, Annie; f; 80 (1852); F; S; Head; yes 2389; yes; Al. 3629

2427; **HAWKBEAR**, Harry; m; 59 (1873); F; M; Head; yes 2390; yes; Al. 2025
2428;　(Twoshield), Jane; f; 57 (1875); F; M; Wife; yes 2391; yes; Al. 3135

2429; **HAWKBEAR**, Josephine; f; 24 (8-25-08); F; S; Head; yes 2392; yes;
Al. 3745

2430; **HAWKEAGLE**, John; m; 48 (1884); F; M; Head; yes 2393; yes; Al. 105
2431;　(Calf), Aloysia; f; 46 (1876); F; M; Wife; yes 2394; yes; Al. 666

2432; **HAWKEAGLE** (Hohewin), Mrs Samuel; f; 67 (1865); F; Wd; Head; yes
2395; yes; Al. 3452

2433; **HAYES**, David; m; 23 (2-11-09); F; S; Head; yes 2396; yes; Al. 3863

2434; **HAYES**, Gideon; m; 30 (9-22-01); F; M; Head; yes 2397; yes; Al. 373
2435;　(Wankicun), Lulu; f; 29 (5-1-02); F; M; Wife; yes 2398; yes; Al. 1030
2436;　" Fannie H; f; 11 (2-26-21); F; S; Dau; yes 2399; yes; An. 1489
2437;　" Raymond; m; 9 (1-13-23); F; S; Son; yes 2400; yes; An. 1490
2438;　" Helen; f; 7 (12-27-24); F; S; Dau; yes 2401; yes; An. 1491
2439;　" Marie E; f; 3 (3-31-29); F; S; Dau; yes 2402; yes; An. 1492

2440; **HAYES**, Julia; f; 68 (1864); F; S; Head; yes 2403; yes; Al. 370

2441; **HENRY**, Charles; m; 38 (1894); F; M; Head; yes 2404; no; Al. 384
2442;　(Dogman), Elizabeth; f; 34 (1898); F; M; Wife; yes 2405; yes; Al. 905

2443; **HER GOOD HORSE** (Tasunkawastewin); f; 69 (1863); F; Wd; Head;
yes 2406; yes; Al. 602

2444; **HIGHCAT**, Bertha; f; 42 (1890); F; Wd; Head; yes 2408; yes; Al. 3027
2445;　" Margaret; f; 16 (6-25-15); F; S; Dau; yes 2409; yes; An. 1497

2446; **HIGHCAT**, Rose; f; 20 (2-3-12); F; S; Head; yes 2410; yes; Al. 4263
2447;　" Louis; m; 1 (1-12-31); F; S; Son; yes 2411; yes; An. 1500

2448; **HIGHCAT**, Mary; f; 25 (1-29-06); F; S; Head; yes 2412; yes; Al. 1448

Census of the **Standing Rock** Reservation of the **Standing Rock** jurisdiction, as of **April 1**, 1932, taken by **E. D. Mossman**, Superintendent. South Dakota

KEY: Number; Surname, Given; Sex; Age at Last Birthday; Tribe (Standing Rock Sioux unless otherwise noted); Degree of Blood; Marital Status; Relationship to Head of Family; At Jurisdiction where enrolled (Yes or No); (If "No", where, if given); Ward (Yes or No); Allotment, Annuity and Identification Numbers.

2449; **HIGHDOG** (Marpiya), Mrs; f; 74 (1858); F; Wd; Head; yes 2413; yes; Al. 3498

2450; **HIGHEAGLE**, Raymond; m; 26 (6-19-05); 1/2; M; Head; yes 2414; yes; Al. 564

2451;   " Raymond C; m; 4 (5-2-27); 1/2; S; Son; yes 2415; yes; An. 1503

2452; **HIGHEAGLE**, Robert; m; 59 (1873); 1/2; Wd; Head; yes 2416; no; Al. 562

2453; **HIGHEAGLE**, Robert, Jr; m; 24 (3-1-08); 1/2; S; Head; yes 2418; yes; Al. 2530

2454; **HISTHUNDERSHIELD**, Julia; f; 37 (1895); F; S; Head; yes 2419; yes; Al. 413

2455;   " Bertha; f; 10 (6-4-21); F; S; Dau; yes 2420; yes; An. 1516
2456;   " Traversie; m; 6 (6-28-25); F; S; Son; yes 2421; yes; An. 1517

2457; **HIS WHITE HORSE**; m; 81 (1851); F; M; Head; yes 2422; yes; Al. 943
2458;   (Goodwoman), Mrs.; f; 75 (1857); F; M; Wife; yes 2423; yes; Al. 3055

~~2459~~; **HOEHNER**, Robert; m; Head
2460;   (Cadotte), Susan; f; 50 (1882); 1/2; M; Wife; yes 2424; no; Al. 91
2461;   " Irene; f; 15 (7-7-16); 1/4; S; Dau; yes 2425; yes; An. 1528
2462;   " Robert V; m; 10 (4-25-21); 1/4; S; Son; yes 2426; yes; An. 1530
2463;   " Bernard; m; 8 (3-27-24); 1/4; S; Son; yes 2427; yes; An. 1531
2464; Cadotte, Adeline; f; 14 (1917); 1/4; S; niece; yes 2428; yes; An. 1529

2465; **HOHEKTE**, Angela; f; 14 (1917); F; S; Alone; yes 2429; yes; An. 1532

2466; **HOHEKTE**, Henry; m; 38 (1894); F; M; Head; yes 2430; no; Al. 988
2467;   (Gayton), Amy; f; 48 (1884); 1/2 F[sic]; M; Wife; yes 2431; no; Al. 1725
2468;   " Henry W; m; 8 (9-27-24); 3/4; S; Son; yes 2432; yes; An. 1535

2469; **HOHEKTE**, Joseph; m; 43 (5-25-89); F; M; Head; yes 2433; no; Al. 987
2470;   " Thelma; f; 14 (12-15-17); F; S; Dau; yes 2434; yes; An. 1537
2471;   " Phoebe; f; 12 (12-9-19) F; S; Dau; yes 2435; yes; An. 1538
2472;   " Percy E; m; 4 (2-8-28); F; S; Son; yes 2436; yes; An. 1539
2473;   " Beatrice; f; 1 (6-11-30); F; S; Dau; yes 2437; yes; An. 1540

2474; **HOHEKTE**, Lawrence; m; 65 (1867); F; Wd; Head; yes 2438; no; Al. 986

2475; **HOLLOW**, Michael; m; 26 (1-24-05); F; M; Head; yes 2439; yes; An. 1546
2476;   (Goodeagle), Olivia; f; 20 (8-22-11); F; M; Wife; yes 2440; yes; Al. 4200
2477;   " Joseph E; m; 8/12 (7-5-31); F; S; Son; yes ---; yes; An. 1548

Census of the __Standing Rock__ Reservation of the __Standing Rock__ jurisdiction, as of __April 1__, 1932, taken by __E. D. Mossman__, Superintendent. South Dakota

KEY: Number; Surname, Given; Sex; Age at Last Birthday; Tribe (Standing Rock Sioux unless otherwise noted); Degree of Blood; Marital Status; Relationship to Head of Family; At Jurisdiction where enrolled (Yes or No); (If "No", where, if given); Ward (Yes or No); Allotment, Annuity and Identification Numbers.

2478; **HOLY WHITEMAN** (Nahotowinla), Mrs; f; 75 (1857); F; Wd; Head; yes 2441; yes; Al. 3485

2479; **HORSETHIEF**, Amos; m; 78 (1854); F; Wd; Head; yes 2442; yes; Al. 73

2480; **HORSETHIEF**, Jasper; m; 42 (4-17-90); F; M; Head; yes 2443; yes; Al. 74
2481;   (LaMonte), Emma; f; 42 (1890); F; M; Wife; yes 2444; yes; Al. 96
2482;   " Cordelia; f; 15 (12-23-16); F; S; Dau; yes 2445; yes; An. 1563
2483;   " Gertrude; f; 11 (4-11-20); F; S; Dau; yes 2446; yes; An. 1564
2484;   " Mary C; f; 9 (1-31-23); F; S; Dau; yes 2447; yes; An. 1565
2485;   " Walter N; m; 8 (12-31-23); F; S; Son; yes 2448; yes; An. 1566
2486;   " Clifford; m; 2 (5-13-29); F; S; Son; yes 2449; yes; An. 1567

2487; **HOURIGAN**, Charles; m; 24 (3-5-08); 1/2; S; Head; no 2450; Mobridge, Walworth Co, SD; yes; Al. 2871

N. E. **HOURIGAN**, James; M; Head
2488;   (Archambault), Emma; f; 62 (1870); 1/2; M; Wife; yes 2451; yes; Al. 4238
2489;   " Clara R; f; 20 (9-1-11); 1/4; S; Dau; yes; 2452; yes; Al. 4238

2490; **HOURIGAN**, Harry; m; 26 (5-4-05); 1/4; S; Head; yes 2453; yes; Al. 2870

2491; **HOURIGAN**, John; m; 35 (1897); 1/4; M; Head; yes 2454; no; Al. 2868
2492;   " Viola; f; 9 (5-22-22); 1/8; S; Dau; yes 2455; yes; An. 1573

2493; **HOURIGAN**, Lawrence; m; 38 (1894); 1/4; M; Head; yes 2456; no; Al. 2866
2494;   " Daisy M; f; 16 (10-15-15); 1/8; S; Dau; yes 2457; yes; An. 1575
2495;   " Henrietta; f; 13 (4-16-18); 1/8; S; Dau; yes 2458; yes; An. 1576

2496; **HOURIGAN**, Sidney; m; 29 (5-16-03); 1/4; S; Head; yes 2460; no; Al. 2869

2497; **HOWARD**, Amos; m; 34 (1898); 1/2; S; Head; yes 2461; yes; Al. 155

2498; **HOWARD**, Charles; m; 46 (1886); 1/2; M; Head; yes 2462; no; Al. 1105
2499;   " Luella; f; 19 (3-10-12); 1/4; S; Dau; yes 2463; yes; Al. 4273
2500;   " Charles D; m; 16 (4-24-15); 1/4; S; Son; yes 2464; yes; An. 1582

2501; **HOWARD**, Edward; m; 32 (5-1-1900); 1/2; S; Head; no; 2465; Yankton Res, Wagner, SD; no; Al. 4227

2502; **HOWARD**, James; m; 50 (1882); 1/2; M; Head; yes 2466; no; Al. 321
2503; Ulysses; m; 19 (1-3-13); 1/4; S; Son; yes 2467; yes; An. 1585

Census of the **Standing Rock** Reservation of the **Standing Rock** jurisdiction, as of **April 1**, 1932, taken by **E. D. Mossman**, Superintendent. South Dakota

KEY: Number; Surname, Given; Sex; Age at Last Birthday; Tribe (Standing Rock Sioux unless otherwise noted); Degree of Blood; Marital Status; Relationship to Head of Family; At Jurisdiction where enrolled (Yes or No); (If "No", where, if given); Ward (Yes or No); Allotment, Annuity and Identification Numbers.

2504; **HOWARD**, Jerome; m; 26 (10-4-04); 1/2; M; Head; yes 2468; yes; Al. 313
2505; (Shields), Matilda E; f; 20 (6-13-11); F; M; Wife; yes 3245; yes; Al. 4155

2506; **HOWARD**, John D; m; 48 (1884); 1/2; M; Head; no 2469; Fort Yuma, Cal;
No; Al. 1103
2507; " Virgil C; m; 4 (2-3-28); 5/8; S; Son; no ---; Fort Yuma, Cal; yes; An. 595

2508; **HOWARD** (Loves War), Kate; f; 27 (12-22-04); 1/2; M; Head; yes 2470; yes;
Al. 1538
2509; " Bernice; f; 4 (6-17-27); 1/2; S; Dau; yes 2471; yes; An. 2641

2510; **HOWARD**, Levi; m; 27 (10-4-04); 1/2; S; Head; no 2472; Yankton Res, SD;
yes; Al. 4228

2511; **HOWARD**, Lydia; f; 22 (9-5-09); F; S; Head; yes 2473; yes; Al. 4009
2512; " Niel[sic] C; m; 11/12 (4-5-31); F; S; Son; yes 2474; yes; An. 1600

2513; **HOWARD**, Michael; m; 38 (10-15-94); 1/2; M; Head; no 2474; Yankton Res,
SD; yes; Al. 4224
2514; " Edith; f; 14 (5-20-17); 1/2; S; Dau; no 2475; Yankton Res, SD; yes;
An. 1604

2515; **HOWARD**, Richard; m; 53 (1879); 1/2; M; Head; yes 2476; no; Al. 318
2516; (Bloodyknife), Emma; f; 47 (1883); F; M; Wife; yes 2477; yes; Al. 344

2517; **HOWARD**, Robert; m; 36 (2-10-96); 1/2; M; Head; no 2478; Yankton Res,
SD; yes; Al. 4226
2518; " Wayne R; m; 10 (6-25-21); 1/2; S; Son; no 2479; Yankton Res, SD;
yes; An. 1606
2519; " Gerald J; m; 9 (6-25-22); 1/2; S; Son; no 2480; Yankton Res, SD; yes;
An. 1607

2520; **HOWARD**, Samuel; m; 53 (1879); 1/2; M; Head; yes 2481; yes; Al. 154
2521; (Standing Bear), Agnes; f; 81 (1851; 1/2; M; Wife; yes 2482; yes; Al.
3632

2522; **HOWARD**, William; m; 23 (3-27-09); 1/2; S; Head; yes 2483; yes; Al. 3894

[sic] **HUBER**, Charles; m; Head;
2523; (Badger), Philomene; f; 43 (1889); F; M; Wife; no 1654; Fort Berthold
Res, ND; yes; Al. 1863

Census of the __Standing Rock__ Reservation of the __Standing Rock__ jurisdiction, as of __April 1__, 1932, taken by __E. D. Mossman__, Superintendent. South Dakota

KEY: Number; Surname, Given; Sex; Age at Last Birthday; Tribe (Standing Rock Sioux unless otherwise noted); Degree of Blood; Marital Status; Relationship to Head of Family; At Jurisdiction where enrolled (Yes or No); (If "No", where, if given); Ward (Yes or No); Allotment, Annuity and Identification Numbers.

2524; **HUGHES**, Jessie M; f; 20 (8-30-11); 1/4; S; Head; no 2484; Gridley, Butte Co, Cal; yes; Al. 4203

2525; " Odessie; f; 18 (6-8-13); 1/4; S; sister; no 2485; Gridley, Butte Co, Cal; yes; Al. 4441

N. E. **IGO**, C. T.; m; Head

2526; (McLaughlin), Ramona; f; 22 (1-12-10); 1/4; M; Wife; no 2935; Rochester, Minn; yes Al. 4026

2527; **INDUSTRIOUS**, Lawrence; m; 65 (1867); F; M; Head; yes 2486; yes; Al. 3880

2528; (Industrious), Alice; F; 65 (1867); F; M; Wife; yes 2487; yes; Al. 3881

N. E. **INGERSOLL**, Lynn; m; Head

2529; (Kempton), Bernice; f; 40 (11-4-92); 1/4; M; Wife; no 2488; Terry, Prairie Co, Mont; no; Al. 2818

2530; " Richard; m; 14 (8-27-17); 1/8; S; Son; no 2489; Terry; Prairie Co, Mont; yes; An. 1623

N. E. **IORNS**[sic], Ben; m; Head

2531; (Waggoner), Luzetta; f; 31 (12-6-1900); 1/4; M; Wife; yes 2490; no; Al. 2826

2532; " June; f; 11 (6-7-20); 1/8; S; Dau; yes 2491; yes; An. 1625

2533; " Ernest F; m; 10 (8-8-21); 1/8; S; Son; yes 2492; yes; An. 1626

2534; " William D; m; 7 (11-16-24); 1/8; S; Son; yes 2493; yes; An. 1627

2535; " Iris May; f; 5 (6-11-26); 1/8; S; Dau; yes 2494; yes; An. 1628

2536; **IRON**, John; m; 31 (8-19-1900); F; M; Head; yes 2495; yes; Al. 792

2537; (Redlegs), Elizabeth; f; 28 (12-20-03); F; M; Wife; yes 2496; yes; Al. 1227

2538; " Ernest; m; 6 (6-3-25); F; S; Son; yes 2497; yes; An. 1641

N. E. **IRON**, Walter; m; Head

2539; (Old Bull), Annie; f; 55 (1877); F; M; Wife; yes 2498; yes; Al. 3392

2540; **IRONCLOUD**, Thomas; m; 8 (12-24-24); F; S; Alone; yes 2500; yes; An. 1649

2541; " Simon; m; 4 (10-26-27); F; S; Alone; yes 2501; yes; An. 1650

2542; " Vermund[sic]; m; 2 (7-30-29); F; S; Alone; yes 2502; yes; An. 1651

2543; **IRONEYES**, Jerome; m; 71 (1861); F; Wd; Head; yes 2504; yes; Al. 191

2544; **IRONEYES**, Louise; f; 82 (1850); F; S; Head; yes 2505; yes; Al. 3587

2545; **IRONHOOP**; m; 81 (1851); F; Wd; Head; yes 2506; yes; Al. 621

Census of the **Standing Rock** Reservation of the **Standing Rock** jurisdiction, as of **April 1**, 1932, taken by **E. D. Mossman**, Superintendent. South Dakota

KEY: Number; Surname, Given; Sex; Age at Last Birthday; Tribe (Standing Rock Sioux unless otherwise noted); Degree of Blood; Marital Status; Relationship to Head of Family; At Jurisdiction where enrolled (Yes or No); (If "No", where, if given); Ward (Yes or No); Allotment, Annuity and Identification Numbers.

2546; **IRONHORN**, Charles; m; 48 (1884); F; M; Head; yes; 2507; no; Al. 622
2547; (Rabbithead) Rose; f; 52 (1880); F; M; Wife; yes 2508; yes; Al. 1648
2548; " Sophie; f; 3-5-17); F; S; Dau; yes 2509; yes; An. 1659
2549; " Elizabeth; f; 10 (12-29-21); F; S; Dau; yes 2510; yes; An. 1660
2550; " Mable; f; 6 (5-9-25); F; S; Dau; yes 2511; yes; An. 1661
2551; Grayspotted, Mark; m; 20 (11-26-11); F; S; St-Son; yes 2512; yes; Al. 4250
2552; Rabbithead; Lee John; m; 14 (11-20-17); F; S; St-Son; yes 2513; yes;
An. 1663

2553; **IRONHORN**, Charles; m; 79 (1853); F; Head; yes 2514; yes; Al. 623
2554; (Ironhorn Elk), Mary; f; 63 (1869); F; M; Wife; yes 2515; yes; Al. 3651

2555; **IRONMAN**, Joseph; m; 49 (1883); F; M; Head; yes 2515; yes; Al. 3651

2556; **IRONNECKLACE**, Eugene; m; 66 (1866); F; M; Head; yes 2519; yes;
Al. 288
2557; (Ironnecklace), Mrs; f; 63 (1869); F; M; Wife; yes 2520; yes; Al. 3599

2558; **IRONSHIELD**, Henry; m; 60 (1872); F; Wd; Head; yes 2521; no; Al. 2412
2559; " Wallace; m; 11 (10-26-20); F; S; Son; yes 2522; yes; An. 1696
2560; Runsaway From Him, George; m; 17 (10-18-14); F; S; St-Son; yes 223; yes;
An. 4668

2561; **IRONTHUNDER**, John; m; 44 (1888); F; M; Head; yes 2524; yes; Al. 1301
2562; " Margaret; f; 14 (7-6-17); F; S; Dau; yes 2525; yes; An. 1707
2563; " Ethel; f; 12 (10-1-19); F; S; Dau; yes 2526; yes; An. 1708
2564; " Mary K; f; 11 (11-25-20); F; S; Dau; yes 2527; yes; An. 2329

2565; **IRONWHITEMAN**, Antoine; m; 46 (1886); F; M; Head; yes 2528; no;
Al. 3895
2566; (Looking Elk), Bessie; f; 50 (1882); F; M; Wife; yes 2529; yes; Al. 981
2567; " " Viola; f; 10 (9-21-22); F; S; Dau; yes 2531; yes; An. 1713
2568; " " Etta J; f; 8 (5-20-22); F; S; Dau; yes 2532; yes; An. 1712

2569; **IRONWINGS**, James; m; 52 (1880); F; Wd; Head; no 2533; Cheyenne
River Res, SD; yes; Al. 1089

2570; **IRONWINGS**, Mary L; f; 23 (12-24-08); F; S; Head; yes 2534; yes; Al. 3700

2571; **IRONWINGS**, Paul; m; 67 (1865); F; M; Head; yes 2535; yes; Al. 725
2572; (Ironwings) Louisa; 54 (1878); F; M; Wife; yes 2536; yes; Al. 3678

Census of the __Standing Rock__ Reservation of the __Standing Rock__ jurisdiction, as of __April 1__, 19**32**, taken by __E. D. Mossman__, Superintendent. South Dakota

KEY: Number; Surname, Given; Sex; Age at Last Birthday; Tribe (Standing Rock Sioux unless otherwise noted); Degree of Blood; Marital Status; Relationship to Head of Family; At Jurisdiction where enrolled (Yes or No); (If "No", where, if given); Ward (Yes or No); Allotment, Annuity and Identification Numbers.

N. E. **JOHNSON**, Owen; m; Head
2573;   (Harris), Alice R; f; 23 (8-14-08); 1/2; M; Wife; no 2359; Kansas City, Kan; yes; Al. 3453
2574;   " Dorothy; f; 2 (2-25-30); 1/2; S; Dau; no 2360; Kansas City, Kan; yes; Al. 1728

2575; **JOHNSON**, Silas; m; 12 (5-14-19); F; S; Alone; no 2537; Crow Creek Res SD; yes; An. 1729

2576; **JORDAN**, John; m; 38 (1894); 1/2; M; Head; yes 2538; no; Al. 1615
2577;   (Defender), Susie; f; 36 (1896); F; M; Wife; yes 2539; yes; Al. 741
2578;   " Peter; m; 11 (2-7-24); F; S; Son; yes 2540; yes; An. 1740
2579;   " Walter; m; 4 (5-1-27); F; S; Son; yes 2541; yes; An. 1741
2580;   " Delores; f; 3 (12-8-28); F; S; Dau; yes 2542; yes; An. 1742
2581;   " Elsie; f; 10/12 (5-28-31); F; S; Dau; yes ---; yes; An. 1743

2582; **JORDAN**, Joseph; m; 36 (1896); 1/2; M; Head; yes 2543; no; Al. 1615
2583;   " Genevieve; f; 4 (1-16-28); 1/2; S; Dau; yes 2544; yes; An. 1745

2584; **JORDAN**, Peter; m; 11 (1921); 1/4; S; Alone; yes 2545; yes; An. 1746

2585; **KEEFE**, Frank; m; 50 (1881); 1/4; S; Head; no 2546; Pollock, Campbell Co, SD; no; Al. 2853

2586; **KELLEY**, Helen L; f; 31 (8-7-1900); 1/4; S; no 2547; St Paul, Ramsey Co, Minn; yes; Al. 1467

2587; **KELLEY**, Theodore; m; 30 (4-1-02); 1/4; M; Head; no 2549; St Paul, Ramsey Co, Minn; yes; Al. 1468

2588; **KELLEY**, Walter; m; 34 (1898); 1/4; M; Head; no 2550; St Paul, Ramsey Co, Minn; yes; Al. 1466

2589; **KEMPTON**, Albert H; m; 25 (10-16-06); 1/8; M; Head; no 2551; Terry, Prairie Co, Mont; no; Al. 2815

2590; **KEMPTON**, Bernard; m; 62 (1870); 1/8; M; Head; no 2552; Terry, Prairie Co, Mont; no; Al. 2817
2591;   " Gerald; m; 19 (6-30-12); 1/16; S; Son; no 2553; Terry; Prairie Co, Mont; yes; Al. 4346
2592;   " John M; m; 18 (2-11-14); 1/16; S; Son; no 2554; Terry, Prairie Co, Mont; yes; Al. 4716
2593;   " Barney E; m; 14 (9-23-17); 11/16; S; Son; no 2555; Terry; Prairie Co, Mont; yes; An. 1782

Census of the **Standing Rock** Reservation of the **Standing Rock** jurisdiction, as of **April 1**, 1932, taken by **E. D. Mossman**, Superintendent. South Dakota

KEY: Number; Surname, Given; Sex; Age at Last Birthday; Tribe (Standing Rock Sioux unless otherwise noted); Degree of Blood; Marital Status; Relationship to Head of Family; At Jurisdiction where enrolled (Yes or No); (If "No", where, if given); Ward (Yes or No); Allotment, Annuity and Identification Numbers.

2594; Kempton, Edmund; m; 18 (11-14-13); 1/16; S; Son; no 2556; Terry, Prairie Co, Mont; yes; Al. 4538

2595; **KEMPTON**, Doris; f; 20 (12-311-10); 1/8; S; Alone; no 2557; Merced, Merced Co, Cal; yes; Al. 3995

2596; **KEMPTON**, Edith; f; 28 (3-16-04); 1/8; S; Head; yes 2558; yes; Al. 2812

2597; **KEMPTON**, Helen; f; 24 (2-7-08); 1/8; S; Head; yes[sic] 2559; Terry, Prairie Co, Mont; yes; Al. 2816

2598; **KEMPTON**, Henry; m; 61 (12-30-71); 1/4; M; Head; yes 2560; no; Al. 2814
2599; " Oswald; m; 18 (7-19-13; 1/8; S; Son; yes 2561; yes; Al. 4507
2600; " Freida L; f; 13 (8-19-18); 1/8; S; Dau; yes 2562; yes; An. 1788

2601; **KEMPTON**, Iris A; f; 29 (11-14-02); 1/8; S; Head; yes 2563; yes; Al. 2807

2602; **KEMPTON**, James; m; 20 (5-15-10)[sic];1/8; S; Head; no 2564; Terry, Prairie Co, Mont; yes; Al. 4053

2603; **KEMPTON**, James G; m; 53 (9-18-79); 1/4; M; Head; no 2565; Merced, Merced Co, Cal; no; Al. 2820
2604; " Willis L; m; 20 (3-27-12); 1/8; S; Son; no 2566; Merced; Merced Co; Cal; yes; Al. 4325
2605; " James, Jr; m; 17 (6-26-14); 1/8; S; Son; no 2567; Merced, Merced Co, Cal; yes; Al. 4710
2606; " Ethel; f; 15 (9-19-16); 1/8; S; Dau; no 2568; Merced, Merced Co, Cal; yes; An. 1794

2607; **KEMPTON**, Joseph; m; 40 (12-22-92); 1/4; M; Head; no 2569; Exeter, Fulone Co, Cal; no; Al. 2301
2608; " Olive; f; 21 (1-23-11); 1/8; S; Dau; no 2570; Exeter, Fulone Co, Cal; yes; Al. 4652
2609; " Joseph G; m; 18 (6-15-13); 1/8; S; Son; no 2571; Exeter, Fulone Co, Cal; yes; Al. 4454

2610; **KEMPTON**, Oliver; m; 23 (7-7-09); 1/8; M; Head; no 2572; Terry, Prairie Co, Mont; yes; Al. 806
2611; " Oliver D; m; 7 (3-17-25); 1/16; S; Son; no 2573; Terry, Prairie Co, Mont; yes; An. 1797

2612; **KEMPTON**, Sanford; m; 57 (10-16-75); 1/4; M; Head; yes 2574; no; Al. 2803
2613; " Sidney; m; 20 (10-6-11); 1/8; W; Son; yes 2575; yes; Al. 4262

101

Census of the **Standing Rock** Reservation of the **Standing Rock** jurisdiction, as of **April 1**, 1932, taken by **E. D. Mossman**, Superintendent. South Dakota

KEY: Number; Surname, Given; Sex; Age at Last Birthday; Tribe (Standing Rock Sioux unless otherwise noted); Degree of Blood; Marital Status; Relationship to Head of Family; At Jurisdiction where enrolled (Yes or No); (If "No", where, if given); Ward (Yes or No); Allotment, Annuity and Identification Numbers.

2614;   "   Vivian; f; 17 (6-6-14); 1/8; S; Dau; yes; 2576; yes; Al. 4602

2615;   "   Norman P; m; 13 (5-13-18); 1/8; S; Son; yes; 2577; yes; An. 1802

2616; **KEMPTON**, Wesley W; m; 35 (1897); 1/4; M; Head; yes 2578; no; Al. 2805

2617;   "   Boyce R; m; 2 (10-22-29); 1/8; S; Son; yes 2579; yes; An. 1807

2618; **KILLS AT NIGHT**, Samuel; m; 65 (1867); F; Wd; Head; yes 2580; yes; Al. 1061

2619; **KILLS CROW**, Annie; f; 27 (4-8-04); F; S; Head; no 2582; Pine Ridge Res, SD; yes; Al. 444

2620; **KILLS CROW**, Anslem; m; 67 (1865); F; M; Head; yes 2583; yes; Al. 402

2621;   (Kills Crow), Alice; f; 57 (1874); F; M; Wife; yes 2584; yes; Al. 3293

2622; **KILLS CROW**, George; m; 24 (8-15-07); F; S; Head; no 2585; Pine Ridge Res, SD; yes; Al. 2521

2623; **KILLS CROW**, Matthew; m; 25 (12-10-96); F; M; Head; yes 2586; yes; Al. 404

2624;   (Shields), Beauty; f; 27 (1-7-04); F; M; Wife; yes 2587; yes; Al. 1114

2625;   "   Iralyn; f; 8 (3-18-23); F; S; Dau; yes 2588; yes; Al. 445

2626; **KILLS CROW INDIAN**, Andrew; m; 29 (4-10-02); F; M; Head; yes 2590; yes; Al. 1086

2627;   (Whitehorse), Esther; f; 25 (4-6-06); F; M; Wife; yes 2591; yes; Al. 958

2628;   "   Leola; f; 6 (5-10-25); F; S; Dau; yes; 2592; yes; An. 1837

2629;   "   Lester; m; 4 (6-30-27); F; S; Son; yes 2593; yes; An. 1838

2630;   "   Fielding; m; 2 (8-12-29); F; S; Son; yes 2594; yes; An. 1839

2631; **KILLSCROWINDIAN**, John; m; 49 (1883); F; M; Head; yes 2595; yes; Al. 1077

2632; (Unknown), Julia; f; 49 (1883); F; M; Wife; yes 2596; yes; Al. 3338

2633;   "   Fannie; f; 10 (2-7-20); F; S; Dau; yes 2597; yes; An. 1842

2634;   "   Josiah; m; 8 (5-12-23); F; S; Son; yes 2598; yes; An. 1843

2635;   "   Cecelia; f; 5 (9-30-26); F; S; Dau; yes 2599; yes; An. 1844

2636; **KILLSCROWINDIAN**, Theodore; m; 26; (9-20-05); F; S; Head; yes 2600; yes; Al. 1087

2637; **KILLS PRETTY ENEMY**; m; 77 (1855); F; M; Head; yes 2601; yes; Al. 1024

2638;   "   Ambrose T; m; 17 (5-23-14); F; S; Son; yes 2602; yes; Al. 4598

Census of the **Standing Rock** Reservation of the **Standing Rock** jurisdiction, as of **April 1**, 1932, taken by **E. D. Mossman**, Superintendent. South Dakota

KEY: Number; Surname, Given; Sex; Age at Last Birthday; Tribe (Standing Rock Sioux unless otherwise noted); Degree of Blood; Marital Status; Relationship to Head of Family; At Jurisdiction where enrolled (Yes or No); (If "No", where, if given); Ward (Yes or No); Allotment, Annuity and Identification Numbers.

2639; **KILLS PRETTY ENEMY**, Felix; m; 23 (11-28-09); F; M; Head; yes 2603; yes; Al. 1025

2640; (Irondog), Alice; f; 33 (1899); F; M; Wife; yes 2604; yes; Al. 1292

2641; " Gilbert; m; 10 (1-21-22); F; S; Son; yes 2505; yes; An. 1851

2642; " Carmille; f; 6 (1925); F; S; Dau; yes 2606; yes; An. 1852

2642; **KILLS SPOTTED**, Emma; f; 37 (1-13-95); F; S; Head; yes 2608; yes; Al. 2334

2644; **KNOCKSTHEMDOWN**, William; m; 57 (1874); F; M; Head; yes 2614; no; Al. 2931

2645; (Unknown), Jane; f; 61 (1871); F; M; Wife; yes 2615; yes; Al. 3452

2646; " James; m; 17 (1914); F; S; Son; yes 2616; yes; An. 1872

2647; **LaFROMBOIS**, Antoine; m; 35 (1897); 1/2; M; Head; yes 2617; no; Al. 422

2648; (Yellow), Virginia; f; 26 (1-15-06); F; M; Wife; yes 2618; yes; Al. 919

2649; " John F; m; 4 (12-26-27); 3/4; S; Son; yes 2619; yes; An. 1872

2650; **LaFROMBOIS**, Frank; m; 64 (1868); 1/2; M; Head; yes 2620; no; Al. 420

2651; (Baine), Sallie; f; 57 (1875); 1/2; M; Wife; yes 2621; no; Al. 3457

2652; **LaFROMBOIS**, Joseph; m; 18 (7-28-13); 1/2; S; Son; yes 2622; yes; Al. 4547

2653; **LaFROMBOIS**, Lillian; f; 24 (6-30-07); 1/2; S; Head; yes 2623; yes; Al. 924

2654; **LaFROMBOIS**, Marjorie; f; 20 (12-13-10); 1/2; S; Alone; yes 2624; yes; Al. 4106

2655; **LaFROMBOIS**, Rose; f; 38 (4-15-93); 1/2; S; Head; no 2625; St Joseph, Stearns Co, Minn; no; Al. 424

2656; **LAMBERT** (Takes The Shield), Angela; f; 34 (1898); F; Wd; Head; no 2626; Fort Peck Res, Mont; yes; Al. 615

2657; **LaMONTE**, Edward; m; 32 (1890); 1/2; M; Head; no 2627; no; Al. 95

2658; " Collins, m; 15 (11-6-16); 1/2; S; Son; no 2628; yes; An. 1900

N. E. **LAWRENCE;** Frank; m; Head

2659; (Agard), Mary; f; 43 (1889); 3/4; M; Wife; yes 2630; no; Al. 1421

2660; " John; m; 20 (3-28-11); 3/8; S; Son; yes 2631; yes; Al. 4087

2661; " Louis; m; 19 (9-7-12); 3/8; S; Son; yes 2632; yes; Al. 4348

2662; " Henry; m; 17 (3-5-15); 3/8; S; Son; yes 2633; yes; Al. 4698

2663; " Frank B; m; 18 (1913); 3/8; S; Son; yes; 2633[sic]; yes; Al. 450222

Census of the __Standing Rock__ Reservation of the __Standing Rock__ jurisdiction, as of __April 1__, 1932, taken by __E. D. Mossman__, Superintendent. South Dakota

2664;   "   Joseph; m; 15 (11-2-16;3/8; S; Son; yes 2634; yes; An. 1908

2665;   "   Benedict; m; 13 (8-29-18); 3/8; S; Son; yes; 2635; yes; An. 1909

2666;   "   Julia; f; 12 (1-21-20); 3/8; S; Dau; yes; 2636; yes; An. 1910

2667;   "   Victoria; f; 11 (6-28-21); 3/8; S; Dau; yes 2637; yes; An. 1911

2668;   "   Helen; f; 6 (3-20-25); 3/8; S; Dau; yes 2638; yes; An. 1912

2669;   "   Arthur; m; 5 (12-15-26); 3/8; S; Son; yes 2639; yes; An. 1913

2670;   **LAWRENCE**, Robert; m; 22 (3-13-10); 3/8; S; Head; yes 2640; yes; Al. 3974

2671;   **LEAF**, Joseph; m; 38 (1892); F; M; Head; yes 2641; no; Al. 1194

2672;   (Brought), Mary; f; 42 (1889); F; M; Wife; yes 2642; yes; Al. 2924

2673;   "   Lizzie; f; 20 (12-15-11); F; S; Dau; yes 2643; yes; Al. 4252

2674;   "   Josephine; f; 15 (12-22-16); F; S; Dau; yes 2644; yes; An. 1916

2675;   "   Emily; f; 10 (1-22-22); F; S; Dau; yes 2645; yes; An. 1917

2676;   Shortbaldhead, Bonnie; f; 13 (3-16-19);F; S; St-Dau; yes 2646; yes; An. 147

2677;   **LEANDOG** (Ptesanamaniwin), Mrs Leo; f; 58 (1874); F; M; Head; yes 2649; yes; Al. 3517

2678;   "   Cecelia; f; 14 (2-18-17); F; S; Dau; yes 2650; yes; An. 1921

2679;   **LEAN WARRIOR**; m; 78 (1854); F; Wd; Head; yes 2651; yes; Al. 2275

2680;   **LeCOMPTE**, Casper O; m; 41 (1891); 1/2; M; Head; no 2652; Cheyenne River Res, SD; no; Al. 5

2681;   **LeCOMPTE**, Cyril; m; 44 (1888); 1/2; M; Head; yes 2653; no; Al. 4

2682;   **LeCOMPTE**, Dennis; m; 27 (9-27-04); 1/2; S; Head; no 2654; Lead, Lawrence Co, SD; yes; Al. 785

2683;   "   Luella E; f; 11/12 (4-13-31); 1/2; S; Dau; no ---; Lead, Lawrence Co, SD; yes; An. 1927

2685;   **LeCOMPTE**, Edward; m; 51 (1881); 1/2; M; Head; yes 2655; no; Al. 2[?]

2686;   "   Martina; f; 13 (3-31-19); 1/2; S; Dau; yes 2656; yes; An. 1929

2687;   **LeCOMPTE**, Elmer; m; 32 (9-22-1900); 1/2; M; Head; yes 2657; yes; Al. 783

2688;   "   Vivian F; f; 12 (9-22-19); 1/2; S; Dau; yes 2658; yes; An. 1931

2689;   "   Doraldine; f; 11 (12-29-21); 1/2; S; Dau; yes 2659; yes; An. 1932

2690;   "   Bernice; f; 7 (12-27-24); 1/2; S; Dau; yes 2660; yes; An. 1933

2691;   "   Darlene; f; 4 (4-14-27); 1/2; S; Dau; yes 2661; yes; An. 1934

2692;   "   Elmer, Jr; m; 2 (4-12 or 22-29); 1/2; S; Son; yes 2662; yes; An. 1935

2693;   "   Clovis; m; 1 (2-17-31); 1/2; S; Son; yes 2663; yes; An. 1936

Census of the **Standing Rock** Reservation of the **Standing Rock** jurisdiction, as of **April 1**, 1932, taken by **E. D. Mossman**, Superintendent. South Dakota

KEY: Number; Surname, Given; Sex; Age at Last Birthday; Tribe (Standing Rock Sioux unless otherwise noted); Degree of Blood; Marital Status; Relationship to Head of Family; At Jurisdiction where enrolled (Yes or No); (If "No", where, if given); Ward (Yes or No); Allotment, Annuity and Identification Numbers.

2694; **LeCOMPTE**, Frank; m; 35 (4-29-95); 1/2; M; Head; yes 2664; yes; Al. 6
2695;   "   Mildred; f; 12 (2-26-19); 1/2; S; Dau; yes 2665; yes; An. 1938
2696;   "   Geo F; m; 10 (2-13-22); 1/2; S; Son; yes 2667; yes; An. 1940
2697;   "   Magdaline   f; 8 (8-3-23); 1/2; S; Dau; yes 2668; yes; An. 1941
2698;   "   Bernice; f; 7 (2-10-25); 1/2; S; Dau; yes 2669; yes; An. 1942

2699; **LeCOMPTE**, Gerald; m; 33 (1-9-99); 1/2; M; Head; no 2670; Salt Lake City,
                                               Salt Lake Co, UT; no; Al. 782
2700;   "   Ellsworth; m; 7 (3-9-25); 1/2; S; Head; yes 2672; yes; Al. 11

2702; **LeCOMPTE**, John; m; 28 (4-19-04); 1/2; S; Head; yes 2673; yes; Al. 12

2703; **LeCOMPTE**, Lawrence; m; 33 (4-12-99); 1/2; S; Head; yes 2675; yes; Al. 9

2704; **LeCOMPTE**, Louis, Jr; m; 46 (1886); 1/2; M; Head; yes 2676; yes; Al. 3

2705; **LeCOMPTE**, Obed; m; 30 (10-13-01); 1/2; M; Head; yes 2677; no; Al. 10
2706; (Skinner), Cecelia; f; 26 (1-25-06); F; M; Wife; yes 2678; yes; Al. 3760
2707;   "   Virgil E; m; 8 (11-10-24); 3/4; S; Son; yes 2679; yes; An. 1952
2708;   "   Adeline   f; 6 (11-16-25); 3/4; S; Dau; yes 2680; yes; An. 1953
2709;   "   Doris D; f; 3 (3-9-28); 3/4; S; Dau; yes 2681; yes; An. 1954,

2710; **LeCOMPTE**, Regina; f; 23 (7-23-09); 1/2; S; Head; yes 2682; yes; Al. 3924

2711; **LeCOMPTE**, Theodore; m; 22 (9-27-09); 1/4; S; Head; no 2683; South Bend,
                                          St Joseph Co, Minn; yes; Al. 3911

2712; **LeCOMPTE**, Vital; m; 57 (1875); 1/4; M; Head; no 2684; Mobridge,
                                          Walworth Co, SD; no; Al. 780

2713; **LeCOMPTE**, Vital, Jr; m; 29 (11-30-02); 1/4; S; Head; no 2685; Bloomfield,
                                          Knox Co, Neb; yes; Al. 784

2714; **LeCOMPTE**, Walter U; m; 24 (2-4-08); 1/4; S; Head; yes 2686; yes;
                                          Al. 3790

N. E. **LEE**, Carl; m; Head
2715;   (Kempton), Hedvig; f; 23 (8-22-09); 1/8; m; Wife; no 2687; Terry,
                                          Prairie Co, Mont; yes; Al. 3996

N. E. **LEE**, Mark; m; Head
2716;   (Mentz), Evaline R; f; 23 (8-18-09); 1/2; M; Wife; no 2689; Stillwell, OK;
                                          yes; Al. 3910

Census of the __Standing Rock__ Reservation of the __Standing Rock__ jurisdiction, as of __April 1__, 1932, taken by __E. D. Mossman__, Superintendent. South Dakota

KEY: Number; Surname, Given; Sex; Age at Last Birthday; Tribe (Standing Rock Sioux unless otherwise noted); Degree of Blood; Marital Status; Relationship to Head of Family; At Jurisdiction where enrolled (Yes or No); (If "No", where, if given); Ward (Yes or No); Allotment, Annuity and Identification Numbers.

2717; **LENDS HIS HORSES**, Emma; f; 53 (1879); F; S; Head; yes 2688; yes; Al. 3698

2718; **LEONARD**, Mildred; f; 24 (4-14-07); 1/4; S; Head; no 2690; Chicago, Cook Co, IL; yes; Al. 2864

2719; **LITTLEBEAR**, John; m; 50 (1882); F; M; Head; yes 2694; no; Al. 1243
2720;   (Firecloud), Etta; f; 39 (1893); F; M; Wife; yes 2695; yes; Al. 939
2721;   "   Eva; f; 17 (1-7-15); F; S; Dau; yes 2696; yes; Al. 4674
2722;   "   Florence; f; 14 (5-29-17); F; S; Dau; yes 2697; yes; An. 1971
2723;   "   Marie; f; 11 (9-20-20); F; S; Dau; yes 2698; yes; An. 1972
2724;   "   Ramona; f; 9 (2-7-23); F; S; Dau; yes 2699; yes; An. 1973
2725;   "   Whitney; m; 7 (5-24-25); F; S; Son; yes 2700; yes; An. 1974
2726;   "   Lydia; f; 3 (7-11-28); F; S; Dau; yes 2701; yes; An. 1975
2727;   "   Melvin; m; 1 (2-23-30); F; S; Son; yes 2702; yes; An. 1976

2728; **LITTLEBEAR**, Joseph; m; 37 (1895); F; M; Head; yes 2703; yes; Al. 17
2729; (Bearsheart), Helen; f; 30 (2-5-02); F; M; Wife; yes 2704; yes; Al. 198
2730;   "   Fremont J; m; 4 (9-18-27); F; S; Son; yes 2705; yes; An. 1979
2731;   "   Rufus; m; 2 (9-16-29); F; S; Son; yes 2706; yes; An. 1980
2732;   "   Cora Fay; f; 9/12 (7-6-31); F; S; Dau; yes none; yes; An. 1981

2733; **LITTLEDOG**, John; m; 32 (3-29-1900); F; M; Head; yes 2710; yes; Al. 966
2734;   (Loves War), Julia; f; 31 (1901); F; M; Wife; yes 2711; yes; Al. 3783
2735;   "   Ramona; f; 9 (9-3-21); F; S; Dau; yes 2712; yes; An. 1990
2736;   "   Irene f; 3 (8-2-28); F; S; Dau; yes 2713; yes; An. 1991
2737;   "   Beatrice; f; 11/12 (4-4-31); F; S; Dau; yes ---; yes; An. 1992

2738; **LITTLEDOG**, Martin; m; 42 (1890); F; M; Head; yes 2714; no; Al. 967
2739;   (Kills Crow), Sarah; f; 31 (1901); F; M; Wife; yes 2715; yes; Al. 888
2740;   "   Norman; m; 7 (2-22-25); F; S; Son; yes 2716; yes; An. 1995
2741;   "   Ross; m; 9 (6-18-22); F; S; Son; yes 2717; yes; An. 1996
2742;   "   Martin, Jr; m; 5 (2-14-27); F; S; Son; yes 2718; yes; An. 1997
2743;   "   Meliner; m; 3 (3-21-29); F; S; Son; yes 2719; yes; An. 1998
2744;   "   Hermus R; m; 9/12 (6-7-31); F; S; Son; yes ---; yes; An. 1999

2745; **LITTLE EAGLE**, Edward; m; 35 (1897); F; M; Head; yes 2372; yes; Al. 1371
2746; (DeRockbraine), Margaret; f; 26 (9-20-05); F; M; Wife; yes 2721; yes; Al. 1265
2747;   "   Harry N; m; 5 (10-20-26); F; S; Son; yes 2722; yes; An. 2002
2748;   "   Mary Ellen; f; 5/12 (10-12-31); F; S; Dau; yes ---; yes; An. 2003

Census of the **Standing Rock** Reservation of the **Standing Rock** jurisdiction, as of **April 1**, 1932, taken by **E. D. Mossman**, Superintendent.   South Dakota

KEY: Number; Surname, Given; Sex; Age at Last Birthday; Tribe (Standing Rock Sioux unless otherwise noted); Degree of Blood; Marital Status; Relationship to Head of Family; At Jurisdiction where enrolled (Yes or No); (If "No", where, if given); Ward (Yes or No); Allotment, Annuity and Identification Numbers.

2749; **LITTLE EAGLE**, George; m; 81 (1851); F; Wd; Head; yes 2723; yes; Al. 1366

2750; **LITTLE EAGLE**, Leo; m; 38 (1895); F; M; Head; yes 2724; yes; Al. 1369
2751;   "   Evelyn; f; 8 (1-10-24); F; S; Dau; yes 2725; yes; An. 2006
2752;   "   Ruth; f; 2 (5-11-28); F; S; Dau; yes 2726; yes; An. 2007

N. E.   **LITTLE EAGLE**, Sam; m; Head
2753;   (Kills Pretty Enemy), Mary; f; 23 (1-4-09); F; M; Wife; yes 2727; yes; Al. 3897
2754;   "   Peter; m; 4 (5-2-27); F; S; Son; yes 2728; yes; An. 2009

2755; **LITTLE HORSE**, Elizabeth; f; 48 (1884); F; S; Head; yes 2729; yes; Al. 843

2756; **LITTLEMOON**; m; 76 (1856); F; M; Head; yes 2730; yes; Al. 213
2757;   (Redeagle), Mrs; f; 69 (1863); F; M; Wife; yes 2731; yes; Al. 3613

2758; **LITTLEMOON**, Andrew; m; 33 (11-24-99); F; M; Head; yes 2732; yes; Al. 214
2759;   (Redeagle), Agnes; f; 31 (1901); F; M; Wife; yes 2733; yes; Al. 587
2760;   "   Amanda; f; 4 (4-10-27); F; S; Dau; yes 2734; yes; An. 2016
2761;   "   Diana; f; 2 (2-11-29); F; S; Dau; yes 2735; yes; An. 2014
2762; Madbear, Celestine; f; 7 (1-7-25); F; S; St-Dau; yes 2736; yes; An. 2017

2763; **LITTLE SOLDIER**, Eugene; m; 70 (1862); F; Wd; Head; yes 2737; yes; Al. 2561

2764; **LONE ELK**, Jesse; m; 26 ((3-10-05); F; M; Head; yes 2738; yes; Al. 1303
2765;   (Primeau), May V; f; 18 (5-12-13); F; M; Wife; yes 2739; yes; Al. 4437

2766; **LONE ELK**, John; m; 56 (1876); F; M; Head; yes 2740; yes; Al. 1299
2767;   (Lone Elk), Agatha; f; 62 (1870); F; M; Wife; yes 2741; yes; Al. 3360

2768; **LONE ELK**, Samuel; m; 24 (7-4-08); F; M; Head; yes 2742; yes; Al. 3361
2769;   "   Ambrose; m; 2 (5-15-29); F; S; Son; yes 2743; yes; An. 2031
2770;   "   Andrew; m; 1 (3-2-31); F; S; Son; yes ---; yes; An. 2032

2771; **LONEMAN**, Benedict; m; 50 (1882); F; M; Head; yes 2744; no; Al. 138
2772;   (Striped Cloud), Louisa; f; 55 (1877); F; M; Wife; yes 2745; yes; Al. 802

2773; **LONGBULL**, Baptiste; m; 37 (1895); F; S; Head; yes 2747; yes; Al. 42

2774; **LONGBULL**, Charles; m; 64 (1868); F; M; Head; yes 2748; yes; Al. 4283
2775;   (Longbull), Lizzie; f; 59 (1873); F; M; Wife; yes 2749; yes; Al. 4284

Census of the **Standing Rock** Reservation of the **Standing Rock** jurisdiction, as of **April 1**, 1932, taken by **E. D. Mossman**, Superintendent. South Dakota

KEY: Number; Surname, Given; Sex; Age at Last Birthday; Tribe (Standing Rock Sioux unless otherwise noted); Degree of Blood; Marital Status; Relationship to Head of Family; At Jurisdiction where enrolled (Yes or No); (If "No", where, if given); Ward (Yes or No); Allotment, Annuity and Identification Numbers.

2776; **LONGBULL**, Dominick; m; 66 (1866); F; M; Head; yes 2750; no; Al. 41

2777; (Eagle On High), Sadie; f; 61 (1871); F; M; Wife; yes 2751; yes; Al. 3597

2778; **LONGBULL**, Joseph; m; 54 (1878); F; M; Head; yes 2752; no; Al. 39

2779; **LONGBULL**, Paul; m; 63 (1869); F; M; Head; yes 2753; yes; Al. 40

2780; (Topaicagewin), Jennie; f; 61 (1871); F; M; Wife; yes 2754; yes; Al. 3359

2781; **LONGBULL**, Sarah; f; 20 (9-1-10); F; S; Alone; yes 2755; yes; Al. 4046

2782; **LONGBULL**, Sophie; f; 26 (6-17-05); F; S; Head; yes 2756; yes; Al. 43

2783; **LONGCHASE**, John; m; 61 (1871); F; M; Head; no 2757; Fort Peck Res, Mont; yes; Al. 951

2784; (Mongram), Bessie; f; 40 (1892); F; M; Wife; no 2758; Fort Peck Res, Mont; yes; Al. 1245

2785; " Samuel; m; 18 (4-11-13); F; S; Son; no 2759; Fort Peck Res, Mont; yes; An. 2051

2786; " Leo; m; 13 (6-22-18); F; S; Son; no 2760; Fort Peck Res, Mont; yes; An. 2048

2787; " Paul; m; 9 (4-26-22); F; S; Son; no 2761; Fort Peck Res, Mont; yes; An. 2049

2788; " Abraham; m; 8 (5-20-25); F; S; Son; no 2762; Fort Peck Res, NT; yes; An. 2050

2789; **LONGCHASE**, Solomon; m; 28 (1-15-04); F; M; Head; yes 2763; yes; Al. 952

2790; (Bruce), Rose; f; 30 (7-12-10); 1/2; M; Wife; yes 2764; yes; Al. 4131

2791; " Cecelia; f; 2 (11-10-29); 3/4; S; Dau; yes 2765; yes; An. 2054

2792; **LONGELK**, Julian; m; 42 (1890); F; M; Head; yes 2766; no; Al. 487

2793; " Angus; m; 16 (3-15-16); F; S; Son; yes 2767; yes; An. 2056

2794; " Chauncey; m; 6 (7-15-25); F; S; Son; yes 2768; yes; An. 2057

2795; " Trivian; f; 3 (7-27-28); F; S; Dau; yes 2769; yes; An. 2058

2796; **LONGFEATHER**, Charles; m; 71 (1861); F; M; Head; yes 2770; no; Al. 968

2797; (Tokicawin), Mrs.; f; 68 (1864); F; M; Wife; yes 2771; yes; Al. 3115

2798; **LONGFEATHER**, Rose; 30 (9-20-01); F; Div; Head; yes 2772; yes; Al. 871

2799; **LONGFEATHER**, Samuel; m; 28 (3-18-04); F; Div; Head; yes 2773; yes; Al. 972

Census of the **Standing Rock** Reservation of the **Standing Rock** jurisdiction, as of **April 1**, 1932, taken by **E. D. Mossman**, Superintendent. South Dakota

KEY: Number; Surname, Given; Sex; Age at Last Birthday; Tribe (Standing Rock Sioux unless otherwise noted); Degree of Blood; Marital Status; Relationship to Head of Family; At Jurisdiction where enrolled (Yes or No); (If "No", where, if given); Ward (Yes or No); Allotment, Annuity and Identification Numbers.

2800; **LONGFEATHER**, William; m; 31 (5-4-1900); F; S; Head; yes 2774; yes; Al. 971

2801; **LOOKING BACK**, Charles; m; 55 (1877); F; M; Head; yes 2775; no; Al. 366

2802; (Bear At Bay), Mrs; f; 67 (1865); F; M; Wife; yes 2776; yes; Al. 1018

2803; **LOOKING BACK**, George; m; 61 (1871); F; M; Head; yes 2777; no; Al. 360

2804; (Ausotapiwin), Sallie; f; 58 (1874); F; M; Wife; yes 2778; yes; Al. 3299

2805; **LOOKING BACK** (White Cow), Mrs; f; 79 (1853); F; Wd; Head; yes 2779; yes; Al. 238

2806; **LOOKINGBACK**, Simon; m; 42 (1890); F; M; Head; yes 2780); no; Al. 364

2807; (Skinner), Kate; f; 40 (1893); F; M; Wife; yes 2781; yes; Al. 218

2808; " Lizzie; f; 17 (7-20-14); F; S; Dau; yes 2782; yes; Al. 4694

2809; " Raymond; m; 12 (1-2-21); F; S; Son; yes 2783; yes; An. 2071

2810; " Melda; f; 8 (4-29-23); F; S; Dau; yes 2784; yes; An. 2072

2811; " Christina; f; 3 (12-27-28); F; S; Dau; yes 2785; yes; An. 2073

2812; " Virgil; m; 9/12 (6-16-31); F; S; Son; yes none; yes; An. 2074

2813; **LOOKING ELK**, Oliver, Jr; m; 48 (1884); F; M; Head; yes 2786; no; Al. 950

2814; (Bluelips), Gertrude; f; 40 (1892); F; M; Wife; yes 2787; yes; Al. 1662

2815; " Lena; f; 7 (3-18-25); F; S; Dau; yes; 2788; yes; An. 2077

2816; " Melvin J; m; 2 (2-5-30); F; S; Son; yes 2789; yes; An. 2078

2817; **LOOKING ELK**, Oliver, Sr; m; 87 (1845); F; M; Head; yes 2790; yes; Al. 979

2818; **LOOKINGHORSE**, Louis; m; 55 (1877); F; M; Head; yes 2792; yes; Al. 1026

2819; (Lookinghorse), Elizabeth; f; 58 (1874); F; M; Wife; yes 2793; yes; Al. 3483

2820; **LOOKINGHORSE**, Isaac; m; 17 (2-4-15); F; S; Head; yes 2794; yes; Al. 4686

2821; **LOOKING HORSE**, Thomas; m; 44 (1888); F; S; Head; no 2795; Eagle Butte, Dewey Co; SD; yes; Al. 273

2822; **LOVES THE WAR**, Henry; m; 40 (1892); F; M; Head; yes 2798; no; Al. 241

2823; (Waters), Jessie; f; 33 (1899); F; M; Wife; yes 2799; yes; Al. 521

KEY: Number; Surname, Given; Sex; Age at Last Birthday; Tribe (Standing Rock Sioux unless otherwise noted); Degree of Blood; Marital Status; Relationship to Head of Family; At Jurisdiction where enrolled (Yes or No); (If "No", where, if given); Ward (Yes or No); Allotment, Annuity and Identification Numbers.

2824;   "   Joseph; m; 3 (4-13-28); F; S; Son; yes 2800; yes; An. 2096
2825;   "   Romaine; f; 1 (6-8-30); F; S; Dau; yes 2801; yes; An. 2097

2826;   **LOVES THE WAR**, James; m; 53 (1879); F; M; Head; yes 2802; yes;
                                                                                    Al. 3782
2827;   (Bloodyknife), Kate; f; 50 (1882); F; M; Wife; yes 2803; yes Al. 3633
2828;   "   James R; m; 17 (4-7-14); F; S; Son; yes 2804; yes; Al. 4581
2829;   "   Vine   m; 12 (1-20-20); F; S; Son; yes 2805; yes; An. 2101

2830;   **LOVES THE WAR**, Louis; m; 45 (1886); F; M; Head; yes 2808; yes; Al. 239
2831;   (Eagle); f; 47 (1884); F; M; Wife; yes 2809; yes; Al. 3635
2832;   "   Nellie; f; 15 (5-27-16); F; S; Dau; yes 2810; yes; An. 1755
2833;   "   Eugenia; f; 13 (5-20-18); F; S; Dau; yes 2811; yes; An. 1756

2834;   **LOWDOG**, Henry; m; 48 (1884); F; M; Head; yes 2812; yes; Al. 799
2835;   "   Augustine; f; 11 (8-17-21); F; S; Dau; yes 2813; yes; An. 2104

2836;   **LOWDOG**, Joshua; m; 84 (1848); F; Wd; Head; yes 2814; yes; Al. 720

2837;   **LOWELL**, Luke; m; 46 (1886); F; Wd; Head; yes; 2815; no; Al. 721

2838;   **MADBEAR**, Robert; m; 43 (1888); 1/2; S; Head; yes 2816; yes; Al. 670

2839;   **MAJHOR**[sic], Gilbert; m; 50 (1882); 1/2; M; Head; yes 2817; no; Al. 531
2840;   "   William; m; 19 (6-12-12); 1/4; S; Son; yes 2818; yes; Al. 4309
2841;   "   Joseph; m; 18 (6-25-13); 1/4; S; Son; yes 2819; yes; Al. 4440
2842;   "   Clay R; m; 16 (10-23-15); 1/4; S; Son; yes 2820; yes; An. 2119
2843;   "   Esther L; f; 15 (11-14-16); 1/4; S; Dau; yes 2821; yes; An. 2120
2844;   "   Alice L; f; 11 (9-19-20); 1/4; S; Dau; yes 2822; yes; An. 2121
2845;   "   Viola; f; 9 (4-6-22); 1/4; S; Dau; yes 2823; yes; An. 2122
2846;   "   Robert; m; 7 (4-6-24); 1/4; S; Son; yes 2824; yes; An. 2123
2847;   "   Clifford; m; 6 (12-15-25); 1/4; S; Son; yes 2825; yes; An. 2124
2848;   "   Theodore; m; 4 (2-1-28); 1/4; S; Son; yes 2826; yes; An. 2125

2849;   **MAKASAN** (Noise), Mrs William; f; 73 (1859); F; Wd; Head; yes 2827; yes;
                                                                                    Al. 2332

2850;   **MAKES TROUBLE**, August; m; 71 (1861); F; M; Head; yes 2828; yes;
                                                                                    Al. 1526
2851;   (Canopa), Mrs; f; 61 (1871); F; M; Wife; yes 2829; yes; Al. 3281
2852;   "   Nellie; f; 19 (9-8-12); F; S; Dau; yes 2830; yes; Al. 4339

Census of the **Standing Rock** Reservation of the **Standing Rock** jurisdiction, as of **April 1**, 1932, taken by **E. D. Mossman**, Superintendent. South Dakota

KEY: Number; Surname, Given; Sex; Age at Last Birthday; Tribe (Standing Rock Sioux unless otherwise noted); Degree of Blood; Marital Status; Relationship to Head of Family; At Jurisdiction where enrolled (Yes or No); (If "No", where, if given); Ward (Yes or No); Allotment, Annuity and Identification Numbers.

2853; **MAKES TROUBLE**, James; m; 38 (1894); F; M; Head; yes 2831; yes; Al. 1528

2854; Lorraine; f; 9 (7-17-22); F; S; Dau; yes 2832; yes; An. 2134

2855; **MALE BEAR**; m; 69 (1889[sic]); F; M: Head; yes 2833; yes; Al. 1052
2856; " Annie; f; 74 (1858); F; M; Wife; yes 2834; yes; Al. 3446

2857; **MANNING**, Gilbert; m; 30 (6-17-02); 1/2; M; Head; no 2835; Portland, Multnoman[sic] Co, OR; yes; Al. 539
2859; (Archambault), Mae E; f; 30 (5-16-01); 1/2; M; Wife; no 2837; Portland, Multnoman Co, OR; no; Al. 1412
2860; " Nora M; f; 9 (8-14-22); 1/2; S; Dau; no 2838; Portland, Multnoman Co, OR; yes; An. 2141

2861; **MANY ELKS**; m; 75 (1857); F; Wd; Head; yes 2839; yes; Al. 1034

2862; **MANY DEEDS**, Clinton; m; 24 (2-15-08); F; S; Head; no 2841; Leavenworth, Kan; yes; Al. 3335

2863; **MANY DEEDS**, Edmund; m; 37 (1895); F; M; Head; yes 2841; no; Al. 1138
2864; (Higheagle), Mary J; f; 33 (6-27-99); 1/2; M; Wife; yes 2842; yes; Al. 563
2865; " Mary M; f; 13 (7-5-18); 3/4; S; Dau; yes 2843; yes; An. 2145
2866; " Lloyd; m; 8 (8-1-23); 3/4; S; Son; yes 2844; yes; An. 2147
2867; " Edmund; m; 10 (7-13-21); 3/4; S; Son; yes 2845; yes; An. 2147

2868; **MANY DEEDS**, Stanton; m; 52 (1870); F; M; Head; yes 2846; no; Al. 1137
2869; (Many Deeds), Nora; f; 57 (1875); F; M; Wife; yes 2847; yes; Al. 3334
2870; " Myrtle; f; 14 (11-21-17); F; S; Dau; yes 2849; yes; An. 2150
2871; " Juanita; f; 11 (1-12-21); F; S; Dau; yes 2850; yes; An. 2151

2872; **MANY HORSES**, Francis; m; 41 (3-20-91); F; M; Head; yes 2851; yes; Al. 323
2873; (Bearcatches), Louisa; f; 41 (1891); F; M; Wife; yes 2852; yes; Al. 463
2874; " Virgil; m; 11 (7-1-20); F; S; Son; yes 2853; yes; An. 2159
2875; " Seraphine; f; 5 (10-26-26); F; S; Dau; yes 2854; yes; An. 2160
2876; " Martha; f; 2 (12-11-28); F; S; Dau; yes 2855; yes; An. 2161
2877; " Lucille; f; 1 (4-13-31); F; S; Dau; yes none; yes; An. 2162

2878; **MANY HORSES**, Francis; m; 68 (1864); F; M; Head; yes 2856; yes; Al. 605
2879; (Snow), Cecelia; f; 53 (1879); F; M; Wife; yes 2857; yes; Al. 3669
2880; " Joseph; m; 11 (3-12-21); F; S; Son; yes 2858; yes; An. 2165
2881; " Jennie; f; 7 (10-16-23); F; S; Dau; yes 2859; yes; An. 2166

Census of the **Standing Rock** Reservation of the **Standing Rock** jurisdiction, as of **April 1**, 1932, taken by **E. D. Mossman**, Superintendent. South Dakota

KEY: Number; Surname, Given; Sex; Age at Last Birthday; Tribe (Standing Rock Sioux unless otherwise noted); Degree of Blood; Marital Status; Relationship to Head of Family; At Jurisdiction where enrolled (Yes or No); (If "No", where, if given); Ward (Yes or No); Allotment, Annuity and Identification Numbers.

2882; **MARSH**, Andrew; m; 26 (3-17-05); 1/4; S; Head; yes 2860; no; Al. 558

2883; **MARSH**, Joseph; m; 39 (3-9-93); 1/4; S; Head; no 2861; Rochester, Olmsted Co, Minn; no; Al. 560

2884; **MARSH**, Miles; m; 25 (7-26-06); 1/4; S; Head; yes 2862; yes; Al. 2862

2885; **MARSHALL**, Albert; m; 45 (1887); F; M; Head; yes 2863; yes; Al. 1551
2886; (Walking Elk), Louisa; f; 23 (4-22-08); F; M; Wife; yes 2864; yes; Al. 2519
2887; " Bertha; f; 6 (3-23-26); F; S; Dau; yes 2865; yes; An. 2181
2888; " Joseph R; m; 3 (9-27-28); F; S; Son; yes 2866; yes; An. 2182
2889; " Theodore; m; 1 (6-25-30); F; S; Son; yes 2867; yes; An. 2183

2890; **MARSHALL**, Charles; m; 72 (1860); F; M; Head; yes 2868; yes; Al. 1548
2891; (Marshall), Mary; f; 63 (1869); F; M; Wife; yes 2869; yes; Al. 3079

2892; **MARSHALL**, Joseph; m; 39 (1893); F; S; Head; yes 2870; Al. 1550

2893; **MARSHALL**, Robert; m; 26 (8-15-04); F; S; Head; yes 2871; yes; Al. 1552

2894; **MARTIN**, Frank; m; 54 (1878); F; M; Head; yes 2872; yes; Al. 628
2895; (Brought), Mary; f; 69 (1863); F; M; Wife; yes 2873; yes; Al. 865
2896; " Mary M; f; 16 (4-5-15); F; S; Dau; yes 2874; yes; An. 2195
2897; " Cecelia; f; 15 (10-26-16); F; S; Dau; yes 2875; yes; An. 2196
2898; " Catherine; f; 14 (3-22-18); F; S; Dau; yes 2876; yes; An. 2197
2899; " Theodore; m; 12 (1-28-20); F; S; Son; yes 2877; yes; An. 2198
2900; " Henry; m; 4 (6-26-27); F; S; Son; yes 2878; yes; An. 2199
2901; " Alfreda R; f; 3 (2-25-29); F; S; Dau; yes 2879; yes; An. 2200

2902; **MARTIN**, Jerome; m; 21 (5-30-10); F; S; Head; yes 2880; yes; Al. 4170

N. E. **MARTIN**, Frank; m; Head
2903; (Ireland), Julia; f; 28 (3-1-04); F; M; Wife; yes 2881; yes; Al. 2737

2904; **MARTIN** (Martin), Margaret; f; 57 (1875); F; Wd; Head; yes 2883; yes; Al. 3591
2905; " Sidney; m; 19 (3-9-12); F; S; Son; yes 2884; yes; Al. 4315
2906; " Esther; f; 17 (10-15-14); F; S; Dau; yes 2885; yes; Al. 4655

2907; **MARTIN**, Julia; f; 17 (11-28-14); F; S; Alone; yes 2886; yes; Al. 4669

2908; **MARTIN**, Maurice; m; 61 (1871); F; M; Head; yes 2887; no; Al. 1118
2909; (Industrious), Julia; f; 41 (1891); F; M; Wife; yes 2888; yes; Al. 3882

112

Census of the **Standing Rock** Reservation of the **Standing Rock** jurisdiction, as of **April 1**, 1932, taken by **E. D. Mossman**, Superintendent. South Dakota

KEY: Number; Surname, Given; Sex; Age at Last Birthday; Tribe (Standing Rock Sioux unless otherwise noted); Degree of Blood; Marital Status; Relationship to Head of Family; At Jurisdiction where enrolled (Yes or No); (If "No", where, if given); Ward (Yes or No); Allotment, Annuity and Identification Numbers.

2910; " Emily; f; 12 (12-24-19); F; S; Dau; yes 2889; yes; An. 2208
2911; " Margaret; f; 8 (9-14-23); F; S; Dau; yes 2890; yes; An. 2209
2912; " Lillian G; f; 5 (1-4-28); F; S; Dau; yes 2891; yes; An. 2210

2913; **MARTIN** (Unknown), Irene; f; 59 (1873); F; M; Head; yes 2892; yes;
Al. 3393
2914; " Gabriel; m; 20 (3-3-12); F; S; Son; yes 2894; yes; Al. 4192
2915; " Agnes; f; 15 (11-3-26); F; S; Dau; yes 2895; yes; An. 2214

N. E. **MARTINEZ**, James; m; Head
2916; (Sudden Brave), Jennie; f; 26 (3-13-07); F; M; Wife; yes 2896; yes;
Al. 1008

N. E. **MARTINEZ**, Richard; m; Head;
2917; (Badhorse), Julia; f; 26 (6-15-07); F; M; Wife; no 1655; Pine Ridge Res,
SD; yes; Al. 3699

N. E. **MATHIESON**, MA; m; Head
2918; (Cadotte), Julia; f; 39 (1893); 1/2; M; Wife; yes 2897; no; Al. 646
2919; " Margaret; f; 20 (2-1-12); 1/4; S; Dau; yes 2898; yes; Al. 4265
2920; " Mary E; f; 18 (1-30-14); 1/4; S; Dau; yes; 2899; yes; Al. 4545
2921; " Lenore L; f; 15 (5-16-16); 1/4; S; Dau; yes 2900; yes; An. 2223
2922; " Helen L; f; 13 (9-27-18); 1/4; S; Dau; yes 2901; yes; An. 2224
2923; " Norma C; f; 11 (3-22-21); 1/4; S; Dau; yes 2902; yes; An. 2225

N. E. **MAXON**, Orlie; m; Head
2924; (Comeau), Maude; f; 28 (11-20-03); 1/4; M; Wife; yes 2903; yes; Al. 1092
2925; " Milo E; m; 6 (5-30-25); 1/8; S; Son; yes 2904; yes; An. 2223
2926; " Lester L; m; 3 (4-7-28); 1/8; S; Son; yes 2905; yes; An. 2224
2927; " Ramona; f; 2 (7-22-30); 1/8; S; Dau; yes 2906; yes; An. 2225
2928; " Joan M; f; 2/12 (1-15-32); 1/8; S; Dau; yes ---; yes; An. ---

N. E. **McCHESNEY**, Elmer; m; Head
2929; (Calf), Mary; f; 43 (1889); 1/2; M; Wife; yes 2907; no; Al. 561
2930; " John E; m; 19 (8-29-12); 1/4; S; Son; yes 2908); yes; Al. 4531
2931; " Hazel; f; 16 (6-18-15); 1/4; S; Dau; yes 2909; yes; An. 2229
2932; " Fern M; f; 12 (10-4-19); 1/4; S; Dau; yes 2910; yes; An. 2230
2933; " Lynn; m; 9 (7-28-22); 1/4; S; Son; yes 2911; yes; An. 2231
2934; " Paul R; m; 4 (12-25-27); 1/4; S; Son; yes 2912; yes; An. 2232

N. E. **McCORMICK**, Joseph; m; Head
2935; (Evans), Mary E; f; 27 (10-5-04); 1/2; M; Wife; yes 2913; yes; Al. 2503
2936; " Joseph E; m; 6 (8-6-25); 1/4; S; Son; yes 2914; yes; An. 3219

Census of the **Standing Rock** Reservation of the **Standing Rock** jurisdiction, as of **April 1**, 1932, taken by **E. D. Mossman**, Superintendent. South Dakota

KEY: Number; Surname, Given; Sex; Age at Last Birthday; Tribe (Standing Rock Sioux unless otherwise noted); Degree of Blood; Marital Status; Relationship to Head of Family; At Jurisdiction where enrolled (Yes or No); (If "No", where, if given); Ward (Yes or No); Allotment, Annuity and Identification Numbers.

N. E. **McDONALD**, H. H.; m; Head
2937;   (Fredette), Clara; f; 63 (1869); 1/8; M; Wife; no 2915; San Diego, Cal; no;
Al. 3347

N. E. **McFARLAND**, H. E.; Head
2938;   (Godfrey), Alene; f; 21 (11-9-10); 1/4; M; Wife; yes 2916; yes; Al. 4084
2939;   " Donald C; m; 7/12 (8-9-31); 1/8; S; Son; yes ---; yes; An. 2235

N. E. **McGILLIS**, John B; m; Head
2940;   (Flying Earth), Eva; f; 35 (1897); F; M; Wife; no 2917; Fort Hall Agcy;
Fort Hall, Idaho; yes; Al. 465

2941; **McLAUGHLIN** (Goodreau), Annie; f; 60 (1872); 1/2; Wd; Head; yes 2918;
no; Al. 3506
2942;   " Jean A; f; 18 (9-25-13); 1/2; S; Dau; yes 2919; yes; Al. 4492

2943; **McLAUGHLIN**, Frank; m; 23 (7-21-08); 1/2; S; Head; no 2920; Rochester,
Olmsted Co, Minn; yes; Al. 2999

2944; **McLAUGHLIN**, Henry; m; 36 (9-8-95); 1/2; M; Head; yes 2921; no; Al. 282
2945;   (Madbear) Mary; f; 37 (1895); F; M; Wife; yes 2922; no; Al. 672
2946;   " Roland, m; 15 (5-4-16); 3/4; S; Son; yes 2923; yes; An. 2243
2947;   " Melda A; f; 13 (9-13-18); 3/4; S; Dau; yes 2924; yes; An. 2244
2948;   " Hugh P; m; 10 (7-20-21); 3/4; S; Son; yes 2925; yes; An. 2245
2949;   " Aleda P; f; 7 (6-30-24); 3/4; S; Dau; yes 2926; yes; An. 2246
2950;   " Rupert S; m; 5 (3-4-27); 3/4; S; Son; yes 2927; yes; An. 2247
2951;   " Philip H; m; 3 (2-2-29); 3/4; S; Son; yes 2928; yes; An. 2248
2952;   " Rita Ann; f; 8/12 (7-17-31); 3/4; S; Dau; yes ---; yes; An. 2249

2953; **McLAUGHLIN**, James L; m; 27 (12-14-04); 1/2; m; Head; no 2929; Hominy,
Osage Co, Okla; yes; Al. 1777

2954; **McLAUGHLIN**, James S; m; 38 (3-18-94); 1/2; Div; Head; yes 2930; no;
Al. 281

2955; **McLAUGHLIN**, Eugene W; m; 23 (5-20-08); 1/2; S; Head; yes 2931; yes;
Al. 2534

2956; **McLAUGHLIN**, Lenore; f; 23 (4-5-08); 1/2; S; Head; yes 2932; yes;
Al. 3503

2957; **McLAUGHLIN**, Mae A; f; 25 (8-22-06); 1/2; S; Head; no 2933; Mankato,
Blue Earth Co, Minn; yes; Al. 1168

Census of the **Standing Rock** Reservation of the **Standing Rock** jurisdiction, as of **April 1**, 1932, taken by **E. D. Mossman**, Superintendent. South Dakota

KEY: Number; Surname, Given; Sex; Age at Last Birthday; Tribe (Standing Rock Sioux unless otherwise noted); Degree of Blood; Marital Status; Relationship to Head of Family; At Jurisdiction where enrolled (Yes or No); (If "No", where, if given); Ward (Yes or No); Allotment, Annuity and Identification Numbers.

2958; **McLAUGHLIN**, Margurita; f; 20 (9-20-11); 1/2; S; Alone; yes 2934; yes; Al. 4207

2959; **McLAUGHLIN**, Robert C; m; 25 (10-4-04); 1/2; S; Head; yes 2936; yes; Al. 568

2960; **McLAUGHLIN** (LeCompte), Zelda; f; 36 (1896); 1/2; Div; Head; no 2937; Bismarck, Burleigh Co, ND; no; Al. 781
2961; " Melvin H; m; 15 (4-17-16); 1/2; S; Son; no 2938; Bismarck, Burleigh Co, ND; yes; An. 2260
2962; " Roletta; f; 14 (5-119-17); 1/2; S; Dau; no 2939; Bismarck, Burleigh Co, ND; yes; An. 2261
2963; " Geraldine; f; 11 (8-20-20); 1/2; S; Dau; no 2940; Bismarck, Burleigh Co, ND; yes; An. 2262
2964; " James S; m; 9 (6-1-22); 1/2; S; Son; no 2941; Bismarck, Burleigh Co, ND; yes; An. 2263
2965; " Willis; m; 7 (1-3-24); 1/2; S; Son; no 2942; Bismarck, Burleigh Co, ND; yes; 2264
2966; " Harry M; m; 6 (6-7-25); 1/2; S; Son; no 2943; Bismarck, Burleigh Co, ND; yes; An. 2265
2967; " Maurine; f; 5 (1-13-27); 1/2; S; Dau; no 2944; Bismarck, Burleigh Co, ND; yes; An. 2266

2968; **McLEAN**, Henry; m; 33 (1899); F; M; Head; yes 2945; yes; Al. 188
2969; (Nationshield), Jennie F; 24 (5-28-08); F; M; Wife; yes 2946; yes; Al. 3279

2970; **McLEAN**, James; m; 42 (12-7-90); 1/2; S; Head; yes 2947; no; Al. 274

2971; **McLEAN**, Margaret; f; 33 (1897); 1/2; S; Head; yes 2948; yes; Al. 187
2972; " Philip; m; 9 (1922); 1/2; S; yes 2949; yes; An. 2271

N. E. **McLEOD**, John; m; Head
2973; (Buckles), Mary; f; 38 (9-1-94); 1/2; M; Wife; yes 2950; yes; Al. 1097
2974; " Elenor J; f; 1 (9-1-30); 1/4; S; Dau; yes 2951; yes; An. 2273

2975; **MEDICINE**, Martin; m; 41 (9-7-91); F; M; Head; yes 2952; no; Al. 180
2976; (Gabe), Annie; f; 36 (4-20-95); F; M; Wife; yes 2953; yes; Al. 124
2977; " Crescensia; f; 15 (10-28-16; F; S; Dau; yes 2954; yes; An. 2280
2978; " Martina; f; 11 (7-9-20); F; S; Dau; yes 2955; yes; An. 2281
2979; " Beatrice; f; 8 (8-1-23); F; S; Dau; yes 2956; yes; An. 2282
2980; " Grace; f; 5 (5-4-26); F; S; Dau; yes 2957; yes; An. 2283
2981; " Lila M; f; 2 (5-17-29); F; S; Dau; yes 2958; yes; An. 2284

Census of the **Standing Rock** Reservation of the **Standing Rock** jurisdiction, as of **April 1**, 1932, taken by **E. D. Mossman**, Superintendent.   South Dakota

KEY: Number; Surname, Given; Sex; Age at Last Birthday; Tribe (Standing Rock Sioux unless otherwise noted); Degree of Blood; Marital Status; Relationship to Head of Family; At Jurisdiction where enrolled (Yes or No); (If "No", where, if given); Ward (Yes or No); Allotment, Annuity and Identification Numbers.

2982;   **MENTZ**, Frank; m; 47 (1885); 1/2; S; Head; no 2959; Crow Agency, Mont;
no; Al. 3017

2983;   **MENTZ**, George; m; 53 (1879); 1/2; M; Head; no 2960; Fort Peck Res,
Poplar, Roosevelt Co, Mont; no; Al. 3493
2984;   "   Gail E; m; 19 (10-2-12); 1/2; S; Son; no 2961; Fort Peck Res, Poplar,
Roosevelt Co, Mont; yes; Al. 4352
2985;   "   Ethel M; f; 17 (10-14-14); 1/2; S; Dau; no 2962; Fort Peck Res, Poplar,
Roosevelt Co, Mont; yes; Al. 4633
2986;   "   Delilah; f; 11 (3-24-21); 1/2; S; Dau; no 2963; Fort Peck Res, Poplar,
Roosevelt Co, Mont; yes; An. 2292
2987;   "   Ada L; f; 7 (4-14-27); 1/2; S; Dau; no 2964; Fort Peck Res, Poplar,
Roosevelt Co, Mont; yes; An. 2293
2988;   "   David R; m; 5 (9-15-24); 1/2; S; Son; no 2966; Fort Peck Res, Poplar,
Roosevelt Co, Mont; yes; An. 2294

2989;   **MENTZ**, Levi; m; 21 (1-6-11); 1/2; M; Head; no 2961; Fort Peck Res,
Poplar, Roosevelt Co, Mont; yes; Al. 4148

2990;   **MIDDLEBULL**, Louis; m; 47 (1885); F; M; Head; yes 2967; no; Al. 1408
2991;   (Fly), Margaret; f; 47 (1885); F; M; Wife; yes 2968; yes; Al. 2892
2992;   "   Rose; f; 8 (10-12-24); F; S; Dau; yes 2969; yes; An. 2326

2993;   **MIDDLEBULL**, Paul; m; 74 (1858); F; M; Head; yes 2970; no; Al. 1406
2994;   (Crawler), Fanny; f; 58 (1874); F; M; Wife; yes 2971; yes; Al. 3104

N. E.   **MIESCH**, Henry; m; Head
2995;   (Cadotte), Lima; f; 20 (8-9-10); 1/2; M; Wife; no 2972; Mobridge,
Walworth Co, SD; yes; Al. 4091

N. E.   **MILLER**, Geo M; m; Head
2996;   (Duncan), Louise; f; 42 (8-19-90); 1/4; M; Wife; no 2973; Pasadena, Cal;
no; Al. 2384
2997;   "   Benjamin; m; 6 (7-24-25); 1/8; S; Son; no 2974; Pasadena, Cal; An. 2333
2998;   Hanley, Helen; f; 17 (8-23-14); 1/8; S; St-Dau; no 2975; Pasadena, Cal;
Al. 4637
2999;   Hanley, Joseph; m; 13 (11-11-18); 1/8; S; St-Son; no 2976; Pasadena, Cal;
yes; An. 1427

3000;   **MOCCASIN NECKLACE** (Wanbliwin), Mrs; f; 87 (1845) F; Wd; Head; yes
2977; yes; Al. 3218

3001;   **MOLASH** (Vermillion), Annie; f; 32 (5-21-1900); 1/2; M; Head; yes 2978;
no; Al. 2907

Census of the **Standing Rock** Reservation of the **Standing Rock** jurisdiction, as of **April 1**, 1932, taken by **E. D. Mossman**, Superintendent. South Dakota

KEY: Number; Surname, Given; Sex; Age at Last Birthday; Tribe (Standing Rock Sioux unless otherwise noted); Degree of Blood; Marital Status; Relationship to Head of Family; At Jurisdiction where enrolled (Yes or No); (If "No", where, if given); Ward (Yes or No); Allotment, Annuity and Identification Numbers.

3002;   "   George; m; 8 (3-9-24); 1/4; S; Son; yes 2979; yes; An. 765
3003;   "   Marie M; f; 6 (7-1-26); 1/4; S; Dau; yes 2980; yes; An. 766
3004;   "   Josephine; f; 3 (10-8-28); 1/4; S; Dau; yes 2981; yes; An. 767
3005;   Demery, Floyd; m; 1 (1930); 1/4; S; Son; yes 2982; yes; An. 768
3006;   Demery, Marie; f; 3/12 (12-2-31); 1/4; S; Dau; yes 2983; yes; An. 760

3007;   **MONGRAN**, Mary; f; 93 (1839); F; S; Head; yes 2983; yes; Al. 3356

3008;   **MOORE**, Edward; m; 20 (8-2-10); 1/4; S; Alone;   yes; 2984; yes; Al. 4308
3009;   "   Warren; m; 10 (1-28-21); P[sic]; S; Alone; yes 2985; yes; An. 2341

3010;   **MOUNTAIN**, Moses; m; 25 (8-17-06); F; M; Head; no 2986; Pine Ridge Res, Pine Ridge, SD; yes; Al. 1009

3011;   **MOUNTAIN**, Willis; m; 36 (1896); F; M; Head; yes 2987; yes; Al. 1003
3012;   (Crazyhawk), Lucy; f; 29 (2-3-03); F; M; Wife; yes 2988; yes; Al. 1146
3013;   "   George; m; 9 (6-3-22); F; S; Son; yes 2989; yes; An. 2348
3014;   "   Mildred; f; 5 (9-15-26); F; S; Dau; yes 2990; yes; An. 2349
3015;   "   Helen J; f; 3 (3-24-29); F; S; Dau; yes; 2991; yes; An. 2350
3016;   "   Joseph; m; 8/12 (7-15-31); F; S; Son; yes ---; yes; An. 2351

3017;   **MUENCH**, Albert; m; 18 (11-29-13); 1/4; S; Alone; yes 2992; yes; Al. 4520
3018;   "   Gladys; f; 15 (12-3-16); 1/4; S; Alone; yes 2993; yes; An. 2353
3019;   "   Violet; f; 11 (12-8-21); 1/4; S; Alone; yes 2994; yes; An. 2354

3020;   **MUTCHLER**, William; m; 50 (1882); 1/2; M; Head; yes 2995; no; Al. 1394
3021;   (Pine), Blanche; f; 42 (11-5-1890); F; M; Wife; yes 2996; yes; Al. 1353
3022;   "   Charles; m; 16 (8-20-15); 3/4; S; Son; yes 2997; yes; An. 2378
3023;   "   Rose L; f; 12 (7-20-19); 3/4; S; Dau; yes 2998; yes; An. 2379

3024;   **NEADE**, Philomene; f; 26 (8-12-05); 1/4; S; Head; yes 2999; yes; Al. 723
3025;   Jordan, Victor B; m; 7 (8-9-24); 3/8; S; Son; yes 3000; yes; An. 2382
3026;   Van Derbarst, Pearl M; f; 4 (12-10-27); 1/8; S; Dau; yes 3001; yes; An. 2383
3027;   Banik, Deloris; f; 2 (3-22-30); 1/8; S; Dau; yes 3002; yes; An. 2384

N. E.   **NELSON**, Otto; m; Head
3028;   (Silk), Louise; f; 52 (9-19-80); 1/4; M; Wife; yes 3003; no; Al. 2951
3029;   "   Mary L; f; 17 (9-4-14); 1/8; S; Dau; yes 3004; yes; Al. 4645

3030;   **NIYAKEKTE**, Henry; m; 78 (1854); F; M; Head; yes 3005; yes; Al. 387
3031;   "   Elizabeth; f; 19 (11-15-12); F; S; Dau; yes 3006; yes; Al. 4397

3032;   **NIYAKEKTE**, James; m; 33 (1-14-99); F; M; Head; yes 3007; yes; Al. 389
3033;   "   Dorothy; f; 6 (7-19-25); F; S; Dau; yes 3008; yes; An. 2390

KEY: Number; Surname, Given; Sex; Age at Last Birthday; Tribe (Standing Rock Sioux unless otherwise noted); Degree of Blood; Marital Status; Relationship to Head of Family; At Jurisdiction where enrolled (Yes or No); (If "No", where, if given); Ward (Yes or No); Allotment, Annuity and Identification Numbers.

3034;   "   Mildred; f; 4 (9-6-27); F; S; Dau; yes 3009; yes; An. 2391
3035;   "   Ethelyn; f; 1 (7-3-30); F; S; Dau; yes 3010; yes; An. 2392

3036;   **NO EYE BROWS** (Star), Mrs; f; 85 (1847); F; Wd; Head; yes 3011; yes; Al. 3137

3037;   **NO HEART**, Esther; f; 24 (8-11-07); F; S; Head; yes 3012; yes; Al. 3701

3038;   **NO HEART**, Marcella; f; 19 (9-20-12); F; S; Head; yes 3013; yes; Al. 4381

3039;   **NOISY HAWK**, Edward; m; 42 (1890); F; M; Head; yes 3014; no; A 950
3040;   (Lowdog), Nancy; f; 23 (5-26-09); F; M; Wife; yes 3015; yes; Al. 3861
3041;   "   Vera; f; 13 (3-10-18); F; S; Dau; yes 3016; yes; An. 2411
3042;   "   Florence; f; 11 (9-24-20); F; S; Dau; yes 3017; yes; An. 2412
3043;   "   Commodore; m; 8 (7-2-24); F; S; Son; yes 3018; yes; An. 413
3044;   "   Gilford, m; 4/12 (11-6-21); F; S; Son; yes ---; yes; An. 2414

3045;   **NOMKTE**, Joseph; m; 52 (1870); F; M; Head; yes 3019; yes; Al. 398
3046;   (Nomkte), Julia; f; 61 (1871); F; M; Wife; yes 3010; yes; Al. 3489
3047;   Fly, Samuel; m; 20 (12-1-11); F; S; Adpt Son; yes 3021; yes; Al. 4241

3048;   **OBERSHAW**, Henry; m; 62 (1870); 1/2; S; Head; no 3022; Pierre, Hughes Co, SD; no; Al. 2763

3049;   **OFTEN KILLS ENEMY**, Louise; f; 46 (1886); F; S; Head; yes 3023; yes; Al. 1171

3050;   **OKA**, Agnes; f; 67 (1865); F; Wd; Head; yes 3024; yes; Al. 3456

3051;   **OKA**, Anna; f; 34 (12-12-99); F; S; Head; no 3025; Yankton Res, Lake Andes, Charles Mix Co, SD; yes; Al. 650
3052;   "   Rose; f; 7 (12-25-24); F; S; Dau; no 3026; Yankton Res, Lake Andes, Charles Mix Co, Div; yes; An. 2841

3053;   **OKA**, Matthew; m; 36 (12-1-96); F; M; Head; yes 3027; yes; Al. 651
3054;   "   Herman; m; 6 (7-12-25); F; S; Son; yes 3028; yes; An. 2429
3055;   "   Madeline; f; 4 (11-22-27); F; S; Dau; yes 3029; yes; An. 2428
3056;   "   Merrill; m; 1 (6-21-30); F; S; Son; yes 3030; yes; An. 2430

3057;   **OLD BULL**; m; 79 (1853); F; M; Head; yes 3031; yes; Al. 1545
3058;   (Kantotowin), Mrs; f; 78 (1854); F; M; Wife; yes 3032; yes; Al. 3421

Census of the **Standing Rock** Reservation of the **Standing Rock** jurisdiction, as of **April 1** , 1932, taken by **E. D. Mossman** , Superintendent. South Dakota

KEY: Number; Surname, Given; Sex; Age at Last Birthday; Tribe (Standing Rock Sioux unless otherwise noted); Degree of Blood; Marital Status; Relationship to Head of Family; At Jurisdiction where enrolled (Yes or No); (If "No", where, if given); Ward (Yes or No); Allotment, Annuity and Identification Numbers.

3059; **OLD CROW**, Joseph; m; 42 (1890); F; M; Head; yes 3033; yes; Al. 2933
3060; (Prays To Him), Annie; f; 59 (1873); F; M; Wife; yes 3034; yes; Al. 3377

3061; **ONE BULL**, Henry; m; 79 (1853); F; M; Head; yes 3035; yes; Al. 990
3062; (Wamniomniluta), Mrs; f; 67 (1865); F; M; Wife; yes 3036; yes; Al. 3398

3063; **ONE BULL**, Margaret; f; 23 (4-7-09); F; S; Head; yes 3037; yes; Al. 3888
3064; Carreaux, Robert L; m; 2 (1-28-30); F; S; Son; yes 3038; yes; An. 2437

3065; **ONE ELK**, Agnes; f; 50 (1882); F; S; Head; yes 3039; yes; Al. 1163
3066; Afraid of Bear, Mary; f; 14 (9-24-17); F; S; Orphan; yes 3040; yes; An. 3
3067; Afraid of Bear, Daniel; m; 11 (8-2-20); F; S; Orphan; yes 3041; yes; An. 4

3068; **ONE ELK**, Andrew; m; 81 (1851); F; M; Head; yes 3042; yes; Al. 1161
3069; (Hehokawin), Mary; f; 78 (1854); F; M; Wife; yes 3043; yes; Al. 3252

3070; **ONEFEATHER**, Frances; f; 65 (1867); F; Wd; Head; yes 3045; yes; Al. 2993

3071; **ONEFEATHER**, Charles; m; 46 (1886); F; M; Head; yes 3046; yes; Al. 1298
3072; " Max; m; 20 (10-20-11); 1/2; S; Son; yes 3047; yes; Al. 4253
3073; " James, m; 18 (1-18-14); 1/2; S; Son; yes 3048; yes; Al. 4523
3074; " Hazel; f; 4 (1-5-27); 1/2; S; Dau; yes 3049; yes; An. 2444
3075; " Pearl; f; 3 (5-12-28); 1/2; S; Dau; yes 3050; yes; An. 2445
3076; " Lorraine; f; 2 (1-17-30); 1/2; S; Dau; yes 3051; yes; An. 2446
3077; " Ruth; f; 3/12 (12-1-31); 1/2; S; Dau; yes --; yes; An. 2447

3078; **ONEFEATHER**, Fred; m; 22 (12-20-09); F; S; Head; yes 3052; yes; Al. 4001

3079; **ONJINCA**, Daniel; m; 75 (1857); F; M; Head; yes 3053; yes; Al. 1379
3080; (Hunkpatesan), Mrs; f; 71 (1861); F; M; Wife; yes 3302; yes; Al. 3302

3081; **ONJINCA**, Emma; f; 24 (12-6-07); F; S; Head; yes 3055; yes; Al. 3304

3082; **ONNESTAD** (Silk), Grace; f; 36 (12-6-96); 1/4; Wd; Head; no 3056;
Pipestone, Pipestone Co, Minn; no; Al. 2955
3083; " Lorraine; f; 13 (12-23-18); 1/8; S; Dau; no 3057; Pipestone, Pipestone
Co, Minn; yes; An. 2471
3084; " Vera M; f; 11 (7-27-20); 1/8; S; Dau; no 3058; Pipestone, Pipestone Co,
Minn; yes; An. 2472
3085; " John J; m; 9 (3-27-23); 1/8; S; Son; no 3059; Pipestone, Pipestone Co,
Minn; yes; An. 2373
3086; " Agnes F; f; 7 (2-11-25); 1/8; S; Dau; no 3060; Pipestone, Pipestone Co,
Minn; yes; An. 2474

Census of the __Standing Rock__ Reservation of the __Standing Rock__ jurisdiction, as of __April 1__, 1932, taken by __E. D. Mossman__, Superintendent. South Dakota

KEY: Number; Surname, Given; Sex; Age at Last Birthday; Tribe (Standing Rock Sioux unless otherwise noted); Degree of Blood; Marital Status; Relationship to Head of Family; At Jurisdiction where enrolled (Yes or No); (If "No", where, if given); Ward (Yes or No); Allotment, Annuity and Identification Numbers.

3087; **OTTERROBE**, Jerome; m; 24 (7-29-07); F; S; Head; yes 3061; yes; Al. 3266

3088; **OTTERROBE**, Joseph; m; 66 (1866); F; Wd; Head; yes 3062; yes; Al. 1332

3089; **OWENS**, Louise; f; 21 (9-8-10); F; S; Head; yes 3063; yes; Al. 3693

3090; **PAINTS BROWN**, Mrs; f; 87 (1864); F; Wd; Head; yes 3064; yes; Al. 3693

N. E. **PARMLEY**, Odie; m; Head
3091; "   Giles; m; 2 (8-13-29); 1/2; S; Son; yes 3065; yes; An. 2493

3092; **PASS BEYOUND**[sic], Melda; f; 17 (10-17-14); F; S; Alone; yes 3066; yes; Al. 4712

N. E. **PATCHEN**, Robert; m; Head
3093;   (McLaughlin), Luella; f; 40 (11-19-92); 1/2; M; Wife; yes 3067; no; Al. 280
3094; "   Florence; f; 17 (8-14-14); 1/4; S; Dau; yes 3068; yes; Al. 4638
3095; "   Melda A; f; 15 (9-28-16); 1/4; S; Dau; yes 3069; yes; An. 2497
3096; "   Etta L; f; 12 (11-12-19); 1/4; S; Dau; yes 3070; yes; An. 2498
3097; "   Emma C; f; 10 (10-9-21); 1/4; S; Dau; yes; 3071; yes; An. 2499
3098; "   Josephine; f; 8 (10-14-23); 1/4; S; Dau; yes 3072; yes; An. 2500
3099; "   Lottie E; f; 6 (7-9-25); 1/4; S; Dau; yes 3073; yes; An. 2501
3100; "   Robert; m; 4 (9-10-27); 1/4; S; Son; yes 3074; yes; An. 2503

N. E. **PETERS**, Edward E; m; Head
3101;   (Powers), Mary; f; 39 (10-28-93); 1/4; M; Wife; yes 3075; no; Al. 2851
3102; "   Vernon; m; 18 (3-13-14); 1/8; S; Son; yes 3076; yes; Al. 4571
3103; "   Dale E; m; 12 (3-8-20); 1/8; S; Son; yes 3077; yes; An. 2507
3104; "   Ellsworth; m; 6 (5-2-25); 1/8; S; Son; yes 3078; yes; An. 2509

3105; **PHEASANT**, Thomas; m; 40 (7-1-92); F; M; Head; yes 3079; no; Al. 1283
3106;   (Firecloud), Mary; f; 73 (1859); F; M; Wife; yes 3080; yes; Al. 826
3107; "   Michael; m; 12 (2-15-20); F; S; Son; yes 3081; yes; An. 2512
3108; "   Catharine; f; 8 (12-2-24); F; S; Dau; yes 3082; yes; An. 2513
N. E. **PHILIPS**, Edward W; m; Head
3109;   (Philips), Mary; f; 51 (1881); 1/4; M; Wife; no 3083; Merced, Merced Co, Cal; no; Al. 2821
3110; "   Joseph; m; 18 (5-2-13); 1/8; S; Son; no 3084; Merced, Merced Co, Cal; yes; Al. 2516

3111; **PHILIPS**, Sarah J; f; 24 (12-7-07); 1/8; S; Head; no 3085; Whereabouts Unknown; yes; Al. 2777

120

Census of the **Standing Rock** Reservation of the **Standing Rock** jurisdiction, as of **April 1**, 1932, taken by **E. D. Mossman**, Superintendent. South Dakota

KEY: Number; Surname, Given; Sex; Age at Last Birthday; Tribe (Standing Rock Sioux unless otherwise noted); Degree of Blood; Marital Status; Relationship to Head of Family; At Jurisdiction where enrolled (Yes or No); (If "No", where, if given); Ward (Yes or No); Allotment, Annuity and Identification Numbers.

3112; **PINE**, Joseph; m; 31 (3-10-01); F; M; Head; yes 3086; yes; Al. 1355

N. E. **PHILIPS**, George; m; Head
3113; (Madbear), Louise; f; 43 (1889); F; M; Wife; yes 3087; yes; Al. 1056
3114; " Lucy; f; 17 (1-19-15); F; S; Dau; yes 3088; yes; Al. 4708

3115; **PINE**, Nancy; f; 63 (1869); F; S; Head; yes 3090; yes; Al. 3375

3116; **PINE**, Straight; m; 36 (1895); F; M; Head; yes 3091; yes; Al. 1354
3117; (One Elk), Susan; f; 39 (10-20-93); F; M; Wife; yes 3092; yes; Al. 1162
3118; " Ambrose; m; 8/12 (7-5-31); F; S; Son; yes ---; yes; An. 2521

3119; **PRAY TO HIM**, Lawrence; m; 67 (1865); F; M; Head; yes 3093; yes;
Al. 1274
3120; (Hintunkasan), Alma; f; 58 (1874); F; M; Wife; yes 3094; yes; Al. 912
3121; " Nellie; f; 12 (11-5-20); F; S; Dau; yes 3095; yes; An. 2548

3122; **PRETENDS EAGLE**, Daniel; m; 24 (8-9-07); F; M; Head; yes 3096; yes;
Al. 2522

3123; **PRETENDS EAGLE**, Martin; m; 79 (1853); F; Wd; Head; yes 3097; yes;
Al. 737

3124; **PRETTY ELK** (Tokahewin), Mrs; f; 89 (1843); F; Wd; Head; yes 3098; yes;
Al. 3486

3125; **PRIMEAU**, Joseph; m; 31 (9-4-1900); 1/2; M; Head; no 3099; Rapid City,
Pennington Co, SD; yes; Al. 1431

3126; **PRIMEAU**, Louis; m; 25 (10-3-06); 1/2; S; Head; yes 3100; yes; Al. 1433

3127; **PRIMEAU**, Louis C; m; 10 (10-28-21); 1/8; S; Alone; no 3101; Kansas City,
Jackson Co, Mo; yes; An. 2568
3128; Primeau, Maurice; m; 9 (3-11-23); 1/8; S; Alone; no 3102; Kansas City,
Jackson Co, Mo; yes; An. 2569

3129; **PRIMEAU**, Mary L; f; 37 (1-10-95); 1/2; S; Head; no 3103; Whereabouts
Unknown; no; Al. 812

3130; **PRIMEAU**, Olive I; f; 34 (3-11-98); 1/4; S; Head; no 3104; Armour, Douglas
Co, SD; no; Al. 814

3131; **PRIMEAU**, Rose F; f; 29 (7-11-02); 1/4; S; Head; no 3105; Armour, Douglas
Co, SD; yes; Al. 815

Census of the __Standing Rock__ Reservation of the __Standing Rock__ jurisdiction, as of __April 1__, 1932, taken by __E. D. Mossman__, Superintendent.   South Dakota

KEY: Number; Surname, Given; Sex; Age at Last Birthday; Tribe (Standing Rock Sioux unless otherwise noted); Degree of Blood; Marital Status; Relationship to Head of Family; At Jurisdiction where enrolled (Yes or No); (If "No", where, if given); Ward (Yes or No); Allotment, Annuity and Identification Numbers.

3132; **PSAKUTIPI**, Thomas; m; 63 (1869); F; M; Head; yes 3106; yes; Al. 3871
3133;   (Village Center), Helen; f; 53 (1879); F; M; Wife; yes 3107; yes; Al. 3364
3134; Village Center, Carl; m; 18 (3-7-13); F; S; St-Son; yes 3108; yes; Al. 4323

N. E. **PUTNAM**, Arthur; m; Head
3135;   (LeCompte), Blanche; f; 35 (1-21-97); 1/2; M; Wife; yes 3109; no; Al. 7
3136; " Louis A; m; 13 (1-27-18); 1/4; S; Son; yes 3110; yes; An. 2576
3137; " Florence; f; 12 (9-28-19); 1/4; S; Dau; yes 3111; yes; An. 2577
3138; " Evelyn; f; 10 (8-30-21); 1/4; S; Dau; yes 3112; yes; An. 2578
3139; " Arthur; m; 8 (4-12-24); 1/4; S; Dau; yes 3112; yes; An. 2578
3140; " Blanche; f; 6 (2-26-26); 1/4; S; Dau; yes 3114; yes; An. 2580

N. E. **QUAY**, Howard F; m; Head
3141;   (Waggoner), Daphne; f; 40 (4-4-91); 1/4; M; Wife; no 3115; Collegeville, Montgomery Co, Pa; no; Al. 2828
3142; " Aurelia; f; 19 (2-1-12); 1/8; S; Dau; no 3116; Collegeville, Montgomery Co, Pa; yes; Al. 4077
3143; " Philmore; m; 16 (9-21-15); 1/8; S; Son; no 3117; Collegeville, Montgomery Co, Pa; yes; An. 2583
3144; " Adria M; f; 7 (2-11-25); 18; S; Dau; no 3118; Collegeville, Montgomery Co, Pa; yes; An. 2584
3145; " Stanley; m; 5 (6-30-26); 1/8; S; Son; no 3119; Collegeville, Montgomery Co, Pa; yes; An. 2585

N. E. **RAINBOW**, Harry; m; Head
3146;   (Redhawk), Martha; f; 25 (5-5-06); F; M; Wife; no 3121; Yankton Res, SD; yes; Al. 1110

3147; **RAWHIDE**, Gust[sic]; m; 62 (1870); F; M; Head; yes 3122; yes; Al. 259
3148; " Jeanette; f; 5 (2-2-27); F; S; Dau; yes 3123; yes; An. 2621

3151; **REDBEAR**, Andrew; m; 30 (1901); F; M; Head; yes 3126; yes; Al. 1012
3152; " Lila Lee; f; 3 (11-25-28); F; S; Dau; yes 3127; yes; An. 2620
3153; " Henrietta; f; 3/12 (12-23-31); F; S; Dau; yes ---; yes; An. 2630

3154; **REDBEAR**, Jacob; m; 19 (10-15-08); F; S[sic]; Head; yes 3129; yes; Al. 2805
3155;   (Leaf), Jennie Mary; f; 18 (9-25-13); F; S[sic]; Wife; yes 2647; yes; Al. 4498

3156; **REDBEAR**, Jennie; f; 19 (12-18-12); F; S; Head; yes 3129; yes; Al. 4388
3157; " Lucille; f; 2 (1930); F; S; Dau; yes 3130; yes; An. 2539

3158; **REDBEAR** Joseph; m; 62 (1880); F; M; Head; yes 3131; no; Al. 1010
3159;   (Redbear), Rose; f; 56 (1876); F; M; Wife; yes 3132; yes; Al. 3324
3160; " Clara; f; 14 (12-5-17); F; S; Dau; yes 3133; yes; An. 2636

Census of the **Standing Rock** Reservation of the **Standing Rock** jurisdiction, as of **April 1**, 1932, taken by **E. D. Mossman**, Superintendent. South Dakota

KEY: Number; Surname, Given; Sex; Age at Last Birthday; Tribe (Standing Rock Sioux unless otherwise noted); Degree of Blood; Marital Status; Relationship to Head of Family; At Jurisdiction where enrolled (Yes or No); (If "No", where, if given); Ward (Yes or No); Allotment, Annuity and Identification Numbers.

3161;   "   Isaac; m; 12 (8-25-19); F; S; Son; yes 3134; yes; An. 2637

3162;   **REDBEAR**, Matilda; f; 75 (1857); F; S; Head; yes 3135; yes; Al. 3258

3163;   **REDBIRD** (Reclining), Mrs Ella; f; 78 (1854); F; Wd; Head; yes 3136; yes; Al. 3167

3164;   **REDEAGLE**, Samuel; m; 25 (5-26-06); F; S; Head; yes 3137; yes; Al. 2710

3165;   **REDFISH**, James; m; 59 (1873); F; M; Head; yes 3138; yes; Al. 641
3166;   (Brownotter), Louise; f; 57 (1875); F; M; Wife; yes 3139; yes; Al. 3349
3167;   "   William; m; 16 (1915); F; S; Son; yes 3140; yes; An. 2662
3168;   "   Charles; m; 12 (5-21-19); F; S; Son; yes 3141; yes; An. 2663
3169;   Shooter, Frank; m; 19 (4-17-12); F; S; St-Son; yes 3142; yes; Al. 4302

3170;   **REDFOX**, George; m; 45 (1887); F; M; Head; yes 3143; no; Al. 2627
3171;   "   Mary; f; 5 (9-17-26); F; S; Dau; yes 3144; yes; An. 2670

3172;   **REDFOX**, William; m; 53 (1879); F; Wd; Head; yes 3147; no; Al. 2625
3173;   "   William, Jr; m; 15 (10-12-16); F; S; Son; yes 3148; yes; An. 2680

3174;   **REDHAWK**, Daniel; m; 36 (2-14-96); F; M; Head; no 3149; Yankton Res, Lake Andes, SD; no; Al. 310
3175;   "   Faith A; f; 3 (9-28-28); F; S; Dau; no 3150; Yankton Res, Lake Andes; SD; yes; An. 2683

3176;   **REDHAWK**, George; m; 18 (1-15-14); F; S; Alone; yes 3151; yes; Al. 4563
3177;   "   Esther; f; 14 (2-7-18); F; S; Alone; yes 3152; yes; An. 2931

3178;   **REDHAWK**, Howard; m; 57 (1875); F; M; Head; no 3153; Yankton Res, Lake Andes, SD; no; Al. 309
3179;   "   May; f; 20 (1-3-12); F; S; Dau; no 3154; Yankton Res, Lake Andes, SD; yes; Al. 4049
3180;   "   Elaine; f; 13 (1-26-19); F; S; Dau; no 3155; Yankton Res, Lake Andes SD; yes; An. 2685
3181;   **REDHAWK**, John; m; 65 (1867); F; M; Head; yes 3156; no; Al. 305
3182;   (Ironcloud), Mrs; f; 68 (1864); F; M; Wife; yes 3157; yes; Al. 29

3183;   **REDHORN**, John G; m; 30 (4-11-01); F; M; Head; yes 3158; yes; Al. 2747
3184;   (Bobtailbear), Grace; f; 25 (10-4-06); F; M; Wife; yes; 3159; yes; Al. 926
3185;   "   Nelson, m; 4 (8-3-27); F; S; Son; yes; 3160; yes; An. 2691
3186;   "   Dewey; m; 4/12 (11-3-31); F; S; Son; yes ---; yes; An. 2692

Census of the **Standing Rock** Reservation of the **Standing Rock** jurisdiction, as of **April 1**, 1932, taken by **E. D. Mossman**, Superintendent. South Dakota

KEY: Number; Surname, Given; Sex; Age at Last Birthday; Tribe (Standing Rock Sioux unless otherwise noted); Degree of Blood; Marital Status; Relationship to Head of Family; At Jurisdiction where enrolled (Yes or No); (If "No", where, if given); Ward (Yes or No); Allotment, Annuity and Identification Numbers.

3187; **REDHORSE**, Zidol; m; 56 (1876); F; M; Head; yes 3161; no; Al. 26
3188; (Shootsnear), Ellen; f; 47 (1885); F; M; Wife; yes 3162; yes; Al. 27
3189; " Rebecca; f; 15 (8-17-14[sic]); F; S; Dau; yes 3163; yes; An. 2700
3190; " Martina; f; 16 (1915); F; S; Dau; yes 3164; yes; An. 2701
3191; " Samuel; m; 7 (3-19-24); F; S; Son; yes 3165; yes; An. 2702
3192; " Jonas T; m; 1 (12-5-30); F; S; Son; yes 3166; yes; An. 2703

3193; **REDLEGS**, Benedict; m; 36 (1895); F; M; Head; yes 3167; no; Al. 1225
3194; (Lookinghorse), Ida; f; 34 (1898); F; M; Wife; yes 3168; yes; Al. 1027
3195; " Gabriel; m; 12 (11-11-19); F; S; Son; yes 3169; yes; An. 2706
3196; " Henry; m; 11 (7-9-21); F; S; Son; yes 3170; yes; An. 2707
3197; " Medina; f; 7 (1-16-25); F; S; Dau; yes 3171; yes; An. 2708
3198; " Sherman; m; 3 (8-9-28); F; S; Son; yes 3172; yes; An. 2709
3199; " Bernice; f; 10/12 (5-17-31); F; S; Dau; yes ---; yes; An. 2710

3200; **REDPHEASANT**, Samuel; m; 54 (1878); F; M; Head; yes 3173; yes;
Al. 704
3201; (Pretends Eagle), Mary; f; 64 (1868); F; M; Wife; yes 3174; yes; Al. 3082

3202; **REDTOMAHAWK**, Francis; m; 54 (1878); F; M; Head; yes 3175; no;
Al. 3276
3203; (Swifthawk), Lucy; f; 56 (1876); F; M; Wife; yes 3176; yes; Al. 1081

3203[sic]; **REEL**, Flora; f; 38 (1-16-94); F; S; Head; yes 3177; yes; Al. 659

3204; **REEL**, Frowin; m; 61 (1871); F; M; Head; yes 3178; yes; Al. 658
3205; (Reel) Mary G; f; 59 (1873); F; M; Wife; yes 3179; yes; Al. 3188
3206; " Faith; f; 17 (10-21-14); F; S; Dau; yes 3180; yes; Al. 4690
3207; " Agatha; f; 13 (10-4-18); F; S; Dau; yes 3181; yes; An. 2739
3208; " Theresa; f; 10 (4-29-21); F; S; Dau; yes 3162; yes; An. 2740

N. E. **REIHER**, William; m; Head
3209; (Moran), Margaret; f; 28 (12-7-03); 1/4; M; Wife; no 3183; Minneapolis,
Ramsey Co, Minn; yes; Al. 2592

N. E. **RICKER**, Richard; m; Head
3210; (Crowghost), Rose; f; 20 (11-12-11); F; M; Wife; no 3184; Fort Peck Res,
Poplar, Mont; yes; Al. 4230
3211; Crowghost, Stephen; m; 2 (4-18-29); F; S; St-Son; no 3185; Fort Peck Res,
Poplar, Mont; yes; An. 712

3212; **RETURNS WOUNDED** (White), Mrs; f; 69 (1863); F; Wd; Head; yes 3186;
yes; Al. 3408

Census of the __Standing Rock__ Reservation of the __Standing Rock__ jurisdiction, as of __April 1__, 1932, taken by __E. D. Mossman__, Superintendent. South Dakota

KEY: Number; Surname, Given; Sex; Age at Last Birthday; Tribe (Standing Rock Sioux unless otherwise noted); Degree of Blood; Marital Status; Relationship to Head of Family; At Jurisdiction where enrolled (Yes or No); (If "No", where, if given); Ward (Yes or No); Allotment, Annuity and Identification Numbers.

N. E. **ROACH**, Joseph; m; Head
3213; (Whitebull), Ellen; f; 32 (1900); F; M; Wife; yes 3187; yes; Al. 870
3214; " Joseph L; m; 3 (2-19-29); F; S; Son; yes 3188; yes; An. 2750
3215; " Isabelle; f; 4 (1927); F; S; Dau; yes; 3189; yes; An. 2749

3216; **ROOT OF CLAWS**, Ernest; m; 72 (1860); F; Wd; Head; no 3190; Cheyenne River Res, SD; yes; Al. 459

N. E. **ROBERTSON**, Wallace; m; Head
3217; (Shields), Lizzie; f; 35 (1897); F; M; Wife; yes 3191; yes; Al. 1112

3218; **ROSEBUD**, Joseph; m; 68 (1864); 1/2; M; Head; yes 3192; yes; Al. 1234
3219; (Onjinca), Agnes; f; 22 (6-11-10); F; M; Wife; yes 3193; yes; Al. 4158

N. E. **ROSS**, Silas; m; Head
3220; (Elk), Rose; f; 33 (1899); F; M; Wife; no 3194; Crow Creek Agency, SD; yes; Al. 2989
3221; " Glorietta; f; 3 (6-29-28); F; S; Dau; no 3195; Crow Creek Agency, SD; yes; An. 2755
3222; " Leroy T; m; 2 (12-30-20[sic]); F; S; Son; no 3196; Crow Creek Agency, SD; yes; An. 2756
3223; " Silas, Jr; m; 7/12 (8-30-31); F; S; Son; no ---; Crow Creek Agency, SD; yes; An. 2757

3224; **ROUGHSURFACE**, Samuel; m; 35 (1896); F; M; Head; yes 3197; no; Al. 717
3225; " Abraham; m; 14 (5-20-17); F; S; Son; yes 3198; yes; An. 2759
3226; " Harriet; f; 8 (2-28-24); F; S; Dau; yes 3199; yes; An. 2760
3227; " Samuel; m; 5 (2-21-27); F; S; Son; yes 3200; yes; An. 2761
3228; " Nora M; f; 3 (6-28-28); F; S; Dau; yes 3201; yes; An. 2762
3229; " Mamie L; f; 1 (5-29-30); F; S; Dau; yes 3202; yes; An. 2763
3230; " Calvin H; m; 1/12 (2-11-32); F; S; Son; yes ---; yes; An. ---

N. E. **ROUILLARD**; m; Head
3231; (Dog), Rose; f; 44 (1888); F; M; Wife; no 3203; Rapid City, Pennington Co, SD; yes; Al. 581
3232; Trudell, Levi; m; 12 (8-26-19); F; S; St-Son; no 3204; Rapid City, Pennington Co, SE; yes; An. 2766
3233; Harris, Lydia; f; 17 (3-10-15); F; S; St-Dau; no 3205; Whereabouts Unknown; yes; Al. 4702

3234; **RUNNINGHAWK**, John; m; 56 (1876); F; M; Head; yes 3206; no; Al. 4577
3235; (Dogeagle), Edith; f; 44 (1888); F; M; Wife; yes 3207; yes; Al. 1058
3236; " Mary E; f; 16 (1-16-16); F; S; Dau; yes 3208; yes; An. 2769

Census of the **Standing Rock** Reservation of the **Standing Rock** jurisdiction, as of **April 1**, 1932, taken by **E. D. Mossman**, Superintendent. South Dakota

KEY: Number; Surname, Given; Sex; Age at Last Birthday; Tribe (Standing Rock Sioux unless otherwise noted); Degree of Blood; Marital Status; Relationship to Head of Family; At Jurisdiction where enrolled (Yes or No); (If "No", where, if given); Ward (Yes or No); Allotment, Annuity and Identification Numbers.

3237; " Ambrose; m; 14 (7-6-17); F; S; Son; yes 3209; yes; An. 2770
3238; " George; m; 13 (11-10-18); F; S; Son; yes 3210; yes; An. 2771
3239; " Sophie; f; 11 (7-16-20); F; S; Dau; yes 3211; yes; An. 2772
3240; " Jane   f; 10 (12-10-21); F; S; Dau; yes 3212; yes; An. 2773
3241; " William; m; 4 (10-24-27); F; S; Son; yes 3213; yes; An. 2774

3242; **SACK**, John; m; 50 (1882); F; M; Head; yes 3214; no; Al. 711
3243;   (Lefthand), Martina; f; 38 (4-20-93); F; M; Wife; yes 3215; yes; Al. 2487
3244; " Lowell R; m; 13 (3-29-19); F; S; Son; yes 3216; yes; An. 2780
3245; " Rose M; f; 15 (5-27-16); F; S; Dau; yes 3217; yes; An. 2783
3246; " Lucille; f; 11 (9-5-20); F; S; Dau; yes 3218; yes; An. 2781
3247; " Ethel; f; 8 (10-15-23); F; S; Dau; yes 3219; yes; An. 2782
3248; " Alvina; f; 6 (10-15-25); F; S; Dau; yes; 3220; yes; An. 2784
3249; " Alma; f; 4 (6-16-27); F; S; Dau; yes 3221; yes; An. 2785
3250; " Mamie; f; 3 (6-25-29); F; S; Dau; yes 3222; yes; An. 2786
3251; " Stella S; f; 8/12 (7-6-31); F; S; Dau; yes ---; yes; An. 2787

3252; **SAVESLIFE**, George M; m; 27 (10-22-04); F; M; Head; no 3224; Pine
                              Ridge Res, Pine Ridge, SD; yes; Al. 1360

3253; **SEE THE BEAR**, Frank; m; 54 (1878); F; M; Head; yes 3225; yes; Al. 2910
3254;   (Carrigewin), Julia; f; 62 (1870); F; M; Wife; yes 3226; yes; Al. 3322

3255; **SEVENTEEN** (Redbird), Nora; f; 57 (1875); F; M; Head; yes 3227; yes;
                                                                    Al. 3264
3256; Redbird, Charles; m; 18 (6-27-13); F; S; Son; yes 3228; yes; Al. 4449

3257; **SHAVEBEAR**, John; m; 41 (1891); F; M; Head; yes 3229; yes; Al. 1365
3258; (Leaf), Kate; f; 37 (1895); F; M; Wife; yes 3230; yes; Al. 1193
3259; " Nellie; f; 11 (12-14-21); F; S; Dau; yes 3231; yes; An. 2799
3260; " Theresa; f; 6 (1925); F; S; Dau; yes 3232; yes; An. 2800
3261; " Wallace; m; 1 (2-4-31); F; S; Son; yes ---; yes; An. 2801

3262; **SHAVEHEAD**, Annie; f; 83 (1849); F; S; Head; yes 3233; no; Al. 817

3263; **SHELL**, William; m; 64 (1868); F; M; Head; yes 3234; no; Al. 68
3264;   (Shell), Mary; f; 61 (1871); F; M; Wife; yes 3235; yes; Al. 3069

N. E. **SHEPARD**, Ralph; m; Head
3265;   (Brings Horses), Lucy; f; 27 (12-4-04); F; M; Wife; yes 3236; yes; Al. 935

N. E. **SHERMAN**, John; m; Head
3266; (Pretty Bear), Emma; f; -32 (1891); F; M; Wife; no 3237; Fort Totten Res,
                                                          ND; yes; Al. 2161

Census of the **Standing Rock** Reservation of the **Standing Rock** jurisdiction, as of **April 1**, 1932, taken by **E. D. Mossman**, Superintendent. South Dakota

KEY: Number; Surname, Given; Sex; Age at Last Birthday; Tribe (Standing Rock Sioux unless otherwise noted); Degree of Blood; Marital Status; Relationship to Head of Family; At Jurisdiction where enrolled (Yes or No); (If "No", where, if given); Ward (Yes or No); Allotment, Annuity and Identification Numbers.

N. E. **SHERWOOD**, H. M.; m; Head
3267;   (Claymore), Martina; f; 50 (1882); 1/2; M; Wife; yes 3238; no; Al. 428
3268;   " William; m; 15 (2-10-17); 1/4; S; Son; yes 3239; yes; An. 2835
3269;   " Donald A; m; 11 (1-19-21); 1/4; S; Son; yes 3240; yes; An. 2836
3270;   " Robert C; m; 9 (11-17-22); 1/4; S; Son; yes 3241; ye; An. 2837

3271; **SHIELDS**, Ambrose; m; 29 (6-3-02); F; M; Head; no 3242; Pawnee, Pawnee, OK; yes; Al. 1113

3272; **SHIELDS**, Isabelle; f; 23 (12-22-09); F; S; Head; yes 3243; yes; Al. 3943

3273; **SHIELDS**, Patrick; m; 54 (1878); F; M; Head; yes 3244; no; Al. 1111
3274;   " Mary; f; 17 (6-25-14); F; S; Dau; yes 3245; yes; Al. 4609
3275;   " Zelda; f; 16 (3-16-16); F; S; Dau; yes 3246; yes; Al. 2845
3276;   " Selina; f; 13 (12-28-18); F; S; Dau; yes; 3248; yes; An. 2846

3277; **SHOESTRING**, James; m; 35 (1-1-97); F; M; Head; yes 3249; yes; Al. 1487
3278; (Little Eagle), Jessie; f; 36 (9-9-96); F; M; Wife; yes 3250; yes; Al. 1370
3279;   " Mary C; f; 3 (8-16-28); F; S; Dau; yes 3251; yes; An. 2850
3280; Kelley, Genevieve; f; 10 (7-27-21); F; S; St-Dau; yes 3252; yes; An. 2849

3281; **SHOOTER**, Barney; m; 39 (1893); F; S; Head; yes 3253; yes; Al. 2885

3282; **SHOOTER**, Edward; m; 77 (1855); F; M; Head; yes 3254; no; Al. 2882
3283; (Littledog), Agnes; f; 74 (1858); F; M; Wife; yes; 3255; yes; Al. 3265

3284; **SHOOTER**, Leo; m; 42 (1890); F; S; Head; yes 3256; yes; Al. 2884

3285; **SHOOTS FIRST**, Pius; m; 63 (1869); F; M; Head; yes 3257; yes; Al. 1593
3286; (White), Mary; f; 63 (1869); F; M; Wife; yes 3258; yes; Al. 544
3287; White, Mary J; f; 15 (11-30-16); F; S; St-Dau; yes 3259; yes; An. 2863

3288; **SHOOTS NEAR**, Jacob; m; 31 (10-16-91); F; S; Head; yes 2360; yes; Al. 33

3289; **SHOOTS THE BEAR**, Garfiled[sic]; m; 27 (12-6-04); F; M; Head; yes 3261; yes; Al. 199
3290; (Amidst), Annie; f; 20 (10-4-11); F; M; Wife; yes 3262; yes; Al. 4812

3291; **SHOOTS THE BEAR**, Maurice; m; 64 (1868); F; M; Head; yes 3264; yes; Al. 102
3292; (Flower), Maggie; f; 60 (1872); F; M; Wife; yes 3266; yes; Al. 3413
3293;   " Edith; f; 19 (8-14-12); F; S; Dau; yes 3265; yes; Al. 4340
3294;   " Stanley; m; 15 (5-4-16); F; S; Son; yes 3267; yes; An. 2869

Census of the **Standing Rock** Reservation of the **Standing Rock** jurisdiction, as of **April 1**, 1932, taken by **E. D. Mossman**, Superintendent. South Dakota

KEY: Number; Surname, Given; Sex; Age at Last Birthday; Tribe (Standing Rock Sioux unless otherwise noted); Degree of Blood; Marital Status; Relationship to Head of Family; At Jurisdiction where enrolled (Yes or No); (If "No", where, if given); Ward (Yes or No); Allotment, Annuity and Identification Numbers.

3295; **SHOOTS THE ENEMY**, Caroline f; 23 (10-20-08); F; S; Head; yes 3268; yes; Al. 3866

3296; **SHOOTS THE ENEMY**, George; m; 48 (1884); F; M: Head; yes 3269; yes; Al. 1045
3297; " Leo; m; 16 (9-4-15); F; S; Son; yes 3270; yes; An. 2873

3298; **SHOOTS WALKING**, Noah; m; 38 (1894); F; Wd; Head; yes 3271; no; Al. 393

3299; **SHOT AT**, Leo; m; 65 (1867); F; M; Head; yes 3274; yes; Al. 960
3300; (Shot At), Catherine; f; 57 (1875); F; M; Wife; yes 3275; yes; Al. 3304

3301; **SILK**, Emma; f; 39 (10-27-92); 1/2; S; Head; yes 3277; no; Al. 2953

3302; **SILK**, Ralph; m; 36 (12-25-95); 1/4; S; Head; yes 3278; yes; Al. 2954

3303; **SITTING DOG**, Robert; m; 32 (10-6-99); F; M; Head; yes 3279; yes; Al. 489
3304; (Firecloud), Martha; f; 30 (1901); F; M; Wife; yes 3280; yes; Al. 942
3305; " Minerva; f; 7 (2-12-25); F; S; Dau; yes 3281; yes; An. 2915
3306; " Elaine J; f; 2 (12-30-29); F; S; Dau; yes 3282; yes; An. 2917

3307; **SKINNER**, William; m; 53 (1878); F; M; Head; yes 3283; no; Al. 217
3308; (Skinner), Lizzie; f; 60 (1873); F; M; Wife; yes 3284; yes; Al. 3068
3309; " James; m; 16 (4-22-15); F; S; Son; yes 3285; yes; Al. 4458

N. E. **SKOGEN**, Henry; m; Head
3310; (Waggoner), Ramona; f; 42 (9-6-1900); 1/4; M; Wife; yes 3286; no; Al. 2823
3311; Braine, Carl; m; 19 (12-10-12); 1/8; S; St-Son; yes 3287; yes; Al. 4375
3312; Braine, Josephine; f; 15 (6-30-16); 1/8; S; St-Dau; yes 3288; yes; An. 325

3313; **SKULL**, John; m; 69 (1863); F; M; Head; yes 3289; yes; Al. 1119
3314; (Manley), Mary; f; 57 (1875); F; M; Wife; yes 3290; yes; Al. 3065

3315; **SKUNK**, Isaac; m; 36 (2-10-96); F; M; Head; yes 3291; no; Al. 312
3316; (Onehawk), Annie; f; 42 (7-4-90); F; M; Wife; yes 3292; yes; Al. 1604
3317; " David; m; 9 (7-21-24); F; S; Son; yes 3293; yes; An. 2926
3318; " Louis; m; 4 (9-14-27); F; S; Son; yes 3294; yes; An. 2927
3319; Redfish, Alma; f; 15 (2-14-27); F; S; St-Dau; yes 3296; yes; An. 2928

N. E. **SMEE**, H. H.; m; Head
3320; (Goodreau), Cecelia; f; 58 (1874); 1/2; M; Wife; no 3297; Spokane, Spokane Co, Wash; no; Al. 204,

Census of the __Standing Rock__ Reservation of the __Standing Rock__ jurisdiction, as of __April 1__, 1932, taken by __E. D. Mossman__, Superintendent. South Dakota

KEY: Number; Surname, Given; Sex; Age at Last Birthday; Tribe (Standing Rock Sioux unless otherwise noted); Degree of Blood; Marital Status; Relationship to Head of Family; At Jurisdiction where enrolled (Yes or No); (If "No", where, if given); Ward (Yes or No); Allotment, Annuity and Identification Numbers.

3321; **SMEE**, Clarence; m; 30 (12-12-01); 1/4; m; Head; no 3298; Spokane,
Spokane Co, Wash; no; Al. 207

3322; **SMEE**, Robert; m; 35 (10-15-97; 1/4; M; Head; no 3299; Spokane, Spokane
Co, Wash; yes; Al. 205

3323; **SNOW**, James; m; 52 (1880); F; M; Head; no 3300; Crow Creek Agency, SD;
no; Al. 2050

3324; **SNOW**, Johnson; m; 24 (2-23-08); F; S; Head; yes 3301; yes; Al. 3702

3325; **SNOW**, Joseph; m; 40 (4-?-01); F; S; Head; no 3302; US Penitentiary,
Leavenworth, Kan; yes; Al. 509

3326; **SNOW**, Michael; m; 68 (1864); F; S; Head; yes 3303; yes; Al. 607

3327; **SOFT**, James; m; 54 (1868); F; M; Head; yes 3304; yes; Al. 242
3328; " Lulu; f; 17 (6-2-14); F; S; Dau; yes 3305; yes; Al. 4599
3329; " Angela; f; 13 (10-20-18); F; S; Dau; yes 3306; yes; An. 2962

3330; **SOFT**, Matthew; m; 28 (8-26-03); F; S; Head; yes 3307; yes; Al. 244

N. E. **SPANGLER**, Roy; m; Head
3331; (Primeau), Grace; f; 48 (1884); 1/4; M; Wife; no 3308; Seattle, King Co,
Wash; no; Al. 1434
3332; " Charles; m; 21 (2-4-11); 1/8; S; Son; no 3309; Seattle, King Co, Wash;
yes; Al. 4112
3333; " Ruth C; f; 19 (2-23-13); 1/8; S; Dau; no 3310; Seattle, King Co, Wash;
yes; Al. 4406
3334; Spangler, Dorothy; f; 17 (1914); 1/8; S; Dau; no 3311 Seattle, King Co, Wash;
yes; An. 2967
3335; **SPANGLER**, John L; m; 22 (7-1-09); 1/8; S; Head; no 3312; Seattle, King
Co, Wash; yes; Al. 3998

3336; **SPEAKSWALKING**, Luke; m; 32 (1900); F; M; Head; yes 3313; yes;
Al. 1755
3337; (DeRockbraine) Josephine; f; 31 (5-31-1900); F; M; Wife; yes 3314; yes;
Al. 1264
3338; " Charlotte; f; 16 (1914); F; S; Dau; yes 3315; yes; An. 2973
3339; " Oscar; m; 4 (10-23-27); F; S; Son; yes 3316; yes; An. 2975

3340; **SPOTTEDBEAR**, H John; m; 66 (1866); F; M; Head; yes 3317; yes;
Al. 930
3341; (Spottedbear) Julia; f; 63 (1869); F; M; Wife; yes 3318; yes; Al. 3339

Census of the **Standing Rock** Reservation of the **Standing Rock** jurisdiction, as of **April 1**, 1932, taken by **E. D. Mossman**, Superintendent. South Dakota

KEY: Number; Surname, Given; Sex; Age at Last Birthday; Tribe (Standing Rock Sioux unless otherwise noted); Degree of Blood; Marital Status; Relationship to Head of Family; At Jurisdiction where enrolled (Yes or No); (If "No", where, if given); Ward (Yes or No); Allotment, Annuity and Identification Numbers.

3342; " Herbert; m; 17 (7-28-13); F; S; Son; yes 3319; yes; Al. 4482

3343; **SPOTTEDHORSE**, Felix; m; 56 (1876); F; M; Head; yes 3321; yes; Al. 440
3344; (Spottedhorse), Mabel; f; 54 (1878); F; M; Wife; yes 3322; yes; Al. 3146
3345; " Elihu; m; 19 (8-6-12); F; S; Son; yes 3323; yes; Al. 4330
3346; " Peter; m; 9 (1-1-23); F; S; Son; yes 3324; yes; An. 3001

3347; **SPOTTEDHORSE**, Henry; m; 52 (1880); F; M; Head; yes 3325; yes;
Al. 438
3348; " Margaret; f; 13 (11-26-18); F; S; Dau; yes 3327; yes; An. 2995

N. E. **SPOTTEDHORSE**, James; m; Head
3349; (Chasealone), Josephine; f; 53 (1879); F; M; Wife; no 1850; Cheyenne
River Res, SD; yes; Al. 3645

3350; **SPOTTEDHORSE**, Joshua; m; 38 (1894); F; M; Head; yes 3328; yes;
Al. 377
3351; (OneBull) Jennie; f; 41 (1-27-91); F; M; Wife; yes 3329; yes; Al. 991
3352; " Charity; f; 2 (11-19-29); F; S; Dau; yes 3330; yes; An. 2999

3353; **SPOTTEDHORSE** (Sungleska), Theresa; f; 58 (1874); F; Wd; Head; yes
3331; yes; Al. 3484
3354; " Daniel; m; 19 (10--12); F; S; Son; yes 3332; yes; Al. 4511
3355; " Annie; f; 14 (5-8-17); F; S; Dau; yes 3333; yes; An. 3003

3356; **STANDINGCLOUD**, John; m; 48 (1-1884); F; M; Head; yes 3334; yes;
Al. 1475
3357; (Industrious) Fannie; f; 39 (1893); F; M; Wife; yes 3335; yes; Al. 3883

3358; **STANDINGCLOUD** (Winyanptecela), Mrs; f; 80 (1851); F; Wd; Head;
yes 3336; yes; Al. 3363
3359; **STARR**, Josephine; f; 79 (1853); F; S; Head; yes 3337; yes; Al. 530

N. E. **STEVENS**, Harry A; m; Head
3360; (Bearking) Rosaline; f; 35 (3-6-97); 1/2; M; Wife; no 3338; San Francisco,
Cal; no; Al. 698

3361; **STRIPEDFACE**, Edward; m; 24 (11-11-07); F; S; Head; yes 3339; yes;
Al. 2524

3362; **STRIPEDFACE**, John; m; 58 (1874); F; M; Head; yes 3340; yes; Al. 224
3363; " Ludia; f; 17 (7-1-14); F; S; Dau; yes 3341; yes; Al. 4663
3364; " Innocent; m; 15 (12-2-16); F; S; Son; yes 3342; yes; An. 3042

Census of the **Standing Rock** Reservation of the **Standing Rock** jurisdiction, as of **April 1**, 1932, taken by **E. D. Mossman**, Superintendent. South Dakota

KEY: Number; Surname, Given; Sex; Age at Last Birthday; Tribe (Standing Rock Sioux unless otherwise noted); Degree of Blood; Marital Status; Relationship to Head of Family; At Jurisdiction where enrolled (Yes or No); (If "No", where, if given); Ward (Yes or No); Allotment, Annuity and Identification Numbers.

3365; **STRIPEDFACE**, Moses; m; 22 (1-1-10); F; M; Head; yes 3343; yes; Al. 3961

3366; (Spottedhorse), Clementine; f; 17 (5-17-14); F; M; Wife; yes 3326; yes; Al. 4584

N. E. **STURGEON**, Sam; m; Head
3367; (Carrier), Louise; f; 34 (4-4-98); F; M; Wife; yes 479; yes; Al. 169

N. E. **SUMMERS**, Milton; m; Head
3368; (Chasealone) Ida; f; 77 (5-11-09); F; M; Wife; no 1849; Cheyenne River Res, SD; yes Al. 693

3369; **SUNGAGLI**, Jack; m; 60 (1872); F; M; Head; yes 3344; yes; Al. 932
3370; (Kirk), Julia; f; 65 (1867); F; M; Wife; yes 3345; yes; Al. 449

3371; **SWIFTCLOUD**, Henry; m; 44 (1888); F; M; Head; yes 3346; yes; Al. 60
3372; (Whitebull), Louisa; f; 32 (1889); F; M; Wife; yes 3347; yes; Al. 664
3373; " Henry J; m; 12 (6-4-19); F; S; Son; yes 3348; yes; An. 3055
3374; " Agatha; f; 3 (12-3-28); F; S; Dau; yes 3349; yes; An. 3056
3375; " Samuel; m; 5/12 (10-4-31); F; S; Son; yes---; yes; An. 3057

3376; **SWIFTCLOUD**, Martin; m; 59 (1873); F; Wd; Head; yes 3350; yes; Al. 56

3377; **TAHNK**, Charles; m; 23 (9-3-09); 1/4; S; Head; no 3352; St Paul, Ramsey Co, Minn; yes; Al. 3969

3378; **TAHNK**, Rose M; f; 24 (9-7-06); 1/4; S; Head; yes 3353; yes; Al. 1107

3379; **TAHNK**, Virginia; f; 24 (10-17-07); 1/4; S; Head; no 3354; St Paul, Ramsey Co, Minn; yes; Al. 3028
3380; " Elsie T; f; 12 (4-28-19); 1/4; S; Sister; no 3355; St Paul, Ramsey Co, Minn; yes; An. 3067

3381; **TAKENALIVE**, Charles; m; 41 (1891); F; M; Head; yes 3356; no; Al. 505
3382; (Kills Crow), Annie; f; 41 (1891); F; M; Wife; yes 3357; yes; Al. 403
3383; " Sophie; f; 13 (5-21-18); F; S; Dau; yes 3358; yes; An. 3075
3384; " Vera; f; 12 (3-28-20); F; S; Dau; yes 3359; yes; An. 3076

3385; **TAKENALIVE**, Jesse; m; 41 (1894); F; M; Head; yes 3360; no; Al. 506
3386; (Brings Horses), Madeline; f; 31 (2-1-01); F; M; Wife; yes; 3361; yes; Al. 934
3387; " Jesse, Jr; m; 11 (5-9-20); F; S; Son; yes 3362; yes; An. 3079
3388; " William; m; 10 (5-19-21); F; S; Dau; yes 3363; yes; An. 3080
3389; " Peter; m; 9 (11-2-22); F; S; Son; yes 3364; yes; An. 3081

Census of the **Standing Rock** Reservation of the **Standing Rock** jurisdiction, as of **April 1**, 1932, taken by **E. D. Mossman**, Superintendent. South Dakota

KEY: Number; Surname, Given; Sex; Age at Last Birthday; Tribe (Standing Rock Sioux unless otherwise noted); Degree of Blood; Marital Status; Relationship to Head of Family; At Jurisdiction where enrolled (Yes or No); (If "No", where, if given); Ward (Yes or No); Allotment, Annuity and Identification Numbers.

3390;　"　Faith M; f; 5 (11-2-26); F; S; Dau; yes 3365; yes; An. 3082

3391;　"　Milton; m; 2 (5-7-29); F; S; Son; yes 3366; yes; An. 3083

3392;　**TAKE THE GUN**, Ben; m; 42 (1890); F; S; Head; yes 3367; yes; Al. 1041

3393;　**TAKE THE GUN**, John, Jr; m; 25 (8-3-06); F; M; Head; yes 3368; yes;
Al. 1043

3394;　(Spottedhorse), Laura; f; 19 (4-10-12); F; M; Wife; yes 3369; yes; Al. 4288

3395;　"　Oliver; m; 1 (9-8-30) F; S; Son; yes 3370; yes; An. 3094

3396;　**TAKE THE GUN**, Joseph; m; 44 (1888); F; S; Head; yes 3371; yes; Al. 1040

3397;　**TAKE THE GUN**, Julia; f; 31 (12-15-1900); F; S; Head; yes 3372; yes;
Al. 1042

3398;　**TAKE THE GUN**, Louis; m; 56 (1876); F; M; Head; yes 3373; yes; Al. 297

3399;　(Boneclub), Maude; f; 62 (1880); F; M; Wife; yes 3374; yes; Al. 235

3400;　"　Lillie; f; 18 (1913); F; S; Dau; yes 3376; yes; Al. 4453

3401;　"　Harry; m; 19 (5-30-12); F; S; Son; yes 3375; yes; Al. 3404

3402;　"　Irene　f; 13 (5-21-18); F; S; Dau; yes 3376; yes; An. 3089

3403;　Boneclub, Clarence; m; 15 (4-15-16); F; S; St-Son; yes 3379; yes; An. 319

3404;　**TAKE THE GUN**, Matilda; f; 22 (6-10-10); F; S; Head; yes 3381; yes;
Al. 4007

3405;　**TAKE THE GUN**, Rose; f; 48 (1884); F; S; Head; yes 3381; yes; Al. 764

3406;　**TAKE THE GUN**, Reuben; m; 64 (1868); F; M; Head; yes 3382; yes;
Al. 1039

3407;　(Horpilutawin), Mrs; f; 65 (1866); F; M; Wife; yes 3383; yes; Al. 3253

3408;　"　Edward; m; 20 (7-21-11); F; S; Son; yes 3384; yes; Al. 4182

3409;　**TAKE THE HAT**, George; m; 33 (9-11-99); F; M; Head; yes 3386; yes;
Al. 1204

3410;　(Catch Bear), Annie; f; 29 (9-16-02); F; M; Wife; yes 3386; yes; Al. 131

3411;　"　Mamie; f; 7 (9-16-24); F; S; Dau; yes 3387; yes; An. 3103

3412;　"　Marie; f; 5 (1926); F; S; Dau; yes 3388; yes; An. 3104

3413;　"　Dennis; m; 3 (4-8-28); F; S; Son; yes 3389; yes; An. 3105

3414;　"　Margie; f; 1 (5-8-30); F; S; Dau; yes 3390; yes; An. 3106

3415;　Crossbear, Michael; m; 11 (10-21-21); F; S; St-Son; yes 3391; yes; An. 514

3416;　**TAKE THE SHIELD**, Joseph; m; 65 (1867); F; M; Head; yes 3392; yes;
Al. 614

Census of the **Standing Rock** Reservation of the **Standing Rock** jurisdiction, as of **April 1**, 1932, taken by **E. D. Mossman**, Superintendent. South Dakota

KEY: Number; Surname, Given; Sex; Age at Last Birthday; Tribe (Standing Rock Sioux unless otherwise noted); Degree of Blood; Marital Status; Relationship to Head of Family; At Jurisdiction where enrolled (Yes or No); (If "No", where, if given); Ward (Yes or No); Allotment, Annuity and Identification Numbers.

3417; **TAYLOR**, Claude; m; 29 (3-24-03); 1/2; M; Head; yes 3393; no; Al. 278
3418; (Bearking), Clara; f; 23 (7-9-08); 1/2; M; Wife; yes 3394; yes; Al. 3850
3419; " Ramona; f; 2 (7-6-29); 1/2; S; Dau; yes 3395; yes; An. 3120
3420; " Hazel G; f; 4 da (3-27-31); 1/2; S; Dau; yes ---; yes; An. ---

3421; **TAYLOR**, Margaret; f; 26 (12-25-05); 1/2; S; Head; yes 3397; yes; Al. 1572

N. E. **TAYLOR**, William; m; Head
3422; (Marsh), Mollie; f; 55 (1876); 1/2; M; Wife; yes 3398; no; Al. 276
3423; " Lavon E; f; 16 (1-18-16); 1/4; S; Dau; yes 3399; yes; An. 3124
3424; " Mae; f; 14 (10-22-18); 1/4; S; Dau; yes 3400; yes; An. 3125

3425; **TAYLOR**, William E; m; 24 (1-9-08); 1/4; S; Head; yes 3401; yes; Al. 3000

3426; **THIEF**, Alphonse; m; 45 (1887); F; M; Head; yes 3402; no; Al. 337
3427; (Whitehorse), Agnes; f; 58 (1874); F; M; Wife; yes 3403; yes; Al. 3166

3428; **THIEF**, David; m; 42 (1896); F; M; Head; yes 3404; no; Al. 1525
3429; " Genevieve; f; 1 (12-9-30); F; S; Dau; yes 3405; yes; An. 3130

3430; **THIEF**, John; m; 38 (8-25-93); F; M; Head; yes 3406; yes; Al. 1524
3431; (Antapeta) Julia; f; 34 (1898); F; M; Wife; yes 3407; yes; Al. 3872
3432; " Bessie; f; 10 (7-7-21); F; S; Dau; yes 3408; yes; An. 3133
3433; " Christine; f; 3 (10-5-28); F; S; Dau; yes 3409; yes; An. 3134
3434; " Sampson; m; 1 (3-3-31); F; S; Son; yes --; yes; An. 3135

3435; **THIEF**, Julia; 71 (1861); F; S; Head; yes 3410; yes; Al. 3620

3436; **THIEF**, Louis; m; 42 (12-25-90); F; S; Head; yes 3411; no; Al. 838

3437; **THIGH**; m; 72 (1860); F; M; Head; yes 3412; yes; Al. 2262
3438; (Ropena), Sarah; f; 77 (1855); F; M; Wife; yes 3413; yes; Al. 3126

3439; **THIGH**, Isaac; m; 29 (11-16-02); F; M; Head; yes 3414; yes; Al. 2264
3440; (Lean Dog), Elizabeth; f; 27 (7-23-04); F; M; Wife; yes 3415; yes;
Al. 1570

N. E. **THOMPSON**, James; m; Head
3441; (Goodboy), Louise; f; 41 (1891); F; M; Wife; yes 3416; yes; Al. 985
3442; " William; m; 9 (8-3-22); F; S; Son; yes 3417; yes; An. 3147
3443; " Face, Andrew; m; 14 (8-10-17); F; S; St-Son; yes 3419; yes; An. 3146

KEY: Number; Surname, Given; Sex; Age at Last Birthday; Tribe (Standing Rock Sioux unless otherwise noted); Degree of Blood; Marital Status; Relationship to Head of Family; At Jurisdiction where enrolled (Yes or No); (If "No", where, if given); Ward (Yes or No); Allotment, Annuity and Identification Numbers.

N. E. **THOMPSON**, John; m; Head
3444;   (Crowghost), Jennie; f; 24 (9-19-07); F; M; Wife; no 3420; Wood
Mountain, Saskeatchewan[sic], Can; yes; Al. 3436

N. E. **THREELEGS**, Henry; m; Head
3445;   (Catchbear), Matilda; f; 23 (3-2-09); F; M; Wife; no 3421; Mobridge,
Walworth Co, SD; yes; Al. 3929

3446; **THUNDERSHIELD**, Ambrose; m; 25 (10-7-05); F; S; Head; yes 3422; yes;
Al. 3704

3447; **THUNDERSHIELD**, Joseph; m; 52 (1880); F; M; Head; yes 3423; yes;
Al. 418
3448;   (Dog) Agnes; f; 30 (1901); F; M; Wife; yes 3424; yes; Al. 577
3449;   "   Rebecca; f; 13 (5-5-18); F; S; Dau; yes 3425; yes; An. 3162
3450;   "   Vincent; m; 10 (1-4-1921); F; S; Son; yes 3426; yes; An. 3163
3451;   "   Bede; m; 8 (12-29-23); F; S; Son; yes 3427; yes; An. 3164
3452;   "   Luella; f; 5 (4-10-26); F; S; Dau; yes 3428; yes; An. 3165
3453;   "   Olive; f; 4 (4-1-28); F; S; Dau; yes 3429; yes; An. 3166
3454;   "   Margaret; f; 1 (2-25-31); F; S; Dau; yes 3430; yes; An. 3167

3455; **TIGER** (Bear Looking Back), Jennie; f; 54 (1878); F; Wd; Head; yes 3431;
yes; Al. 267
3456;   "   Ralph; m; 19 (8-4-12); F S; Son; yes 3432; yes; Al. 4333

3457; **TIGER**, Nicholas; m; 46 (1886); F; S; Head; yes 3433; yes; Al. 135

3458; **TIGER** (Caddy), Theresa; f; 77 (1855); F; Wd; Head; yes 3434; yes; Al. 1957

3459; **TIGER**, William; m; 55 (1875); F; M; Head; yes 3435; yes; Al. 133
3460;   (Tiger), Annie; f; 56 (1876); F; M; Wife; yes 3436; yes; Al. 3418

N. E. **TIYONA**, David; m; Head
3461;   (Reel), Bessie; f; 23 (12-16-09); F; M; Wife; yes 1312; yes; Al. 3957
3462;   " Ray; m; 3/12 (12-25-31); F; S; Son; yes ---; yes; An. 3192

3463; **TOKAOLA**, (Winyanwaste), Mrs; f; 86 (1846); F; Wd; Head; yes 3439; yes;
Al. 3246

3464; **TREETOP**, Michael; m; 22 (3-6-10); F; S; Head; yes 3438; yes; Al. 4099

N. E. **TURNINGHEART**, John; m; Head
3465; (Takenalive), Pauline f; 28 (1903); F; M; Wife; yes 3439; yes; Al. 508
3466; Wawokiya, William; m; 8 (3-24-23); F; S; St-Son; yes 3440; yes; An. 3205

Census of the **Standing Rock** Reservation of the **Standing Rock** jurisdiction, as of **April 1**, 1932, taken by **E. D. Mossman**, Superintendent. South Dakota

KEY: Number; Surname, Given; Sex; Age at Last Birthday; Tribe (Standing Rock Sioux unless otherwise noted); Degree of Blood; Marital Status; Relationship to Head of Family; At Jurisdiction where enrolled (Yes or No); (If "No", where, if given); Ward (Yes or No); Allotment, Annuity and Identification Numbers.

3467;　　" 　　Delmas V; f; 5 (11-23-26); F; S; St-Dau; yes 3441; yes; An. 3206
3468;　Turningheart, Samuel; m; 3/12 (12-4-31); F; S; Son; yes ---; yes; An. 3207

3469;　**TWIGGS**, Jesse; m; 41 (1891); F; M; Head; no 3442; Rosebud Res, Rosebud,
　　　　　　　　　　　　　　　　　　　　　　　　　　　SD; no; Al. 790
3470;　　" 　　Sidney S; m; 20 (12-21-11); F; S; Son; no 3443; Rosebud Res, Rosebud,
　　　　　　　　　　　　　　　　　　　　　　　　　　　SD; yes; Al. 4269
3471;　　" 　　Vern J; m; 18 (1-27-14); F; S; Dau; no 3444; Rosebud Res, Rosebud, SD;
　　　　　　　　　　　　　　　　　　　　　　　　　　　yes; Al. 4555
3472;　　" 　　Cyril; m; 16 (1-8-16); F; S; Son; no 3445; Rosebud Res, Rosebud, SD;
　　　　　　　　　　　　　　　　　　　　　　　　　　　yes; An. 3218

3473;　**TWOFACE**; m; 73 (1859); F; M; Head; yes 3446; yes; Al. 1501

3474;　**TWOFURS** (TakeTheShield), Flora; f; 48 (1884); F; Wd; Head; yes 3448;
　　　　　　　　　　　　　　　　　　　　　　　　　　　yes; Al. 3574
3475;　　" 　　Jacob; m; 7 (2-6-25); F; S; Son; yes 3449; yes; An. 3254
3476;　White, Joseph; m; 13 (6-24-18); F; S; Son; yes 3450; yes; An. 3255
3477;　White, Mary; f; 11 (10-3-20); F; S; Dau; yes 3451; yes; An. 3256

3478;　**TWO GENERATION**; f; 87 (1845); F; Wd; Head; yes 3452; yes; Al. 669

3479;　**TWOHEARTS**, Edward; m; 42 (12-15-90); F; M; Head; yes 3453; yes;
　　　　　　　　　　　　　　　　　　　　　　　　　　　Al. 525
3480;　　　(Bearlooking), Annie; f; 41 (1891); F; M; Wife; yes 3454; yes; Al. 266
3481;　　" 　　Johnson; m; 18 (10-15-13); F; S; Son; yes 3455; yes; Al. 4534
3482;　　" 　　Stephen; m; 12 (2-12-20); F; S; Son; yes 3456; yes; An. 3260
3483;　　" 　　Irene 　f; 5 (2-2-24); F; S; Dau; yes 3457; yes; An. 3261
3484;　　" 　　Lucille; f; 2 (11-21-26); F; S; Dau; yes 3458; yes; An. 3262

3485;　**TWOHEARTS**, Sallie; f; 57 (1875); F; Wd; Head; yes 3460; yes; Al. 415
3486;　　" 　　Roy; m; 14 (2-13-17); F; S; Son; yes 3461; yes; An. 3265
3487;　**TWOHEARTS**, Samuel; m; 23 (2-17-09); F; S; Head; yes 3463; yes;
　　　　　　　　　　　　　　　　　　　　　　　　　　　Al. 3794

3488;　**UBERSETZIG**, Eleanor K; f; 20 (1-18-12); 1/4; S; Alone; no 3464; Oakland,
　　　　　　　　　　　　　　　　　　　　　　　　Alameda Co, Cal yes; Al. 4261

N. E.　**VATLAND**, Louis; m; Head
3489;　　　(Waggoner), Maude; 38 (1-12-94); 1/4; M; Wife; yes 3465; yes;
　　　　　　　　　　　　　　　　　　　　　　　　　　　Al. 2825

3490;　**VERMILLION**, Arthur; m; 51 (9-8-91); 1/2; M; Head; yes; 3466; yes;
　　　　　　　　　　　　　　　　　　　　　　　　　　　Al. 2881

Census of the __Standing Rock__ Reservation of the __Standing Rock__ jurisdiction, as of __April 1__, 1932, taken by __E. D. Mossman__, Superintendent. South Dakota

3491; **VERMILLION**, Charles; m; 46 (1886); 1/2; M; Head; yes; 3467; no;
Al. 2854

3492;   (Ironwing), Marcella; f; 32 (3-28-1900); 1/2; M; Wife; yes; 3468; yes;
Al. 734

3493; "   Chas, Jr; m; 18 (2-12-14); 1/2; S; Son; yes 3469; yes; Al. 4557

3494; "   Frank; m; 14 (10-2-17); 1/2; S; Son; yes 3470; yes; An. 3298

3495; "   Jerome; m; 8 (11-28-23); 1/2; S; Son; yes 3471; yes; An. 3296

3496; "   William; m; 4 (7-11-27); 1/2; S; Son; yes 3472; yes; An. 3297

3497; **VILLAGE CENTER**, Charles; m; 48 (1884); F; Wd; Head; yes 3473; yes;
Al. 1183

3498; **VILLAGE CENTER**, Frank; m; 26 (3-11-05); F; S; Head; yes 3474; yes;
Al. 1220

3499; **VILLAGE CENTER**, Herbert; m; 24 (4-14-07); F; S; Head; yes 3475; yes;
Al. 1221

3500; **VILLAGE CENTER** (Cetanwambliwin), Mrs; 83 (1849); F; Wd; Head; yes
3476; yes; Al. 3366

3501; **VILLAGE CENTER**, Joseph; m; 43 (1889); F; M; Head; yes 3477; no;
Al. 1182

3502;   (Looking Elk), Agnes; f; 36 (1896); F; M; Wife; yes 3478; yes; Al. 983

3503; "   Patrick; m; 8 (4-10-23); F; S; Son; yes 3479; yes; An. 3311

3504; "   Alexander; m; 7 (11-13-24); F; S; Son; yes 3480; yes; An. 3312

3505; "   Floyd; m; 5 (4-19-26); F; S; Son; yes 3481; yes; An. 3313

3506; "   Carl; m; 3 (2-11-29); F; S; Son; yes 3482; yes; An. 3314

3407; "   Michael; m; 1 (11-7-30); F; S; Son; yes 3483; yes; An. 3315

3408; Looking Elk, Verling; m; 12 (2-24-20); F; S; St-Son; yes 3484; yes; An. 3309

3409; Looking Elk, Dorothy; f; 10 (10-30-21); F; S; St-Dau; yes 3485; yes; An. 3310

N. E. **VLANDRY**, Louis; m; Head

3510;   (Archambault), Blanche; f; 36 (12-7-96); 1/4; M; Wife; no 3486; Rosebud
Agency, SD; yes; Al. 1393

3511; **WAGGONER**, Aurelia; f; 27 (3-18-05); 1/4; S; Head; yes 3487; yes;
Al. 2824

3512; **WAGGONER**, Erne st; m; 27 (1905); 1/4; M; Head; yes 3488; yes; Al. 2827

3513; "   Gary Leo; m; 2 (8-1-29); 1/8; S; Son; yes 3489; yes; An. 3318

3514; "   Donald F; m; 10/12 (5-15-31); 1/8; S; Son; yes ---; yes; An. ---

Census of the **Standing Rock** Reservation of the **Standing Rock** jurisdiction, as of **April 1**, 1932, taken by **E. D. Mossman**, Superintendent. South Dakota

3515; **WAGGONER**, John; m; 33 (4-8-98); 1/4; M; Head; no 3490; Leavenworth, Kan; no; Al. 2839

3516; (Forte), Genevieve; f; 36 (1-26-96); 1/2; M; Wife; yes 3491; yes; Al. 1896

3517; " Virginia; f; 10 (1-3-22); 3/8; S; Dau; yes 3492; yes; An. 3321

3518; " Joseph L; m; 8 (7-17-23); 3/8; S; Son; yes 3493; yes; An. 3323

3519; " Joanitta D; f; 11/12 (4-3-31); 3/8; S; Dau; yes ---; yes; An. ---

3520; Archambault, Olivia; f; 15 (7-3-16); 1/2; S; St-Dau; yes 3494; yes; An. 3323

3521; Archambault, May T; f; 13 (2-15-18); 1/2; S; St-Dau; yes 3495; yes; An. 3324

N. E. **WAGGONER**, Frank; m; Head

3522; (McCarthy), Josephine; f; 63 (1869); 1/2; M; Wife; yes 3496; no; Al. 2822

3523; **WAGGONER**, Lester; m; 25 (3-4-07); 1/4; M; Head; no 3497; Pringle, SD; yes; Al. 2829

3524; **WAGGONER**, Wayne; m; 3 (8-21-09); 1/4; S; Head; no 3498; yes; Al. 3997

3525; **WALKINGBULL**, John; m; 76 (1886); F; M; Head; no; 3499; Cheyenne River Res, SD; yes; Al. 1542

3526; " Minnie; f; 19 (9-5-12); F; S; Dau; no 3500; Cheyenne River Res, SD; yes; Al. 4362

3527; " Julia; f; 17 (8-13-14); F; S; Son; no 3501; Cheyenne River Res, SD; yes; Al. 4619

3528; **WALKINGELK**, Francis; m; 62 (1870); F; M; Head; yes 3502; no; Al. 591

3529; **WALKING ELK** (Walking Elk), Lucy; f; 86 (1846); F; Wd; Head; yes 3503; yes; Al. 3201

3530; **WALKING ELK**, Mark; m; 38 (1894); F; M; Head; yes 3504; no; Al. 592

3531; (Bobtail Bear), Jessie; F; 29 (12-15-02); F; M; Wife; yes 3505; yes; Al. 647

3532; " Kenneth; m; 5/12 (10-11-31); F; S; Son; yes ---; yes; An. 3341

3533; **WALKINGELK**, Mark; m; 56 (1876); F; M; Head; yes 3506; yes; Al. 703

3534; " Mark L; m; 4 (2-13-27); F; S; Son; yes 3507; yes; An. 3344

3535; " Gloria M; f; 1 (7-16-30); F; S; Dau; yes 3508; yes; An. 3345

3536; **WALKINGSHIELD**, George; m; 32 (2-24-99); F; S; Head; yes 3509; yes; Al. 48

3537; **WALKINGSHIELD**, William; m; 33 (1849); F; M; Head; yes 3510; yes; Al. 46

Census of the **Standing Rock** Reservation of the **Standing Rock** jurisdiction, as of **April 1**, 1932, taken by **E. D. Mossman**, Superintendent. South Dakota

KEY: Number; Surname, Given; Sex; Age at Last Birthday; Tribe (Standing Rock Sioux unless otherwise noted); Degree of Blood; Marital Status; Relationship to Head of Family; At Jurisdiction where enrolled (Yes or No); (If "No", where, if given); Ward (Yes or No); Allotment, Annuity and Identification Numbers.

3538; **WALKS IN THE WIND**; m; 62 (1860); F; M; Head; yes 3511; yes; Al. 147
3539; (Four Horses), Mrs; f; 64 (1868); F; M; Wife; yes 3512; yes; Al. 3460

3540; **WALKS QUIETLY** (Catkawin), Mrs; f; 71 (1861); F; Wd; Head; yes 3513; yes; Al. 3471

3541; **WALKS QUIETLY**, Amos; m; 34 (1898); F; M; Head; yes 3514; yes; Al. 1279
3542; (Seventeen), Margaret; f; 29 (1902); F; M; Wife; yes 3515; yes; Al. 1442
3543; " Ada; f; 5 (6-29-26); F; S; Dau; yes 3516; yes; An. 3355

3544; **WANKICUN**, Daniel; m; 25 (4-7-06); F; M; Head; yes 3517; yes; Al. 1033
3545; (Wawokiya), Ruth; f; 28 (1903); F; M; Wife; yes 3518; yes; Al. 1071
3546; " Evelyn; f; 4 (4-11-27); F; S; Dau; yes 3519; yes; An. 3365
3547; " Bernadine; f; 5/12 (10-5-31); F; S; Dau; yes ---; yes; An. 3366

3548; **WANKICUN**, Suibert; m; 65 (1867); F; M; Head; yes 3520; yes; Al. 1029
3549; (Wankicun), Angela; f; 57 (1875); F; M; Wife; yes 3521; yes; Al. 3354
3550; " Dora; f; 15 (1916); F; S; Dau; yes 3522; yes; An. 3370
3551; " Percy; m; 11 (6-4-20); F; S; Son; yes 3523; yes; An. 3369
3552; " Isabelle; f; 9 (10-1-22); F; S; Dau; yes 3524; yes; An. 3371

3553; **WANKICUN**, Nellie; f; 20 (2-8-12); F; S; Head; yes 2525; yes; Al. 4630

3554; **WARBONNETT** (Wiciska), Mrs; f; 89 (1853); F; Wd; Head; yes 3527; yes; Al. 3917

N. E. **WARD**, Buck; Head
3555; (LeCompte), Florence; f; 32 (4-12-99); 1/2; M; Wife; yes 3528; yes; Al. 8
3556; " James G; m 9 (9-12-22); 1/4; S; Son; yes 3529; yes; An. 3385
3557; " Robert; m; 7 (4-30-24); 1/4; S; Son; yes 3530; yes; An. 3386
3558; " Rita C; f; 5 (10-19-26); 1/4; S; Son; yes 3531; yes; An. 3387
3559; " Kenneth; m; 3 (2-24-29); 1/4; S; Son; yes 3532; yes; An. 3388
3560; " Richard L; m; 8/12 (7-12-31); 1/4; S; Son; yes ---; yes; An. 3389

3561; **WATERS**, Isadore; m; 63 (1869); F; M; Head; yes 3533; no; Al. 519
3562; (Tamahen), Mrs; f; 65 (1867); F; M; Wife; yes 3534; yes; Al. 3658

N. E. **WATKINS**, HT; m; Head
3563; (Marsh), Elizabeth; f; 42 (1890); 1/4; M; Wife; no 3535; Rochester, Olmsted Co, Minn; no; Al. 559
3564; " Alethea; f; 20 (3-30-12); 1/8; S; Dau; no 3536; Rochester, Olmsted Co, Minn; yes; Al. 4269

Census of the __Standing Rock__ Reservation of the __Standing Rock__ jurisdiction, as of __April 1__, 1932, taken by __E. D. Mossman__, Superintendent. South Dakota

KEY: Number; Surname, Given; Sex; Age at Last Birthday; Tribe (Standing Rock Sioux unless otherwise noted); Degree of Blood; Marital Status; Relationship to Head of Family; At Jurisdiction where enrolled (Yes or No); (If "No", where, if given); Ward (Yes or No); Allotment, Annuity and Identification Numbers.

3565; " Hugh L; m; 14 (2-23-18); 1/8; S; Son; no 3537; Rochester, Olmsted Co, Minn; yes; An. 3399

3566; **WAWOKIYA** (Ramsey), Benedicta; f; 58 (1874); 1/2; Wd; Head; yes 3538; yes; Al. 3410
3567; " Alma; f; 15 (6-26-17); 3/4; S; Dau; yes 3539; yes; Al. 1064

3568; **WAWOKIYA**, Julia; f; 20 (8-8-11); 3/4; S; Head; yes 3540; yes; Al. 4146

3569; **WAWOKIYA**, Wallace; m; 24 (1-9-08); F; M; Head; yes 3541; yes; Al. 3321
3570; (Eagledog), Julia; f; 20 (8-10-10); F; M; Wife; yes 2098; yes; Al. 4149
3571; " Emma; f; 6/12 (9-3-31); F; S; Dau; yes --; yes; An. 3406

3572; **WEARS HORNS**; m; 63 (1869); F; M; Head; yes 3542; yes; An. 3413
3573; (Pankeskalutewin), Mrs; f; 64 (1868); F; M; Wife; yes 3543; yes; Al. 4587

3574; **WEASEL**, George; m; 36 (1895); F; M; Head; yes 3544; yes; Al. 913
3575; (Iron), Helen; f; 22 (6-1-09); F; M; Wife; yes 3545; yes; Al. 3386
3576; " Leonard; m; 8 (10-1-23); F; S; Son; yes 3546; yes; An. 3418
3577; " Oscar; m; 6 (4-5-25); F; S; Son; yes 3547; yes; An. 3419
3578; " Gerald; m; 4 (4-20-27); F; S; Son; yes 3548; yes; An. 3420
3479; " Harold; m; 1 (7-5-30); F; S; Son; yes 3549; yes; An. 3417

N. E. **WELLS**, Jack; m; Head
3580; (Redfox), Mollie; f; 34 (6-20-98); F; M; Wife; no 3550; Bixley, Perkins Co, SC; no; Al. 2638
3581; " John E; m; 9 (10-3-22); 1/2; S; Son; no 3551; Bixley, Perkins Co, SD; yes; An. 3431
3582; Harris; Effie; f; 13 (6-22-18); 1/2; S; St-Dau; no 3552; Bixley, Perkins Co, SD; yes; An. 3430

3583; **WELLS**, Rush E; m; 23 (12-20-09); 1/4; S; Head; no 3553; Phoenix, AZ; yes; Al. 4089
3584; **WHITE**, Abel; m; 35 (2-18-97); F; M; Head; yes 3554; yes; Al. 547
3585; (Redbear), Elizabeth; f; 39 (12-24-92); F; M; Wife; yes 3555; yes; Al. 639

3586; **WHITE**, Ralph; m; 58 (1884); F; M; Head; yes 3556; no; Al. 477
3587; (Jordan) Bessie; f; 44 (1888); F; M; Wife; yes 3557; yes; Al. 1613
3588; " Florence; f; 8 (3-4-24); F; S; Dau; yes 3558; yes; An. 3451
3589; " Jacob; m; 6 (9-29-25); F; S; Son; yes 3559; yes; An. 3452
3590; " Bertha; f; 13 (6-14-18); F; S; Dau; yes 3560; yes; An. 3449
3591; " Ralph; m; 11 (4-28-20); F; S; Son; yes 3561; yes; An. 3450
3592; " Jeanette; f; 8 (12-27-22); F; S; Dau; yes 3562; yes; An. 1321
3593; " Evelyn; f; 3 (1929); F; S; Dau; yes 3563; yes; An. 3453

KEY: Number; Surname, Given; Sex; Age at Last Birthday; Tribe (Standing Rock Sioux unless otherwise noted); Degree of Blood; Marital Status; Relationship to Head of Family; At Jurisdiction where enrolled (Yes or No); (If "No", where, if given); Ward (Yes or No); Allotment, Annuity and Identification Numbers.

3594; Spottedhorse, Catherine; f; 14 (5-27-17); F; S; St-Dau; yes 3564; yes; An. 3454

3595; **WHITEBEARCLAWS**, Adelia; f; 21 (3-10-11); F; S; Head; yes 3567; yes; Al. 4135

3596; " Sylvester; m; 2/12 (1-4-32); F; S; Son; yes ---; yes; An. 3463

3597; **WHITEBEARCLAWS**, Frank; m; 49 (1883); F; M; Head; yes 3565; no; Al. 1350

3598; (Often Kills The Enemy), Jane; f; 51 (1881); F; M; Wife; yes 3566; yes; Al. 2903

3599; " Helen; f; 17 (10-23-14); F; S; Dau; yes 3569; yes; An. 3459

3600; " Sophie; f; 16 (11-7-16); F; S; Dau; yes ---; yes; An. 3460

3601; **WHITEBEARPAWS**; m; 75 (1857); F; Wd; Head; yes 3570; yes; Al. 1349

3602; **WHITE BIRD**, Henry; m; 36 (1895); F; M; Head; yes 3571; yes; Al. 1319

3603; (Bravethunder), Bessie; f; 29 (4-26-02); F; M; Wife; yes 3572; yes; Al. 1211

3604; **WHITE BIRD**, Joseph; m; 74 (1858); F; M; Head; yes 3573; yes; Al. 1315

3605; (Whitebird), Augustine; f; 67 (1865); F; M; Wife; yes 3574; yes; Al. 3380

3606; **WHITE BUFFALOBOY** (Ptesanhoksila), Mrs; f; 72 (1864); F; Wd; Head; yes 3575; yes; Al. 3352

3607; **WHITEBULL**, George; m; 57 (1875); F; M; Head; yes 3576; no; Al. 869

3608; (Whitebull), Rose; f; 54 (1878); F; M; Wife; yes 3577; yes; Al. 3383

3609; " Jane; f; 16 (12-6-16); F; S; Dau; yes 3578; yes; An. 3477

3610; **WHITEBULL**, Jacob; m; 36 (10-22-95); F; M; Head; yes 3579; no; Al. 1532

3611; (Redfish), Julia; f; 26 (6-2-05); F; M; Wife; yes 3580; yes; Al. 543

3612; Cecil J; m; 6 (2-6-26); F; S; Son; yes 3581; yes; An. 3480

3613; Melvin J; m; 4 (9-4-27); F; S; Son; yes 3582; yes; An. 3481

3614; Cynthia; f; 3 (11-28-28); F; S; Dau; yes 3583; yes; An. 3482

3615; **WHITEBULL**, James; m; 27 (3-25-05); F; S; Head; yes 3584; yes; Al. 677

3616; **WHITEBULL**, Louis; m; 55 (1877); F; M; Head; yes 3585; yes; Al. 665

3617; **WHITECOAT**, Frederick; m; 63 (1869); F; M; Head; yes 3586; yes; Al. 1334

3618; (Whitecoat), Helen; f; 63 (1869); F; M; Wife; yes 3587; yes; Al. 3371

3619; Crowghost, Seraphine; f; 8 (1924); F; S; Son; yes 3588; yes; An. 3489

Census of the **Standing Rock** Reservation of the **Standing Rock** jurisdiction, as of **April 1**, 1932, taken by **E. D. Mossman**, Superintendent. South Dakota

KEY: Number; Surname, Given; Sex; Age at Last Birthday; Tribe (Standing Rock Sioux unless otherwise noted); Degree of Blood; Marital Status; Relationship to Head of Family; At Jurisdiction where enrolled (Yes or No); (If "No", where, if given); Ward (Yes or No); Allotment, Annuity and Identification Numbers.

3620; **WHITECOAT**, Mary; f; 36 (1895); F; S; Head; yes 3589; yes; Al. 1335

3621; **WHITE DEER** (Wasu), Mrs; f; 87 (1845); F; Wd; Head; yes 3590; yes;
Al. 3845

3622; **WHITE EAGLE**, Benjamin; m; 24 (8-16-07); F; M; Head; yes 3591; yes;
Al. 3163
3623; (Wankicun), Angeline; f; 22 (2-10-10); F; M; Wife; yes 3592; yes; Al. 4629
3624; " Rita Rose; f; 1 (1-23-31); F; S; Dau; yes 3593; yes; An. ---

3625; **WHITEEAGLE**, Samuel; m; 70 (1862); F; M; Head; yes 3594; yes; Al. 54
3626; (Tasina), Mrs; f; 70 1862); F; M; Wife; yes 3595; yes; Al. 3164

N. E. **WHITEFACE**, Oliver; m; Head
3627; (Dogeagle), Hannah; f' 31 (4-27-1900); F; M; Wife; yes 3596; yes; Al. 3839

3628; **WHITEHORSE**, Jane; f; 28 (4-1-04); F; S; Head; yes 3597; yes; Al. 955

3629; **WHITEHORSE**, Louis; m; 59 (1873); F; M; Head; yes 3598; yes; Al. 954

3630; **WHITEHORSE**, Scholastica; f; 42 (1890); F; Wd; Head; yes 3599; yes;
Al. 351
3631; " Etta M; f; 5 (5-28-26); F; S; Dau; yes 3600; yes; An. 3527

3632; **WHITEHORSE**, Sebastian; m; 73 (1859); F; M; Head; yes 3601; yes;
Al. 1579
3633; (Whitehorse), Josephine; f; 77 (1855); F; M; Wife; yes 3602; yes; Al. 3169

3634; **WHITEHORSE**, Thomas; m; 66 (1866); F; Wd; Head; yes 3603; yes;
Al. 350

3635; **WHITEMAN**, George; m; 43 (1899); F; M; Head; yes 3604; yes; Al. 2717
3636; (Hawkbear), Lucy; f; 28 (7-11-03); F; M; Wife; yes 3605; yes; Al. 2026
3637; " Mildred; f; 4 (4-14-27); F; S; Dau; yes 3606; yes; An. 3546;
3638; " Matthew; m; 8 (9-22-23); F; S; Son; yes 3607; yes; An. 3545
3639; " Wilma; f; 8/12 (7-7-31); F; S; Dau; yes --; yes; An. 3547

3640; **WHITESELL**, Charles; m; 40 (1-25-92); 1/2; M; Head; yes 3608; no; Al. 556
3641; " Annie E; f; 17 (6-25-14); 1/2; S; Dau; yes 3609; yes; Al. 4615

3642; **WHITESELL**, Diel; m; 24 (10-10-07); 1/2; M; Head; yes 3610; yes; Al. 2879

3643; **WHITESELL**, John; m; 55 (1877); 1/2; M; Head; yes 3611; no; Al. 551
3644; (Whitesell), Clara; f; 55 (1877); 1/2; M; Wife; yes 3612; no; Al. 3403

Census of the **Standing Rock** Reservation of the **Standing Rock** jurisdiction, as of **April 1**, 1932, taken by **E. D. Mossman**, Superintendent. South Dakota

KEY: Number; Surname, Given; Sex; Age at Last Birthday; Tribe (Standing Rock Sioux unless otherwise noted); Degree of Blood; Marital Status; Relationship to Head of Family; At Jurisdiction where enrolled (Yes or No); (If "No", where, if given); Ward (Yes or No); Allotment, Annuity and Identification Numbers.

3645; **WHITESELL**, Irvin; m; 33 (2-12-99); 1/2; M; Head; yes 3613; no; Al. 553

3646; (Cadotte), Phoebe; f; 26 (3-16-06); F; M; Wife; yes 3614; yes; Al. 915

3647; " Jeanette; f; 1 (12-18-30); 3/4; S; Dau; yes 3615; yes; An. 3555

3648; Thorton, Fremont J; m; 5 (8-9-26); 1/2; S; St-Son; yes 3616; yes; An. 3554

3649; **WHITESELL**, Lavina; f; 21 (3-15-11); 1/2; S; Head; yes 3617; yes; Al. 4275

3650; **WHITESELL**, William; m; 29 (1-1-03); 1/2; M; Head; yes 3618; yes; Al. 554

3651; " Jean P; f; 4 (10-29-27); 1/4; S; Dau; yes 3619; yes; An. 3559

3652; **WHITESHIELD**, John; m; 58 (1874); F; M; Head; yes 3620; no; Al. 875

3653; (Wiciqna), Lottie; f; 58 (1874); F; M; Wife; yes 3621; yes; Al. 3422

3654; " Elsie; f; 11 (6-30-20); F; S; Dau; yes 3622; yes; An. 3562

3655; **WHITESHIELD**, Joshua; m; 32 (6-22-99); F; M; Head; yes 3624; yes; Al. 1088

3656; (Archambault), Mary L; f; 28 (12-25-03); F; M; Wife; yes 3625; yes; Al. 1889

3657; " Stanton, m; 6 (6-12-25); F; S; Son; yes 3626; yes; Al. 1088-A

3658; " Helen; f; 3 (11-17-28); F; S; Dau; yes 3627; yes; Al. 1088-B

3659; **WHITE TEMPLE**, Gilbert; m; 24 (10-2-08); F; S; Head; yes 3628; yes; Al. 3747

3660; **WHITE TEMPLE**, Joseph; m; 64 (1868); F; M; Head; yes 3629; no; Al. 1544

3661; (White Temple), Fannie; f; 59 (1873); F; M; Wife; yes 3630; yes; Al. 3348

3662; **WHITE THUNDER**, Anthony; m; 82 (1850); F; M; Head; yes 3631; yes; Al. 619

3663; " Mary; f; 8 (4-18-23); F; S; Dau; yes 3632; yes; An. 3542

3664; **WHITE THUNDER**, Evelyn; f; 17 (9-29-14); F; S; Alone; yes 3633; yes; Al. 4660

N. E. **WILLIAMS**, Henry; m; Head

3665; (LaFrombois), Amy; f; 33 (6-29-99); 1/2; M; Wife; no 3634; Mobridge, Walworth Co, SD; no; Al. 423

3666; Forman, Frank V; m; 7 (9-14-24); 1/4; S; St-Son; no 3635; Mobridge, Walworth Co, SD; yes; An. 3589

3667; " John H; m; 2 (11-25-29); 1/4; S; Son; no ---; Mobridge, Walworth Co, SD; yes; An. 3590

3668; **WISESPIRIT**, John; m; 43 (1889); F; S; Head; yes 3636; yes; Al. 1284

Census of the **Standing Rock** Reservation of the **Standing Rock** jurisdiction, as of **April 1**, 1932, taken by **E. D. Mossman**, Superintendent. South Dakota

KEY: Number; Surname, Given; Sex; Age at Last Birthday; Tribe (Standing Rock Sioux unless otherwise noted); Degree of Blood; Marital Status; Relationship to Head of Family; At Jurisdiction where enrolled (Yes or No); (If "No", where, if given); Ward (Yes or No); Allotment, Annuity and Identification Numbers.

3669; **WOLF**, Henry; m; 21 (2-21-91); F; S; Head; yes 3637; yes; Al. 4109

3670; **YELLOW**, Charles; m; 23 (4-5-09); F; S; Head; yes 3638; yes; Al. 3792

3671; **YELLOW**, Laura; f; 27 (8-4-04); F; S; Head; yes 3639; yes; Al. 190

3672; **YELLOW**, Proteus; m; 55 (1877); F; M; Head; yes 3640; no; Al. 185
3673;   (McLean); Lizzie; f; 55 (1877); F; M; Wife; yes 3641; yes; Al. 3930
3674;   "   Rose; f; 20 (6-3-11); F; S; Dau; yes 3642; yes; Al. 4153
3675;   "   Allen; m; 19 (2-21-13); F; S; Son; yes 3643; yes; Al. 4405
3676;   "   Vivian; f; 17 (11-27-14); F; S; Dau; yes 3644; yes; Al. 4665
3677;   "   Adeline; f; 15 (11-7-16); F; S; Dau; yes 3645; yes; An. 3628
3678;   "   James A; m; 12 (5-16-19); F; S; Son; yes 3646; yes; An. 3629
3679;   "   Marie; f; 11 (2-22-21); F; S; Dau; yes 3647; yes; An. 3630

3680; **YELLOWEARRING**, Alvin; m; 18 (1-16-14); F; S; Alone; yes 3648; yes; Al. 4536

3681; **YELLOWEARRING**, Daniel; m; 46 (1886); F; M; Head; yes 3649; no; Al. 2921
3682;   "   James; m; 19 (1-30-13); F; S; Son; yes 3650; yes; Al. 4416
3683;   "   Luke; m; 16 (2-18-16); F; S; Son; yes 3651; yes; An. 3635
3684;   "   Andrew; m; 2 (4-4-29); F; S; Son; yes 3652; yes; An. 3637
3685;   "   Annie; f; 1 (11-16-30); F; S; Dau; yes 3653; yes; An. 3636

3686; **YELLOWEARRING**, Harriet; f; 52 (1880); F; M; Head; yes 3654; yes; Al. 2922
3687;   "   Alma; f; 19 (6-3-12); F; S; Dau; yes 3655; yes; Al. 4422
3688;   "   Ambrose; m; 10 (6-6-21); F; S; Head; yes 3656; yes; An. 3640

3689; **YELLOWEARRING**, Thomas; m; 61 (1871); F; M; Head; yes 3657; yes; Al. 1502
3690; Brought Plenty, Annie; f; 15 (1-23-16); F; S; St-Dau; yes 3658; yes; An. 373
3691; Brought Plenty, Mary; f; 10 (12-29-21); F; S; St-Dau; yes 3659; yes; An. 374
3692; Yellowearring, Louise; f; 4 (10-15-28); F; S; Dau; yes 3660; yes; An. 3642

3693; **YELLOWFAT**, James; m; 38 (2-24-94); F; M; Head; yes 3661; no; Al. 769
3694;   (Edgar), Mary; f; 34 (6-22-97); F; M; Wife; yes 3663; yes; Al. 851
3695;   "   Alice; f; 15 (3-116-17); F; S; Dau; yes 3663; yes; An. 3645
3696;   "   James, Jr; m; 12 (2-11-20); F; S; Son; yes 3664; yes; An. 3646
3697;   "   Raymond; m; 9 (1-20-23); F; S; Son; yes 3665; yes; An. 3647
3698;   "   Robert; m; 6 (12-11-25); F; S; Son; yes 3666; yes; An. 3648
3699;   "   Theresa; f; 2 (6-29-29); F; S; Dau; yes 3667; yes; An. 3649

Census of the __Standing Rock__ Reservation of the __Standing Rock__ jurisdiction, as of __April 1__, 1932, taken by __E. D. Mossman__, Superintendent. South Dakota

KEY: Number; Surname, Given; Sex; Age at Last Birthday; Tribe (Standing Rock Sioux unless otherwise noted); Degree of Blood; Marital Status; Relationship to Head of Family; At Jurisdiction where enrolled (Yes or No); (If "No", where, if given); Ward (Yes or No); Allotment, Annuity and Identification Numbers.

3700; **YELLOWFAT**, Joseph; m; 63 (1869); F; M; Head; yes 3668; yes; Al. 768
3701;   (Yellowfat), Maggie; f; 56 (1876); F; M; Wife; yes 3669; yes; Al. 3206
3702;   "   Mary R; f; 14 (12-10-17); F; S; Dau; yes 3670; yes; An. 3652

3703; **YELLOWWINGS** (Birdbear), Mrs; f; 77 (1855); F; Wd; Head; yes 3671;
                                                                yes; Al. 3124

3704; **YOUNGEAGLE**, Albert; m; 70 (1862); F; M; Head; yes 3672; yes; Al. 493
3705;   (Jordan), Annie; f; 87 (1845); F; M; Wife; yes 3673; yes; Al. 859

3706; **YOUNGHAWK**, Alberta; f; 4 (1-11-28); F; S; Alone; yes 3675; yes;
                                                                An. 3678

3707; **YOUNGHAWK**, Eugene; m; 46 (1886); F; S; Head; yes 3676; no; Al. 1150

3708; **YOUNGHAWK**, John; m; 36 (1895); F; M; Head; yes 3677; yes; Al. 145
3709;   (Redhawk), Lizzie; f; 24 (5-5-07); F; M; Wife; yes 3678; yes; Al. Al. 2509
3710;   "   Cyprian; m; 12 (5-24-19); F; S; Son; yes; 3679; yes; An. 3682
3711;   "   Eva; f; 11 (11-5-21); F; S; Dau; yes 3680; yes; An. 3683
3712;   "   Unnamed; m; 2/12 (1-26-32); F; S; Son; yes ---; yes; An. ---

Supplemental Sheet

3715; **LONEMAN**, Mary; f; 62 (1850); F; S; Head; yes 2746; yes; Al. 3445

3716; **DEFENDER;** Michael; m; 9; F; S; Son; yes 1876; yes; An. 749

Standing Rock Agency

Births - North Dakota

July 1, 1924 to March 31, 1932

Standing Rock Reservation

NORTH DAKOTA SIOUX

Live Births

July 1, 1924 - June 30, 1925

State ___North Dakota___ Reservation ___Standing Rock___ Agency or jurisdiction ___Standing Rock___ Office of Indian Affairs

Births Occurring Between the Dates of July 1, 1924 and June 30, 1925 to Parents Enrolled at Jurisdiction

Key: 1925 Census Roll Number; Surname, Given; Date of Birth (Year-Month-Day); Live Births (blank unless otherwise given); Still Births (blank unless otherwise given); Sex; Tribe (Standing Rock Sioux unless given otherwise); Ward (Yes/No); Degree of Blood (Father; Mother; Child); At Jurisdiction Where Enrolled (Yes/No); (If no – Where)

127; BAILEY, William Wesley; 25-6-1; m; yes; W; F; 1/2; yes
203; BIGHORN ELK, William; 24-11-3; m; yes; F; F; F; yes
247; BLACKHOOP, Pearl; 25-3-18; f; yes; F; F; F; yes
not recorded; BUCKLEY, Rebecca Monica; 24-11-16; f; yes; 1/2; 1/2; 1/2; yes
not recorded; CALLOUSLEG, Oliver; 25-5-29; m; yes; F; F; F; yes
501; CHAPMAN, Clyde; 25-4-9; m; yes; 3/4; 3/4; 3/4; yes
not recorded; CRAZYWALKING, Charles; 24-9-3; m; yes; F; F; F; yes
687; CROWNECKLACE, Henry; 24-11-27; m; yes; F; F; F; yes
not recorded; DIFFERENT OWL, James; 25-4-12; m; yes; F; F; F; yes
not recorded; DIFFERENT OWL, Nellie; 25-4-12; f; yes; F; F; F; yes
800; DOGSKIN, Lawrence; 24-10-28; m; yes; F; F; F; yes
936; EVANS, Charlotte K; 24-8-26; f; yes; W; 1/2; 1/4; yes
not recorded; FASTHORSE, Eugene; 24-11-4; m; yes; F; F; F; yes
not recorded; FORTE, Charles Mayo; 24-8-12; m; yes; 1/2; 1/2; 1/2; yes
not recorded; GOODIRON, Alice; 25-1-27; f; yes; F; F; F; yes
1271; GROVER, Milton; 25-1-20; m; yes; W; 3/4; 3/8; yes
1325; HALSEY, Thomas Alvin; 24-8-28; m; yes; 3/4; F; 7/8; yes
1398; HAWKSHIELD, Aline; 25-4-4; f; yes; F; F; F; yes
1433; HIS HORSE APPEARS, Job; 25- 4-23; m; yes; F; F; F; yes
1562; IRELAND, Agatha; 25-1-22; f; yes; F; F; F; yes
1683; JORDAN, Mary; 24-8-1; f; yes; 1/2; F; 3/4; yes
1885; KELLEY, Susan Louise; 25-1-22; f; yes; 1/4; 3/4; 1/2; yes
1789; KING, Amos; 25-2-18; m; yes; W; 1/2; 1/4; yes
1817; LAMBIE, Patrick; 25-3-17; m; yes; W; 1/2; 1/4; no; Swastika, N. Dak.
1916; LITTLE CROW, Wesley; 25-5-1; m; yes; F; F; F; yes
1997; LOOKING ELK, Lena; 25-3-18; f; yes; F; F; F; yes
2079; MANYHORSES, Carl; 25-5-29; m; yes; F; F; F; yes
1926-2072; MANNING, Aileen Gertrude; 25-1-29; f; yes; 1/2; 1/2; 1/2; no; Vader, Wash.
2185; MEANS, Wesley; 25-3-13; m; yes; 1/4; 1/4; 1/4; yes
2224; MENTZ, Melda; 24-11-11; f; yes; 1/2; F; 3/4; yes
2212; MENTZ, Marcella; 25-3-25; f; yes; 1/2; W; 1/4; yes
2272; MURPHY, Calvin Henry; 24-12-14; m; yes; F; F; F; yes
not recorded; MURPHY, Robert Chas; 24-10-2; m; yes; 1/2; 1/2; 1/2; yes
1926-2587; REDFOX, Virginia; 24-5-4; f; yes; F; F; F; yes
2737; SHELL TRACK, Victoria; 25-2-25; f; yes; F; F; F; yes
2795; SIAKA, Felix; 24-12-3; m; yes; F; F; F; yes
2840; SLATER, Christopher; 24-12-1; m; yes; 1/2; F; 3/4; yes
2855; SMITE, Mathew; 25-3-25; m; yes; F; F; F; yes
665; STANDING CROW, Marie; 25-4-1; f; yes; F; F; F; yes
3043; TATTOO, Morris Vern; 25-2-22; m; yes; F; 1/2; 3/4; yes
3104; TIOKASIN, Claude; 24-7-1; m; yes; F; F; F; yes
3163; TWO BEAR, Verna; 25-4-30; m; yes; F; F; F; yes

State ___ North Dakota ___ Reservation ___ Standing Rock ___ Agency or jurisdiction
___ Standing Rock ___ Office of Indian Affairs

Births Occurring Between the Dates of July 1, 1924 and June 30, 1925 to Parents Enrolled at Jurisdiction

Key: 1925 Census Roll Number; Surname, Given; Date of Birth (Year-Month-Day); Live Births (blank unless otherwise given); Still Births (blank unless otherwise given); Sex; Tribe (Standing Rock Sioux unless given otherwise); Ward (Yes/No); Degree of Blood (Father; Mother; Child); At Jurisdiction Where Enrolled (Yes/No); (If no – Where)

3206; TWOSHIELDS, Jerry; 25-2-12; m; yes; F; F; F; yes
2395; WAYMAN, Warren Melvin; 25-1-1; m; yes; W; 1/2; 1/4; yes
3308; WAREHAM, Shirley Mae; 25-3-18; f; yes; W; 1/4; 1/8; no; St. Paul, Minn.
 192; WEASELBEAR, Geraldine; 24-12-27; f; yes; F; F; F; yes
3413; WHITECLOUD, Chauncey; 24-11-21; m; yes; F; F; F; yes
3422; WHITEEAGLE, Sarah; 25-4-29; f; yes; F; F; F; yes
2220; WICKS, Caske; 25-5-10; m; yes; W; 1/2; 1/4; yes

NORTH DAKOTA SIOUX

Live Births

July 1, 1925 - June 30, 1926

LIVE BIRTHS

State __North Dakota__ Reservation __Standing Rock__ Agency or jurisdiction __Standing Rock__ Office of Indian Affairs

Births Occurring Between the Dates of July 1, 1925 and June 30, 1926 to Parents Enrolled at Jurisdiction

Key: 1926 Census Roll Number; Surname, Given; Date of Birth (Year-Month-Day); Live Births (blank unless otherwise given); Still Births (blank unless otherwise given); Sex; Tribe (Standing Rock Sioux unless given otherwise); Ward (Yes/No); Degree of Blood (Father; Mother; Child); At Jurisdiction Where Enrolled (Yes/No); (If no – Where)

not recorded; BABBITT, None; 26-6-4; Stillbirth; m; yes; W; F; 1/2; yes
174; BEARGHOST, Viola; 26-3-19; f; yes; F; F; F; yes
1928-199; BEARSHIELD, Cecilia; 25-12-3; f; yes; F; F; F; yes
198; BENDIKSON, Lucille; 26-2-3; f; yes; W; 1/2; 1/4; yes
214; BIGSHIELD, Ned; 26-2-26; m; yes; F; F; F; yes
267; BLACK, Virginia; 26-6-22; f; yes; F; F; F; yes
318; BRAVEBULL, John, Jr; 25-5-4; m; yes; F; W; 1/2; yes
1927-349; BREINER, Marie C; 25-8-11; f; yes; W; 1/2; 1/4; yes
387; BUCKLEY, Lorraine; 26-3-5; f; yes; 1/2; 1/4; 3/8; yes
425; BYINGTON, Dorothy; 26-3-21; f; yes; W; 1/2; 1/4; yes
466; CALLOUSLEG, Francis; 25-10-1; m; yes; F; F; F; yes
not recorded; CALLOUSLEG, Theresa; 25-12-23; f; yes; F; F; F; yes
not recorded; CASKE, Frederick; 26-2-2; m; yes; F; F; F; yes
not recorded; CHASINGBEAR, John, Jr; 25-7-22; m; yes; F; F; F; yes
2679; COMES LAST, Donald; 26-3-19; m; yes; F; F; F; yes
678; CROWFEATHER, Grace; 25-11-10; f; yes; F; F; F; yes
723; DEFENDER, Daniel; 25-12-4; m; yes; F; 1/2; 3/4; yes
821; DOUGLAS, Virginia; 26-2-21; f; yes; F; F; F; yes
963; FASTHORSE, Crusantius; 26-2-6; m; yes; F; F; F; yes
1031; FOLLOWS THE ROAD, Ella; 25-11-28; f; yes; F; F; F; yes
1931-469; GAYTON, Lorraine; 26-4-26; f; yes; 1/2; W; 1/4; yes
1155; GIPP, Christine; 26-3-14; f; yes; W; 1/2; 1/4; yes
not recorded; GOODIRON, Josephine; 26-2-6; f; yes; F; F; F; yes
not recorded; GOODIRON, Samuel; 26-5-24; m; yes; F?; F; F; yes
1234; GRAYBEAR, Josephine; 26-3-19; f; yes; F; F; F; yes
1252; GREYBULL, Elmer; 25-11-8; m; yes; F; F; F; yes
1333; HALSEY, Rose; 26-2-20; f; yes; 1/2; 1/2; 1/2; yes
1927-3066; HOPKINS, Benjamin; 26-6-25; m; yes; F; F; F; yes
1641; IRONROAD, Charlotte; 26-1-20; f; yes; F; F; F; yes
1650; IRONSHIELD, Sylvan; 25-8-23; f; yes; F; F; F; yes
1814; KRAUSER, Helen; 26-5-5; f; yes; W; 1/2; 1/4; yes
2164; McCORMICK, Joseph; 25-8-6; m; yes; W; 1/2; 1/4; yes
2243; MENTZ, William; 25-8-7; m; yes; 1/2; 1/2; 1/2; yes
2284; MULHERN, Patrick; 26-3-25; m; yes; 1/2; 1/2; 1/2; yes
2317; NOEL, Leon Weston; 25-8-1; m; yes; W; 1/4; 1/8; yes
not recorded; NOHEART, Coolidge; 25-7-1; m; yes; F; F; F; yes
2405; PANHICIYA, Julia; 26-1-19; f; yes; F; F; F; yes
3600; RAMEY, James; 25-2-25; m; yes; W; 1/2; 1/4; yes
2521; RAMSEY, Regina; 26-6-1; f; yes; F; F; F; yes
not recorded; RATTLINGHAIL, Marie; 26-3-7; f; yes; F; F; F; yes
2960; RUNS THE HOOP, Margaret; 26-3-10; f; yes; F; F; F; yes
114; SCHOCK, Jacqueline; 26-1-18; f; yes; W; 1/4; 1/8; yes
2739; SEE THE ELK, Cyril; 25-11-4; m; yes; F; F; F; yes

153

State ___North Dakota___ Reservation ___Standing Rock___ Agency or jurisdiction ___Standing Rock___ Office of Indian Affairs

Births Occurring Between the Dates of July 1, 1925 and June 30, 1926 to Parents Enrolled at Jurisdiction

Key: 1926 Census Roll Number; Surname, Given; Date of Birth (Year-Month-Day); Live Births (blank unless otherwise given); Still Births (blank unless otherwise given); Sex; Tribe (Standing Rock Sioux unless given otherwise); Ward (Yes/No); Degree of Blood (Father; Mother; Child); At Jurisdiction Where Enrolled (Yes/No); (If no – Where)

2762;   SHELL TRACK, Wesley; 26-3-20; m; yes; F; F; F; yes
2812;   SHORT, Thomasine; 26-5-31; f; yes; 1/4; 3/4; 1/2; yes
2822;   SIAKA, Margaret; 25-12-10; f; yes; F; F; F; yes
2944;   STANDING SOLDIER, Virginia; 26-6-9; f; yes; F; F; F; yes
2963;   STREKED[sic] EYE, Edna; 26-3-27; f; yes; F; F; F; yes
3088;   THOMPSON, Ambrose; 26-2-20; m; yes; F; F; F; yes
3356;   VIDOVICH, Geraldine; 26-6-14; f; yes; F; 1/2; 3/4; yes
 658;   WALKER, Charles; 25-12-30; m; yes; F; F; F; yes
3365;   WHITE, Victor; 26-4-4; m; yes; F; F; F; yes
not reported; WHITEEAGLE, Mary; 25-7-26; f; yes; F; F; F; yes
3462;   WHITELIGHTNING, John; 25-10-20; m; yes; F; F; F; yes
3500;   WINDY, Francis; 25-9-23; m; yes; F; F; F; yes
3584;   YOUNGBEAR, Calvin; 26-2-6; m; yes; F; F; F; yes
3612;   ZAHN, Geraldine; 26-3-29; f; yes; 1/2; F; 3/4; yes

NORTH DAKOTA SIOUX

Live Births

July 1, 1926 - June 30, 1927

State   North Dakota   Reservation   Standing Rock   Agency or jurisdiction

    Standing Rock   Office of Indian Affairs

Births Occurring Between the Dates of July 1, 1926 and June 30, 1927 to Parents Enrolled at Jurisdiction

Key: 1927 Census Roll Number; Surname, Given; Date of Birth (Year-Month-Day); Live Births (blank unless otherwise given); Still Births (blank unless otherwise given); Sex; Tribe (Standing Rock Sioux unless given otherwise); Ward (Yes/No); Degree of Blood (Father; Mother; Child); At Jurisdiction Where Enrolled (Yes/No); (If no – Where)

15;   AGARD, Bernardine; 27-1-14; f; yes; 3/4; 3/4; 3/4; yes
42;   ALKIRE, Ruth; 27-3-24; f; yes; 3/4; F; 7/8; yes
107;   ARCHAMBAULT, Richard, Jr; 27-2-24; m; yes; 1/2; 1/4; 3/8; yes
181;   BEARGHOST, Nelson; 27-4-7; m; yes; F; F; F; yes
213;   BIGHORNELK, Louis, Jr; 27-5-12; m; yes; F; F; F; yes
248;   BLACKCLOUD, Anastasia; 27-5-1; f; yes; F; F; F; yes
350;   BREINER, Joseph Paul; 26-9-15; m; yes; W; 1/4; 1/8; yes
488;   CALLOUSLEG, Beatrice; 27-1-24; f; yes; F; F; F; yes
522;   CHAPAMAN, Margaret V; 26-7-28; f; yes; 3/4; 1/2; 5/8; yes
2034;   CHAPMAN, Paul Irvin; 26-10-19; m; yes; 3/4; F; 7/8; yes
1928-507; CASKE, Josephine; 27-6-23; f; yes; F; F; F; yes
547;   CHASINGBEAR, Catherine; 26-9-9; f; yes; F; F; F; yes
624;   CONICA, Marcelian; 26-7-1; m; yes; F; F; F; yes
1928-839; DOGSKIN, Allen; 27-2-29; m; yes; F; F; F; yes
834;   DOUGLAS, Gene; 26-10-22; m; yes; F; F; F; yes
936;   ELK, Justus John; 27-3-15; m; yes; F; F; F; yes
1928-985; EVANS, Francis P; 27-3-17; m; yes; W; 1/4; 1/8; yes
1929-975; EVANS, Lawrence D; 26-8 9-18; yes; W; 1/2; 1/4; yes
1210;   GOODIRON, Magdalene; 27-5-14; f; yes; 3/4; 3/4; 3/4; yes
1259;   GRAYBULL, Vincent; 27-3-19; m; yes; F; 1/2; 3/4; yes
1308;   GROVER, Memoree Jean; 26-11-11; f; yes; W; 3/4; 3/8; yes
1343;   HALSEY, Gladys Mae; 26-7-18; f; yes; 1/2; F; 3/4;   yes
1457;   HIS CHASE, Pius, Jr; 26-2-26; m; yes; F; F; F; yes
not reported; HOPKINS, Cecelia Irene; 27-5-3; f; yes; F; F; F; yes
1583;   IRELAND, Christina; 27-3-28; f; yes; F; F; F; yes
267;   JACKSON, Helen; 26-11-7; f; yes; W; F; 1/2; yes
1681;   JAMERSON, Wm; 27-5-6; m; yes; 1/2; F; 3/4; yes
not reported; JORDAN, Albert; 26-7-20[sic]; m; yes; 1/2; F; 3/4; yes
1904;   KELLEY, Theodora; 27-3-6; f; yes; 1/4; 3/4; 1/2; yes
1752;   KEOGH, Elmer; 26-7-14; m; yes; W; 1/4; 1/8; yes
1928-1854; KILLSPOTTED, Wilfred; 27-4-28; m; yes; F; F; F; yes
1808;   KING, Melvin; 27-4-11; m; yes; W; 1/2; 1/4; yes
1927;   LITTLECHIEF, Germaine; 27-2-12; f[sic]; yes; F; F; F; yes
1935;   LITTLE CROW, Pearl; 26-11-15; f; yes; F; F; F; yes
not reported; LOON, Herbert Carl; 26-8-25; m; yes; F; 1/2; 3/4; yes
2125;   MANYWOUNDS, George, Jr; 26-8-26; m; yes; F; 1/2; 3/4; yes
1929-2287; MENTZ, Antoine Chas; 27-2-12; m; yes; 1/2; W; 1/4; yes
3238;   MOLASH, Marie; 26-7-1; f; yes; W; 1/4; 1/8; yes
2311;   MURPHY, Cyril; 27-5-15; m; yes; F; F; F; yes
2336;   NOEL, Eloise; 26-10-6; m[sic]; yes; W; 1/4; 1/8; yes
2398;   ONEHORN, Pauline Ann; 27-2-6; f; yes; F; F; F; yes
2419;   PAINTSBROWN, Jerome; 27-5-27; m; yes; F; F; F; yes
2481;   PLEETS, Henrietta; 26-12-30; f; yes; 3/4; F; 7/8; yes

LIVE BIRTHS

State ___North Dakota___ Reservation ___Standing Rock___ Agency or jurisdiction
___Standing Rock___ Office of Indian Affairs

Births Occurring Between the Dates of July 1, 1926 and June 30, 1927 to Parents Enrolled at Jurisdiction

Key: 1927 Census Roll Number; Surname, Given; Date of Birth (Year-Month-Day); Live Births (blank unless otherwise given); Still Births (blank unless otherwise given); Sex; Tribe (Standing Rock Sioux unless given otherwise); Ward (Yes/No); Degree of Blood (Father; Mother; Child); At Jurisdiction Where Enrolled (Yes/No); (If no – Where)

604;   PLENTYCHIEF, Irvin; 26-7-22; m; yes; F; F; F; yes
2548;   RATTLINGHAIL, Cyril; 27-3-5; m; yes; F; F; F; yes
1928-2695; REDSTONE, Melvin; 27-6-26-; m; yes; F?; F; F; yes
2670;   RED TOMAHAWK, Peter; 26-11-16; m; yes; F; F; F?; yes
2773;   SHELLTRACK, Viola; 26-7-27; f; yes; F; F; F; yes
2854;   SILK, Chas Bernard; 27-2-10; m; yes; 1/2; F; 3/4; yes
690;   STANDING CROW, Theron; 26-10-11; m; yes; F; F; F; yes
3073;   TATTOE, Margaret; 27-5-11; f; yes; F; 1/2; 3/4; yes
3105;   THUNDERHAWK, Jacob; 26-8-10; m; yes; F; F; F; yes
3135;   TIOKASIN, Joseph; 27-6-15; m; yes; F; W; 1/2; yes
3160;   TUSK, Chas, Jr; 27-1-9; m; yes; F; F; F; yes
3186;   TWOBEARS, Patrick; 27-5-17; m; yes; F; F; F; yes
1932-*; WAREHAM, John Robert; 26-8-19; m; yes; W; 1/4; 1/8; no; St. Paul, Minn.
3373;   WELLS, Aurelia Mae; 27-4-21; f; yes; 1/4; F; 5/8; yes
3534;   WHITECLOUD, Cordon; 26-7-26; m; yes; F; F; F?; yes
3457;   WHITEEAGLE, Irene May; 26-7-19; f; yes; 1/2; 1/2; 1/?; yes
3449;   WHITEEAGLE, Melvin; 26-9-27; m; yes; F; F; F; yes
3486;   WHITEMAN, Mildred L; 27-4-1; f; yes; F; F; F; yes
2253;   WICKS, Joseph James; 27-2-26; m; yes; W; 1/2; 1/4; yes

* Not yet reported.

158

NORTH DAKOTA SIOUX

Live Births

July 1, 1927 - June 30, 1928

LIVE BIRTHS

State   North Dakota   Reservation   Standing Rock   Agency or jurisdiction
   Standing Rock   Office of Indian Affairs

Births Occurring Between the Dates of July 1, 1927 and June 30, 1928 to Parents Enrolled at Jurisdiction

Key: 1928 Census Roll Number; Surname, Given; Date of Birth (Year-Month-Day); Live Births (blank unless otherwise given); Still Births (blank unless otherwise given); Sex; Tribe (Standing Rock Sioux unless given otherwise); Ward (Yes/No); Degree of Blood (Father; Mother; Child); At Jurisdiction Where Enrolled (Yes/No); (If no – Where)

219;   BIGHORNELK, William; 28-4-24; m; yes; F; F; F; yes
263;   BLACKHOOP, Arnold; 28-3-14; m; yes; F; 1/2; 3/4; yes
269;   BLACKHOOP, Robert; 27-12-20; m; yes; F; F; F; yes
528;   CHAPMAN, Clement; 28-4-18; m; yes; 3/4; 1/2; 5/8; yes
not reported; CONICA, Earl; 27-9-25; m; yes; F; F; F; yes
634;   COTTONWOOD, Christine; 28-5-8; f; yes; F; F; F; yes
679;   CRAZYWALKING, Henry; 28-2-1; m; yes; F; F; F; yes
714;   CROWNECKLACE, Robert; 27-8-11; m; yes; F; F; F; yes
1929-838; DOUGLAS, Jacob; 28-5-11; m; yes; F; F; F; yes
993;   FASTHORSE, Edward; 27-10-6; m; yes; F; F; F; yes
1668;   FISHER, Narodny; 28-1-24; m; yes; W; 1/2; 1/4; no; Bismarck, N. Dak.
1092;   FOUR, Eugene; 28-3-8; m; yes; 1/2; F; 3/4; yes
1240;   GOODIRON, Lucille; 28-2-19; f; yes; F; F; F; yes
1235;   GOODIRON, Theresa; 28-2-15; f; yes; F; F; F; yes
1932-*; GOODREAU, Patricia I; 28-3-10; f; yes; 1/4; W; 1/8; no; St Paul, Minn
1293;   GRAYDAY, Gladys; 27-9-11; f; yes; F; W; 1/2; yes
1291;   GREYBULL, Teddy; 28-4-1; m; yes; F; F; F; yes
1376;   HALSEY, George Jay; 28-4-26; m; yes; 1/2; 1/2; 1/2; yes
1405;   HARMON, Charles; 27-9-14; m; yes; 1/4; W; 1/8; yes
1417;   HARRISON, James; 27-10-11; m; yes; 1/4; W; 1/8; yes
1935-*; HOWARD, Virgil Charles; 28-2-3; m; yes; 1/4; F; 5/8; no; Western Navajo
     Agency, AZ
1682;   IRONROAD, Leon; 28-1-26; m; yes; F; F; F; yes
1929-1689; IRONSHIELD, Jane; 28-5-13; f; yes; F; F; F; yes
1732;   JORDAN, Genevieve; 28-1-16; f; yes; 1/2; W; 1/4; yes
1803;   KEOGH, Margaret Grace; 28-2-17; f; yes; W; 1/4; 1/8; yes
3405;   LaPLANT, Kenneth Dale; 28-6-18; m; yes; 1/4; 1/2; 3/8; yes
2144;   MANYHORSES, Raymond; 28-3-9; m; yes; F; F; F; yes
2256;   MEANS, Mary Janet; 27-7-13; f; yes; 1/4; 1/4; 1/4; yes
not reported; MENTZ, William; 28-1-7; m; yes; 1/2; F; 3/4; yes
2338;   MULHERN, Hildagard[sic]; 27-12-22; f; yes; 1/2; 3/4; 5/8; yes
2426;   ONEFEATHER, Henry, Jr; 28-2-2; m; yes; F; F; F; yes
3647;   RAMEY, Mae Adeline; 27-8-19; f; yes; W; 1/2; 1/4; yes
1929-2574; RAMSEY, Sidney; 28-5-22; m; yes; F; F; F; yes
2581;   RATTLINGHAIL, Irwin; 27-7-28; m; yes; F; F; F; yes
2650;   REDFOX, Alvina Marie; 27-8-12; f; yes; F; F; F; yes
2728;   RETURNS LAST, Thos, Jr; 28-6-21; m; yes; F; F; F; yes
121;   SCHOCK, Evangeline; 27-10-8; f; yes; W; 1/4; 1/8; yes
3056;   SEE WALKER, Margaret; 28-6-12; f; yes; F; F; F; yes
2862;   SIAKA, Cecelia; 27-7-18; f; yes; F; F; F; yes
3020;   STRETCHES HIMSELF, Virgil; 28-5-5; m; yes; F; F; F; yes
3133;   THOMPSON, Veronica; 28-5-13; f; yes; F; F; F; yes
* Not yet reported

State___North Dakota___Reservation___Standing Rock___Agency or jurisdiction
___Standing Rock___Office of Indian Affairs

Births Occurring Between the Dates of July 1, 1927 and June 30, 1928 to Parents Enrolled at Jurisdiction

Key: 1928 Census Roll Number; Surname, Given; Date of Birth (Year-Month-Day); Live Births (blank unless otherwise given); Still Births (blank unless otherwise given); Sex; Tribe (Standing Rock Sioux unless given otherwise); Ward (Yes/No); Degree of Blood (Father; Mother; Child); At Jurisdiction Where Enrolled (Yes/No); (If no – Where)

3125; TIBBITTS, Florienne; 28-5-27; f; yes; F; F; F; yes
3244; TWOBEARS, Grady; 27-10-8; m; yes; F; F; F; yes
3550; WINDY, Edna Rose; 28-2-28; m[sic]; yes; F; F; F; yes
3481; WHITEEAGLE, Margaret; 28-1-14; f; yes; F; F; F; yes
3507; WHITELIGHTNING, Luke; 27-9-2θ[sic]; m; yes; F; F; F; yes

NORTH DAKOTA SIOUX

Live Births

July 1, 1928 - June 30, 1929

LIVE BIRTHS

State __North Dakota__ Reservation __Standing Rock__ Agency or jurisdiction
__Standing Rock__ Office of Indian Affairs

Births Occurring Between the Dates of July 1, 1928 and June 30, 1929 to Parents Enrolled at Jurisdiction

Key: 1929 Census Roll Number; Surname, Given; Date of Birth (Year-Month-Day); Live Births (blank unless otherwise given); Still Births (blank unless otherwise given); Sex; Tribe (Standing Rock Sioux unless given otherwise); Ward (Yes/No); Degree of Blood (Father; Mother; Child); At Jurisdiction Where Enrolled (Yes/No); (If no – Where)

211; BENDIKSON, John, Jr; 28-11-8; m; yes; W; 1/4; 1/8; yes
not reported; BIGSHIELD, Berdie; 28-11-17; f; yes; F; F; F; yes
not reported; BLACKCLOUD, Susanne; 28-9-27; f; yes; F; F; F; yes
292; BLACK TOMAHAWK, William; 29-5-12; m; yes; F; F; F; yes
334; BRAVEBULL, Frank; 28-8-8; m; yes; F; W; 1/2; yes
356; BREINER, Alfred W; 28-10-17; m; yes; W; 1/4; 1/8; yes
438; BYINGTON, Lawrence; 28-7-16; m; yes; W; 1/2; 1/4; yes
496; CARIGNAN, Alfred Joseph; 28-9-28; m; yes; W; 1/8; 1/16; yes
1930-515; CHASING EAGLE, Jennie; 29-6-5; f; yes; F; F; F; yes
619; CONICA, Stella; 28-8-10; f; yes; F; F; F; yes
not reported; COTTONWOOD, Alvina; 28-8-2; f; yes; F; F; F; yes
636; COTTONWOOD, Eunice; 29-3-30; f; yes; F; F; F; yes
834; DOGSKIN, Thomas; 29-2-12; m; yes; F; F; F; yes
1061; FOOLBEAR, Wilbur; 29-5-21; m; yes; F; F; F; yes
1150; GAYTON, Dorothy Mae; 29-4-6; f; yes; 1/2; W; 1/4; yes
1229; GOODIRON, Carl; 29-1-23; m; yes; F; F; F; yes
1265; GRAYBEAR, Joseph; 29-2-15; m; yes; F; F; F; yes
1270; GRAYBEAR, Raymond B; 29-4-29 5; m; yes; F; 1/4; 5/8; yes
1370; HALSEY, Michael, Jr; 28-10-17; m; yes; 1/2; F; 3/4; yes
3076; HOPKINS, Benedict; 28-9-12; m; yes; F; F; F; yes
1670; IRONROAD, Grace; 29-6-2; f; yes; F; F; F; yes
1686; IRONSHIELD, Evelyn; 28-10-19; f; yes; F; F; F; yes
1054; KARNIGA, Leo; 29-1-30[sic]; m; yes; F; F; F; yes
1751; KELLEY, Calvin T; 28-7-8; m; yes; 1/4; 3/4; 1/2; yes
1804; KIDDER, Magdalene; 28-8-27; f; yes; F; F; F; yes
1856; KING, Leora Mae; 29-4-25; f; yes; W; 1/2; 1/4; yes
2163; MANYWOUNDS, Peter; 29-5-30; m; yes; F; 1/2; 3/4; yes
2301; MENTZ, Thomas, Jr; 29-3-4; m; yes; 1/2; F; 3/4; yes
2888; MENTZ, Walter James; 28-9-26; m; yes; 1/2; W; 1/4; yes
2355; MURPHY, Harold Michael; 29-5-23; m; yes; F; F; F; yes
2359; MURPHY, Sylvia Maye; 29-3-3; f; yes; 1/2; W; 1/4; yes
2380; NOEL, Ronald; 28-9-11; m; yes; W; 1/4; 1/16; yes
1164; NORD, Raymond; 28-12-14; m; yes; W; 1/2; 1/4; yes
1930-2493; PLEETS, Laverne; 28-12-30; m; yes; 3/4; F; 7/8; yes
3633; RAMEY, Aaron Edward; 29-4-7; m; yes; W; 1/2; 1/4; yes
122; SCHOCK, Agnes Marian; 29-4-15; f; yes; W; 1/4; 1/8; yes
2848; SHORT, Bernice; 28-8-13; f; yes; 1/4; 3/4; 1/2; yes
1932-*; SIAKA, Veronica; 29-3-4; f; yes; F; F; F; yes
2880; SILK, Edith; 29-3-11; f; yes; 1/2; F; 3/4; yes
2786; SHELLTRACK, Elmer; 28-10-7; m; yes; F; F; F; yes
2695; RED TOMAHAWK, Courtney; 29-5-22; m; yes; F; 1/2; 3/4; yes
* Not yet reported

State ___North Dakota___ Reservation ___Standing Rock___ Agency or jurisdiction ___Standing Rock___ Office of Indian Affairs

Births Occurring Between the Dates of July 1, 1928 and June 30, 1929 to Parents Enrolled at Jurisdiction

Key: 1929 Census Roll Number; Surname, Given; Date of Birth (Year-Month-Day); Live Births (blank unless otherwise given); Still Births (blank unless otherwise given); Sex; Tribe (Standing Rock Sioux unless given otherwise); Ward (Yes/No); Degree of Blood (Father; Mother; Child); At Jurisdiction Where Enrolled (Yes/No); (If no – Where)

682;   STANDINGCROW, Lavern Bruno; 29-5-17; m; yes; F; F; F; yes
2979;   STANDING SOLDIER, Bernard, Jr; 28-7-29; m; yes; F; F; F; yes
3149;   TIOKASIN, Louis; 28-10-3; m; yes; F; F; F; yes
3176;   TUSK, Leonard; 29-6-11; m; yes; F; F; F; yes
3328;   USES HIS ARROWS, Calvin; 29-4-30; m; yes; F; F; F; yes
3254;   VAULTER, Alice; 28-8-8; f; yes; F; F; F; yes
3433;   WHITEBULL, Cynthea; 28-11-28; f; yes; F; F; F; yes
3457;   WHITEEAGLE, Wesley; 28-10-7; m; yes; F; F; F; yes
3486;   WHITELIGHTNING, Peter; 28-10-18; m; yes; F; F; F; yes
3529;   WHITETWIN, Margaret; 29-3-15; f; yes; F; F; F; yes
3550;   WISESPIRIT, Muriel; 29-3-1; f; yes; F; F; F; yes
3613;   YOUNGBEAR, Estella; 28-8-18; f; yes; F; F; F; yes
3546;   ZAHN, Lavonne; 28-7-2; f; yes; 1/2; 1/2; 1/2; yes

NORTH DAKOTA SIOUX

Live Births

July 1, 1929 - June 30, 1930

State ___North Dakota___ Reservation ___Standing Rock___ Agency or jurisdiction
___Standing Rock___ Office of Indian Affairs

Births Occurring Between the Dates of July 1, 1929 and June 30, 1930 to Parents Enrolled at Jurisdiction

Key: 1930 Census Roll Number; Surname, Given; Date of Birth (Year-Month-Day); Live Births (blank unless otherwise given); Still Births (blank unless otherwise given); Sex; Tribe (Standing Rock Sioux unless given otherwise); Ward (Yes/No); Degree of Blood (Father; Mother; Child); At Jurisdiction Where Enrolled (Yes/No); (If no – Where)

8; AFRAID OF HAWK, Verne; 29-7-14; m; yes; F; F; F; yes
44; ALKIRE, Maude; 29-11-7; f; yes; 3/4; F; 7/8; yes
119; AZURE, Henry; 30-3-27; m; yes; 1/4; 7/8; 9/16; yes
1931-57; BARDSLEY, Floyd, Jr; 30-5-31; m; yes; W; 1/2; 1/4; yes
180; BEARSGHOST, Elmer; 29-10-14; m; yes; F; F; F; yes
1931-100; BIGSHIELD, Angela; 30-6-1; f; yes; F; F; F; yes
284; BLACK PRAIRIE DOG, Martin; 29-11-7; m; yes; F; F; F; yes
1931-128; BLACK TOMAHAWK, Michael; 30-6-15; m; yes; F; F; F; yes
1931-234; CARRY MOCCASIN, Jessie; 30-4-14; m; yes; F; F; F; yes
532; CHASE THE BEAR, Florence; 29-10-~~30~~29; f; yes; F; F; F; yes
1931-1899; COLLIS, Chas. R; 30-4-2; m; yes; W; 1/2; 1/4; yes
600; CONICA, Maclina; 29-9-1; f; yes; F; F; F; yes
605; CONICA, Marvin; 30-1-13; m; yes; F; F; F; yes
620; COTTONWOOD, Abel; 30-1-25; m; yes; F; F; F; yes
1931-301; COTTONWOOD, Ramona; 30-6-4; f; yes; F; F; F; yes
854; DWARF, Mary; 30-3-27; f; yes; F; F; F; yes
1931-431; FOLLOWS THE ROAD, John; 30-1-31; m; yes; F; F; F; yes
1130; GAYTON, Waldo Chas; 30-2-10; m; yes; 1/2; 1/4; 3/8; yes
1271; GREYBULL, Matt; 30-2-6; m; yes; F; F; F; yes
1273; GREYDAY, Joseph D; 30-1-29; m; yes; F; W; 1/2; yes
1322; GROVER, John Cyril; 29-7-25; m; yes; W; 3/4; 3/8; yes
1470; HIS CHASE, Joan Rita; 29-8-13; f; yes; F; F; F; yes
1475; HIS HORSE APPEARS, Isaac, Jr; 29-8-26; m; yes; F; F; F; yes
1512; HOLY ELK FACE, Agatha; 30-1-2; f; yes; F; F; F; yes
1518; HOPKINS, Daniel V; 29-12-8; m; yes; F; F; F; yes
1601; IRELAND, Irene; 29-10-6; f; yes; F; F; F; yes
not reported; IRONROAD, George; 30-4-12; m; yes; F; F; F; yes
1733; KELLEY, Patrick C; 29-11-14; m; yes; 1/4; 3/4; 1/2; yes
1931-798; KIDDER, Daniel, Jr; 30-5-21; m; yes; F; F; F; yes
1931-813; KITTELSTVEDT, Ronald; 30-6-6; m; yes; W; 3/4; 3/8; yes
2032; LOOKING ELK, Melvin J; 30-2-5; m; yes; F; F; F; yes
2040; LOON, Rita Ella; 29-11-22; f; yes; F; 1/2; 1/4; yes
2069; LYONS, Ramona I; 29-10-21; f; yes; 1/8; W; 1/16; yes
2421; ONEHORN, Edward Lucas; 30-1-12; m; yes; F; F; F; yes
2701; RETURNS LAST, Christine L; 29-7-24; f; yes; F; F; F; yes
3020; SEE WALKER, Milton; 29-8-31; m; yes; F; F; F; yes
2835; SIAKA, Virginia; 29-9-27; f; yes; F; F; F; yes
3090; THOMPSON, Olive Marie; 30-3~~0~~-30; f; yes; F; F; F; yes
1931-1305; TIOKASIN, Clifford; 30-6-26; m; yes; F; F; F; yes
not reported; TWO BEAR, Cerena; 29-7-29; f; yes; F; 3/4; 7/8; yes
3176; TWO BEAR, Neal V; 29-12-9; m; yes; F; F; F; yes
3394; WHITEBIRD, Josephine; 30-2-19; f; yes; F; F; F; yes

State ___ North Dakota ___ Reservation ___ Standing Rock ____ Agency or jurisdiction
___ Standing Rock ____ Office of Indian Affairs
Births Occurring Between the Dates of July 1, 1929 and June 30, 1930 to Parents Enrolled at Jurisdiction

Key: 1930 Census Roll Number; Surname, Given; Date of Birth (Year-Month-Day); Live Births (blank unless otherwise given); Still Births (blank unless otherwise given); Sex; Tribe (Standing Rock Sioux unless given otherwise); Ward (Yes/No); Degree of Blood (Father; Mother; Child); At Jurisdiction Where Enrolled (Yes/No); (If no – Where)

3420;   WHITECLOUD, Victoria; 29-10-21; f; yes; F; F; F; yes
3527;   WISESPIRIT, Quenton; 30-9-20; m; yes; F; F; F; yes
3530;   WISESPIRIT, Veronica; 30-3-11; f; yes; F; F; F; yes
1931-1539; YELLOWHAMMER, Angeline; 30-6-20; f; yes; F; F; F; yes
3618;   ZAHN, Carmen L; 29-10-1; f; yes; 1/2; 1/2; 1/2; yes

NORTH DAKOTA SIOUX

Live Births

April 1, 1930 - March 31, 1931

LIVE BIRTHS

State   North Dakota   Reservation   Standing Rock   Agency or jurisdiction
    Standing Rock   Office of Indian Affairs

Births Occurring Between the Dates of April 1, 1930 and March 31, 1931 to Parents Enrolled at Jurisdiction

Key: 1931 Census Roll Number; Surname, Given; Date of Birth (Year-Month-Day); Live Births (blank unless otherwise given); Still Births (blank unless otherwise given); Sex; Tribe (Standing Rock Sioux unless given otherwise); Ward (Yes/No); Degree of Blood (Father; Mother; Child); At Jurisdiction Where Enrolled (Yes/No); (If no – Where)

57;   BARDSLEY, Floyd, Jr; 30-5-31; m; yes; W; 1/2; 1/4; yes
78;   BEARSHIELD, Mary Ann; 30-8-15; f; yes; F; F; F; yes
100;   BIGSHIELD, Angela; 30-6-1; f; yes; F; F; F; yes
112;   BLACKCLOUD, Pauline; 30-7-15; f; yes; F; F; F; yes
128;   BLACK TOMAHAWK, Michael; 30-6-15; ɟ m; yes; F; F; F; yes
234;   CARRY MOCCASIN, Jessie; 30-4-14; f; yes; F; F; F; yes
242;   CASKE, Leo; 30-9-1; m; yes; F; F; F; yes
249;   CHAPMAN, Delphine A; 31-3-30; f; yes; 3/4; 3/4; 3/4; yes
1899;   COLLIS, Chas. R; 30-4-2; m; yes; W; 1/2; 1/4; yes
290;   CONICA, Henry, Jr; 30-7-1; m; yes; F; F; F; yes
301;   COTTONWOOD, Ramona; 30-6-4; f; yes; F; F; F; yes
316;   COTTONWOOD, Stephen; 30-12-27; m; yes; F; F; F; yes
344;   DEFENDER, Olivia; 30-10-14; f; yes; F; F; F; yes
368;   DOUGLAS, Cynthea Ann; 30-10-31; f; yes; F; F; F; yes
441;   FOOLBEAR, Flossie; 3-22-31[sic]; f; yes; F; F; F; yes
454;   GAYTON, Ralph Merlin; 30-11-26; m; yes; 1/2; W; 1/4; yes
1932 -*;   GILLAND, Robert, Jr; 30-10-27; m; yes; 1/4; W; 1/8; yes
490;   GIPP, Albert Louis; 30-12-4; m; yes; 1/4; 1/4; 1/4; yes
515;   GOODIRON, Margaret M; 31-1-14; f; yes; F; F; F; yes
623;   HALSEY, Wesley B; 30-12-7; m; yes; 1/2; F; 3/4; yes
642;   HARRISON, Chas. Henry; 30-7-24; m; yes; 1/4; W; 1/8; yes
659;   HIS CHASE, Elizabeth M; 31-3-22; f; yes; F; F; F; yes
670;   HOISINGTON, Richard K; 30-10-8; m; yes; W; 1/4; 1/8; yes
718;   IRONEYES, Jerome; 31-2-25; m; yes; F; F; F; yes
not reported; IRONROAD, George; 30-4-12; m; yes; F; F; F; yes
798;   KIDDER, Daniel, Jr; 30-5-21; m; yes; F; F; F; yes
3687;   KILLSPOTTED, Lucille; 31-3-31; f; yes; F; F; F; yes
813;   KITTELSTVEDT, Ronald; 30-6-6; m; yes; W; 3/4; 3/8; yes
837;   LITTLE WARRIOR, Joseph; 31-1-28; m; yes; F; F; F; yes
1410;   LOAN HIM ARROW, Lorene; 30-7-23; f; yes; F; F; F; yes
897;   MENTZ, Marie Ramona; 31-2-1; f; yes; 1/2; W; 1/4; yes
922;   MOORHEAD, Beatrice A; 31-3-9; f; yes; 1/2; W; 1/4; no; Flasher, N. Dak.
929;   MURPHY, Doris May; 31-11-16; f; yes; 1/2; W; 1/4; yes
936;   MURPHY, Rita Aurelia; 30-10-15; f; yes; F; F; F; yes
953;   NOEL, Paul R; 30-8-10; m; yes; W; 1/4; 1/8; yes
963;   NORD, Wayne Raymond; 30-9-13; m; yes; W; 1/2; 1/4; yes
980;   ONIHAN, Lynas; 31-3-30; m; yes; F; F; F; yes
1106;   REDSTONE, Cecilia; 30-8-2; f; yes; F; F; F; yes
1169;   SHORT, Colleen M; 30-11-25; f; yes; 1/4; 3/4; 1/2; yes
1221;   SPOTTED ELK, Hermina; 31-2-11; f; yes; F; F; F; yes
1242;   STRAMPHER, Doris E; 30-12-27; f; yes; W; 1/4; 1/8; yes
1258;   STRETCHES HIMSELF, Laura; 31-2-24; f; yes; F; F; F; yes
* not yet reported

State ___North Dakota___ Reservation ___Standing Rock___ Agency or jurisdiction ___Standing Rock___ Office of Indian Affairs

Births Occurring Between the Dates of April 1, 1930 and March 31, 1931 to Parents Enrolled at Jurisdiction

Key: 1931 Census Roll Number; Surname, Given; Date of Birth (Year-Month-Day); Live Births (blank unless otherwise given); Still Births (blank unless otherwise given); Sex; Tribe (Standing Rock Sioux unless given otherwise); Ward (Yes/No); Degree of Blood (Father; Mother; Child); At Jurisdiction Where Enrolled (Yes/No); (If no – Where)

1284; TATTOOED, Torrence; 30-10-14; m; yes; F; 1/2; 1/4; yes

1296; THUNDERHAWK, Alma; 31-3-12; f; yes; F; F; F; yes

1310; TIOKASIN, Antoine; 30-8-21; m; yes; F; W; 1/2; yes

1305; TIOKASIN, Clifford; 30-6-26; m; yes; F; F; F; yes

1335; TWIN, Joseph, Jr; 30-10-18; m; yes; F; F; F; yes

1026; PRETENDS EAGLE, Leo Don; 30-9-25; m; yes; F; F; F; yes

1385; VAULTERS, Evelyn; 30-11-5; f; yes; F; F; F; yes

1472; WHITEEAGLE, Leonard; 30-7-1; m; yes; F; 1/2; 3/4; yes

1465; WHITEEAGLE, Earl; 30-11-1; m; yes; F; F; F; yes

not reported; WHITEEAGLE, Jacob, Jr; 31-3-16; m; yes; F; F; F; yes

1486; WHITELIGHTNING, Edward; 30-7-24; m; yes; F; F; F; yes

1495; WHITETWIN, Agnes; 31-3-19; m[sic]; yes; F; F; F; yes

1510; WINDY, Chester; 30-7-23; m; yes; F; F; F; yes

1539; YELLOWHAMMER, Angeline; 30-6-20; f; yes; F; F; F; yes

not reported; ZAHN, Keith; 31-2-6; m; yes; 1/2; 1/2; 1/2; yes

NORTH DAKOTA SIOUX

Live Births

April 1, 1931 - March 31, 1932

LIVE BIRTHS

State ___North Dakota___ Reservation ___Standing Rock___ Agency or jurisdiction ___Standing Rock___ Office of Indian Affairs

Births Occurring Between the Dates of April 1, 1931 and March 31, 1932 to Parents Enrolled at Jurisdiction

Key: 1932 Census Roll Number; Surname, Given; Date of Birth (Year-Month-Day); Live Births (blank unless otherwise given); Still Births (blank unless otherwise given); Sex; Tribe (Standing Rock Sioux unless given otherwise); Ward (Yes/No); Degree of Blood (Father; Mother; Child); At Jurisdiction Where Enrolled (Yes/No); (If no – Where)

26; ALKIRE, Ione; 31-11-3; f; yes; F; F; F; yes
6; AFRAID OF HAWK, (Unnamed); 32-3-7; f; yes; F; F; F; pes
60; BARDSLEY, Margaret M; 31-10-20; f; yes; W; 1/2; 1/4; yes
Not recorded ; BEARSGHOST, Virgil; 31-12-2; m; yes; F; F; F; yes
87; BIGHORNELK; Mary; 31-9-25; f; yes; F; F; F; yes
117; BLACKTOMAHAWK, James; 31-9-19; m; yes; F; F; F; yes
143; BRAVEBULL, Florence; 31-10-30; f; yes; F; W; 1/2; yes
284; COTTONWOOD, Agnes; 31-4-26; f; yes; F; F; F; yes
306; COTTONWOOD, Isabelle; 31-12-22; f; yes; F; F; F; yes
298; COTTONWOOD, Walter; 32-2-23; m; yes; F; F; F; yes
322; CROW, Duane L; 31-12-28; m; yes; F; F; F; yes
351; DOGSKIN, Tony; 31-5-9; m; yes; F; F; F; yes
363; DOUGLAS, Florence; 31-5-9; f; yes; F; F; F; yes
376; EAGLEBOY, Serena; 31-7-18; f; yes; F; F; F; yes
410; FASTHORSE, Frederick; 31-11-7; m; yes; F; F; F; yes
405; FASTHORSE, Herbert K; 31-4-6; m; yes; F; F; F; yes
1274; FOLLOWS THE ROAD, Eli; 31-4-5; m; yes; F; F; F; yes
425; FOLLOWS THE ROAD, Nellie; 32-3-29; f; yes; F; F; F; yes
431; FOUR, Alvera; 31-9-5; f; yes; F; F; F; yes
485; GIPP, Frank B; 31-11-26; m; yes; 1/2; 1/2; 1/2; yes
507; GOODIRON, Percy; 31-9-13; m; yes; F; F; S; yes
515; GOODLEFTHAND, Wilmer; 31-10-10; m; yes; F; F; F; yes
542; GRAYBEAR, Eva; 32-3-8; f; yes; F; F; F; yes
583; GROVER, Marie; 31-4-27; f; yes; W; 1/2; 1/4; yes
629; HARRISON, David; 32-3-30; m; yes; 1/4; W; 1/8; yes
696; IRELAND, Alvin; 32-3-24; m; yes; F; F; F; yes
718; IRONROAD, Albert J; 31-6-27; m; yes; F; F; F; yes
728; IRONROAD, Shirley; 32-2-3; f; yes; F; F; F; yes
725; IRONSHIELD, Ironshield[sic]; 31-4-22; f; yes; F; F; F; yes
749; JONES, Marlene; 31-11-15; f; yes; F; 1/2; 3/4; yes
Not recorded; JORDAN, Joan; 31-5-6; f; yes; 1/2; 1/2; 1/2; yes
787; KEOGH, Audrey P; 31-5-23; f; yes; W; 1/8; 1/16; yes
793; KIDDER, Bertha; 31-6-12; f; yes; F; F; F; yes
Not recorded; KIDDER, Marcella; 31- 6-12; f; yes; F; F; F; yes
800; KING, Renee D; 31-5-13; f; yes; W; 1/2; 1/4; yes
836; LITTLEBEAR, Aleck C; 32-3-24; m; yes; F; 1/2; 3/4; yes
852; LOOKINGHORSE, Peter, Jr; 31-6-30; m; yes; F; F; F; yes
Not recorded; MURPHY, Ellen B; 31-12-8; f; yes; F; F; F; yes
952; MURPHY, Elenor June; 31-4-13; f; yes; 1/2; W; 1/4; yes
936; MURPHY, Woodrwo[sic]; 32-3-7; m; yes; 1/2; W; 1/4; yes
1017; PLEETS, Jean; 31-6-20; f; yes; F; F; F; yes
1060; RAMSEY, Julia A; 31-6-14; f; yes; F 1/2; F; 3/4; yes

State ___North Dakota___ Reservation ___Standing Rock___ Agency or jurisdiction ___Standing Rock___ Office of Indian Affairs

Births Occurring Between the Dates of April 1, 1931 and March 31, 1932 to Parents Enrolled at Jurisdiction

Key: 1932 Census Roll Number; Surname, Given; Date of Birth (Year-Month-Day); Live Births (blank unless otherwise given); Still Births (blank unless otherwise given); Sex; Tribe (Standing Rock Sioux unless given otherwise); Ward (Yes/No); Degree of Blood (Father; Mother; Child); At Jurisdiction Where Enrolled (Yes/No); (If no – Where)

1089;   REDEARS, Irene M; 31-8-27; f; yes; F; F; F; yes
1125;   REDTOMAHAWK, Bernard; 31-12-16; m; yes; F; F; F; yes
1288;   SEE WALKER, Dorothy E; 31-4-15; f; yes; F; F; F; yes
1164;   SHELL TRACK, Alvin; 31-10-11; m; yes; F; F; F; yes
1207;   SILK, Elizabeth; 31-6-26; f; yes; 1/2; F; 3/4; yes
1212;   SKYE, Harriet; 31-12-6; f; yes; 1/2; 1/2; 1/2; no; Rosebud Res, S.D.
1314;   TIBBETS, Wayne A; 31-8-18; m; yes; F; F; F; yes
1361;   TWOBEARS, June; 31-6-26; f; yes; F; F; F; yes
1370;   TWOBEARS, Selma; 31-11-2; f; yes; F; F; F; yes
1395;   TWOSHIELDS, Nora; 31-8-5; f; yes; F; F; F; yes
1467;   WHITEBIRD, Gloria M; 31-10-26; f; yes; F; F; F; yes
1476;   WHITEEAGLE, Jacob; 31-3-16; m; yes; F; F; F; yes
1499;   WHITELIGHTNING, Jerome; 32-1-19; m; yes; F; F; F; yes
1539;   WISESPIRIT, Unnamed; 32-3-15; m; yes; F; F; F; yes
1562;   YELLOWLODGE, Agatha; 31-9-20; f; yes; F; F; F; yes
1585;   ZAHN, Keith; 32-2-6; m; yes; F 1/2; 1/2; 1/2; yes

Standing Rock Agency

Births - South Dakota

July 1, 1924 to June 30, 1932

Standing Rock Reservation

SOUTH DAKOTA SIOUX

Live Births

July 1, 1924 - June 30, 1925

State __South Dakota__ Reservation __Standing Rock__ Agency or jurisdiction __Standing Rock__ Office of Indian Affairs

Births Occurring Between the Dates of July 1, 1924 and June 30, 1925 to Parents Enrolled at Jurisdiction

Key: 1925 Census Roll Number; Surname, Given; Date of Birth (Year-Month-Day); Live Births (blank unless otherwise given); Still Births (blank unless otherwise given); Sex; Tribe (Standing Rock Sioux unless given otherwise); Ward (Yes/No); Degree of Blood (Father; Mother; Child); At Jurisdiction Where Enrolled (Yes/No); (If no – Where)

1926-33; AGARD, Quentin; 25-6-20; m; yes; 3/4; 1/2; 5/8; yes
180; BEARSGHOST, Nellie; 25-4-28; f; yes; F; F; F; yes
318; BRAVECROW, Effie Roletta; 24-12-6 ~~22~~; f; yes; F; F; F; yes
not reported; BROUGHT PLENTY, Thomas; 24-10-6; m; yes; F; F; F; yes
374; BUCKLEY, Philomene; 24-12-28; f; yes; F; F; F; yes
464; CADOTTE, Mary Julia; 25-4-5; f; yes; F; F; F; yes
1926-539; CHASINGHAWK, Lora; 25-6-30; f; yes; F; F; F; yes
637; CRAZYBEAR, Philip; 24-8-26; m; yes; F; F; F; yes
721; DEFENDER, Marie Agnes; 24-7-2; f; yes; F; 1/2; 3/4; yes
842; EAGLE, George, Jr; 25-4-28; m; yes; F; F; F; yes
867; EAGLEHORN, Sophie; 24-9-11; f; yes; F; F; F; yes
890; EAGLESHIELD, Collis; 24-12-14; m; yes; F; F; F; yes
896; FASTBEAR, Jessie; 25-4-25; f; yes; F; F; F; no; Sisseton Agency, S. Dak.
1801; FOREMAN, Frank Vincent; 24-9-4; m; yes; W; 5/8; 5/16; no; Mobridge, S. Dak.
1043; FOSTER, Selina; 25-2-28; f; yes; F; F; F; yes
1054; FRANK, Agnes Lulu; 24-12-22; f; yes; W; F; 1/2; yes
1086; GARTER, Solomon John; 25-3-8; m; yes; F; F;F P; yes
1160; GOODEAGLE, Ethel; 25-1-14; f; yes; F; F; F; yes
1404; HAYES, Vera or Helen; 24-12-27; f; yes; F; F; F; yes
1460; HOHEKTE, Harry or Henry; 24-9-27; m; yes; F; 1/2; 3/4; yes
1465; HOHEKTE, Melvin; 25-3-19; m; yes; F; F; F; yes
1479; HOLYMAN, Sarah; 24-8-7; f; yes; F; F; F; yes
1926-1535; HOWARD, Eileen Mary; 25-6-11; f; yes; 3/4; W; 3/8; no; Yankton Agency, S.D.
not reported; HOWARD, Sherman; 25-6-11; m; yes; 3/4; W; 3/8; no; Yankton Agency, S.D.
1566; IORNS[sic], William; 24-11-16; m; yes; W; 1/4; 1/8; yes
1569; IRON, Ernest; 25-6-3; m; yes; F; F; F; yes
1583; IRONCLOUD, Thomas; 24-12-24; m; yes; F; F; F; yes
1647; IRONWHITEMAN, Philip; 24-9-14; m; yes; F; F; F; yes
1673; JORDAN, Peter J; 24-7-23; m; yes; 1/2; 1/2; 1/2; yes
1926-1738; KEMPTON, Oliver Dale; 25-3-17; m; yes; 1/4; W; 1/8; yes
1758; KILLS CROW INDIAN, Leola; 25-5-10; f; yes; F; F; F; yes
1799; KRAUSER, John Chas; 25-1-24; m; yes; W; 1/2; 1/4; yes
1834; LAWRENCE, Helen; 25-3-20; f; yes; W; 3/4; 3/8; yes
1860; LeCOMPTE, Bernice; 24-12-27; f; yes; 1/4; W; 1/8; yes
1869; LeCOMPTE, Bernice C; 25-2-10; f; yes; 1/4; W; 1/8; yes
1926-1884; LeCOMPTE, Elsworth; 25-3-9; m; yes; 1/4; W; 1/8; yes
1877; LeCOMPTE, Virgil Dean; 24-11-10; m; yes; 1/4; 3/4; 1/2; yes
1926-1917; LITTLEBEAR, Whitney; 25-5-24; f; yes; F; F; F; yes
1924; LITTLE DOG, Norman; 25-2-22; m; yes; F; F; F; yes
not reported; LITTLE DOG, Solomon, 24-7-21; m; yes; F; F; F; yes

State ___ South Dakota ___ Reservation ___ Standing Rock ___ Agency or jurisdiction
___ Standing Rock ___ Office of Indian Affairs

Births Occurring Between the Dates of July 1, 1924 and June 30, 1925 to Parents Enrolled at Jurisdiction

Key: 1925 Census Roll Number; Surname, Given; Date of Birth (Year-Month-Day); Live Births (blank unless otherwise given); Still Births (blank unless otherwise given); Sex; Tribe (Standing Rock Sioux unless given otherwise); Ward (Yes/No); Degree of Blood (Father; Mother; Child); At Jurisdiction Where Enrolled (Yes/No); (If no – Where)

1965;   LONGCHASE, Abraham; 25-5-20; m; yes; F; F; F; yes
not reported; LONGFEATHER, Jesse; 25-3-27; m; yes; F; F; F; yes
1990;   LOOKINGBACK, Seraphine; 25-3-18; f; yes; F; F; F; yes
 255;   MADBEAR, Celesta; 25-1-7; f; yes; F; F; F; yes
2083:   MANYHORSES, Innocent; 24-10-16; m; yes; F; F; F; yes
2106;   MARSHALL, Mae Rose; 24-11-2; f; yes; F; F; F; yes
 585;   MAXON, Milo, Jr; 25-5-30; m; yes; W; 1/4; 1/8; yes
2176;   McLAUGHLIN, Harry M; 25-6-7; m; yes; 1/4; 1/4; 1/4; yes
2204;   MENTZ, Ada Louise; 24-9-15; f; yes; 1/2; 1/2; 1/2; yes
2234;   MIDDLEBULL, Rose; 24-10-12; f; yes; F; F; F; yes
2255;   MOUNTAIN, Bertha J; 24-10-7; f; yes; F; F; F; yes
2309;   NOISYHAWK, Commodore; 24-7-2; m; yes; F; F; F; yes
2360;   ONNESTAD, Agnes Florence; 25-2-11; f; yes; W; 1/2; 1/4; yes
2319;   OKA, Rose; 24-12-25; f; yes; F; F; F; yes
not reported; PASS BEYOND, Vernon D; 25-11-12; m; yes; F; F; F; yes
2409;   PETERS, Elsworth; 25-5-2; m; yes; W; 1/2; 1/4; yes
1926-1721; PLOOG, Hugo; 25-4-25; m; yes; W; 1/4; 1/8; yes
2488;   QUAY, Adria Marie; 25-2-11; f; yes; W; 1/4; 1/8; no; Lansdale, Pa.
2539;   REDBIRD, Hazel; 25-2-13; f; yes; F; F; F; yes
2593;   REDHAWK, Zelda Goldie; 24-8-22; f; yes; F; F; F; no; Yankton Agency,
        S.D.
2619;   REDLEGS, Martina; 25-1-16; f; yes; F; F; F; yes
2819;   SITTING DOG, Minerva; 25-2-12; f; yes; F; F; F; yes
2830;   SKUNK, David; 24-7-21; m; yes; F; F; F; yes
2845;   SLEEPS FROM HOME, William; 24-9-5; m; yes; F; F; F; yes
not recorded; SPOTTEDHORSE, Not given; 25-6-25; m; yes; F; F; F; yes
2965;   SWIFTCLOUD, Isaac William; 25-1-15; m; yes; F; F; F; yes
2996;   TAKEN ALIVE, Charlotte; 24-11-14; f; yes; F; F; F; yes
3002;   TAKEN ALIVE, Nelson; 24-9-10; m; yes; F; F; F; yes
3016;   TAKE THE GUN, Sarah; 24-10-17; f; yes; F; F; F; yes
3026;   TAKE THE HAT, Mamie; 24-9-16; f; yes; F; F; F; yes
1439;   THUNDERSHIELD, Traversie; 25-5-28; m; yes; F; F; F; yes

SOUTH DAKOTA SIOUX

Live Births

July 1, 1925 - June 30, 1926

LIVE BIRTHS.

State ___South Dakota___ Reservation ___Standing Rock___ Agency or jurisdiction
___Standing Rock___ Office of Indian Affairs

Births Occurring Between the Dates of July 1, 1925 and June 30, 1926 to Parents Enrolled at Jurisdiction

Key: 1926 Census Roll Number; Surname, Given; Date of Birth (Year-Month-Day); Live Births (blank unless otherwise given); Still Births (blank unless otherwise given); Sex; Tribe (Standing Rock Sioux unless given otherwise); Ward (Yes/No); Degree of Blood (Father; Mother; Child); At Jurisdiction Where Enrolled (Yes/No); (If no – Where)

1129;   ADAMS, Nora; 26-6-1; f; yes; W; 3/4; 3/8; yes
20;   AGARD, Miles; 26-1-1; m; yes; 3/4; F; 7/8; yes
50;   ANKLE, Corinne; 26-3-27; f; yes; F; F; F; yes
60;   ANTELOPE, Noble; 25-9-11; m; yes; F; F; F; yrs
157;   BEARKING, Bernice Rose; 25-11-1; f; yes; F; F; F; yes
519;   CHASE ALONE, Evelyn; 25-7-6; f; yes; F; F; F; yes
571;   CLAYMORE, Mary S; 26-2-4; f; yes; 3/4; 1/2; 5/8; yes
not recorded; CRAZYHAWK, James; 26-4-28; m; yes; F; F; F; yes
1927-686;   CROSSBEAR, Frank Elgin; 26-4-15; m; yes; F; F; F; yes
700;   CROWNECKLACE, Andrew; 25-12-31; m; yes; F; F; F; yes
730;   DEFENDER, Othmar[sic]; 25-11-30; m; yes; F; 1/2; 3/4; yes
751;   DEMERY, Albert Chas; 25-7-16; m; yes; 1/2; 1/2; 1/2; yes
740;   DEMERY, Ernest; 25-12-18; m; yes; F; F; F; yes
766;   DeROCKBRAINE, Joseph; 25-12-23; m; yes; F; F; F; yes
788;   DISTRIBUTE, Lillian, 25-12-17; f; yes; F; F; F; yes
874;   DOGEAGLE, James; 26-2-25; m; yes; F; F; F; yes
999;   FLY, Felix; 26-1-12; m; yes; F; F; F; yes
1025;   FLYINGHORSE, Edna; 26-1-14; f; yes; F; F; F; yes
1071;   FRANK, Annie Hermina; 26-5-21; f; yes; W; F; 1/2; yes
1099;   GABE, Berneta; 25-8-5; f; yes; F; F; F; yes
1265;   GREYEAGLE, Elaine; 26-1-2; f; yes; F; F; F; yes
1287;   GRINDSTONE, Amy; 25-7-7; f; yes; F; F; F; yes
1311;   HAIRYCHIN, Joseph; 10-26; m; yes; F; F; F; yes
not recorded; HORSETHIEF, Sarah; 25-12-13; f; yes; F; F; F; yes
1927-1588; IORNS, Iris May; 26-6-11; f; yes; W; 1/4; 1/8; yes
not recorded; JORDAN, Not given; 26-6-2; f; yes; 1/2; 1/2; 1/2; yes
2313;   KILLS ALIVE, Dorothy; 25-7-19; f; yes; F; F; F; yes
1892;   LeCOMPTE, Arlene; 25-11-16; f; yes; 1/4; 3/4; 1/2; yes
1936;   LITTLEDOG, Joseph; ?-?-?; m; yes; F; F; F; yes
not recorded; LITTLE EAGLE, Gladys; 26-2-22; f; yes; F; F; F; yes
1985;   LONGELK, Chauncey; 25-7-15; m; yes; F; F; F; yes
2057;   MAJHOR, Clifford; 25-12-17; m; yes; 1/2; W; 1/4; yes
2117;   MARSHALL, Bertha; 26-3-23; f; yes; f; yes; F; F; F; yes
2207;   MEDICINE, Grace; 26-5-4; f; yes; F; F; F; yes
2257;   MILLER, Benjamin L; 25-7-24; m; yes; W; 1/4; 1/8; yes
2364;   ONEFEATHER, Rita; 25-10-26; f; yes; F; F; F; yes
2429;   PATCHEN, Lottie; 25-7-29; f; yes; W; 1/4; 1/8; yes
2509;   PUTMAN, Blanche; 26-2-26; f; yes; W; 1/4; 1/8; yes
1927-2528; QUAY, Stanley Wayne; 26-6-30; m; yes; W; 1/4; 1/8; no; Lansdale, Pa.
not recorded; RAWHIDE, Jennie; 26-1-20; f; yes; F; F; F; yes
not recorded; ROACH, Melvin; 25-12-5; m; yes; F; F; F; yes
1927-2702; ROMAN NOSE, Rebecca; 26-5-28; f; yes; F; F; F; yes
2715;   SACK, Alvina; 25-10-15; f; yes; F; F; F; yes

LIVE BIRTHS.

State ___ South Dakota ___ Reservation ___ Standing Rock ___ Agency or jurisdiction ___ Standing Rock ___ Office of Indian Affairs

Births Occurring Between the Dates of July 1, 1925 and June 30, 1926 to Parents Enrolled at Jurisdiction

Key: 1926 Census Roll Number; Surname, Given; Date of Birth (Year-Month-Day); Live Births (blank unless otherwise given); Still Births (blank unless otherwise given); Sex; Tribe (Standing Rock Sioux unless given otherwise); Ward (Yes/No); Degree of Blood (Father; Mother; Child); At Jurisdiction Where Enrolled (Yes/No); (If no – Where)

2873; SLEEPS FROM HOME, Mary; 26-1-25; f; yes; F; F; F; yes
3075; THIEF, Percy; 26-1-31; m; yes; F; F; F; yes
4106; THUNDERSHIELD, Luella; 26-4-10; f; yes; F; F; F; yes
not recorded; VILLAGE CENTER, Floyd; 26-4-19; m; yes; F; F; F; yes
3290; WANKICUN, Noah; 25-8-14; m; yes; F; F; F; yes
not recorded; WAWOKIYA, Lillian; 25-11-9; f; yes; F; F; F; yes
3351; WELLS, Ferdinand; 25-10-31; m; yes; 1/4; F; 5/8; yes
3377; WHITE, Jacob Wm; 25-9-29; m; yes; F; 1/2; 3/4; yes
3407; WHITEBULL, Cecil; 26-2-6; m; yes; F; F; F; yes
3442; WHITEFACE, Hermit; 25-10-24; m; yes; F; F; F; yes
1927-3470; WHITEHORSE, Etta; 26-5-28; f; yes; F; F; F; yes
3559; YELLOWFAT, Robert; 25-12-11; m; yes; F; F; F; yes
3617; ZAHN, George B; 25-7-28; m; yes; 1/2; W; 1/4; yes

SOUTH DAKOTA SIOUX

Live Births

July 1, 1926 - June 30, 1927

LIVE BIRTHS

State _____ South Dakota _____ Reservation _____ Standing Rock _____ Agency or jurisdiction _____ Standing Rock _____ Office of Indian Affairs

Births Occurring Between the Dates of July 1, 1926 and June 30, 1927 to Parents Enrolled at Jurisdiction

Key: 1927 Census Roll Number; Surname, Given; Date of Birth (Year-Month-Day); Live Births (blank unless otherwise given); Still Births (blank unless otherwise given); Sex; Tribe (Standing Rock Sioux unless given otherwise); Ward (Yes/No); Degree of Blood (Father; Mother; Child); At Jurisdiction Where Enrolled (Yes/No); (If no – Where)

1928-180; BEARRIBS, Bernard; 27-2-18; m; yes; F; F; F; yes
225; BIRDHORSE, Wilmer; 26-9-28; m; yes; F; F; F; yes
239; BLACKCLOUD, Loretta; 26-11-11; f; yes; F; F; F; yes
364; BROUGHT PLENTY, Genevieve; 27-5-18; f; yes; F; F; F; yes
390; BUCKLES, Mary Margaret; 26-10-8; f; yes; W; 1/2; 1/4; yes
564; CHEYENNE, Mary; 26-10-2; f; yes; F; F; F; yes
not recorded; CLOWN, Mary; 26-7-3; f; yes; F; F; F; yes
767; DEMERY, Dorothy; 26-11-13; f; yes; 1/2; 1/2; 1/2; yes
1928-787; DeROCKBRAINE, Nelson; 27-2-7; m; yes; F; F; F; yes
817; DOG, Evelyn Marie; 27-5-28; f; yes; F; F; F; yes
807; DOG, Helen Alberta; 27-1-3; f; yes; F; F; F; yes
928; ECKMAN, Elizabeth; 27-1-16; f; yes; W; 1/2; 1/4; yes
929; ECKMAN, Julia; 27-1-16; f; yes; W; 1/2; 1/4; yes
996; FERRO, Mary Lou; 26-12-6; f; yes; W; 1/4; 1/8; yes
1011; FLY, Regina Mae; 26-12-3; f; yes; F; W; 1/2; yes
not recorded; FLYINGBY, Barney; 27- 6-18; m; yes; F; F; F; yes
1069; FOSTER, Mary Jane; 26-12-14; f; yes; F; F; F; yes
not recorded; GABE, Carmen; 27-6-17; f; yes; W; F; 1/2; yes
1928-1214; GOODEAGLE, Leon; 27-5-1; m; yes; F; F; F; yes
1289; GRINDSTONE, Adel Fae; 26-7-10; f; yes; F; F; F; yes
1325; HALIBURTON, Paul; 27-1-16; m; yes; W; 1/4; 1/8; yes
1398; HAS HORNS, Irwin; 26-8-28; m; yes; F; F; F; yes
1410; HAWK, Reynold; 26-12-29; m; yes; F; F; F; yes
not recorded; HAYES, Lawrence; 26-9-22; m; yes; F; F; F; yes
1928-1488; HIGHEAGLE, Raymond, Jr; 27-5-2; m; yes; F; 1/2; 3/4; yes
1519; HORSETHIEF, Irene; 26-12-14; f; yes; F; F; F; yes
1928-1729; JORDAN, Walter; 27-5-1; m; yes; 1/2; 1/2; 1/2; yes
1772; KILLSCROW, Wilma; 26-11-2; f; yes; F; F; F; yes
1782; KILLS CROW INDIAN, Cecilia; 26-9-30; f; yes; F; F; F; yes
1928-1824; KILLS CROW INDIAN, Lester; 27-6-30; m; yes; F; F; F; yes
1928-1838; KILLS PRETTY ENEMY, Peter; 27-5-2; m; yes; F; F; F; yes
1856; LAWRENCE, Arthur; 26-12-15; m; yes; F; F; F; yes
1887; LeCOMPTE, Melvin Gerald; 27-1-23; m; yes; 1/4; W; 1/8; yes
1361; LEFTHAND, Theodore; 26-7-4; m; yes; F; F; F; yes
not recorded; LITTLE DOG, Dale; 27-2-14; m; yes; F; F; F; yes
not recorded; LITTLE DOG, James; 26-10-24; m; yes; F; F; F; yes
1953; LITTLE EAGLE, Grace; 26-10-20; f; yes; F; F; F; yes
1948; LITTLE EAGLE, Harry; 26-10-20; m; yes; F; F; F; yes
1960; LITTLEMOON, Amanda; 27-4-10; f; yes; F; F; F; yes
2014; LOOKINGBACK, Cecilia; 27-3-13; f; yes; F; F; F; yes
not recorded; LOVES WAR, Lester; 27-1-16; m; yes; F; F; F; yes
1928-2184; MARTIN, Henry; 27-6-26; m; yes; F; F; F; yes

191

State ___South Dakota___ Reservation ___Standing Rock___ Agency or jurisdiction ___Standing Rock___ Office of Indian Affairs

Births Occurring Between the Dates of July 1, 1926 and June 30, 1927 to Parents Enrolled at Jurisdiction

Key: 1927 Census Roll Number; Surname, Given; Date of Birth (Year-Month-Day); Live Births (blank unless otherwise given); Still Births (blank unless otherwise given); Sex; Tribe (Standing Rock Sioux unless given otherwise); Ward (Yes/No); Degree of Blood (Father; Mother; Child); At Jurisdiction Where Enrolled (Yes/No); (If no – Where)

2209;   McLAUGHLIN, Maurine; 27-1-13; f; yes; 1/4; 1/4; 1/4; yes

2197;   McLAUGHLIN, Rupert; 27-3-4; m; yes; 1/4; F; 5/8; yes

not recorded; NOISY HAWK, Jacob; 27-11-26; m; yes; F; F; F; yes

2380;   ONEFEATHER, Hazel; 27-1-3; f; yes; F; F; F; yes

2495;   PRETENDS EAGLE, Bernard; 27-4-4; m; yes; F; F; F; yes

2553;   RAWHIDE, Jeannette, 27-3-2; f; yes; F; F; F; yes

2602;   REDFOX, Mary; 26-9-17; f; yes; F; F; F; yes

2626;   REDHAWK, Faith Agnes; 26-9-28; f; yes; F; F; F; yes

not recorded; REDHORSE, Ennis Lordet; 26-10-5; f; yes; F; F; F; yes

1928-2765; SACK, Alma; 27-6-16; f; yes; F; F; F; yes

2858;   SILK, Mark Thomas; 26-7-26; m; yes; 1/2; F; 3/4; yes

not recorded; SITTING DOG, Hazel; 26-11-17; f; yes; F; F; F; yes

not recorded; STANDING CLOUD, Reva; 26-11-18; f; yes; F; F; F; yes

2969;   STRAMPHER, Geo. H; 27-2-1; m; yes; W; 1/4; 1/8; yes

3036;   TAKEN ALIVE, Faith; 26-11-2; f; yes; F; F; F; yes

 448;   THORNTON, James F; 26-8-9; m; yes; W; 1/2; 1/4; yes

3205;   TWOHEARTS, Irene; 26-11-21; m[sic]; yes; F; F; F; yes

3293;   WALKINGELK, Mack L; 27-2-13; m; yes; F; 1/2; 3/4; yes

1928-3339; WANKICUN, Evelyn; 27-4-11; f; yes; F; F; F; yes

1878;   WARD, Rita C; 26-10-19; f; yes; W; 1/4; 1/8; yes

3339;   WATERS, Rose; 27-4-5; f; yes; F; F; F; yes

3346;   WAWOKIYA, Delma Bernice; 26-12-23; f; yes; F; F; F; yes

1928-3379; WEASEL, Gerald, Jr; 27-4-20; m; yes; F; F; F; yes

3391;   WHITE, Ione; 27-3-9; f; yes; F; F; F; yes

2292;   WHITE MOUNTAIN, Mildred; 26-?-?; f; yes; 3/4; F; 7/8; yes

3502;   WHITESHIELD, Catherine; 27-3-29; f; yes; F; 1/2; 3/4; yes

3576;   YELLOWEARRINGS, Patrick; 27-4-7; f[sic]; yes; F; F; F; yes

SOUTH DAKOTA SIOUX

Live Births

July 1, 1927 - June 30, 1928

LIVE BIRTHS

State ___South Dakota___ Reservation ___Standing Rock___ Agency or jurisdiction ___Standing Rock___ Office of Indian Affairs

Births Occurring Between the Dates of July 1, 1927 and June 30, 1928 to Parents Enrolled at Jurisdiction

Key: 1928 Census Roll Number; Surname, Given; Date of Birth (Year-Month-Day); Live Births (blank unless otherwise given); Still Births (blank unless otherwise given); Sex; Tribe (Standing Rock Sioux unless given otherwise); Ward (Yes/No); Degree of Blood (Father; Mother; Child); At Jurisdiction Where Enrolled (Yes/No); (If no – Where)

35; AGARD, Wyln Marie; 27-9-11; f; yes; 3/4; 1/2; 5/8; yes

87; ARCHAMBAULT, Germaine; 27-7-1; f[sic]; yes; 1/2; F; 3/4; yes

158; BEARFACE, Doraphine; 27-10-17; f; yes; F; F; F; yes

234; BLACKBEAR, Joseph; 28-3-8; m; yes; F; F; F; yes

346; BRAVETHUNDER, Joseph; 28-2-22; m; yes; F; F; F; yes

396; BUCKLEY, Zelda; 27-9-28; f; yes; F; F; F; yes

1929-444; CADOTTE, Lillian E; 28-2-4; f; yes; F; F; F; yes

not recorded; CADOTTE, William W; 27-7-2; m; yes; F; F; F; yes

560; CHASING HAWK, Jennie; 27-12-10; f; yes; F; F; F; yes

793; DeROCKBRAINE, Dorothy; 27-12-10; f; yes; F; F; F; yes

819; DOG, Elaine; 28-3-22; f; yes; F; F; F; yes

831; DOGEAGLE, George; 28-5-10; m; yes; F; F; F; yes

875; EAGLE, Elmer; 27-11-24; m; yes; F; F; F; yes

907; EAGLEHORN, Annabelle; 28-1-6; f; yes; F; F; F; yes

929; EAGLESHIELD, Inez; 27-12-25; f; yes; F; F; F; yes

1010; FENELON, Eugene V; 28-5-12; m; yes; W; 1/4; 1/8; yes

1054; FLYINGHORSE, Irene; 27-12-21; f; yes; F; F; F; yes

1929-1085; FOSTER, Stanley John; 28-6-15; m; yes; F; F; F; yes

1108; FRANK, Michael; 27-8-3; m; yes; W; F; 1/2; yes

1223; GOODFUR, Joshua; 27-9-30; m; yes; F; F; F; yes

1531; HOHEKTE, Perry; 28-2-8; m; yes; F; F; F; yes

1929-1789; HOISINGTON, Clarence, Jr; 28-6-17; m; yes; W; 1/8; 1/16; yes

1639; IRONCLOUD, Simon Peter; 27-10-26; m; yes; F; F; F; yes

not recorded; IRONHORN, Ernest F; 28-6-6; m; yes; F; F; F; yes

2372; KILLS ALIZE, Mildred; 27-8-6; f; yes; F; F; F; yes

1843; KILLS PRETTY ENEMY, Vincent; 27-11-1; m; yes; F; F; F; yes

1870; KRAUSER, Deloris; 28-4-12; f; yes; W; 1/2; 1/4; yes

1875; LaFROMBOISE, John Francis; 27-12-26; m; yes; 1/2; 3/4; 5/8; yes

1950; LeCOMPTE, Doris; 28-3-9; f; yes; 1/4; 3/4; 1/2; yes

1968; LITTLEBEAR, Fremont; 27-9-18; f[sic]; yes; F; F; F; yes

not recorded; LONGELK, Melvin Nelson; 27-7-21; m; yes; F; F; F; yes

2053; LOVES WAR, Joseph; 28-4-13; m; yes; F; F; F; yes

2108; MAJHOR, Theodore; 28-2-2; m; yes; 1/2; W; 1/4; yes

not recorded; MANYHORSES, Patrick; 27-2-4; m; yes; F; F; F; yes

2191; MARTIN, Lillian Grace; 28-1-4; f; yes; F; F; F; yes

2214; McCHESNEY, Paul Elmer; 27-12-25; m; yes; W; F; 1/2; yes

not recorded; MIDDLEBULL, Royal Joseph; 28-3-6; m; yes; F; F; F; yes

2364; NEAD, Pearl May; 27-12-10; f; yes; W; 1/2; 1/4; yes

2406; OKA, Madeline; 27-11-22; f; yes; F; F; F; yes

2670; REDHORN, Nelson; 27-8-3; m; yes; F; F; F; yes

not recorded; ROMAN NOSE, Lessie; 28-6-27; m; yes; F; F; F; yes

1929-955; ROSS, Gloriette J; 28-6-29; f; yes; F; F; F; yes

2753; RUNNINGHAWK, William; 27-10-24; m; yes; F; F; F; yes

State ___South Dakota___ Reservation ___Standing Rock___ Agency or jurisdiction ___Standing Rock___ Office of Indian Affairs

Births Occurring Between the Dates of July 1, 1927 and June 30, 1928 to Parents Enrolled at Jurisdiction

Key: 1928 Census Roll Number; Surname, Given; Date of Birth (Year-Month-Day); Live Births (blank unless otherwise given); Still Births (blank unless otherwise given); Sex; Tribe (Standing Rock Sioux unless given otherwise); Ward (Yes/No); Degree of Blood (Father; Mother; Child); At Jurisdiction Where Enrolled (Yes/No); (If no – Where)

not recorded; SHAVEBEAR, John, Jr; 27-11-4; m; yes; F; F; F; yes
2889; SILK, Louis M; 28-1-30; m; yes; 1/2; F; 3/4; yes
2918; SLEEPS FROM HOME, Margaret; 27-11-7; f; yes; F; F; F; yes
2952; SPEAKSWALKING, Oscar; 27-10-23; m; yes; F; F; F; yes
3090; TAKE THE HAT, Dennis; 28-4-8; m; yes; F; F; F; yes
3147; THUNDERSHIELD, Olive; 28-4-1; f; yes; F; F; F; yes
3275; VERMILLION, William; 27-11-27; m; yes; 1/4; F; 5/8; yes
3299; WAGGONER, Mamie or Marie; 28-4-19; f; yes; 1/4; 1/4; 1/4; yes
3448; WHITEBULL, Melvin; 27-9-4; m; yes; F; F; F; yes
3520; WHITESELL, Jean; 27-10-29; f; yes; 1/2; W; 1/4; yes
3602; YELLOWEARRINGS, Samuel; 27-11-5; m; yes; F; F; F; yes
3632; YOUNGHAWK, Alberta; 28-1-11; f; yes; F; F; F; yes

SOUTH DAKOTA SIOUX

Live Births

July 1, 1928 - June 30, 1929

LIVE BIRTHS

State ___South Dakota___ Reservation ___Standing Rock___ Agency or jurisdiction
___Standing Rock___ Office of Indian Affairs

Births Occurring Between the Dates of July 1, 1928 and June 30, 1929 to Parents Enrolled at Jurisdiction

Key: 1929 Census Roll Number; Surname, Given; Date of Birth (Year-Month-Day); Live Births (blank unless otherwise given); Still Births (blank unless otherwise given); Sex; Tribe (Standing Rock Sioux unless given otherwise); Ward (Yes/No); Degree of Blood (Father; Mother; Child); At Jurisdiction Where Enrolled (Yes/No); (If no – Where)

109; ARCHAMBAULT, Mary Vivian; 29-3-22; f; yes; 3/4; F; 7/8; yes
2388; BELASQUES, Bernice Dorothy; 29-5-6; f; yes; F; F; F; yes
230; BIRDHORSE, Dallas Reno; 28-10-26; m; yes; F; F; F; yes
245; BLACKCLOUD, Aloysius; 28-10-5; m; yes; F; F; F; yes
317; BOBTAIL TIGER, Rhoda; 29-6-25; f; yes; F; F; F; yes
2565; BONECLUB, Agnes Julia; 29-5-15; f; yes; F; F; F; yes
387; BROWNOTTER, Henry; 28-8-26; m; yes; F; F; F; yes
696; BROWNOTTER, Steven; 29-4-18; m; yes; F; F; F; yes
not recorded; CADOTTE, Unnamed; 29-1-31; f; yes; 1/2; F; 3/4; yes
583; CLAYMORE, Evelyn; 28-8-15; f; yes; 1/2; 1/2; 1/2; yes
657; CRAZYBEAR, Victor George; 29-3-13; m; yes; F; F; F; yes
714; CROWNECKLACE, Cernia Rose; 29-3-26; f; yes; F; F; F; yes
764; DEMERY, Irvin C; 28-9-18; m; yes; W; 1/2; 1/4; yes
752; DEMERY, Matilda May; 28-10-30; f; yes; 1/2; 9/16; 5/8; yes
801; DISTRIBUTE, Delphine; 28-12-26; f; yes; F; F; F; yes
895; DOG, Davis; 29-4-10; ƒ m; yes; F; F; F; yes
897; DOGEAGLE, Lily M; 28-11-11; f; yes; F; F; F; yes
1015; FIRECLOUD, Christopher; 29-4-9; m; yes; F; F; F; yes
1930-1018; FLY, Maxine; 29-5-31; f; yes; F; W; 1/2; yes
1099; FRANK, Martin R; 28-10-6; m; yes; W; 1/4; 1/2[sic]; yes
2072; GRINDSTONE, May Ramona; 29-5-28; f; yes; F; F; F; yes
1347; HAIRYCHIN, Grace; 29-4-26; f; yes; F; 1/2; 3/4; yes
Not recorded; HAWK, Unnamed; 29-1-4; f; yes; F; 1/4; 5/8; yes
1469; HAYES, Marie Elenor; 29-3-31; f; yes; F; F; F; yes
1548; HORSETHIEF, Clifford M; 29-5-13; m; yes; F; 1/2; 3/4; yes
1726; JORDAN, Deloris M; 28-12-8; f; yes; 1/2; 3/4; 5/8; yes
1930-1898; LeCOMPTE, Elmer, Jr; 29-4-12; m; yes; 1/2; 1/2; 1/2; yes
1389; LEFTHAND, Elaine; 28-11-22; f; yes; F; F; F; yes
1964; LITTLEBEAR, Lidia; 28-7-11; f; yes; F; F; F; yes
1979; LITTLE DOG, Irene May; 28-8-2; f; yes; F; F; F; yes
1985; LITTLE DOG, Meliner Grant; 29-3-21; m; yes; F; F; F; yes
1993; LITTLE EAGLE, Ruth; 28-5-11; f; yes; F; F; F; yes
2010; LONE ELK, Ambrose; 29-5-15; m; yes; F; F; F; yes
Not recorded; LONGCHASE, Daniel; 29-6-21; m; yes; F; F; F; yes
Not recorded; LONGCHASE, Joseph; 29-6-21; m; yes; F; F; F; yes
1930-2015; LONGFEATHER, Willard D; 29-5-25; m; yes; F; F; F; yes
2055; LOOKINGBACK, Christine; 28-12-27; f; yes; F; F; F; yes
2082; LOVES WAR, Gloretta H; 29-6-24; f; yes; F; F; F; yes
2150; MANY HORSES, Martha; 28-12-11; f; yes; F; F; F; yes
2172; MARSHALL, Joseph R; 28- 8-27; m; yes; F; F; F; yes
2189; MARTIN, Alfreda Rose; 29-2-25; f; yes; F; F; F; yes
Not recorded; MARTINEZ, Aloysius; 29-4-21; m; yes; F; 3/4; 7/8; yes

State ___ South Dakota ___ Reservation ___ Standing Rock ___ Agency or jurisdiction
___ Standing Rock ___ Office of Indian Affairs

Births Occurring Between the Dates of July 1, 1928 and June 30, 1929 to Parents Enrolled at Jurisdiction

Key: 1929 Census Roll Number; Surname, Given; Date of Birth (Year-Month-Day); Live Births (blank unless otherwise given); Still Births (blank unless otherwise given); Sex; Tribe (Standing Rock Sioux unless given otherwise); Ward (Yes/No); Degree of Blood (Father; Mother; Child); At Jurisdiction Where Enrolled (Yes/No); (If no – Where)

Not recorded; MARTINEZ, James, Jr; 28-11-19; m; yes; F; F; F; yes
2240;   McLAUGHLIN, Philip Henry; 29-2-2; m; yes; 1/2; F; 3/4; yes
 389;   McLEOD, Unnamed; 29-5-17; f; yes; W; 1/4; 1/8; yes
2266;   MEDICINE, Lila Marie; 29-5-11; f; yes; 3/4; F; 7/8; yes
2372;   NOISY HAWK, Roy Edward; 29-5-11; m; yes; F; F; F; yes
2521;   POWERS, Doris Ann; 28-10-16; f; yes; 1/8; W; 1/16; yes
2532;   PRETENDS EAGLE, James; 28-12-11; m; yes; F; F; F; yes
2727;   ROUGH SURFACE, Nora May; 28-8-28; f; yes; F; 1/4; 5/8; yes
Not recorded; ROUGH SURFACE, Seraphine; 28-12-18; f; yes; F; F; F; yes
2595;   REDBEAR, Lila Lee; 28-11-25; f; yes; F; F; F; yes
2704;   ROACH, Joseph L; 29-2-19; m; yes; F; F; F; yes
2751;   SACK, Mamie; 29-6-25; f; yes; F; F; F; yes
2775;   SHAVEBEAR, Mayo; 29-1-24; m; yes; F; F; F; yes
2809;   SHOESTRING, Mary C; 28-8-16; f; yes; F; F; F; yes
Not recorded; SKUNK, Philip; 28-12-25; m; yes; F; F; F; yes
Not recorded; STANDING CLOUD, Lena; 28-12-22; f; yes; F; F; F; yes
3027;   SWIFTCLOUD, Agatha; 28-12-3; f; yes; F; F; F; yes
3045;   TAKEN ALINE, Milton; 29-5-7; m; yes; F; F; F; yes
3098;   THIEF, Christine; 28-10-5; f; yes; F; F; F; yes
Not recorded; USES HIS ARROWS, Danver; 29-4-3; m; yes; F; F; F; yes
3257:   VERMILLION, Jacqueline; 28-10-8; f; yes; W; 1/4; 1/8; yes
3277;   VILLAGE CENTER, Carl; 29-2-11; m; yes; F; F; F; yes
3306;   WALKING ELK, Thelma; 28-9-22; f; yes; F; F; F; yes
1930-3316; WARD, Kenneth; 29-2-24; m; yes; 1/2; 1/2; 1/2; yes
2332;   WHITE MOUNTAIN, Helen J; 29-3-24; f; yes; F; F; F; yes
3513;   WHITESHIELD, Helen; 28-11-17; f; yes; F; F; F; yes
Not recorded; YELLOWEARRINGS, Unnamed; 28-10-15; f; yes; F; F; F; yes
3598;   YELLOWFAT, Theresa B; 29-6-29; f; yes; F; F; F; yes

SOUTH DAKOTA SIOUX

Live Births

July 1, 1929 - June 30, 1930

LIVE BIRTHS

State ___South Dakota___ Reservation ___Standing Rock___ Agency or jurisdiction ___Standing Rock___ Office of Indian Affairs

Births Occurring Between the Dates of July 1, 1929 and June 30, 1930 to Parents Enrolled at Jurisdiction

Key: 1929 Census Roll Number; Surname, Given; Date of Birth (Year-Month-Day); Live Births (blank unless otherwise given); Still Births (blank unless otherwise given); Sex; Tribe (Standing Rock Sioux unless given otherwise); Ward (Yes/No); Degree of Blood (Father; Mother; Child); At Jurisdiction Where Enrolled (Yes/No); (If no – Where)

54; ANKLE, Loraine; 30-2-8; f; yes; F; F; F; yes
162; BEARKING, Leonard G; 29-12-15; m; yes; F; F; F; yes
1931-1715; BLACKBEAR, Chauncey; 30-5-7; m; yes; F; F; F; yes
247; BLACKCLOUD, Melvin; 29-10-18; m; yes; F; F; F; yes
1931-1797; BUCKLEY, Ruth; 30-6-30; f; yes; F; F; F; yes
Not recorded; CADOTTE, Mary; 30-3-8; f; yes; F; F; F; yes
754; DEMERY, Iola; 29-11-7; f; yes; W; 1/2; 1/4; yes
744; DEMERY, Ray Bird; 29-12-17; m; yes; 1/2; 1/4; 3/8; yes
Not recorded; DeROCKBRAINE, Effie; 30-2-19; f; yes; F; F; F; no; Rapid City, S. Dak.
1931-2037; DOG, Unnamed; 30-5-2; f; yes; F; F; F; yes
Not recorded; DOG EAGLE, Louise; 30-6-26; f; yes; F; F; F; yes
861; EAGLE, Cherolyn M; 29-9-12; f; yes; F; F; F; yes
889; EAGLE DOG, Nelson; 30-3-25; m; yes; F; F; F; yes
Not recorded; EAGLEMAN, Unnamed; 30-2-8; f; yes; F; F; F; yes
918; EAGLESHIELD, Clarence; 30-9-24; m; yes; F; F; F; yes
980; FASTHORSE, Mary; 29-8-17; f; yes; F; F; F; yes
1041; FLYINGHORSE, Elmer; 30-1-20; m; yes; F; F; F; yes
1080; FOSTER, Theresa A; 30-1-13; f; yes; F; F; F; yes
1114; GABE, Geraldine; 29-12-11; f; yes; F; F; F; yes
1931-2257; GABE, Madeline R; 30-4-27; f; yes; F; 1/2; 3/4; yes
1931-2281; GOINS, Frank; 29 30-9-13; m; yes; F; F; F; yes
1203; GOODFUR, Lucile M; 29-12-24; f; yes; F; F; F; yes
1389; HARRIS, Dorothy N; 30-2-25; f; yes; 1/2; 3/4; 5/8; yes
Not recorded; HAWK, Wilmot C; 30-1-16; f; yes; 1/2; 1/4; 3/4; yes
1931-2437; HOHEKTE, Beatrice O; 30-6-11; f; yes; F; F; F; yes
Not recorded; IRON, Jerry W; 30-3-15; m; yes; F; F; F; yes
1618; IRONCLOUD, Vernon N; 29-7-30; m; yes; F; F; F; yes
1931-2479; KEMPTON, Boyce R; 29-10-22; m; yes; 1/8; W; 1/16; yes
1799; KILLS CROW INDIAN, Freding; 29-8-12; m; yes; F; F; F; yes
1814; KILLS PRETTY ENEMY, Sidney; 30-2-16; m; yes; F; F; F; yes
1864; LaMONTE, Edward; 29-10-9; m; yes; F; F; F; yes
1931-2702; LITTLE BEAR, Melvin; 30-2-23; m; yes; F; F; F; yes
1938; LITTLE BEAR, Rufus F; 29-9-16; m; yes; F; F; F; yes
1971; LITTLE MOON, Diana; 29-12-11; f; yes; F; F; F; yes
2006; LONGCHASE, Cecelia; 29-11-10; f; yes; F; F; F; yes
2010; LONGELK, Treban; 29-7-27; f; yes; F; F; F; yes
1931-2982; MOLASH, Floyd; 30-3-11; m; yes; W; 1/2; 1/4; yes
1931-3002; NEADE, Deloris; 30-3-22; f; yes; W; 1/2; 1/4; yes
2397; ONE BULL, Robert L; 30-1-28; m; yes; 1/4; 1/2; 3/4; yes
2414; ONE FETHER[sic], Clifford; 29-12-15; m; yes; F; F; F; yes
2411; ONE FEATHER, Lauraine; 30-1-17; f; yes; F; F; F; yes
1931-3030; OKA, Merrill; 30-6-21; m; yes; F; F; F; yes

LIVE BIRTHS

State ___South Dakota___ Reservation ___Standing Rock___ Agency or jurisdiction ___Standing Rock___ Office of Indian Affairs

Births Occurring Between the Dates of July 1, 1929 and June 30, 1930 to Parents Enrolled at Jurisdiction

Key: 1929 Census Roll Number; Surname, Given; Date of Birth (Year-Month-Day); Live Births (blank unless otherwise given); Still Births (blank unless otherwise given); Sex; Tribe (Standing Rock Sioux unless given otherwise); Ward (Yes/No); Degree of Blood (Father; Mother; Child); At Jurisdiction Where Enrolled (Yes/No); (If no – Where)

2454; PARMLEY, Giles; 29-8-13; m; yes; W; F; 1/2; yes

2652; RED HORN, Lawrence; 29-8-29; m; yes; F; F; F; yes

1931-3202; ROUGH SURFACE, Mamie; 30-5-29; f; yes; 1/2; 1/4; 3/8; yes

2863; SITTING DOG, Elaine J.; 30-12-30; f; yes; F; F; F; yes

2888; SLEEPS FROM HOME, Margaret; 29-9-5; f; yes; F; F; F; yes

2947; SPOTTED HORSE, Cherity; 29-11-19; f; yes; F; F; F; yes

1931-3390; TAKES THE HAT, Margie; 30-5-8; f; yes; F; F; F; yes

3066; TAYLOR, Ramona Mae; 29-7-6; f; yes; 1/2; 1/2; 1/2; yes

Not recorded; THOMPSON, Ida A; 30-6-26; f; yes; 1/2; F; 3/4; yes

Not recorded; TIYONA, Felix; 30-5-21; m; yes; F; F; F; yes

3195; TWOHEARTS, Lucille; 29-11-4; f; yes; F; F; F; yes

1931-3526; WANKICUN, Emerson L; 30-5-2; m; yes; F; F; F; yes

Not recorded; WHITEMAN, John; 30-6-24; m; yes; F; F; F; yes

Not recorded; WILLIAMS, John H; 29-11-25; m; yes; W; 5/8; 5/16; no; Mobridge, S.D.

Not recorded; YOUNGHAWK, Henry; 30-1-6; m; yes; F; F; F; yes

SOUTH DAKOTA SIOUX

Live Births

July 1, 1930 - June 30, 1931

LIVE BIRTHS

State ___South Dakota___ Reservation ___Standing Rock___ Agency or jurisdiction
___Standing Rock___ Office of Indian Affairs

Births Occurring Between the Dates of April 1, 1930 and March 31, 1931 to Parents Enrolled at Jurisdiction

Key: 1931 Census Roll Number; Surname, Given; Date of Birth (Year-Month-Day); Live Births (blank unless otherwise given); Still Births (blank unless otherwise given); Sex; Tribe (Standing Rock Sioux unless given otherwise); Ward (Yes/No); Degree of Blood (Father; Mother; Child); At Jurisdiction Where Enrolled (Yes/No); (If no – Where)

1591; AGARD, Theresa; 30-7-14; f; yes; 3/4; 1/2; 5/8; yes
1641; ARCHAMBAULT, Maurice; 30-8-8; m; yes; 1/2; 1/4; 3/4; yes
1706; BIRDHORSE, Ernest; 30-7-14; m; yes; F; F; F; yes
1715; BLACKBEAR, Chauncey; 30-5-7; m; yes; F; F; F; yes
Not Recorded; BLACKCLOUD, Vendeline J; 31-3-26; m; yes; F; 1/2; 3/4; yes
1748; BOBTAIL TIGER, Malenia Fay; 30-10-29; f; yes; F; F; F; yes
1777; BROWN, Nora; 30-12-4; f; yes; 1/2; F; 3/4; yes
1797; BUCKLEY, Ruth; 30-6-3; f; yes; F; F; F; yes
1818; CADOTTE, Dorothy I; 30-11-7; f; yes; 3/4; F; 7/8; yes
1910; COMEAU, Madonna Jean; 30-8-21; f; yes; 1/4; W; 1/8; yes
2024; DeROCKBRAINE, Bertha; 31-1-1; f; yes; F; 1/2; 3/4; yes
2037; DOG, Unnamed; 30-5-2; f; des; F; F; F; yes
Not Recorded; DOGEAGLE, Louisa; 30-6-26; f; yes; F; F; F; yes
2069; DUNCAN, Richard James; 30-9-29; m; yes; 1/4; W; 1/8; yes
2160; END OF HORN, Merrill A; 30-9-2; m; yes; F; F; F; yes
2191; FLY, Lawrence S; 31-1-31; m; yes; F; W; 1/2; yes
2197; FLYINGBY, Grace; 30-12-4; f; yes; F; F; F; yes
Not Recorded; FRANK, Andrew; 30-8-23; m; yes; W; 1/2; 1/4; yes
2257; GABE, Madeline R; 30-4-27; f; yes; F; 1/2; 3/4; yes
Not Recorded; HALIBURTON, John Lowell; 30-8-3; m; yes; W; 1/4; 1/8; yes
2437; HOHEKTE, Beatrice O; 30-6-11; f; yes; F; F; F; yes
2663; LeCOMPTE, Clovis; 31-2-17; f; yes; 1/2; 1/2; 1/2; yes
2693; LITTLE BEAR, Bernice I; 30-10-6; f; yes; 3/4; 1/2; 3/4; yes
Not Recorded; LONE ELK, Andrew; 31-3-2; m; yes; F; F; F; yes
2906; MAXON, Ramona; 30-7-22; f; yes; W; 1/4; 1/8; yes
2951; McLEOD, Elenor J; 30-9-1; f; yes; W; 1/4; 1/8; yes
Not Recorded; MEISCH[sic], Rolland J; 30-7-28; m; yes; W; 1/2; 1/4; yes
3030; OKA, Merrill; 30-6-21; m; yes; F; F; F; yes
3166; REDHORSE, Jonas T; 30-12-5; m; yes; F; F; F; yes
3202; ROUGH SURFACE, Mamie; 30-5-29; f; yes; 1/2; 1/4; 3/8; yes
3370; TAKES THE GUN, Oliver; 30-9-8; m; yes; F; F; F; yes
3390; TAKES THE HAT, Margie, 30-5-8; f; yes; F; F; F; yes
Not Recorded; TAYLOR, Hazel Grace; 31-3-27; f; yes; 1/2; 1/2; 1/2; yes
3405; THIEF, Genevia; 30-12-9; f; yes; F; F; F; yes
3066; THOMPSON, Ida A; 30-6-26; f; yes; 1/4; 1/2; 3/4; yes
3430; THUNDERSHIELD, Margaret R; 31-2-25; f; yes; F; F; F; yes
Not Recorded; TIYONA, Felix; 30-5-21; m; yes; F; F; F; yes
3483; VILLAGE CENTER, Michael; 30-11-7; m; yes; F; F; F; yes
3508; WALKING ELK, Gloria M; 30-7-15; f; yes; F; W; 3/4; yes
3526; WANKICUN, Emerson L; 30-5-2; m; yes; F; F; F; yes
3549; WEASEL, Harold; 30-7-5; m; yes; F; F; F; yes

State ___South Dakota___ Reservation ___Standing Rock___ Agency or jurisdiction ___Standing Rock___ Office of Indian Affairs

Births Occurring Between the Dates of April 1, 1930 and March 31, 1931 to Parents Enrolled at Jurisdiction

Key: 1931 Census Roll Number; Surname, Given; Date of Birth (Year-Month-Day); Live Births (blank unless otherwise given); Still Births (blank unless otherwise given); Sex; Tribe (Standing Rock Sioux unless given otherwise); Ward (Yes/No); Degree of Blood (Father; Mother; Child); At Jurisdiction Where Enrolled (Yes/No); (If no – Where)

3593;   WHITEEAGLE, Rita Rose; 31-1-23; f; yes; F; F; F; yes
Not Recorded; WHITEMAN, John; 30-6-24; m; yes; F; F; F; yes
1931-3615; WHITESELL, Janette Mary; 30-12-18; f; yes; 1/2; 1/2; 1/2; yes
3653;   YELLOWEARRINGS, Annie; 30-11-16; f; yes; F; F; F; yes
Not Recorded; YOUNGHAWK, Daniel; 31-1-7; m; yes; F; F; F; yes

SOUTH DAKOTA SIOUX

Live Births

July 1, 1931 - June 30, 1932

State _____ South Dakota _____ Reservation _____ Standing Rock _____ Agency or jurisdiction _____ Standing Rock _____ Office of Indian Affairs

Births Occurring Between the Dates of April 1, 1931 and March 31, 1932 to Parents Enrolled at Jurisdiction

Key: 1932 Census Roll Number; Surname, Given; Date of Birth (Year-Month-Day); Live Births (blank unless otherwise given); Still Births (blank unless otherwise given); Sex; Tribe (Standing Rock Sioux unless given otherwise); Ward (Yes/No); Degree of Blood (Father; Mother; Child); At Jurisdiction Where Enrolled (Yes/No); (If no – Where)

1644; ARCHAMBAULT, Roy; 31-8-29; m; yes; 1/2; F; 3/4; yes
1698; BEARKING, Loretta; 31-10-3; f; yes; 1/2; 1/2; 1/2; yes
1770; BOBTAILTIGER, Genevieve; 31-10-23; f; yes; F; F; F; yes
1776; BONECLUB, Minerva; 31-11-16; f; yes; F; F; F; yes
1797; BROUGHTPLENTY, Cyril E; 31-8-12; m; yes; F; F; F; yes
Not recorded; BROWNOTTER, Wilma C; 31-4-1; f; yes; F; F; F; yes
1851; CADOTTE, Daniel; 31-7-8; m; yes; F; F; F; yes
1863; CATCHBEAR, Abel; 31-10-6; m; yes; F; F; F; yes
1873; CHAPMAN, Guy, Jr; 31-10-24; m; yes; F; F; F; yes
3006; DEMERY, Marie; 31-12-4; f; yes; 1/2; 1/4; 3/8; yes
2023; DEMPSEY, Benj L; 31-[?-?]; m; yes; W; 1/2; 1/4; yes
2054; DISTRIBUTE, Amelia; 31-1-7; f; yes; F; F; F; yes
2121; DOGEAGLE, Irene Mae; 31-6-22; f; yes; F; F; F; yes
2778; DOGEAGLE, Theresa; 32-1-11; f; yes; F; F; F; yes
Not recorded; EAGLEMAN, Unnamed; 31-11-10; m; yes; F; F; F; yes
Not recorded; EAGLEHORN, Unnamed; 31-12-7; m; yes; F; F; F; yes
2193; END OF HORN, Vincent; 32-2-2; m; yes; F; F; F; yes
2281; FRANK, Cecelia; 31-4-10; f; yes; WF; F; 1/2; yes
2339; GOODFUR, Charlotte J; 31-12-1; f; yes; F; F; F; yes
2390; HAND LEFT, Catherine; 31-2-7; f; yes; F; F; F; yes
2392; HAND, Henry L; 32-2-19; m; yes; F; F; F; yes
Not recorded; HAYES, Irwin W; 31-8-31; m; yes; F; F; F; yes
2477; HOLLOW, Joseph; 7-5; m; yes; F; F; F; yes
2512; HOWARD, Niel[sic] Cullen; 31- 4-5; m; yes; F; F; F; yes
2581; JORDAN, Elsie; 31-4-13; f; yes; F; F; F; yes
2683; LeCOMPTE, Luella; 31-4-13; f; yes; 1/2; 1/2; 1/2; yes
2732; LITTLEBEAR, Cora Fay; 31-7-6; f; yes; F; F; F; yes
2737; LITTLEDOG, Bernice; 31-4-4; f; yes; F; F; F; yes
2744; LITTLEDOG, Hermus R; 31-6-7; m; yes; F; F; F; yes
2748; LITTLE EAGLE, Mary E; 31-10-12; f; yes; F; F; F; yes
2812; LOOKING BACK, Virgil; 31-6-16; m; yes; F; F; F; yes
2877; MANYHORSES, Lucille; 31-4-13; f; yes; F; F; F; yes
2928; MAXON, Joan; 32-1-5; f; yes; W; 1/4; 1/8; yes
Not recorded; MARTINEZ, Manuel; 31-8-3; m; yes; F; F; F; yes
2939; McFARLAND, Donald C; 31-8-9; m; yes; W; 1/4; 1/8; yes
2952; McLAUGHLIN, Rita Ann; 31-7-17; f; yes; 1/2; F; 3/4; yes
3016; MOUNTAIN, Joseph; 31-7-15; m; yes; F; F; F; yes
3077; ONEFEATHER, Ruth; 31-12-1; f; yes; F; W; 1/2; yes
3118; PINE, Ambrose; 31-7-5; m; yes; F; F; F; yes
3153; REDBEAR, Henrietta; 31-12-23; f; yes; F; F; F; yes
3186; REDHORN, Dewey; 31-11-3; m; yes; F; F; F; yes
3199; REDLEGS, Bernice; 31-5-17; f; yes; F; F; F; yes

State ___ South Dakota ___ Reservation ___ Standing Rock ___ Agency or jurisdiction
___ Standing Rock ___ Office of Indian Affairs

Births Occurring Between the Dates of April 1, 1931 and March 31, 1932 to Parents Enrolled at Jurisdiction

Key: 1932 Census Roll Number; Surname, Given; Date of Birth (Year-Month-Day); Live Births (blank unless otherwise given); Still Births (blank unless otherwise given); Sex; Tribe (Standing Rock Sioux unless given otherwise); Ward (Yes/No); Degree of Blood (Father; Mother; Child); At Jurisdiction Where Enrolled (Yes/No); (If no – Where)

3223; ROSS, Silas, Jr; 31-8-30; m; yes; F; F; F; yes
3230; ROUGH SURFACE, Calvin H; 32-2-11; m; yes; F; F; F; yes
3251; SACK, Stella; 31-12-6; f; yes; F; F; F; yes
1220; SLEEPS FROM HOME, Wallace; 32-3-31; m; yes; F; F; F; yes
3375; SWIFTCLOUD, Samuel; 31-10-4; m; yes; F; F; F; yes
Not recorded; TAKE THE GUN, Fred; 31-7-1; m; yes; F; F; F; yes
3420; TAYLOR, Hazel G; 31-3-27; f; yes; 1/2; 1/2; 1/2; yes
3462; TIYONA, Roy; 31-12-25; m; yes; F; F; F; yes
3468; TURNINGHEART, Samuel; 31-12-4; m; yes; F; F; F; yes
3514; WAGGONER, Donald F; 31-5-15; m; yes; 1/2; W; 1/8[sic]; yes
3519; WAGGONER, Joenitta[sic]; 31-4-3; f; yes; 1/4; 1/2; 3/8; yes
3547; WANKICUN, Bernadine; 31-10-5; f; yes; F; F; F; yes
3532; WALKING ELK, Kenneth; 31-10-11; m; yes; F; F; F; yes
3560; WARD, Richard L; 31-7-12; m; yes; W; 1/2; 1/4; yes
3571; WAWOKIYA, Emma; 31-9-3; f; yes; F; F; F; yes
3526; WHITEBEARCLAWS, Sylvester; 32-1-4; m; yes; F; F; F; yes
3639; WHITEMAN, Wilma; 31-7-7; f; yes; F; F; F; yes
3712; YOUNGHAWK, Unnamed; 32-1-27; m; yes; F; F; F; yes

Standing Rock Agency

<u>Deaths</u> - - North Dakota

Standing Rock Reservation

July 1, 1924 - June 30, 1925

State ___ North Dakota ___ Reservation___ Standing Rock ___ Agency or jurisdiction, ___ Standing Rock ___ Office of Indian Affairs

Deaths Occurring Between the Dates of July 1, 1924 and June 30, 1925 of Indians Enrolled at Jurisdiction

Key: Year and Number Last Census Roll; Surname, Given; Date of Birth (Year-Month-Day); Age at Death; Sex; Tribe (NC Cherokee unless stated otherwise); Ward (Yes/No); Degree of Blood; Cause of Death (if given); At Jurisdiction Where Enrolled (Yes/No); (If no – Where)

1924- 666;   BAILEY, Elizabeth; 25-1-14; 36; f; yes; 1/2; Infection; yes

1924- 902;   BLUE EARTH, Julia; 25-2-19; 1; f; yes; F; Not reported; yes

1924-2892;   BRISTLING, Lucas; 24-8-23; 79; m; yes; F; Senility; yes

Not recorded; BROUGHT PLENTY, Thomas; 25-2-10; 4 hrs; m; yes; F; Not
    reported; yes

1924-2879;   BUFFALOBOY, Sophia; 25-4-12; 10; f; yes; F; Pul. Tuberculosis; yes

1924- 752;   CANTEWANICA; 24-[?-?]; 80; m; yes; F; Old Age; yes

1924-1106;   COMES LAST, Victoria; 25-5-5; 1; f; yes; F; Not reported; yes

1925- 652;   CRAZYWALKING, Paul, Jr; 25-1-8; 5/12; m; yes; F; Pneumonia; yes

Not recorded; DIFFERENT OWL, James; 25-4-13; 1 da; m; yes; F; Atelectosis[sic];
    yes

Not recorded; DIFFERENT OWL, Nellie; 25-4-14; 2 da; f; yes; F; Atelectosis; yes

1924- 800;   DOUGLAS, LeRoy; 25-1-30; 11; m; yes; F; Not reported; yes

1924-2939;   DWARF, Mary; 24-9-5; 6; f; yes; F; Pneumonia; yes

1924-3283;   GAYTON, Mrs Annie; 24-8-31; 33; f; yes; 1/4; Apoplexy; yes

Not recorded; GOODIRON, Alice; 25-1-27; 2 hrs; f; yes; F; Not reported; yes

1924-3395;   GRAYSTONE, Alice; 24-12-30; 48; f; yes; F; Apoplexy; yes

1924-3358;   IAPIPANINKIYA; 25-4-15; 82; f; yes; F; Old age; yes

Not recorded; IRELAND, Philip; 24-10-15; 1; m; yes; F; Not reported; yes

Not recorded; IRONROAD, Solomon; 25-1-27; 8/12; m; yes; F; Not reported; yes

1924-3057;   KIDDER, Thomas; 24-8-14; 55; m; yes; F; Dropsy; yes

1924- 982;   LITTLE CROW, Adelina; 24-11-13; 11/12; f; yes; F; Not reported; yes

Not recorded; MARTIN, Sylvester; 25-2-5; 11/12; m; yes; 3/4; Not reported; yes

1934-1010;   MULHERN, Wm. F; 25-3-20; 1; m; yes; 5/8; Not reported; yes

Not recorded; MURPHY, Robt. Chas; 24-10-10; 10 da; m; yes; F; Pneumonia; yes

1924-3097;   PLEETS, John; 24-11-20; 63; m; yes; F; Mitral Regurgitation; yes

1924-1047;   PRETTY BEAR, Amy; 24-10-1; 48; f; yes; F; Not reported yes

1924-1078;   RED BEANS, Alice; 25-4-30; 3; f; yes; F; Not reported; yes

1924-3472;   RUNS THE MIDDLE, John; 24-1-13; 71; m; yes; F; Pneumonia; yes

1924-3502;   SMITE, Abraham; 24-7-31; 1; m; yes; F; Not reported; yes

1924-1123;   SPOTTED ELK, John; 24-[?-?]; 31; m; yes; F; Not reported; yes

1924-3135;   SWIFT ELK, Jennie; 24-8-28; 75; f; yes; F; Fever; yes

1924-1171;   TAIL, Martin; 24-12-18; 51; m; yes; F; Kidney Trouble; yes

1924-2857;   THOMPSON, Helen; 24-8-19; 24; f; yes; F; Not reported; yes

Not recorded; THOMPSON, Mary; 24-11-13; 1; f; yes; F; Not known; yes

1924-1215;   TWO BEAR, Benjamin; 25-1-27; 11; m; yes; F; Not reported; yes

1924-1211;   TWO BEAR, Kenneth; 24-7-30; 1; m; yes; F; Not reported; yes

1924-1218;   TWO BEARS, Leon; 25-5-26; 1; m; yes; F; Not reported; yes

State _____ North Dakota _____ Reservation _____ Standing Rock _____ Agency or jurisdiction,
_____ Standing Rock _____ Office of Indian Affairs

Deaths Occurring Between the Dates of July 1, 1924 and June 30, 1925 of Indians Enrolled at Jurisdiction

Key: Year and Number Last Census Roll; Surname, Given; Date of Birth (Year-Month-Day); Age at Death; Sex; Tribe (NC Cherokee unless stated otherwise); Ward (Yes/No); Degree of Blood; Cause of Death (if given); At Jurisdiction Where Enrolled (Yes/No); (If no – Where)

1924-1122;   WELCH, Maggie; 25-5-31; 24; f; yes; F; Tuberculosis; yes

1924- 810;   WINTERS, Carl; 24-12-6; 15; m; yes; F; Tuberculosis; yes

1924-2831;   WHITE, Melda; 25-5-7; 18; f; yes; F; Pul. Tuberculosis; yes

Not recorded; WHITE, Robert; 25-2-26; 4; m; yes; F; Cerebral Meningitis; yes

1920-1276;   WHITELIGHTNING, Roy; 24- 8-23; 4; m; yes; F; Not known; yes

Not recorded; YANKEWIN, Annnie[sic]; 25-4-16; 93; f; yes; F; Senility; yes

1924-1306;   YELLOWHAWK; 25-2-9; 77; m; yes; F; Not reported; yes

1925-3605;   ZAHN, George; 25-6-13; 1; m; yes; 5/8; Not reported; yes

Standing Rock Agency

<u>Deaths</u> - - North Dakota

Standing Rock Reservation

July 1, 1925 - June 30, 1926

State _____ North Dakota _____ Reservation _____ Standing Rock _____ Agency or jurisdiction,
_____ Standing Rock _____ Office of Indian Affairs

Deaths Occurring Between the Dates of July 1, 1925 and June 30, 1926 of Indians Enrolled at Jurisdiction

Key: Year and Number Last Census Roll; Surname, Given; Date of Birth (Year-Month-Day); Age at Death; Sex; Tribe (NC Cherokee unless stated otherwise); Ward (Yes/No); Degree of Blood; Cause of Death (if given); At Jurisdiction Where Enrolled (Yes/No); (If no – Where)

1925-   3;   AFRAID OF BEAR, Katie; 26-3-19; 7; f; yes; F; Lobar Pneumonia; yes

1925- 35;   ALKIRE, Sallie Mrs; 26-5-22; 34; f; yes; F; Tuberculosis; yes

1925- 330;   BRINGS THEM, Joseph; 26-6-10; 44; m; yes; F; Pul. Tuberculosis; yes

1925-2664;   BEARSHIELD, Mrs; 26-3-30; 67; f; yes; F; Not known; yes

1925- 349;   BROWN, Joseph; 25-9-13; 33; m; yes; F; Not known; yes

1925- 404;   BULLBEAR, Frank; 25-11-11; 68; m; yes; F; Stomach Trouble; yes

1925- 446;   CALLOUSLEG, Mrs; 26-1-8; 63; f; yes; F; Chronic Rheumatism; yes

Not recorded; CALLOUSLEG, Theresa; 26-3-31; 3/12; f; yes; F; Not known; yes

Not recorded; CASKE, Frederick; 26-2-2; 1 da; m; yes; F; Premature; yes

1925- 501;   CHAPMAN, Clyde; 25-10-20; 6/12; m; yes; F; Peritonitis; yes

Not recorded; CHASING BEAR, John R; 25-9-5; 1/12; m; yes; F; Not known; yes

1925- 607;   COTTONWOOD, Margaret; 26-4-29; 14; f; yes; F; Tuberculosis; yes

1925- 687;   CROWNECKLACE, Henry; 25-8-4; 8/12; m; yes; F; Summer Complaint; yes

1925- 854;   EAGLEBOY, Samuel Mrs; 26-3-24; 54; f; yes; F; Not known; yes

1925- 881;   EAGLENATION, Mrs; 26-3-5; 59; f; yes; F; Not known; yes

1925-1093;   GAYTON, Christopher; 25-11-13; 16; m; yes; 1/2; Peritonitis; yes

Not recorded; GOODIRON, Josephine; 26-4-26; 2/12; f; yes; F; Not known; yes

1925-1276;   GOODIRON, Margaret; 26-4-10; 23; f; yes; F; Pul. Tuberculosis; yes

Not recorded; GOODIRON, Sam, Jr; 26-5-23; 1 hr.; m; yes; F; Enclosed Liver; yes

1925-2303;   GOOD NEST WOMAN; 26-3-2; 63; f; yes; F; Acute Indigestion; yes

1925-1221;   GREYBULL, Lorene; 25-10-11; 2; f; yes; F; Meningitis; yes

1925-1225;   HALSEY, Thomas; 26-5-19; 1; m; yes; F; Not reported; yes

1925-1398;   HAWKSHIELD, Alene; 25-9-14; 5/12; f; yes; F; Pneumonia; yes

1925-1442;   HIS WHITE HORSE; 26-1-26; 78; m; yes; F; Pneumonia; yes

1925-1476;   HOLY ELK FACE, Morris; 25-10-28; 9/12; m; yes; F; Pneumonia; yes

1925-1483;   HONA, Mrs. Adam; 25-9-18; 72; f; yes; F; Liver Trouble; yes

1925-3035;   HOPKINS, Benjamin; 25-8-25; 2; m; yes; F; Summer Complaint; yes

1925-1488;   HORNCLOUD, Joseph; 25-8-13; 39; m; yes; F; Not reported; yes

1925-1561;   IRELAND, Claude; 25-7-7; 6/12; m; yes; F; Not reported; yes

Not recorded; IRONSHIELD, Clement; 26-2-20; 1/12; m; yes; F; Not reported; yes

1925-1641;   IRONTOMAHAWK, Julia; 26-1-25; 15; f; yes; F; Tuberculosis; yes

1925-1653;   ITATEWIN; 26-3-4; 93; f; yes; F; Old age; yes

1925-1916;   LITTLECROW, Wesley; 25-12-3; 7/12; m; yes; F; Pneumonia; yes

1925-1995;   LOOKING ELK, Oliver, Jr; 26-3-12; 5; m; yes; F; Not reported; yes

1925-1683;   JORDAN, Mary; 25-7-20; 1; f; yes; 3/4; Pneumonia; yes

1923- 403;   MAKALUTAWIN; 26-4-4; [?]; f; yes; F; Old age; yes

Deaths Occurring Between the Dates of July 1, 1925 and June 30, 1926 of Indians Enrolled at Jurisdiction

Key: Year and Number Last Census Roll; Surname, Given; Date of Birth (Year-Month-Day); Age at Death; Sex; Tribe (NC Cherokee unless stated otherwise); Ward (Yes/No); Degree of Blood; Cause of Death (if given); At Jurisdiction Where Enrolled (Yes/No); (If no – Where)

1925-2074; MANY HORSES: Annie; 26- 4-28; 13; f; yes; F; Not reported; yes

1925-2160; McLAUGHLIN, Ruth; 25-10-4; 7; f; yes; 3/4; Acute appendicitis; yes

1925-2225; MENTZ, William; 25-8-3; 34; m; yes; 1/2; Cancer of stomach; yes

Not recorded; NOHEART, Coolidge; 26-6-29; 1; m; yes; F; Pneumonia; yes

1925-2427; PLEETS, Frank; 26-5-11; 13; m; yes; F; Pul. Tuberculosis; yes

1925-2437; PLEETS, Mary; 25-11-3; 59; f; yes; F; Mitral insufficiency; yes

1925-2458; PRETTY BEAR, Lucy; 26-2-27; 15; f; yes; F; Tuberculosis; yes

Not recorded; RAINBOW, Hermine; 25- 9-29; 5/12; f; yes; F; Not reported; yes

1925-2555; REDEARS, Bessie; 25-9-26; 61; f; yes; F; Not reported; yes

1924-3113; REDHORSE, Joseph; 25-5-3; 16; m; yes; F; Pul. Tuberculosis; yes

1925-2840; SLATER, Christopher; 25-7-31; 8/12; m; yes; F; Not reported; yes

1925-2881; SPEAKS WALKING, Mrs Luke; 26-5-20; 27; f; yes; F; Tuberculosis; yes

1925-2884; SPOTTED ELK, Luke; 26-5-26; 54; m; yes; F; Tuberculosis; yes

1925- 665; STANDING CROW, Marie Jean; 25-8-25; 7/12; f; yes; F; Summer complaint, yes

1924-3159; STANDING SOLDIER, Louise; 25-[?-?]; 69; f; yes; F; Not reported; yes

1925-3110; TABONA, Mrs Henry; 25-12-6; 59; f; yes; F; Not reported; yes

1925-3027; TAKES THE SHIELD; 26-2-26; 78; m; yes; F; Ulcers; yes

1925-1045; TAWIPABLAYEWASTEWIN; 26-1-18; 70; f; yes; F; Carcinoma of Liver; yes

1925-3104; TIOKASIN, Claude; 26-4-14; 1; m; yes; F; Meningitis; yes

1925-3099; TIOKASIN, Cora; 26-1-23; 15; f; yes; F; Tuberculosis; yes

1925-3103; TIOKASIN, Evelyn; 26-2-14; 2; f; yes; F; Pneumonia; yes

1925-3115; TRACKHIDER; 25-10-24; 65; m; yes; F; Tuberculosis; yes

1925-3127; TREETOP, Teresa; 25-11-19; 72; f; yes; F; Apoplexy; yes

1925- 806; TWOPARENTS, Alice; 26-1-2; 10/12; f; yes; F; Bronchial Pneumonia; yes

1925-3206; TWOSHIELDS, Jerry; 26-1-2; 10/12; m; yes; F; Bronchial pneumonia; yes

Not recorded; WALKER, Caroline; 25-10-[?]; 12; f; yes; F; Tuberculosis; yes

1925-3372; WHITE, Moses B; 25-9-10; 40; m; yes; F; Injury; yes

1925-3309; WHITE, Winifred; 26-6-18; 24; f; yes; 1/2; Not reported; yes

Not recorded; WHITEEAGLE, Mary; 25-2-5; 1 da; f; yes; F; Premature Birth; yes

1325-3421; WHITEEAGLE, Theodore; 26-2-5; 9/12; m; yes; F; Pneumonia; yes

1925-3438; WHITE EYELASH, Mrs; 26-1-30; 85; f; yes; F; Tuberculosis; yes

State ___North Dakota___ Reservation___ Standing Rock ___ Agency or jurisdiction, ___ Standing Rock ___ Office of Indian Affairs

Deaths Occurring Between the Dates of July 1, 1925 and June 30, 1926 of Indians Enrolled at Jurisdiction

Key: Year and Number Last Census Roll; Surname, Given; Date of Birth (Year-Month-Day); Age at Death; Sex; Tribe (NC Cherokee unless stated otherwise); Ward (Yes/No); Degree of Blood; Cause of Death (if given); At Jurisdiction Where Enrolled (Yes/No); (If no – Where)

1925-3459;   WHITELIGHTNING, Michael; 25-8-25; 1; m; yes; F; Gastro
             Entrities[sic]; yes
1925-3565;   YELLOWHAWK, Mrs; 26-3-14; 63; f; yes; F; Not reported; yes

Standing Rock Agency

Deaths - - North Dakota

Standing Rock Reservation

July 1, 1926 - June 30, 1927

State ___ North Dakota ___ Reservation ___ Standing Rock ___ Agency or jurisdiction, ___ Standing Rock ___ Office of Indian Affairs

Deaths Occurring Between the Dates of July 1, 1926 and June 30, 1927 of Indians Enrolled at Jurisdiction

Key: Year and Number Last Census Roll; Surname, Given; Date of Birth (Year-Month-Day); Age at Death; Sex; Tribe (NC Cherokee unless stated otherwise); Ward (Yes/No); Degree of Blood; Cause of Death (if given); At Jurisdiction Where Enrolled (Yes/No); (If no – Where)

1926-   10;   AFRAID OF HIS PLUME, Mrs; 26-12-24; 91; f; yes; F; Not reported; yes

1927- 211;   BIGHORNELK, Mary; 26-7-24; 4; f; yes; F; Not reported; yes

1926- 266;   BLACK PRAIRIE DOG, Pridget; 27-5-14; 3; f; yes; F; Not reported; yes

1926- 335;   BROWN, John S; 27-2-16; 55; m; yes; 1/2; Gasinoma[sic] Stomach; yes

1926-3520;   BULLHEAD, Frank; 27-1-1; 65; m; yes; F; Chronic Bronchitis; yes

1926- 730;   DEFENDER, Lincoln; 26-8-15; 9/12; m; yes; F; Bronchial Pneumonia; yes

1926- 781;   DIFFERENT TRACK BULL; 26-10-28; 78; m; yes; F; Not reported; yes

1926- 821;   DOUGLAS, Virginia; 26-9-7; 6/12; f; yes; F; Gastro Entrities[sic]; yes

1926- 863;   FASTHORSE, Crusantius; 27-1-6; 6 da; f; yes; F; Not reported; yes

1926- 996;   FIREHEART, Henry; 26-10-47; 75; m; yes; F; Pul. Tuberculosis; yes

1926-1203;   GOOD MEDICINE, Mrs; 27-2-26; 84; f; yes; F; Senility; yes

1927-1249;   GRAYBEAR, Christine; 27-6-25; 10; f; yes; 3/4; Tuberculosis; yes

1926-1934:   GRAYBEAR, Josephine; 27-4-26; 1; f; yen; F; Pul. Tuberculosis; yes

Not recorded; HOPKINS, Cecelia I; 27-5-5-1920; 2 da; f; yes; F; Unknown; yes

Not recorded; HOPKINS, Benjamin; 27-7-9; 14 da; m; yes; F; Not reported; yes

Not recorded; JORDAN, Albert; 27-4-28; 9/12; m; yes; F; Tuberculosis; yes

1926-1704;   KARNIGA, Laura; 27-5-13; 19; f; yes; F; Pul. Tuberculosis; yes

1926-1956;   LOAN HIM ARROWS, Mrs; 26-12-6; 71; f; yes; F; Pul. Tuberculosis; yes

Not recorded; LOON, Herbert C; 26-12-11; 3/12; m; yes; F; Not reported; yes

1926-2194;   McLAUGHLIN, William; 27-4-14; 27; m; yes; 1/2; Meningitis; yes

1926-2284;   MULHERN, Patrick; 27-2-21; 11/12; m; yes; 1/2; Unknown; yes

1928-2452;   OWNS MEDICINE, Annie; 27-6-18; 13; f; yes; F; Meningitis; yes

1926-2443;   PIERRE, Louise Mrs; 27-6-17; 75; f; yes; F; Not reported; yes

1926-2454;   PLEETS, Irene; 27-5-22; 15; f; yes; F; Pul. Tuberculosis; yes

1926-2538;   RECLINING BEAR, Mrs; 27-3-27; 64; f; yes; F; Unknown; yes

1926-2585;   REDFISH, Mrs Mark; 27-5-8; 84; f; yes; F; Pneumonia; yes

1926-2598;   REDFOX, Mrs Leo; 27-1-26; 81; f; yes; F; Not reported; yes

1926-2681;   ROACH, John; 26-10-3; 72; m; yes; F; Chronic Bronchitis; yes

1926-2758;   SHELL TRACK, Samuel; 27-4-4; 30; m; yes; F; Tuberculosis; yes

1926-2787;   SHOOTER, Philip; 27-3-26; 72; m; yes; F; Unknown; yes

1926-2944;   STANDING SOLDIER, Virginia; 27-3-30; 9/12; f; yes; F; Not reported; yes

1926-2990;   SWIFTBIRD, Mrs Hugh; 27-2-18; 60; f; yes; F; Unknown; yes

1926-3003;   SWIFTELK, Abe; 26-7-19; 62; m; yes; F; Tuberculosis; yes

1926-3299;   USES HIS ARROWS, Hattie; 26-9-15; 26; f; yes; F; Not reported; yes

1926-3503;   WINYANLA; 26-8-11; 62; f; yes; F; Decompensation; yes

1926-3421;   WHITEEAGLE, Mrs Adam; 26-10-14; 88; f; yes; F; Senility; yes

1926-3434;   WHITEEAGLE, Margaret; 26-12-5; 10; f; yes; F; Not reported; yes

1926-1445;   YELLOWHAIR, Mrs; 26-8-22; 81; f; yes; F; Unknown; yes

Standing Rock Agency

Deaths - - North Dakota

Standing Rock Reservation

July 1, 1927 - June 30, 1928

State ___ North Dakota ___ Reservation___ Standing Rock ___ Agency or jurisdiction, ___ Standing Rock ___ Office of Indian Affairs

Deaths Occurring Between the Dates of July 1, 1927 and June 30, 1928 of Indians Enrolled at Jurisdiction

Key: Year and Number Last Census Roll; Surname, Given; Date of Birth (Year-Month-Day); Age at Death; Sex; Tribe (NC Cherokee unless stated otherwise); Ward (Yes/No); Degree of Blood; Cause of Death (if given); At Jurisdiction Where Enrolled (Yes/No); (If no – Where)

1927- 130; BADHORSE, Maude; 27-11-14; 77; f; yes; F; Not reported; yes
1927- 213; BIGHORNELK, Louis; 27-8-1; 2; m; yes; F; Lobar Pneumonia; yes
1927- 212; BIGHORNELK, William; 28-4-9; 3; m; yes; F; Peritonitis; yes
1927-2461; BLACKHAWK, Peter; 27-8-27; 54; m; yes; F; Cordiac Dilitation[sic];
            yes
1927- 258; BLACKHOOP, Agnes; 27-12-30; 54; f; yes; F; Diabetes; yes
1927- 292; BLACKTONGUE, Grace; 29-1-27; 2; f; yes; F; Measles; yes
1927- 372; BROWNFOREHEAD, William; 27-11-21; 68; m; yes; F; Not reported;
            yes
1927- 538; CHASE FLYING; 28-3-14; 82; m; yes; F; Diarrhea; yes
1927- 617; CONICA, Mrs Louisa; 28-2-20; 30; f; yes; F; Pul. Tuberculosis; yes
1927- 699; CROWGHOST, Lawrence; 27-9-16; 64; m; yes; F; Senility; yes
1927- 834; DOUGLAS, Gene; 27-8-4; 1; m; yes; F; Meningitis; yes
1927- 831; DOUGLAS, Jacob; 27-10-21; 30; m; yes; F; Not reported; yes
1927-1204; GOODIRON, Paul; 27-7-3; 30; m; yes; F; Unknown; yes
1927-1361; HAND, Theodore; 28-1-10; 2; m; yes; F; Lobar pneumonia; yes
1927-1505; HOLY ELK FACE, Fannie; 27-10-8; 10; f; yes; F; Pul. Tuberculosis;
            yes
1927-3065; HOPKINS, Ernest; 28-4-17; 6; m; yes; F; Meningitis; yes
1927-2019; LOOKING ELK, Chas; 29-3-11; 6; m; yes; F; Pneumonia; yes
1927-2234; MENTZ, Marcella; 28-1-9; 11; f; yes; 1/2; Pul. Tuberculosis; yes
Not recorded; MENTZ, William; 28-3-23; 3; m; yes; 7/8; Unknown; yes
1927-2392; ONIHAN, William; 28-3-23; 3; m; yes; F; Not reported; yes
1927-2412; OYATE or NATION; 28-6-21; 90; f; yes; F; Senility; yes
1927-1602; PAINTS BROWN, Phoebe; 28-4-28; 18; f; yes; F; Pul. Tuberculosis;
            yes
1927-2415; PAINTS BROWN, Samuel; 28-1-1; 26; m; yes; F; Pul. Tuberculosis;
            yes
1927-2677; REE or PADANI; 27-12-23; 76; m; yes; F; Pul. Tuberculosis; yes
1927-2621; REDHAWK, Fletcher; 27-11-11; 17; m; yes; F; Meningitis; yes
1927-2661; REDSTONE, David; 27-9-26; 52; m; yes; F; Unknown; yes
1927-2754; SEE THE ELK, Cyril; 28-1-20; 2; m; yes; F; Not reported; yes
1927-2801; SHOOTS HOLY, Mrs. Paul; 27-12-3; 80; f; yes; F; Pul. Tuberculosis;
            yes
1927-2891; STETCHES[sic] HIMSELF, John; 27-8-20; 12; m; yes; F; Tuberculosis;
            yes
1927-2899; STRETCHES HIMSELF, Sylvester; 27-7-15; 4; m; yes; F; Not
            reported; yes
1927-3274; WAKANKECAMNAWIN; 28-3-11; 92; f; yes; F; Pneumonia; yes
1927-3435; WHITECLOUD, Cordon; 28-3-17; 1; m; yes; F; Lobar pneumonia; yes
1927-3437; WHITE COW WALKING, Mrs; 27-10-7; 70; f; yes; F; Pneumonia; yes

Standing Rock Agency

Deaths - - North Dakota

Standing Rock Reservation

July 1, 1928 - June 30, 1929

State_____North Dakota_____Reservation_____Standing Rock_____Agency or jurisdiction,
_____Standing Rock_____ Office of Indian Affairs

Deaths Occurring Between the Dates of July 1, 1928 and June 30, 1929 of Indians Enrolled at Jurisdiction

Key: Year and Number Last Census Roll; Surname, Given; Date of Birth (Year-Month-Day); Age at Death; Sex; Tribe (NC Cherokee unless stated otherwise); Ward (Yes/No); Degree of Blood; Cause of Death (if given); At Jurisdiction Where Enrolled (Yes/No); (If no – Where)

1928- 46; ALL YELLOW, Mary; 29-6-3; 58; f; yes; F; Tuberculosis; yes
Not recorded; BIGSHIELD, Burdie; 29-2-2; 4/12; f; yes; F; Unknown; yes
1928- 253; BLACKCROW, John Lee; 28-8-4; 25; m; yes; F; Tuberculosis; yes
1928- 249; BLACKCLOUD, Pauline; 29-3-21; 9; f; yes; F; Tuberculosis; yes
1928- 319; BRAVE, Paul; 29-2-26; 63; m; yes; F; Tuberculosis; yes
1928- 326; BRAVEBULL, Mrs; 29-6-24; 81; f; yes; F; Pneumonia; yes
1928- 436; BYINGTON, Harriet; 29-5-25; 15; f; yes; 1/4; Acute appendicitis; yes
1928- 478; CALLOUSLEG, Nellie; 28-10-23; 31; f; yes; F; Tuberculosis; yes
1928- 468; CALLOUSLEG, Mrs Sarah; 28-8-11; 84; f; yes; F; Jaundice; yes;
1928- 512; CASKE, Henry; 28-10-19; 16; m; yes; F; Pul. Tuberculosis; yes
1928- 509; CASKE, Mary Lucy; 28-7-22; 60; f; yes; F; General Edema; yes
1928- 574; CHOPPER, Amos; 28-7-9; 10; m; yes; F; Killed by Lightning; yes
1928- 572; CHOPPER, Benjamin; 28-7-9; 13; m; yes; F; Killed by Lightning; yes
1928- 570; CHOPPER, Lizzie; 28-7-9; 39; f; yes; F; Killed by Lightning; yes
1928- 569; CHOPPER, Mark; 28-7-9; 43; m; yes; F; Killed by Lightning; yes
Not recorded; COTTONWOOD, Alvina; 29-4-19; 8/12; f; yes; F; Pneumonia; yes
1928- 636; COTTONWOOD, Julia; 29-1-1; 70; f; yes; F; Heart Failure; yes
1928- 676; CRAZYWALKING, Bernard; 28-12-22; 14; m; yes; F; Tuberculosis; yes
1928- 714; CROWNECKLACE, Robert; 29-1-2; 1; m; yes; F; Pneumonia; yes
1928-1058; FOLLOWS THE ROAD, Nellie; 28-11-30; 62; f; yes; F; Gangrene; yes
1928-1201; GOODCROW, Walter; 29-5-23; 23; m; yes; F; Pul. Tuberculosis; yes
1928-1248; GOODWOOD, Benedict; 28-8-17; 51; m; yes; F; Unknown; yes
1928-1291; GREYBULL, Teddy; 28-9-26; 6/12; m; yes; F; Whooping Cough; yes
1928-1285; GREYBULL, Vincent; 29-1-11; 2; m; yes; F; Unknown; yes
1928-1405; HARMON, Charles F; 29-1-2; 1; m; yes; 1/8; Convulsions; yes
1928-1496; HIS HORSE APPEARS; 29-1-16; 77; m; yes; F; Pneumonia; yes
1928-1497; HIS HORSE APPEARS, Mrs; 29-1-13; 76; f; yes; F; Pneumonia; yes
1928-1495; HIS HOLY HORSE, Moses; 29-6-15; 75; m; yes; F; Pneumonia; yes
1928-2156; HOWARD, Daisy Ida; 29-4-26; 15; f; yes; 1/2; Pul. Tuberculosis; yes
Not recorded; HOPKINS, Benedict; 28-9-16; 4 da; m; yes; F; Unknown; yes
1928-1923; LITTLECHIEF, Joseph; 29-9-12; 50; m; yes; F; Dropsy; yes
Not recorded; MARTIN, Lucy E; 28-12-12; 4/12; f; yes; F; Unknown; yes
1928-2295; MENTZ, Louise; 29-4-13; 30; f; yes; F; Childbirth; yes
1928-2458; PAINTS BROWN, Jerome; 28-7-23; 1; m; yes; F; Gastro-Entrities[sic]; yes
1928-2580; RATTLING HAIL, George; 29-3-27; 13; m; yes; F; Tuberculosis; yes
1928-2620; REDDOG, James; 29-1-9; 60; m; yes; F; Pul. Tuberculosis; yes
1928-2637; REDFOX, Virginia; 28-7-25; 3; f; yes; F; Tuberculosis; yes
1928-2655; REDHAWK, Mrs Jesse; 29-2-9; 59; f; yes; F; Cancer of Breast; yes
1928-2728; RETURNS LAST, Thos. Joseph; 28-8-3; 1/12; m; yes; F; Convulsions; yes
1928-2768; SANTEE, Haskell; 28-11-7; 73; m; yes; F; Old age; yes
1928- 934; SANTEE, Samuel; 28-8-14; 73; m; yes; F; Auto Accident; yes

233

State _____ North Dakota _____ Reservation _____ Standing Rock _____ Agency or jurisdiction,
_____ Standing Rock _____ Office of Indian Affairs

Deaths Occurring Between the Dates of July 1, 1928 and June 30, 1929 of Indians Enrolled at Jurisdiction

Key: Year and Number Last Census Roll; Surname, Given; Date of Birth (Year-Month-Day); Age at Death;
Sex; Tribe (NC Cherokee unless stated otherwise); Ward (Yes/No); Degree of Blood; Cause of Death (if
given); At Jurisdiction Where Enrolled (Yes/No); (If no – Where)

1928-2784; SEE THE ELK, Lawrence; 28-7-14; 42; m; yes; F; Tuberculosis; yes
1928-2791; SHARPHORN BULL, Emma; 28-10-21; 64; f; yes; F; Carcinoma of
             scalp; yes
1928-2929; SMITE, Matthew; 28-12-25; 4; m; yes; F; Influenza; yes
1928- 935; SWEETCORN, James; 28-8-2; 4; m; yes; F; Tuberculosis; yes
1928-3057; TAIL, Philip; 29-5-4; 20; m; yes; F; Tuberculosis; yes
1928-1470; TAIL, Solomon; 28-8-7; 9; m; yes; F; Tuberculosis; yes
1928-3619; YELLOWLODGE, Eugene; 29-2-5; 55; m; yes; F; Exposure; yes
1928-3624; YOUNG BEAR, Moses; 29-1-4; 71; m; yes; F; Heart Failure; yes
1928-3249; TWO PARENTS, Stephen; 28-10-2; 48; m; yes; F; Tuberculosis; yes

Standing Rock Agency

<u>Deaths</u> - - North Dakota

Standing Rock Reservation

July 1, 1929 - June 30, 1930

State   North Dakota   Reservation   Standing Rock   Agency or jurisdiction,
       Standing Rock   Office of Indian Affairs

Deaths Occurring Between the Dates of July 1, 1929 and June 30, 1930 of Indians Enrolled at Jurisdiction

Key: Year and Number Last Census Roll; Surname, Given; Date of Birth (Year-Month-Day); Age at Death;
Sex; Tribe (NC Cherokee unless stated otherwise); Ward (Yes/No); Degree of Blood; Cause of Death (if
given); At Jurisdiction Where Enrolled (Yes/No); (If no – Where)

1929-   8;   AFRAID OF HAWK; 30-1-2; 79; m; yes; F; Brights Disease; yes

1929- 103;   ARCHAMBAULT, Richard; 30-3-5; 22; m; yes; 1/2; Tuberculosis; yes

1929- 125;   AZURE, McHenry; 30-2-25; 27; m; yes; 1/2; Snake bite; yes

1929- 136;   BAILEY, Warren; 30-2-4; 17; m; yes; 1/4; Pul. Tuberculosis; yes

1929- 275;   BLACKHOOP, Chas.; 30-5-30; 17; m; yes; F; Tuberculosis; yes

Not recorded; BLACK TOMAHAWK, Wm.; 29-8-26; 3/12; m; yes; F; Diarrhea; yes

1929- 507;   CHAPMAN, Mamie; 30-6-6; 28; f; yes; 1/2; Tuberculosis; yes

1929- 975;   EVANS, Lawrence; 29-8-13; 2; m; yes; 1/2; Bronchial Pneumonia; yes

1929-1021;   FLY, George; 29-8-3; 25; m; yes; F; Tuberculosis; yes

1929-1053;   FOLLOWS THE ROAD, Ella; 29-10-13; 4; f; yes; F; Not reported; yes

1929-1127;   GATES, Frank; 29-11-19; 79; m; yes; F; Heart Failure; yes

1929-1381;   HALSEY, Clara J; 29-12-15; 22; f; yes; 3/4; Tuberculosis; yes

1929-1477;   HIGH DOG, Pierre; 29-9-6; 77; m; yes; F; Pneumonia; yes

Not recorded; HIS HORSE APPEARS, Junior; 30-5-5; 10/12; m; yes; F; Meningitis;
yes

Not recorded; IRONROAD, George; 30-6-8; 1/12; m; yes; F; Meningitis; yes

1929-1704;   JAMERSON, Susan; 30-1-30; 38; f; yes; 1/2; Tuberculosis; yes

1929-2003;   LITTLE WARRIOR, Stanislaus; 30-6-12; 15; m; yes; F; Intestinal TB;
yes

1929-2087;   LOW BEAR; 29-7-10; 74; m; yes; F; Paraglegia[sic]; yes

1929-2088;   LOW BEAR, Mrs; 29-8-7; 69; f; yes; F; Chronic Nephritis; yes

1929-2145;   MANY HORSES, Raymond; 29-8-4; 1; m; yes; F; Pneumonia; yes

1929-2164;   MANYWOUNDS, Loretta; 29-8-13; 1; f; yes; 7/8; Gastro Entrities[sic];
yes

1929-2354;   MURPHY, James; 29-9-13; 2; m; yes; 1/2; Gastro Entrities; yes

1929-2511;   PLEETS, Martina; 29-12-23; 29; f; yes; 7/8; Tuberculosis; yes

1929-3647;   RAMEY, May A; 29-7-25; 1; f; yes; 1/4; Convulsions; yes

1929-2577;   RATTLINGHAIL, Leo; 29-9-21; 18; m; yes; F; Tuberculosis; yes

1929-2904;   SLATER, Michael; 29-12-26; 20; m; yes; 3/4; Tuberculosis; yes

1929-3001;   STRETCHES HIMSELF, Paul; 30-4-27; 62; m; yes; F; Tuberculosis;
yes

1929-3015;   STRONG HEART; 30-4-8; 86; m; yes; F; Nephrities[sic]; yes

Not recorded; TIBBETS, Florina Ann; 30-3-1; 13/4 hrs; f; yes; F; Ecephaletes[sic]; yes

Not recorded; TWO BEARS, Cerena; 29-8-1; 3 da; f; yes; 7/8; Accidental Abortion;
yes

Standing Rock Agency

Deaths - - North Dakota

Standing Rock Reservation

April 1, 1930 - March 31, 1931

State ____ North Dakota ____ Reservation ____ Standing Rock ____ Agency or jurisdiction,
____ Standing Rock ____ Office of Indian Affairs

Deaths Occurring Between the Dates of April 1, 1930 and March 31, 1931 of Indians Enrolled at Jurisdiction

Key: Year and Number Last Census Roll; Surname, Given; Date of Birth (Year-Month-Day); Age at Death; Sex; Tribe (NC Cherokee unless stated otherwise); Ward (Yes/No); Degree of Blood; Cause of Death (if given); At Jurisdiction Where Enrolled (Yes/No); (If no – Where)

1929- 125;   AZURE, McHenry; 30-5-25; 27; m; yes; 1/2; Snake bite; yes
1929- 275;   BLACKHOOP, Charles; 30-5-10; 17; m; yes; F; Tuberculosis; yes
1929- 517;   CHAPMAN, Mamie; 30-6-6; 28; f; yes; 1/2; Tuberculosis; yes
1930- 554;   CHOPPER, Mamie; 30-7-3; 14; f; yes; F; Meningitis; yes
1930-3395;   CHAPMAN, Paul I; 30-11-29; 4; m; yes; F; Tuberculosis; yes
1930-1055;   FOOLBEAR, Wilbert; 30-11-14; 11/12; m; yes; F; Rachitis; yes
1930-1181;   GOOD DAY, Mrs; 30-8-10; 90; f; yes; F; Old Age; yes
1930-1232;   GOODREAU, Mrs Agnes; 31-2-22; 25; f; yes; F; Tuberculosis; yes
Not recorded; HIS HORSE APPEARS, Issac[sic], Jr; 30-5-5; 10/12; m; yes; F;
              Pneumonia; yes
Not recorded; IRONROAD, George; 30-6-8; 1/12; m; yes; F; Tuberculosis; yes
1930-1669;   IRONSHIELD, Thomas; 31-1-11; 25; yes; F; Exposure; yes
1930-2003;   LITTLE WARRIOR, Stanislaus; 30-6-12; 15; m; yes; F; Intestinal
              Tuberculosis; yes
1930-2327;   MURPHY, Cyril; 30-7-11; 5; m; yes; F; Meningitis; yes
1930-2565;   RATTLINGHAIL, Annie; 30-7-15; 43; f; yes; F; Tuberculosis; yes
1930-2628;   REDFOX, Joshua; 31-2-24; 21; m; yes; F; Tuberculosis; yes
1930-2619;   REDFOX, Mary P; 31-3-30; 11; f; yes; F; Tuberculosis; yes
1930-2687;   RED TOMAHAWK, Marcellus Mrs.; 31-2-16; 82; f; yes; F; Old age;
              yes
1930-2765;   SHAVE ON ONE SIDE, Mrs; 30-12-31; 92; f; yes; F; Possibly freezing;
              yes
1930-2839;   SIAKA, Josephine; 30-12-25; 5; f; yes; F; Convulsions; yes
1929-3001;   STRETCHES HIMSELF, Paul; 30-42-27; 62; m; yes; F; Tuberculosis;
              yes
1929-3015;   STRONG HEART; 30-4-8; 86; m; yes; F; Nephritis; yes
1930-2993;   STRUCKMANY, Mrs Leo; 31-1-10; 65; f; yes; F; Tuberculosis; yes
1930-3167;   TUSK, Rueben[sic]; 30-8-6; 59; m; yes; F; Concussion of Cerebri[sic]; yes
1930-3420;   WHITECLOUD, Victoria; 31-1-7; 2; f; yes; F; Bronchial Pneumonia;
              yes
1930-3463;   WHITE LIGHTNING, Annie; 30-9-4; 52; f; yes; F; Tuberculosis; yes

Standing Rock Agency

Deaths - - North Dakota

Standing Rock Reservation

April 1, 1931 - March 31, 1932

State ___North Dakota___ Reservation___ Standing Rock ___ Agency or jurisdiction, ___ Standing Rock ___ Office of Indian Affairs

Deaths Occurring Between the Dates of April 1, 1931 and March 31, 1932 of Indians Enrolled at Jurisdiction

Key: Year and Number Last Census Roll; Surname, Given; Date of Birth (Year-Month-Day); Age at Death; Sex; Tribe (NC Cherokee unless stated otherwise); Ward (Yes/No); Degree of Blood; Cause of Death (if given); At Jurisdiction Where Enrolled (Yes/No); (If no – Where)

1932-   9;   AFRAID OF HAWK, Mrs; 31-7-21; 81; f; yes; F; Senility; yes
1932- 45;   AZURE, Laura; 31-8-14; 20; f; yes; 1/2; Gunshot wounds; yes
Not recorded; BEARSHEART, Virgil S; 31-12-8; 7 da; m; yes; F; Unknown; yes
1932- 120;   BLACKPRAIRIEDOG, Alice; 31-[?-?]; 31; f; yes; F; Unknown; yes
1932- 128;   BLACKTOMAHAWK, Michael; 31-9-29; 1; m; yes; F; Enteritis; yes
1932- 182;   BUFFALOBOY; Herbert; 31-1-2; 51; m; yes; F; Hemorrhagic Pancreatitis; yes
1932- 210;   CALLOUSLEG, Alma; 31-4-26; 15; f; yes; F; Meningitis; yes
1932- 243;   CASKE, Louise; 31-[?-?]; 43; f; yes; F; Unknown; yes
1932- 306;   COTTONWOOD, Ignatius; 31-11-5; 10; m; yes; F; Unknown; yes
1932- 316;   COTTONWOOD, Stephen; 31-10-[?]; 1; m; yes; F; Not reported; yes
1932- 386;   EAGLEBOY, Marcella; 31-10-30; 9; f; yes; F; Unknown; yes
1932- 473;   GAYTON, Samuel; 31-6-8; 73; m; yes; 1/2; Pyeletis suppurative[sic]; yes
1932- 515;   GOODIRON, Margaret; 31-5-30; 4 mo; f; yes; F; Erysipelas; yes
1932- 585;   GRAYWHIRLWIND; 31-7-13; 89; m; yes; F; Senility; yes
1932- 635;   HARRIS, Ione; 31-7-19; 8; f; yes; 1/2; Drowned; no; Hopeville, GA
1932- 636;   HARRIS, Marion; 31-7-19; 6; f; yes; 1/2; Drowned; no; Hopeville, GA
1932- 671;   HOLYELKFACE, John; 31-12-10; 50; m; yes; F; Fracture of skull, hemorrhage; yes
Not recorded; JORDAN, Joan; 31-5-7; 17 hrs; yes; 1/2; Premature birth; yes
Not recorded; KIDDER, Marcella; 31-9-26; 3 mo; f; yes; F; Enteritis; yes
1932- 923;   MULHERN, John B; 31-5-15; 31; m; yes; 1/2; Hemorrhage; yes
Not recorded; MURPHY, Ellen; 31-12-13; 5 da; f; yes; 1/2; Not reported; yes
1932-1032;   PRETTY BIRD, Mrs; 31-6-12; 86; f; yes; F; Unknown; yes
1932- 76;   REDDOOR, Albert J; 31-[?-?]; 13; m; yes; F; Unknown; yes
1962 1115;   REDTOMAHAWK, Marcellus; 31-8-7; 79; m; yes; F; Unknown; yes
1932-1145;   SHARPHORNBULL; 32-1-2; 75; m; yes; F; Uremia; yes
1932- 915;   SHORT, Edgar B; 31-8-27; 18; m; yes; 1/4; Railroad accident; yes
1932-1197;   SLATER, Jesse; 31-9-16; 48; m; yes; F; Tuberculosis; yes
1932-1236;   STONEMAN, Mrs; 31-11-21; 79; f; yes; F; Old age; yes
1932-1253;   STRETCHES HIMSELF, Peter; 31-4-11; 38; m; yes; F; Poisoning; yes
1932-1868;   TWOHORSES, Leo; 31-5-4; 79; m; yes; F; Tuberculosis; yes
1932-1373;   TWOSHIELDS, Adam; 31-4-28; 94; m; yes; F; Old age; yes
1932-1381;   TWOSHIELDS, Mrs; 31-12-?; 77; f; yes; F; Unknown; yes
1932-1433;   WHITE, Helen; 32-3-15; 32; f; yes; F; Chronic Nephritis; yes
1932-1474;   WHITE LIGHTNING; 31-12-17; 78; m; yes; F; Old age; yes
1932-1524;   WORDPECKER, Tail; 32-1-15; 61; m; yes; F; Unknown; yes

Standing Rock Agency

Deaths - - South Dakota

Standing Rock Reservation

July 1, 1924 - June 30, 1925

State _____ South Dakota ____ Reservation____ Standing Rock ____ Agency or jurisdiction, _____ Standing Rock _____ Office of Indian Affairs

Deaths Occurring Between the Dates of July 1, 1924 and June 30, 1925 of Indians Enrolled at Jurisdiction

Key: Year and Number Last Census Roll; Surname, Given; Date of Birth (Year-Month-Day); Age at Death; Sex; Tribe (NC Cherokee unless stated otherwise); Ward (Yes/No); Degree of Blood; Cause of Death (if given); At Jurisdiction Where Enrolled (Yes/No); (If no – Where)

1924-2818; ALKIRE, Susan; 24-12-13; 28; f; yes; F; Pneumonia; yes
1924-2745; BALDHEAD, Benjamin; 24-8-16; 37; m; yes; F; Heart Failure; yes
1224- 28; BLACKBEAR, Mrs. Louis; 24-7-14; 73; f; yes; F; Old age; yes
1924- 41; BROWNELK, Mrs. Leo; 25-5-29; 66; f; yes; F; Cancer & Kidney trouble; yes
1924-2632; CROWFEATHER, Albert; 24-10-29; 9/12; m; yes; F; Tuberculosis; yes
1924-2630; CROWFEATHER, Clara; 24-7-28; 8; f; yes; F; Tuberculosis; yes
1925- 509; CHASE ALONE, George; 25-6-30; 60; m; yes; F; Bronchial trouble; yes
1924- 151; DID NOT BUTCHER, Mrs; 25-5-26; 66; f; yes; F; Heart Failure; yes
1924-2160; DOGMAN, James; 25-1-26; 76; m; yes; F; Heart Failure; yes
Not recorded; FORTE, Charles Mayro; 24-9-1; 19 da; m; yes; F; Bowel trouble; yes
1924- 195; GABE, Charles, Sr; 25-5-26; 66; m; yes; Kidney trouble; yes
1924-1612; GRAYEAGLE, Levi; 24-8-25; 1; m; yes; F; Stomach Trouble; yes
1924-1811; IRON TUSK; 24-12-14; 75; m; yes; F; Heart Trouble; yes
1924-2281; IRON WHITEMAN, Lucille; 25-5-21; 12; f; yes; F; Hemorrhage; yes
1924-1585; JAW, Charlie; 24-7-22; 69; m; yes; F; Old age; yes
1926-1866; LeCOMPTE, Nancy; 25-4-18; 41; f; yes; 1/2; Not reported; yes
1924-1774; LITTLE DOG, Hover; 24-11-19; 1; m; yes; F; Stomach Trouble; yes
Not recorded; LITTLE DOG, Solomon; 24-7-23; 2 da; m; yes; F; Not reported; yes
1924-2347; LONGCHASE, Albert; 24-10-20; 4; m; yes; F; Stomach trouble; yes
Not recorded; LONGFEATHER, Jesse; 25-5-31; 2/12; m; yes; F; Fever; yes
Not recorded; LOOKING ELK, Norma; 24-11-19; 1 da; f; yes; F; Stomach trouble; yes
1924-2360; LOW DOG, Garfield; 25-6-27; 18; m; yes; F; Tuberculosis; yes
1924- 385; MARTIN, Leo; 24-7-17; 9/12; m; yes; F; Meningitis; yes
1924- 387; MARTIN, Maggie; 24-10-28; 36; f; yes; F; Tuberculosis; yes
1924-2379; MARTIN, Victoria; 25-2-9; 12; f; yes; F; Tuberculosis; yes
1924-2383; McLAUGHLIN, R. S.; 24-9-17; 48; m; yes; 1/4; Heart Trouble; yes
1924-1833; ONEBEAR, Sanford; 25-1-3; 68; m; yes; F; Pneumonia; yes
1924-1867; ONEFEATHER, Antoine Mrs.; 24-10-2; 69; f; yes; F; Heart Trouble; yes
1924-1846; ONJINCA, Mary; 25-2-10; 13; f; yes; F; Tuberculosis; yes
1925-2560; RATTLINGTHUNDER, Nellie; 25-4-19; 15; f; yes; F; Tuberculosis; yes
1924-1057; REDBIRD, Mrs.; 25-5-21; 86; f; yes; F; Old Age; yes
1924-3133; REDHORSE, Joseph; 25-5-31; 16; m; yes; F; Pul. Tuberculosis; yes
1925-2675; ROUGH SURFACE, Thomas; 25-3-23; 70; m; yes; F; Injury; yes
1924-1976; SHOESTRING, Alice; 24-7-3; 19; f; yes; F; Snake Bite; yes
1924-2432; SHOOT THE ENEMY, Helen; 24-10-23; 13; f; yes; F; Spinal trouble; yes
1925-3123; SPOTTEDHORSE, Clara; 25-25-5[sic]; 8; f; yes; F; Tuberculosis; yes
1924- 552; SWIFTBIRD, Samuel; 24-8-31; 84; m; yes; F; Old age; yes
1924- 614; WHITEBULL, Isaac; 25-5-28; 80; m; yes; F; Influenza; yes

State ___ South Dakota ___ Reservation ___ Standing Rock ___ Agency or jurisdiction,
___ Standing Rock ___ Office of Indian Affairs

Deaths Occurring Between the Dates of July 1, 1924 and June 30, 1925 of Indians Enrolled at Jurisdiction

Key: Year and Number Last Census Roll; Surname, Given; Date of Birth (Year-Month-Day); Age at Death; Sex; Tribe (NC Cherokee unless stated otherwise); Ward (Yes/No); Degree of Blood; Cause of Death (if given); At Jurisdiction Where Enrolled (Yes/No); (If no – Where)

1924-2821; WHITEHORSE, Patrick; 25-5-22; 22; m; yes; F; Tuberculosis; yes
1924-2810; WALKING ELK, Mrs. Maude; 25-1-4; 50; f; yes; F; Tumor; yes
1924-2533; WAWOKIYA, Norman J; 25-3-5; 2; m; yes; F; Stomach trouble; yes
1924-2088; YELLOWEARRINGS, Bessie; 24-7-10; 21; f; yes; F; Tuberculosis; yes
1924- 657; YOUNGHAWK, Bridget; 25-5-26; 32; f; yes; F; Tuberculosis; yes

Standing Rock Agency

Deaths - - South Dakota

Standing Rock Reservation

July 1, 1925 - June 30, 1926

State _____ South Dakota _____ Reservation _____ Standing Rock _____ Agency or jurisdiction,
_____ Standing Rock _____ Office of Indian Affairs

Deaths Occurring Between the Dates of July 1, 1925 and June 30, 1926 of Indians Enrolled at Jurisdiction

Key: Year and Number Last Census Roll; Surname, Given; Date of Birth (Year-Month-Day); Age at Death; Sex; Tribe (NC Cherokee unless stated otherwise); Ward (Yes/No); Degree of Blood; Cause of Death (if given); At Jurisdiction Where Enrolled (Yes/No); (If no – Where)

1925- 695;   ANPETELUTAWIN, 25[sic]; 25-8-16; 69; f; yes; F; Not reported; yes

Not recorded; ARCHAMBAULT, Gladys; 2-23; 1 da; f; yes; 3/4; Pneumonia; yes

1925- 757;   BANGLE EYE, Lillian; 26-6-12; 20; f; yes; F; Tuberculosis; yes

1925- 142;   BEARCATCHES, Mrs.; 26-1-12; 78; f; yes; F; Old age; yes

1925- 180;   BEARSHART, Nellie; 26-3-24; 10/12; f; yes; F; Pneumonia; yes

1925- 187;   BEARSHOLDIER[sic], Mrs.; 25-9-26; 66; f; yes; F; Stomach trouble; yes

1925- 627;   CRAWLER, Louis J; 25-8-9; 28; m; yes; F; Injury; yes

1927- 669;   CRAZYHAWK, Douglas; 25-10-17; 2; m; yes; F; Not reported; yes

1925- 999;   FLYINGEARTH, Bessie; 25-2-19; 14; f; yes; F; Tuberculosis; yes

1925-1409;   HIGHBULL, Mrs.; 26-1-9; 77; f; yes; F; Suicide; yes

1925-3373;   HIS THUNDERSHIELD, Agnes; 26-4-9; 87; f; yes; F; Old age; yes

Not recorded; HORSETHIEF, Sarah; 25-12-31; 1 da; f; yes; F; Not reported; yes

1925-1546;   HUNGRY CROW; 26-6-17; 76; m; yes; F; Old age; yes

1925-1571;   IRON, Walter; 26-2-27; 57; m; yes; F; Pneumonia; yes

1925-1588;   IRONEYES, Mrs. Jerome; 26-3-3; 64; f; yes; F; Cancer of stomach; yes

1925-1647;   IRONWHITEMAN, Philip; 26-3-26; 1; m; yes; F; Pneumonia; yes

1925-1649;   IRONWINGS, Agnes; 25-12-31; 40; f; yes; F; Tuberculosis; yes

Not recorded; JORDAN, Unnamed; 26-6-2; 1/2 hr; f; yes; F; Not reported; yes

Not recorded; KILLS PRETTY ENEMY, Marcella; 25-9-20; 2; f; yes; F; Bowel
                trouble; yes

1925-1465;   LAWRENCE, Melvin; 26-2-25; 11/12; m; yes; F; Pneumonia; yes

Not recorded; LONGCHASE, Marie E; 26-4-7; 1/12; f; yes; F; Not reported; yes

1925-1970;   LONGELK; 25-11-8; 78; m; yes; F; Old age; yes

1925-1968;   LONG ELK, Mary Mercy; 25-8-20; 14; f; yes; F; Tuberculosis; yes

1925 1990;   LOOKING BACK, Seraphine; 26-6-13; 1; f; yes; F; Pneumonia; yes

1925-2035;   LOVES WAR, Dora; 26-3-31; 53; f; yes; F; Heart Attack; yes

1925-2053;   MALE BEAR, Annie; 26-5-23; 2; f; yes; F; Stomach trouble; yes

1925-2255;   MOUNTAIN, Bertha; 26-4-20; 1; f; yes; F; Tuberculosis; yes

1925-2396;   PASS BEYOND, Jessie; 26-6-16; 43; f; yes; F; Brights Disease; yes

1925-2466;   PRIMEAU, Leon; 25-9-3; 68; m; yes; F; Diabetes Mellitus; yes

1925- 2538; REDBIRD, John; 25-9-15; 2; m; yes; F; Stomach Flu; yes

1925-2533;   REDBIRD, Samuel; 26-2-11; 35; m; yes; F; Tuberculosis; yes

1925-2531;   REDBIRD, William; 26-6-22; 79; m; yes; F; Old age; yes

1925- 476;   RED EAGLE; 26-4-26; 84; m; yes; F; Acute Indigestion; yes

1925-2574;   REDFOX, John; 26-6-7; 89; m; yes; F; Not reported; yes

Not recorded; RED FOX, Priscialla[sic]; 25-10-7; 2; f; yes; F; Gastro Entrities[sic]; yes

1925-2657;   RETURNS, Victoria; 25-10-27; 67; f; yes; F; Heart Trouble; yes

Not recorded; ROACH, Melvin; 26-1-13; 1/12; m; yes; F; Pneumonia; yes

State _____South Dakota_____ Reservation_____ Standing Rock_____ Agency or jurisdiction, _____Standing Rock_____ Office of Indian Affairs

Deaths Occurring Between the Dates of July 1, 1925 and June 30, 1926 of Indians Enrolled at Jurisdiction

Key: Year and Number Last Census Roll; Surname, Given; Date of Birth (Year-Month-Day); Age at Death; Sex; Tribe (NC Cherokee unless stated otherwise); Ward (Yes/No); Degree of Blood; Cause of Death (if given); At Jurisdiction Where Enrolled (Yes/No); (If no – Where)

1925-2712; SCRAPER, Annie; 25-11-24; 86; f; yes; F; Not reported; yes

1925-2910; SPOTTEDHORSE, Ruth; 26-2-26; 20; f; yes; F; Stomach trouble; yes

1925- 999; SWIFT DOG, Mrs.; 25-7-15; 91; f; yes; F; Old age; yes

1925-2996; TAKEN ALIVE: Charlotte; 25-10-7; 1; f; yes; F; Stomach Trouble; yes

1926-3038; TAKE THE GUN, Sarah; 26-3-12; 1; f; yes; F; Pneumonia; yes

1925-3062; THIEF, Robert; 25-10-21; 69; m; yes; F; Not reported; yes

1925-3291; USES HIS ARROW, Alma; 25-10-5; 17; f; yes; F; Not reported; yes

1925-3220; VILLAGE CENTER; 25-7-2; 76; m; yes; F; Pneumonia; yes

1925-3220[sic]; VILLAGE CENTER, Bessie; 26-6-24; 48; f; yes; F; Tuberculosis; yes

1925-3304; WAONSILA; 25-7-29; 85; f; yes; F; Old age; yes

Not recorded; WAWOKIYA, Lillian M; 26-4-16; 2/12; f; yes; F; Pneumonia; yes

1925-3387; WHITE PAW, Mary; 25-10-2; 68; f; yes; F; Tuberculosis; yes

Standing Rock Agency

Deaths - - South Dakota

Standing Rock Reservation

July 1, 1926 - June 30, 1927

State ___ South Dakota ___ Reservation___ Standing Rock ___ Agency or jurisdiction, ___ Standing Rock ___ Office of Indian Affairs

Deaths Occurring Between the Dates of July 1, 1926 and June 30, 1927 of Indians Enrolled at Jurisdiction

Key: Year and Number Last Census Roll; Surname, Given; Date of Birth (Year-Month-Day); Age at Death; Sex; Tribe (NC Cherokee unless stated otherwise); Ward (Yes/No); Degree of Blood; Cause of Death (if given); At Jurisdiction Where Enrolled (Yes/No); (If no – Where)

1926- 47; AMIDST, Martin; 26-11-11; 24; m; yes; F; Tuberculosis; yes
1926- 162; BEAR NECKLACE: Jacob; 27-6-15; 18; m; yes; F; Tuberculosis; yes
1926- 240; BLACKFOX, William, Jr; 26-8-5; 37; m; yes; F; Stomach trouble; yes
1926- 542; CHEYENNE; 26-8-5; 71; m; yes; F; Stomach trouble; yes
1926-2554; CLOWN, Mary; 27-3-22; 8/12; f; yes; F; Pneumonia; yes
1926- 643; CRAZY BEAR, Philip; 26-7-18; 2; m; yes; F; Pneumonic Empyema; yes
1927- 741; DEFENDER, Mrs Jennie; 27-6-27; 30; f; yes; F; Bladder trouble; yes
1926- 879; EAGLEHORN, Sophie; 26-8-4; 1; f; yes; F; Stomach trouble; yes
1926- 885; EAGLEMAN, Bertha; 27-3-25; 14; f; yes; F; Tuberculosis; yes
1926- 991; FIRECLOUD, Lucy; 26-9-17; 44; f; yes; F; Tuberculosis; yes
1926-1010; FLYINGEARTH, Margaret; 26-8-15; 21; f; yes; F; Tuberculosis; yes
1926-1025; FLYINGHORSE, Edna; 26-12-7; 11/12; f; yes; 1/2; Convulsions; yes
1926-1038; FOOLISH THUNDER, Mrs; 26-9-1; 87; f; yes; F; Senility; yes
1926-1052; FOSTER, John; 27-5-26; 53; m; yes; F; Tuberculosis; yes
1926-1103; GARTER, Genevieve; 26-10-30; 5; f; yes; F; Not reported; yes
1926-1205; GOOD THUNDER, Mrs; 26-8-19; 84; f; yes; F; Exophthaline[sic] Goitre; yes
Not recorded; HALIBURTON, Paul; 27-1-19; 3 da; m; yes; 1/4; Mitral insufficiency; yes
Not recorded; HAYES, Lawrence; 26-9-24; 2 da; m; yes; F; Hemmorhage[sic] Umbilical; yes
1926-1434; HIGHCAT, Paul; 27-4-29; 45; m; yes; F; Peritonitis; yes
1926-1544; HOWARD, Ella; 27-6-12; 14; f; yes; F; Appendicitis; yes
1926-1564; HUNGRY CROW, Mrs; 27-2-17; 77; f; yes; F; Old age; yes
1926-1759; KILLS AT NIGHT, Mrs He[sic]; 26-9-20; 51; f; yes; F; Heart disease; yes
1926-1857; LEAN DOG, Leon; 26-7-10; 58; m; yes; F; Heart disease; yes
Not recorded; LITTLE BEAR, Florine; 26-11-22; 2/12; f; yes; F; Not reported; yes
1926-1931; LITTLE DOG; 27-2-26; 74; m; yes; F; Brights Disease; yes
Not recorded; LITTLE DOG, James; 27-2-13; 4/12; m; yes; F; Pneumonia; yes
Not recorded; LITTLE DOG, John; 27-2-13; 3/12; m; yes; F; Pneumonia; yes
1926-1932; LITTLE DOG, Mrs Mary; 26-8-3; 76; f; yes; F; Old age; yes
1926-1986; LONGELK, Mrs; 27-6-14; 77; f; yes; F; Heart Failure; yes
1926-1992; LOOKINGBACK; 26-11-26; 82; m; yes; F; Old age; yes
1926-2021; LOUD VOICE; 27-1-19; 83; m; yes; F; Old age; yes
1926-2033; LOVES WAR, Ardmore; 27-3-29; 5; m; yes; F; Appendicitis; yes
Not recorded; LOVES WAR, Lester; 27-2-13; 28 da; m; yes; F; Pneumonia; yes
1926-2342; OKA, Louis; 26-8-5; 66; m; yes; F; Rheumatism; yes
1926-2364; ONEFEATHER, Rita; 26-10-19; 1; f; yes; F; Acute bronchitis; yes
1926-2422; PASS BEYOND, Joseph; 26-9-18; 7; m; yes; F; Bronchial Pneumonia; yes
1926-2465; PINE, Robert; 27-5-31; 62; m; yes; F; Heart Trouble; yes

State _____ South Dakota _____ Reservation_____ Standing Rock _____ Agency or jurisdiction,
_____ Standing Rock _____ Office of Indian Affairs

Deaths Occurring Between the Dates of July 1, 1926 and June 30, 1927 of Indians Enrolled at Jurisdiction

Key: Year and Number Last Census Roll; Surname, Given; Date of Birth (Year-Month-Day); Age at Death; Sex; Tribe (NC Cherokee unless stated otherwise); Ward (Yes/No); Degree of Blood; Cause of Death (if given); At Jurisdiction Where Enrolled (Yes/No); (If no – Where)

Not recorded; REDHORSE, Ennis Lordet; 27-1-28; 3/12; m; yes; F; Whooping cough;
     yes
1926-2657; RED TOMAHAWK, Jacob; 26-7-30; 13; m; yes; F; Not reported; yes
1926-2695; ROUGH SURFACE, Mrs; 27-4-7; 73; f; yes; F; Tuberculosis; yes
1926-2756; SEVENTEEN, Philip; 27-5-9; 44; m; yes; F; Tuberculosis; yes
Not recorded; SITTING DOG, Hazel B; 27-2-19; 3/12; f; yes; F; Tuberculosis; yes
1926-2843; SITTING DOG, Mrs; 27-11-8; 69; f; yes; F; Old Age; yes
1926-2867; SLEEPS FROM HOME, Oliver; 27-2-18; 69; m; yes; F; Gallstones; yes
1926-2932; SPOTTEDHORSE, Ramona; 26-7-22; 4; f; yes; F; Tuberculosis; yes
Not recorded; STANDING CLOUD, Reva; 26-11-10; 2 da; f; yes; F; Not reported;
     yes
1926-2891; SUDDEN BRAVE, Hiram; 26-12-4; 73; m; yes; F; Tuberculosis; yes
1926-2982; SWIFTCLOUD, Eugene; 27-5-6; 28; m; yes; F; Tuberculosis; yes
1926-2470; SWIFTCLOUD, Jennie; 27-4-8; 13; f; yes; F; Tuberculosis; yes
1926-3025; TAKEN ALIVE, Nelson; 26-8-28; 1; m; yes; F; Stomach trouble; yes
1926-3027; TAKE THE GUN, Brown; 26-11-19; 48; m; yes; F; Not reported; yes
1925-3012; TAKE THE GUN, Johnson; 26-7-6; 11; m; yes; F; Drowned; yes
1926-3314; WASICUINOPIWIN; 27-5-24; 97; f; yes; F; Old age; yes
1927-3347; WAWOKIYA, William; 27-5-9; 57; m; yes; F; Diabetes; yes
1926-3366; WHITE, Elaine; 27-3-12; 41; f; yes; F; Pneumonia; yes
1926-3401; WHITEBULL, Cecelia; 27-2-2; 18; f; yes; F; Tuberculosis; yes
1927-3526; WAINYANLUTA; 27-4-29; 90; f; yes; F; Senility; yes

Standing Rock Agency

Deaths - - South Dakota

Standing Rock Reservation

July 1, 1927 - June 30, 1928

State ___ South Dakota ___ Reservation___ Standing Rock ___ Agency or jurisdiction, ___ Standing Rock ___ Office of Indian Affairs

Deaths Occurring Between the Dates of July 1, 1927 and June 30, 1928 of Indians Enrolled at Jurisdiction

Key: Year and Number Last Census Roll; Surname, Given; Date of Birth (Year-Month-Day); Age at Death; Sex; Tribe (NC Cherokee unless stated otherwise); Ward (Yes/No); Degree of Blood; Cause of Death (if given); At Jurisdiction Where Enrolled (Yes/No); (If no – Where)

1927-   1;   AFRAID OF BEAR, Leo; 28-3-21; 79; m; yes; F; Senility; yes
1927-   28;   AMIDST, John; 28-2-20; 19; m; yes; F; Tuberculosis; yes
1927-   54;   ANKLE, Corinne; 28-5-17; 1; f; yes; F; Tuberculosis; yes
1927-   62;   ANTELOPE, Noble; 28-5-28; 16; m; yes; F; Tuberculosis; yes
1927-1226;   BADGER, Martha; 28-2-21; 18; f; yes; F; Tuberculosis; yes
1927- 151;   BEARFACE, Christine; 28-2-28; 23; f; yes; F; Tuberculosis; yes
Not recorded; BLACKBEAR, Joseph; 28-7-4; 1/12; m; yes; F; Influenza; yes
1927-3304;   BRAVETHUNDER, Fanny; 27-7-26; 79; f; yes; F; Brights Disease; yes
1927- 306;   BOBTAIL ELK, Mary; 28-5-27; 80; f; yes; F; Tuberculosis; yes
1927- 376;   BROWNOTTER, Henry; 27-12-8; 27; m; yes; F; Tuberculosis; yes
1928- 392;   BUCKLEY, Nathan; 28-6-10; 16; m; yes; F; Pneumonia; yes
1927- 677;   CROSS, George H; 28-1-22; 27; m; yes; F; Tuberculosis; yes
1927- 671;   CROSS, Nellie; 28-2-3; 23; f; yes; F; Tuberculosis; yes
1927- 931;   ELK, Finton; 27-7-4; 31; m; yes; F; Drowned; yes
Not recorded; FLYINGBY, Barney; 28-4-16; 10/12; m; yes; F; Pneumonia; yes
1927-1023;   FLYINGEARTH, Mrs. Mary; 27-9-22; 49; f; yes; F; Typhoid Fever; yes
1927-1024;   FLYINGEARTH, Viola; 27-2-1; 19; f; yes; F; Tuberculosis; yes
Not recorded; GABE, Cormen; 28-1-17; 7/12; f; yes; F; Stomach trouble; yes
1927-1218;   GOODSHOT, Amos; 28-5-14; 57; m; yes; F; Tuberculosis; yes
1927-1317;   HAIRYCHIN, Mrs. Geo; 27-11-20; 60; f; yes; F; Tuberculosis; yes
1927-1377;   HARRIS, William; 28-6-14; 24; m; yes; F; Tuberculosis; yes
1927-1426;   HAWKEAGLE, Samuel; 27-7-27; 64; m; yes; F; Leakage of Heart; yes
1927-1496;   HOLLOW, Michael; 28-5-14; 59; m; yes; F; Influenza; yes
1928-1543;   HOLY MEDICINE, Julia; 28-5-12; 74; f; yes; F; Stomach trouble; yes
1927-1497;   HOLY WHITEMAN, Charles; 27-12-31; 33; m; yes; F; Tuberculosis; yes
1927-1519;   HORSETHIEF, Irene; 27-2-29; 1; f; yes; F; Pneumonia; yes
1927-1613;   IRONHORN, Mrs Alice; 28-6-5; 34; f; yes; F; Childbirth; yes
Not recorded; IRONHORN, Ernest; 28-6-26; 20 da; m; yes; F; Stomach trouble; yes
1927-1953;   LITTLE EAGLE, Grace; 27-10-26; 1; f; yes; F; Meningitis; yes
1927-1947;   LITTLE EAGLE, James; 27-11-10; 5; m; yes; F; Brain Fever; yes
1927-3287;   LITTLESHIELD, Genevieve; 28-1-15; 61; f; yes; F; Tuberculosis; yes
Not recorded; LONGELK, Nelson; 27-7-24; 3 da; m; yes; F; Stomach trouble; yes
1927-2014;   LOOKINGBACK, Cecelia; 28-3-9; 11/12; f; yes; F; Pneumonia; yes
1927-1814;   KNOCKS THEM DOWN, Herbert; 27-8-22; 17; m; yes; F; Tuberculosis; yes
1927-2087;   MANY DEEDS Theodore; 27-12-26; 24; m; yes; F; Tuberculosis; yes
1927-2110;   MANY HORSES, Innocent; 27-7-28; 2; f; yes; F; Cramps; yes
Not recorded; MANY HORSES, Patrick; 28-5-9; 4/12; f; yes; F; Meningitis; yes
1928-2201;   MARTIN, William; 27-7-18; 51; m; yes; F; Tuberculosis; yes
1927-2283;   MOORE, Gertrude; 27-8-26; 40; f; yes; 1/4; Mitral Insufficiency; yes
Not recorded; MIDDLEBULL, Royal; 28-4-19; 2/12; m; yes; F; Bowel trouble; yes
1927-2293;   MUENCH, Nellie; 27-10-9; 36; f; yes; 1/4; Neserterecthrombosis[sic]; yes

261

State _____ South Dakota _____ Reservation _____ Standing Rock _____ Agency or jurisdiction,
_____ Standing Rock _____ Office of Indian Affairs

Deaths Occurring Between the Dates of July 1, 1927 and June 30, 1928 of Indians Enrolled at Jurisdiction

Key: Year and Number Last Census Roll; Surname, Given; Date of Birth (Year-Month-Day); Age at Death; Sex; Tribe (NC Cherokee unless stated otherwise); Ward (Yes/No); Degree of Blood; Cause of Death (if given); At Jurisdiction Where Enrolled (Yes/No); (If no – Where)

Not recorded; NOISY HAWK, Jacob; 28-2-12; 1; m; yes; F; Otitis Media; yes

1927-2368; OLOWAN, Mary; 27-9-2; 67; f; yes; F; Eczema; yes

1927-2567; REDBEAR, Gladys; 28-6-1; 7; f; yes; F; Shot accidentally; yes

1927-2597; RED FOX, Cecelia; 28-4-6; 22; f; yes; F; Pul. Tuberculosis; yes

1927-2696; RETURNS WOUNDED, Joshua; 28-6-6; 66; m; yes; F; Enlargement of Liver; yes

1927-2698; ROMAN NOSE; 27-7-2; 62; m; yes; F; Heart Failure; yes

Not recorded; ROMAN NOSE, Lusie[sic]; 28-6-28; 2 da; f; yes; F; Stomach trouble; yes

1927-2710; ROUGH SURFACE, Bernice; 28-1-15; 2; f; yes; F; Measles; yes

Not recorded; SHAVEBEAR, John, Jr; 28-1-1; 2/12; m; yes; F; Pneumonia; yes

1927-1997; SHOOTS THE ENEMY; Sylvia; 28-3-12; 5; f; yes; F; Meningitis; yes

1927-2857; SILK, Annie; 28-5-28; 24; f; yes; F; Tuberculosis; yes

1927-2858; SILK, Mark T; 28-2-29; 1; m; yes; 1/2; Measles; yes

1927-2861; SITTING WHITE COW; 27-8-27; 73; m; yes; F; Tuberculosis; yes

1927-3000; SUTESNI, Agnes; 28-3-20; 66; f; yes; F; Heart Failure; yes

3117[sic]-3117; TIGER, Walter; 28-1-15; 48; m; yes; F; Choledochastomy; yes

1927-3273; USES AS A SHIELD, James; 27-10-11; 74; a; yes; F; Cholrea[sic] Morbus[sic]; yes

1927-3339; WATERS, Rose; 27-7-23; 3/12; f; yes; F; Stomach trouble; yes

1927-3343; WAWOKIYA, Saul; 28-2-10; 27; m; yes; F; Pul. Tuberculosis; yes

1927-3355; WEASEL, Mrs Eunice; 27-12-19; 27; f; yes; F; Not reported; yes

1927-3421; WHITEBULL, William; 28-4-28; 9; m; yes; F; Hemorrhage; yes

1927-3502; WHITESHIELD, Catherine; 28-2-4; 1; f; yes; F; Pneumonia; yes

1927-3562; YELLOWEARRINGS, Dan, Jr; 28-2-5; 4; f[sic]; yes; F; Tuberculosis; yes

1927-3571; YELLOWEARRINGS, Rose; 28-5-15; 12; 12[sic]; yes; F; Tuberculosis; yes

Standing Rock Agency

<u>Deaths</u> - - South Dakota

Standing Rock Reservation

July 1, 1928 - June 30, 1929

State ___ South Dakota ___ Reservation ___ Standing Rock ___ Agency or jurisdiction,
___ Standing Rock ___ Office of Indian Affairs

Deaths Occurring Between the Dates of July 1, 1928 and June 30, 1929 of Indians Enrolled at Jurisdiction

Key: Year and Number Last Census Roll; Surname, Given; Date of Birth (Year-Month-Day); Age at Death; Sex; Tribe (NC Cherokee unless stated otherwise); Ward (Yes/No); Degree of Blood; Cause of Death (if given); At Jurisdiction Where Enrolled (Yes/No); (If no – Where)

1928- 56; ANTELOPE; 29-2-15; 82; m; yes; F; Pneumonia; yes
1928- 152; BEAR CATCHES; 29-5-29; 87; m; yes; F; Gen. Debility; yes
1928-2732; BEAR LOOKING, Genevieve; 28-10-12; 18; f; yes; F; Tuberculosis; yes
1928- 181; BEARRIBS, Bernard; 29-5-2; 2; m; yes; F; Tuberculosis; yes
1928- 311; BONE, Agatha; 29-2-24; 60; f; yes; F; Intestinal T. B.; yes
1928- 312; BONECLUB, Joseph; 28-11-28; 86; m; yes; F; Old age & Flu; yes
1928- 313; BONECLUB, Mrs.; 28-10-30; 81; f; yes; F; Cancer of Liver; yes
1928- 360; BROKEN HORN BULL, Mrs.; 28-7-6; 71; f; yes; F; Old age; yes
1928- 382; BRUIGIER, Samuel; 29-6-7; 74; m; yes; 1/2; Paripligia[sic]; yes
1928- 384; BRUSHHORNS, Maurice; 29-5-18; 60; m; yes; F; Auto Accident; yes
Not recorded; CADOTTE, Unnamed; 29-2-7; 7 da; f; yes; 1/2; Lack of Vitality; yes
1928- 685; CROSSBEAR, Esther; 27- 8-12; 27; f; yes; F; Tuberculosis; yes
1928- 687; CROSSBEAR, Frank; 29-1-18; 9; m; yes; F; Tuberculosis; yes
1928- 804; DISTRIBUTE, Mrs. John; 29-2-18; 40; f; yes; F; Childbirth; yes
1928- 875; EAGLE, Elmer; 28-8-19; 8/12; m; yes; F; Pul. Tuberculosis; yes
1928- 916; EAGLEMAN, Adeline; 28-9-15; 5; f; yes; F; Not reported; yes
1928- 933; EAGLESTAFF, Ruth; 28-8-4; 35; f; yes; F; Pul. Tuberculosis; yes
Not recorded; END OF HORN, Seraphine; 29-2-5; 1/12; f; yes; F; Not reported; yes
1928-1027; FLANK, Francis; 29-2-13; 77; m; yes; F; Old age & Flu; yes
1928-1195; GOODBOY, Mrs. Paul; 78[sic]-4-2; 29; f; yes; F; Influenza; yes
1928-1223; GOODFUR, Joshua; 28-7-8; 9/12; m; yes; F; Tuberculosis; yes
1928-1357; HAIRYCHIN, Geo; 29-1-28; 61; m; yes; F; Tuberculosis; yes
Not recorded; HAWK, Unnamed; 29-1-11; 8 da; f; yes; F; Influenza; yes
1928-1502; HIS THUNDERSHIELD, Mrs.; 28-10-18; 77; f; yes; F; Old age; yes
1928-1353; HOLY WHITEMAN, Sarah; 28-7-28; 4; f; yes; F; Tuberculosis; yes
1928-1654; IRONHORN, Mrs. Mary; 29- 2-10; 81; f; yes; F; Tuberculosis; yes
1928-1812; KILLS CROW, Evelyn; 28-9-9; 17; f; yes; F; Meningitis; yes
1928-1819; KILLS CROW, Wilmar; 28-7-2; m; yes; F; Tuberculosis; yes
1928-1843; KILLS PRETTY ENEMY, Vincent; 28-11-21; 1; m; yes; F; Pneumonia; yes
1928-1862; KIRK, Susan; 29-1-16; 89; f; yes; 1/2; Old age; yes
1928-1480; LITTLEHORSE, Mrs.; 29-2-14; 73; f; yes; F; Tuberculosis; yes
Not recorded; LONGCHASE, Daniel; 29-6-24; 3d; m; yes; F; Cramps; yes
Not recorded; LONGCHASE, Joseph; 29-9-23; 2d; m; yes; F; Cramps; yes
1928-2087; LOW DOG, Mary; 29-6-12; 14; f; yes; F; Tuberculosis; yes
1928-2098; MAJHOR, Clara; 28-12-28; 23; f; yes; F; Pneumonia Flu; yes
Not recorded; MARTINEZ, James, Jr; 29-1-30; 3/12; m; yes; 7/8; Stomach trouble; yes
1928-2446; OTTERROBE, Helen; 28-12-26; 57; f; yes; F; Tuberculosis; yes
1928-2453; PAINTS BROWN, Joseph; 29-4-10; 84; m; yes; F; Old age; yes
1928-2598; REDBEAR, Charles; 29-5-28; 38; m; yes; F; Tuberculosis; yes;
1928-2608; REDBEAR, William; 29-1-16-; 86; m; yes; F; Old age; yes
1928-2707; RED TOMAHAWK, Marcella; 29-1-10; 11; f; yes; F; Influenza; yes

State ____ South Dakota ____ Reservation ____ Standing Rock ____ Agency or jurisdiction,
____ Standing Rock ____ Office of Indian Affairs
Deaths Occurring Between the Dates of July 1, 1928 and June 30, 1929 of Indians Enrolled at Jurisdiction

Key: Year and Number Last Census Roll; Surname, Given; Date of Birth (Year-Month-Day); Age at Death; Sex; Tribe (NC Cherokee unless stated otherwise); Ward (Yes/No); Degree of Blood; Cause of Death (if given); At Jurisdiction Where Enrolled (Yes/No); (If no – Where)

1928-2733;   ROMAN NOSE, Rebecca; 29-1-19; 2; f; yes; 7/8; Influenza; yes
1928-2742;   RUNNING HAWK, George; 28-7-3; 79; m; yes; F; Tuberculosis; yes
1928-2751;   RUNNING HAWK, Lillie; 29-1-8; 5; f; yes; F; Pneumonia; yes
1928-2779;   SEE CLOUD; 28-10-16; 72; m; yes; F; Tuberculosis; yes
1928-2787;   SEVENTEEN, Mrs. David; 29-1-8; 70; f; yes; F; Pneumonia; yes
Not recorded; SKUNK, Philip; 29-3-26; 3/12; m; yes; F; Abscess on Hips; yes
1928-2918;   SLEEPS FROM HOME, Margaret; 28-11-22; 1; f; yes; F; Accident; yes
1928-2921;   SMEE, Elmer; 29-10-22; 29; m; yes; 3/4; Tuberculosis; yes
1928-2975;   SPOTTEDHORSE, James; 29-2-6; 59; m; yes; F; Influenza; yes
1928-2968;   SPOTTEDHORSE, Ludlow; 29- 6-23; 52; m; yes; F; Brain Fever; yes
1928-3063;   TAKEN ALIVE, Lorene; 29-4-8; 6; f; yes; F; Influenza; yes
Not recorded: STANDING CLOUD, Lena; 28-12-23; 1 da; f; yes; F; Not reported;
                   yes
1928-3039;   SWIFTCLOUD, Isaac; 28-7-17; 3; m; yes; F; Unknown; yes
1928-3071;   TAKE THE GUN, Charles; 28-8-25; 72; m; yes; F; Cancer of throat; yes
1928-3121;   THIEF, Surah; 29-4-28; 3; f; yes; F; Pneumonia; yes
1628 3236;   TWOHEARTS, Nettie; 28-10-30; 13; f; yes; F; Tuberculosis; yes
Not recorded; USES HIS ARROWS, Danver; 29-5-20; 21 da; m; yes; F; Stomach
                   trouble; yes
1928-3315;   WALKING ELK, Virgil; 29-6-14; 5; m; yes; F; Liver trouble; yes
1928-3363;   WATERS, Rose; 28-11-19; 21; f; yes; F; Child birth; yes
1928- 205;   WEASEL BEAR, Geraldine; 29-4-14; 4; f; yes; F; Meningitis; yes
1928- 533;   WEBSTER, Mrs. Peter; 29-5-15; 74; f; yes; F; Tuberculosis; yes
1928-3451;   WHITEBULL, Mrs. Louis; 28-12-16; 54; f; yes; F; Influenza; yes
1928-3521;   WHITESHIELD, Jessie; 28-7-2; 25; m; yes; F; Tuberculosis; yes
1928-3566;   WAWICAGEWIN; 28-11-5; 84; f; yes; F; Old age; yes
1928-3587;   YELLOWEARRINGS, Andrew; 29-3-13; 15; m; yes; F; Heart Disease;
                   yes
1928-3599;   YELLOWEARRINGS, Martin; 29-1-1; 44; m; yes; F; Tuberculosis; yes
1928-3600;   YELLOWEARRINGS, Samuel; 29-4-22; 22; m; yes; F; Tuberculosis;
                   yes

Standing Rock Agency

Deaths - - South Dakota

Standing Rock Reservation

July 1, 1929 - June 30, 1930

State _____ South Dakota _____ Reservation_____ Standing Rock _____ Agency or jurisdiction, _____ Standing Rock _____ Office of Indian Affairs

Deaths Occurring Between the Dates of July 1, 1929 and June 30, 1930 of Indians Enrolled at Jurisdiction

Key: Year and Number Last Census Roll; Surname, Given; Date of Birth (Year-Month-Day); Age at Death; Sex; Tribe (NC Cherokee unless stated otherwise); Ward (Yes/No); Degree of Blood; Cause of Death (if given); At Jurisdiction Where Enrolled (Yes/No); (If no – Where)

1929- 238; BLACKBEAR, Mrs. Walter; 30;2-27; 75; f; yes; F; Tuberculosis; yes
1929- 239; BLACKBIRD, Mrs.; 29-9-14; 74; f; yes; F; Dropsy; yes
1929- 309; BOBTAILBEAR, Rose; 30-6-7; 14; f; yes; F; Tuberculosis; yes
1929- 364; BROUGHT, Mrs. Pius; 30-3-11; 78; f; yes; F; Kidney trouble; yes
Not recorded; CADOTTE, Mary; 30-3-8; 4 hrs; f; yes; F; Unknown; yes
1929- 699; CROWHEAD, Thos; 29-9-30; 70; m; yes; F; Tuberculosis; yes
Not recorded; EAGLEMAN, Unnamed; 30-2-8; 1½ hrs; m; yes; F; No vitality; yes
1929- 913; EAGLEMAN, Robert; 30-2-4; 20; m; yes; F; Pul. Tuberculosis ; yes
1929- 957; ELK NATION, Clara; 29-8-5; 40; f; yes; F; Gallstones; yes
1929-1062; FOOLBULL, Rose; 29-7-6; 25; f; yes; F; Tuberculosis; yes
1929-1085; FOSTER, Stanley; 29-8-19; 1; m; yes; F; Stomach trouble; yes
1929-1323; GRINDSTONE, Julia; 30-6-3; 21; f; yes; F; Meningitis; no; Chey. River Agcy, S.D.
1929-1423; HAS HORNS, Fedilia; 30-1-1; 18; f; yes; F; Tuberculosis; yes
Not recorded; HAWK, Wilmot; 30-1-19; 3 da; f; yes; F; Unknown; yes
1929-1527; HOHEKTE, Hazel; 30-3-1; 9; f; yes; F; Brain fever; yes
Not recorded; IRON, Jerry W; 30-4-5; 21 da; m; yes; F; Cramps; yes
1929-1662; IRONSHIELD, Susan; 30-6-8; 55; f; yes; F; Meningitis; yes
1929-1887; LaMONTE, Cecelia; 30-1-1; 60; f; yes; 1/2; Cancer of Stomach; yes
1929-1879; LEAF, Elizabeth; 30-6-23; 41; f; yes; F; Heart trouble; yes
1929-2672; REDHORSE, Nancy; 30- 2-27; 1; f; yes; F; Pneumonia; yes
1929-2710; REEL, Giles; 29-10-13; 20; m; yes; F; Electrocution; yes
1929-3582; SEVEN ELK, Rose; 29-12-3; 39; f; yes; F; Heart trouble; yes
1929-2775; SHAVEBEAR, Joseph; 30 5-14; 1; m; yes; F; Tuberculosis; yes
1929-3029; SWIFTCLOUD, Mrs. Martin; 30-3-16; 58; f; yes; F; Cancer of stomach; yes
1929-3023; TAKEN ALIVE, Bertha; 30-6-4; 14; f; yes; F; Tuberculosis; yes
1929- 317; TIGER, Rhoda; 29-12-13; 5 mo; f; yes; F; Pneumonia; yes
Not recorded; TURNING HEART, Arol E; 30-2-22; 1/12; m; yes; F; Influenza; yes
1929-3222; TWOHEARTS, Thos; 29-8-18; 5; m; yes; F; Tuberculosis; yes
1929-3316; WALKS QUIETLY; 29-7-21; 71; m; yes; F; Paralysis; yes
1929-3320; WARRIOR, Mrs.; 30-6-18; 64; f; yes; F; Heart trouble; yes
1929-3403; WHITEBULL, Emma; 30-4-2; 16; f; yes; F; Tuberculosis; yes
1929-3462; WHITEHANDBEAR, Sophie; 29-11-30; 13; f; yes; F; Intestinal T.B.; yes
Not recorded; YOUNGHAWK, Henry; 30-1-11; 5 da; m; yes; F; Lack of vitality; yes

Standing Rock Agency

<u>Deaths</u> - - South Dakota

Standing Rock Reservation

April 1, 1930 - March 31, 1931

State _____ South Dakota _____ Reservation _____ Standing Rock _____ Agency or jurisdiction,
_____ Standing Rock _____ Office of Indian Affairs

Deaths Occurring Between the Dates of April 1, 1930 and March 31, 1931 of Indians Enrolled at Jurisdiction

Key: Year and Number Last Census Roll; Surname, Given; Date of Birth (Year-Month-Day); Age at Death; Sex; Tribe (NC Cherokee unless stated otherwise); Ward (Yes/No); Degree of Blood; Cause of Death (if given); At Jurisdiction Where Enrolled (Yes/No); (If no – Where)

1930- 97; ARCHAMBAULT, Annie; 31-3-26; 48; f; yes; 3/4; Nephritis; yes

1930- 148; BEARFACE, John; 30-10-16; 22; m; yes; F; Tuberculosis; yes

1930- 174; BEARRIBS, Jennie; 31-1-23; 14; f; yes; F; Tuberculosis; yes

1929- 238; BLACKBEAR, Mrs. Walter; 30-4-27; 75; f; yes; F; Heart Trouble; yes

1930- 256; BLACKFOX, Herman; 30-8-2; 76; m; yes; F; Nephritis; yes

1929- 309; BOBTAIL BEAR, Rose; 30-6-7; 14; f; yes; F; Tuberculosis; yes

1930-2567; BROWNOTTER, Alfred; 30-11-7; 16; m; yes; F; Tuberculosis; yes

1930- 550; CHEYENNE, Mrs.; 30-7-5; 77; f; yes; F; Old age; yes

1930- 688; CROWHEAD, Mrs. Thos; 31-3-5; 67; f; yes; F; Heart trouble; yes

1930- 559; CLAYMORE, Antoine Mrs.; 30-11-12; 70; f; yes; 1/2; Dropsy; yes

1930- 611; CONICA, Mrs. Oscar; 31-2-22; 77; f; yes; F; Old age; yes

1930- 889; DOGEAGLE, Nelson; 30-8-11; 4/12; m; yes; F; Cholera Infantrum[sic]; yes

Not recorded; DOGEAGLE, Louise; 30-7-16; 2 da; f; yes; F; Unknown; yes

1930-1091; FLYINGBY, George; 30-11-26; 78; m; yes; F; Heart trouble; yes

Not recorded; FRANK, Andrew; 30-8-26; 3 da; m; yes; 1/2; Unknown; yes

1930-1191; GOODEAGLE, Pearl; 30-30-13; 10/12; f; yes; F; Tuberculosis; yes

1930-1203; GOODFUR, Lucille M; 30-9-24; 9/12; f; yes; F; Stomach trouble; yes

1929-1323; GRINDSTONE, Julia; 30-6-3; 21; f; yes; F; Meningitis; no; Chey. River Agcy, S.D.

Not recorded; HALIBURTON, John Lowell; 30-9-14; 1/12; m; yes; 1/8; Ileocolitis[sic]; yes

1930- 259; HAWK, Gladys; 30-7-2; 15; f; yes; F; Tuberculosis; yes

Not recorded; IRON, Jerry; 30-4-5; 21 da; m; yes; F; Cramps; yes

1929-1662; IRONSHIELD, Susan; 30-6-8; 55; f; yes; F; Tuberculosis; yes

1929-1879; LEAF, Elizabeth; 30-5-23; 41; f; yes; F; Heart trouble; yes

1930-2021; LOOKING BACK, Annie; 20[sic]-7-29; 16; f; yes; F; Tuberculosis; yes

1930-1623; MANY DOGS, Mrs. Mary; 31-3-20; 80; f; yes; F; Old age; yes

1930-2244; MEDICINE, Mary; 30-12-22; 68; f; yes; F; Dropsy; yes

1930-2347; NIYAKEKTE, Alice; 31-1-12; 70; f; yes; F; Heart failure; yes

1930-2366; NOHEART, Philip; 30-11-2; 27; m; yes; F; Railroad accident; yes

1930-2372; NOISY HAWK, Ed, Jr; 31-1-25; 2; m; yes; F; Influence; yes

Not recorded; ONEFEATHER, Chas; 30-8-19; 3 da; m; yes; F; Entrites[sic]; yes

1930- 862; REDBIRD, Mary E; 30-11-5; 16; f; yes; F; Tuberculosis; yes

1930-2635; REDFOX, Julia; 30-11-9; 46; f; yes; F; Stomach trouble; yes

1930-2652; REDHORN, Alvin L; 30-10-29; 1; m; yes; F; Bloat; yes

1930-2706; ROMAN NOSE, Rufus; 30-9-3; 24; m; yes; F; Tuberculosis; yes

1929-2775; SHAVEBEAR, Joseph M; 30-4-15; 1; m; yes; F; Tuberculosis; yes

Deaths Occurring Between the Dates of April 1, 1930 and March 31, 1931 of Indians Enrolled at Jurisdiction

Key: Year and Number Last Census Roll; Surname, Given; Date of Birth (Year-Month-Day); Age at Death; Sex; Tribe (NC Cherokee unless stated otherwise); Ward (Yes/No); Degree of Blood; Cause of Death (if given); At Jurisdiction Where Enrolled (Yes/No); (If no – Where)

1930-2899; SNOW, Benjamin; 30-12-1; 27; m; yes; F; Poison Liquor; yes

1930-2805; SNOW, Philip; 30-11-5; 30; m; yes; F; Tuberculosis; yes

1930-2906; SOFT, Esther; 30-7-3; 20; f; yes; F; Tuberculosis; yes

1930-2955; STANDING ROCK, Mrs.; 30-8-11; 86; f; yes; F; Mitral Stenosis; yes

1929-3023; TAKEN ALIVE, Bertha; 30-6-4; 14; f; yes; F; Tuberculosis; yes

Not recorded; THOMPSON, Ida A; 30-7-7; 11 da; f; yes; F; Premature birth; yes

Not recorded; TIYONA, Felix; 30-9-5; 3½ mo; m; yes; F; Pneumonia; yes

1930-3252; WAGGONER, Helen or M; 30-8-12; 2; f; yes; 1/2; Entrites[sic]; yes

1930-3273; WALKING ELK, Elma T; 31-3-30; 3; f; yes; F; Tuberculosis; yes

1929-3320; WARRIOR, Mrs.; 30-6-17; 64; f; yes; F; Heart trouble; yes

1930-3402; WHITEBULL, Agnes; 30-11-2; 18; f; yes; F; Tuberculosis; yes

1929-3403; WHITEBULL, Emma; 30-4-2; 16; f; yes; F; Tuberculosis; yes

1930-3443; WHITE EARTH, Moses; 31-3-13; 22; m; yes; F; Tuberculosis; yes

1930-3449; WHITEHORSE, Mrs. Louis; 30-10-17; 70; f; yes; F; Stomach trouble; yes

1930-3511; WINONA, Angela; 30-9-2; 99; f; yes; F; Old age; yes

1930-3584; YELLOWFAT, Jerome; 30-11-30; 16; m; yes; F; Poison Liquor; yes

Not recorded; YELLOWHAWK, Daniel; 31-1-21; 21 da; m; yes; F; Pneumonia; yes

Standing Rock Agency

<u>Deaths</u> - - South Dakota

Standing Rock Reservation

April 1, 1931 - March 31, 1932

State _____ North Dakota _____ Reservation _____ Standing Rock _____ Agency or jurisdiction, _____ Standing Rock _____ Office of Indian Affairs

Deaths Occurring Between the Dates of April 1, 1931 and March 31, 1932 of Indians Enrolled at Jurisdiction

Key: Year and Number Last Census Roll; Surname, Given; Date of Birth (Year-Month-Day); Age at Death; Sex; Tribe (NC Cherokee unless stated otherwise); Ward (Yes/No); Degree of Blood; Cause of Death (if given); At Jurisdiction Where Enrolled (Yes/No); (If no – Where)

1932-1572; AGARD, James; 31-5-25; 39; m; no; 1/2; Gunshot wounds; yes

1932-1613; ARCHAMBAULT, Harry; 31-[?-?]; 22; m; yes; 1/2; Unknown; yes

1932-1706; BIRDHORSE, Ernest; 31-[?-?]; 1; m; yes; F; Unknown; yes

1932-1705; BIRDHORSE, Lillie; 31-5-3; 24; f; yes; F; Tuberculosis; yes

1932-3295; BLACKHOOP, Francis; 31-10-30; 19; m; yes; Tuberculosis; yes

Not recorded; BROWNOTTER, Wilma; 31-4-2; 2 da; f; yes; F; Unknown; yes

1932-1783; BROWNOTTER, Virginia; 31-12-18; 25; f; yes; F; Unknown; yes

1932-1951; CROWNECKLACE, Thaner; 31-6-30; 13; m; yes; F; Tuberculosis; yes

1932-1968; DAVIS, David; 31-6-17; 14; m; yes; F; Tuberculosis; yes

1932-2037; DOG, Unnamed; 31-[?-?]; m; yes; F; Unknown; yes

1932-2139; ELK, Catherine; 31-9-17; 50; f; yes; F; Intestinal Trouble; yes

1932-2144; ELK, Robert; 31-5-9; 61; m; yes; F; Growth in throat; yes

Not recorded; EAGLEMAN, Unnamed; 31-11-10; 1 da; m; yes; F; Premature; yes

Not recorded; EAGLEHORN, Unnamed; 31-12-7; 10 min; m; yes; F; Choked; yes

1932-3418; FACE, Henry; 31-9-20; 19; m; yes; F; Tuberculosis; yes

1932-2197; FLYINGBY, Grace; 31-5-26; 6 mo; f; yes; F; Tuberculosis; yes

1932- 484; GILLAND, Elizabeth; 31-[?-?]; 64; f; no; 1/2; Unknown; yes

1932-2285; GOODEAGLE, Joseph; 32-3-13; 49; m; yes; F; Unknown; yes

1932-2326; GRINDSTONE, David; 31-9-22; 17; m; yes; F; Unknown; yes

1932-2146; HALF, Octavia; 31-5-11; 12; f; yes; F; Tuberculosis; yes

Not recorded; HAYES, Irvin W; 31-11-16; 3 mo; m; yes; F; Unknown; yes

1932-2417; HIGHEAGLE, Louise; 31-10-29; 55; f; yes; 1/2; Heart trouble; yes

1932-2499; IRONCLOUD, Jasper; 31-11-21; 30; m; yes; F; Tuberculosis; yes

1932-2528; IRONHORN, Edward; 31-9-1; 19; m; yes; F; Tuberculosis; yes

1932-2517; IRONMAN, Emma; 32-3-11; 49; f; yes; F; Unknown; yes

1932-2530; IRONWHITEMAN, Lillian; 31-12-25; 17; f; yes; F; Unknown; yes

1932-2648; KELLEY, Louise; 31-12-?; 73; f; no; 1/2; Unknown; no; St Paul, Minn

1932-2581; KILLS AT NIGHT, Mrs. Sam; 31-9-30; 62; f; yes; F; Intestinal; yes

1932-2609; KILLS THE ENEMY, Mrs.; 31-6-1; 72; f; yes; F; Dropsy; yes

1932-2648; LEAF, Robert; 31-[?-?]; 3; m; yes; F; Unknown; yes

1932-2666; LeCOMPTE, Evelyn; 32-3-18; 13; f; yes; 1/2; Meningitis; yes

1932-2791; LOOKING ELK, Lucy; 31-11-14; 81; f; yes; F; Burned; yes

1932-2591; MANY DEEDS, David; 31-9-15; 15; m; yes; F; Tuberculosis; yes

1932-2882; MARTIN, John; 31-9-29; 56; m; yes; F; Hardening Arteries; yes

1932-2892; MARTIN, Thomas; 32-1-2; 59; m; yes; N; T.B. Kidneys; yes

1932-3044; ONEFEATHER, Antoine; 32-3-1; 81; m; yes; F; Old age; yes

1932-3089; PINE, Josephine; 31-8-2; 27; f; yes; F; Epilepsy; yes

1932-3144; REDFOX, Mrs. Alice; 32-3-7; 42; f; yes; F; Unknown; yes

State   North Dakota   Reservation   Standing Rock   Agency or jurisdiction,
    Standing Rock   Office of Indian Affairs

Deaths Occurring Between the Dates of April 1, 1931 and March 31, 1932 of Indians Enrolled at Jurisdiction

Key: Year and Number Last Census Roll; Surname, Given; Date of Birth (Year-Month-Day); Age at Death; Sex; Tribe (NC Cherokee unless stated otherwise); Ward (Yes/No); Degree of Blood; Cause of Death (if given); At Jurisdiction Where Enrolled (Yes/No); (If no – Where)

1932-3264;   SHOOTS THE BEAR, Martin; 31-9-21; 11 mo; m; yes; F; Intestinal
    trouble; yes
1932-3644;   SHOOTS ENEMY, Mrs.; 31-5-27; 88; f; yes; F; Heart disease; yes
1932-3273;   SHOOTS WALKING, Wolcott; 31-7-15; 82; m; yes; F; Tuberculosis;
    yes
1932-3351;   SWIFTCLOUD, Mrs. Sam; 31-5-3; 82; f; yes; F; Auto accident; yes
1932-3178;   TAKE THE GUN, Ernest; 32-2-6; 10; m; yes; F; Paralysis; yes
Not recorded; TAKE THE GUN, Fred; 31-11-21; 4 mo; m; yes; F; Stomach trouble;
    yes
1932-3447;   TWOFURS, Walter; 31-12-[?]; 73; m; yes; F; Unknown; yes
1932-3462;   TWOHEARTS, Alice; 31-3-15; 13; f; yes; F; Tuberculosis; yes
1932-3469;   TWOHEARTS, Luke; 31-11-16; 67; m; yes; F; Liver & bladder trouble;
    yes
1932-3526;   WANKICUN, Emerson; 31-7-4;1; m; yes; F; Whooping cough; yes
1932-3622;   WHITESHIELD, Nellie; 31-6-26; 16; f; yes; F; Tuberculosis; yes
1932-3674;   YOUNGHAWK, Ed; 32-3-5; 76; m; yes; F; Hardening arteries; yes

278

www.ingramcontent.com/pod-product-compliance
Lightning Source LLC
Chambersburg PA
CBHW032101040426
42336CB00040B/637